UNDOING
MULTICULTURALISM

PITT LATIN AMERICAN SERIES

Catherine M. Conaghan, Editor

UNDOING
MULTICULTURALISM

Resource Extraction *and*
Indigenous Rights *in* Ecuador

CARMEN MARTÍNEZ NOVO

University *of* Pittsburgh Press

Published by the University of Pittsburgh Press, Pittsburgh, Pa., 15260
Copyright © 2021, University of Pittsburgh Press
All rights reserved
Manufactured in the United States of America
Printed on acid-free paper
10 9 8 7 6 5 4 3 2 1

Cataloging-in-Publication data is available from the Library of Congress

ISBN 13: 978-0-8229-4663-2
ISBN 10: 0-8229-4663-7

Cover art: Paula Barragán, *Renacer II*, 2013. Técnica mixta y dibujo digital, impresión de pigmento sobre papel de algodón (mixed technique and digital drawing, pigment impression over cotton paper), 130 × 110 cm.

Cover design: Alex Wolfe

To my parents,

Inmaculada Novo & José Miguel Martínez

CONTENTS

Acknowledgments

ix

List of Abbreviations

xiii

INTRODUCTION

Undoing Multiculturalism

3

CHAPTER 1

Being Indigenous in Ecuador

35

CHAPTER 2

Dispensing and Curtailing Rights through Policy and Practice

46

CHAPTER 3

The Minimization of Indigenous Numbers and the Fragmentation of Civil Society

67

CHAPTER 4

Creating and Dismantling Intercultural Bilingual Education

104

CHAPTER 5

Anthropology and Indigenous Peoples: Collaborations and Estrangements

153

CHAPTER 6

The Salesian Missions: Navigating Neoliberalism and Nationalist-Extractivism with the Indigenous Movement

203

CHAPTER 7

Ventriloquism, Racism, and the Politics of Decolonial Scholarship

238

CONCLUSION

Neoliberalism, Nationalist-Extractivism, and Racial Formations in Ecuador

267

References

277

Index

295

ACKNOWLEDGMENTS

Many people have inspired and facilitated my research in Ecuador. Francisco Rhon, of the Andean Center for Popular Action (Centro Andino de Acción Popular), first encouraged me to visit Zumbahua, Cotopaxi, and he made me aware of the important work of the Salesian order there. I always learned new perspectives from my long conversations with him. Fathers José Manangón and Luiggi Ricchiardi were kind enough to receive me in Zumbahua and enabled my research there. Rodrigo Guanotuña, Nelly Guanotuña, and the rest of the family welcomed me during my stay in Zumbahua and taught me a great deal about indigenous livelihoods.

Deborah Poole first encouraged me to investigate the history of anthropology and the relationship between anthropologists and indigenous peoples in Ecuador. Víctor Bretón, Fernando García, Teodoro Bustamante, Andrés Guerrero, Hernán Ibarra, Pepe Yánez, Consuelo Yánez, Segundo Moreno, José Juncosa, and many others have shared their deep understanding of Ecuador's intellectual history. The indigenous graduate students of the masters in ethnic studies at FLACSO Ecuador taught me a great deal about being indigenous in Ecuador and elsewhere in Latin America. I admired their courage when they opened previously white-mestizo spaces to indigenous academics. Today they are professionals and scholars. I am proud of the work they have done and glad that I had the opportunity to teach them and to learn from them. I would like to specially recognize the friendship and assistance of Luis Alberto Tuaza, Juan Illicachi, Antonio Duchi, and Raul Cevallos Calapi. Kar Atamaint, as my research assistant on several occasions, introduced me to Shuar culture, history, and politics and was fun to work with. At FLACSO Ecuador, Felipe Burbano de Lara has always been a great friend and colleague and has helped with institutional affiliation on several occasions. I am grateful to Fernando Carrión for giving me the opportunity to work on this research at FLACSO.

I am indebted to my mother-in-law Noemí Espinosa Correa, her sister María, and brother José for sharing their stories about the old times and for deepening my understanding of the highlands hacienda. I appreciate the linguists who taught me the first rudiments of the Kichwa language: Adrián Suarez, Teodoro Gallegos, Pepe Yánez, Luis Alberto Tuaza, and Razu Paza were patient and dedicated teachers who opened my eyes to a deeper layer of indigenous culture. Alberto Acosta and Gina Chávez provided access to the 2008 Constituent Assembly, contacts, documents and bibliography. Ana María Varea shared her contacts in the southern Amazon. Francisco Sánchez and Simón Pachano organized a wonderful workshop at Universidad de Salamanca in Spain where an interdisciplinary team discussed various aspects of the government of Rafael Correa. The workshop demonstrated the importance of interdisciplinary exchange.

This book was written thanks to a research leave funded by the American Council of Learned Societies in the year 2017–2018. I am thankful to Associate Dean Ted Schatzki and the Department of Anthropology at the University of Kentucky for granting the leave and for complementing it with a sabbatical semester. This book would not have been possible without the time away from other responsibilities. Some of the preliminary fieldwork was conducted with a 2008–2009 Post-PhD Grant from the Wenner Gren Foundation for Anthropological Research. The Wenner Gren has consistently supported me at several stages of my academic career. FLACSO Ecuador and its director, Adrián Bonilla, funded some of the research on intercultural bilingual education. Joanne Rappaport and Rudi Colloredo were kind enough to find time in their busy schedules to send letters of recommendation for me so that I could have funding for research and writing. Joanne has encouraged me to publish this work and to do it right. Rudi's genuine anthropological style and personal kindness have been a great inspiration.

At the University of Kentucky, I am grateful to Mark Kornbluh, Chris Pool, and the Department of Anthropology for offering me a job when I needed one and for the opportunity to learn about Kentucky, a beautiful state that became a new home for us and our children. At the University of Kentucky, Ann Kingsolver and Mark Whitaker helped with grant proposals and publication strategies. Ann's generosity and wisdom has been a great role model.

In the writing stages of this book, the advice of Nancy Postero and Joanne Rappaport was invaluable. I thank them for reading the manuscript more than once and for taking the time to provide detailed suggestions for revision. I am sure that the book is much stronger with their help. I am also thankful to Catherine Conaghan and Josh Shanholtzer at the University of Pittsburgh Press for their support and guidance navigating from manuscript to publication, and to Terry Malhame for her careful copyediting. Catherine is an example of academic rigor and personal integrity. Pavel Shlossberg was a generous reader for some of the chapters of this book and a supportive friend. I have admired the work of Paula Barragán Miller for some time. I am grateful for her contribution to the book cover.

I have published previous and different versions of some chapters in this book. A previous and different version of chapter 2 was published as "Managing Diversity in Post-Neoliberal Ecuador," *Journal of Latin American and Caribbean Anthropology* 19, no. 1 (2014): 399–422. Chapter 3 originated partially from an article published as "The Minimization of Indigenous Numbers and the Fragmentation of Civil Society in the 2010 Census in Ecuador," *Journal of Iberian and Latin American Research* 20, no. 3 (2014): 399–422, copyright Taylor and Francis, available at http://tandfonline.com/10.1080/13260219.2014.995877. Chapter 7 is based in part on an article published as "Ventriloquism, Racism and the Politics of Decoloniality in Ecuador in *Cultural Studies* 32, no. 3 (April 2018): 389–413, copyright Taylor and Francis, available at http://tandfonline.com/10.1080/09502386.2017.1420091.

Finally, I would like to thank my husband, Carlos de la Torre, for introducing me to Ecuador and for teaching me a lot of what I know about that country and about Latin America in general. He has a critical eye and is a great reader and an enthusiastic supporter.

LIST OF ABBREVIATIONS

CAAP	Andean Center for Popular Action (Centro Andino de Acción Popular)
CEAACES	Council for the Evaluation, Accreditation, and Assessment of the Quality of Higher Education (Consejo de Evaluación, Acreditación y Aseguramiento de la Calidad de la Educación Superior)
CEPAL	Economic Comission for Latin America (Comisión Económica Para América Latina)
CIESAS	Center for Advanced Studies and Research in Social Anthropology (Centro de Investigaciones y Estudios Superiores en Antropología Social)
CODAE	Corporation of Afro-Ecuadorian Development (Corporación de Desarrollo Afroecuatoriano)
CODENPE	Council for the Development of the Nationalities and Peoples of Ecuador (Consejo de Desarrollo de las Nacionalidades y Pueblos del Ecuador)
CODEPMOC	Council for the Development of the Montubio People of the Coast (Consejo de Desarrollo del Pueblo Montubio de la Costa)
CONAIE	Confederation of Indigenous Nationalities of Ecuador (Confederación de Nacionalidades Indígenas del Ecuador)
CONEPIA	National Statistics Commission for Indigenous and Afro-Ecuadorian Peoples (Comisión Nacional de Estadísticas de Pueblos Indígenas y Afro-Ecuatorianos)
COOTAD	Organic Code of Territorial Organization, Autonomy, and Decentralization (Código Orgánico de Organización Territorial, Autonomía y Descentralización)

CORMONLIT	Montubio Corporation of the Coast (Corporación Montubia del Litoral)
CRCC	Chinese Railroads and Construction Company, a public construction company
DINEIB	National Directorate of Intercultural Bilingual Education (Dirección Nacional de Educación Intercultural Bilingüe)
DIPEIB	Provincial Directorate of Intercultural Bilingual Education (Dirección Provincial de Educación Intercultural Bilingüe)
ECLA	Economic Commission for Latin America (Comisión Económica Para América Latina)
ECORAE	Institute for Regional Ecodevelopment of the Ecuadorian Amazon (Instituto para el Ecodesarrollo Regional de la Amazonía Ecuatoriana)
ECSA	A Chinese mining company (Ecuacorriente Sociedad Anónima)
ECUARUNARI	Awakening of the Ecuadorian Runa (Ecuador Runakunapak Rikcharimuy), an organization of the Kichwa of the highlands, a regional branch of CONAIE.
EIB	Intercultural bilingual education (Educación Intercultural Bilingüe)
FEI	Ecuadorian Federation of Indians (Federación Ecuatoriana de Indios)
FEINE	Ecuadorian Federation of Protestant Evangelical Indigenous Peoples (Federación Ecuatoriana de Indígenas Evangélicos)
FENOCIN	National Federation of Peasant, Indigenous, and Black Organizations (Federación Nacional de Organizaciones Campesinas, Indígenas y Negras)
FICSH	Interprovincial Federation of Shuar Centers (Federación Interprovincial de Centros Shuar)
FLACSO	Latin American Faculty of Social Sciences (Facultad Latinoamericana de Ciencias Sociales)
FODERUMA	Development Fund for Rural and Marginal Areas (Fondo de Desarrollo Rural Marginal)

ICCI	Scientific Institute of Indigenous Cultures (Instituto Científico de Culturas Indígenas)
INEC	National Institute of Statistics and Censuses (Instituto Nacional de Estadísticas y Censos)
LOEI	Organic Law of Intercultural Education (Ley Orgánica de Educación Intercultural)
MAS	Movement toward Socialism (Movimiento al Socialismo)
MICC	Indigenous and Peasant Movement of Cotopaxi (Movimiento Indígena y Campesino de Cotopaxi)
NBI	Unsatisfied basic needs (necesidades básicas insatisfechas), a statistical indicator
PAC	Cotopaxi Academic Program (Programa Académico Cotopaxi)
PRODEPINE	Indigenous and Afro-Ecuadorian Peoples Development Project (Programa de Desarrollo de los Pueblos Indígenas y Negros)
PUCE	Pontifical Catholic University of Ecuador (Pontificia Universidad Católica del Ecuador)
SEIC	System of Indigenous Schools of the Cotopaxi Province (Sistema de Escuelas Indígenas de Cotopaxi)
SENPLADES	National Secretariat for Planning and Development (Secretaría Nacional de Planificación y Desarrollo)
SERBISH	Shuar Intercultural Bilingual Radio Education System (Sistema Educativo Radiofónico Bicultural Shuar)
SIISE	System of Social Indicators of Ecuador (Sistema de Indicadores Sociales del Ecuador)
UINPI	Intercultural University of Indigenous Nationalities and Peoples (Universidad Intercultural de las Nacionalidades y Pueblos Indígenas Amawta Wasi)
UNE	National Teachers' Union (Unión Nacional de Educadores)
UPS	Unit of Social Participation, a working group of the 2007–2008 Constituent Assembly (Unidad de participación social)

UNDOING
MULTICULTURALISM

Map 1. Administrative map of Ecuador, from the Perry-Castañeda Library Map Collection, University of Texas Libraries.

INTRODUCTION

UNDOING MULTICULTURALISM

Twenty-first-century Left governments in Latin America promised to "decolonize" their societies by advancing indigenous and Afrodescendant protections and rights and by redistributing resources to the most vulnerable, who often happened to be ethnic and racialized groups (Escobar 2010; Lander 2017). On the basis of almost two decades of ethnographic research, this book discusses why these good intentions were not implemented and why indigenous rights came to be the Achilles heel of turn to the Left governments (Angosto Ferrández 2015). Seeking independence from multilateral organizations and the United States and in the context of skyrocketing commodity prices, twenty-first-century Left governments became highly reliant on natural resource extraction. Indigenous, Afrodescendant, and other organized groups resisted the expansion of extractive industries into their territories as they threatened their livelihood and safety. As governments struggled to finance budgets and keep themselves in power, they watered down subnational forms of self-government, slowed down land redistribution, weakened the politicized cultural identities that gave strength to social movements, and reversed other fundamental gains of the multicultural era. The twenty-first-century Left was particularly effective in undoing multiculturalism because its radical discourses legitimized the regimes, its leaders justified sacrificing indigenous and environmental protections as a trade-off for redistributive policies and the alleviation of poverty, and government officials with a trajectory on leftist organizations knew well the internal dynamics of social movements.

This book analyzes the paradoxical reversal of multiculturalism under the rule of the Left through an examination of Ecuador's Citizens' Revolution, led by President Rafael Correa (2007–2017). The book argues that this government's dependency on natural resources and its choice of centralized, authoritarian rule underpin this reversal. The book does not look at resource extraction per se and does not focus exclusively on the areas of the country where this activity takes place. It examines the deterioration of multiculturalism at the national level and analyzes this process within multiple layers of context. To do so, the book examines the consequences for indigenous people of the transition between neoliberalization and the regime of Rafael Correa, that has self-identified as and has been called postneoliberal. By "postneoliberal," I do not mean that all neoliberal policies and logics were radically and permanently transformed under Correa to give way to a better and fairer economic model. The book argues instead that some processes characteristic of neoliberalism such as the reduction and privatization of the public sector and the promotion of globalization and free trade were reversed and replaced by a stronger, centralized state and nationalist economic policies funded with the revenues from oil and other natural resources. For this reason, I prefer to use the term "nationalist-extractivism" to refer to the political-economic configuration that characterized Correa's decade. The book also argues that neoliberal forms of governance first weakened and depoliticized indigenous movements. When Correa came to power, he found organizations that were already fragile. Indigenous organizations challenged the regime's development and centralization policies, which further circumscribed the rights of this population.

By multiculturalism, I mean the policies and state institutions seeking to recognize and include indigenous peoples and Afro-Ecuadorians. However, the book focuses mostly on the indigenous sector, given the difficulties of examining both social movements in sufficient depth. Multicultural policies such as intercultural bilingual education, the official recognition of indigenous systems of justice, and the official acknowledgment of territorial autonomy were achievements of social movement struggles in the previous decades. Under neoliberalization the state and multilateral organizations privileged symbolic and cultural forms of recognition over the redistribution of resources and deeper structural transformations (Hale 2002). Superficial forms of recognition encouraged leaders and organizations to focus on short-term technical and cultural goals rather than working toward more radical changes (Bretón 2005). However, under Correa even these limited forms of recognition and participation typical of neoliberalism were reversed in the context of weak indigenous organization and the regime's emphasis on centralized rule and resource extraction. This book shows that indigenous rights did not advance in Ecuador beyond vague declarations, indigenous autonomy was curtailed, and some colonial legacies were able to come back and thrive. I now turn to how I arrived at this argument.

I first came to Ecuador in 1996, a few years after the first nationwide indigenous uprising and at the peak of indigenous organizational vitality. Two years later, a new constitution recognized Ecuador as a pluricultural and multiethnic nation and granted indigenous people and Afro-Ecuadorians collective rights that included tax-free communal property, intercultural bilingual education, and the official recognition of their systems of social organization and authority. In addition, the 1998 constitution conceded indigenous people the right to be consulted about the extraction of nonrenewable resources from their territories or to benefit from it, as well as the prerogative to receive compensation from any negative effects of extraction.

At the time, I was still working on my PhD dissertation, which focused on how whites and mestizos in positions of power were able to shape the identities of indigenous migrants to the Mexico–United States border. During my Mexican fieldwork, I observed that government officials were particularly influential in defining what it meant to be indigenous and in helping organize migrants on the basis of that definition. I also studied how intellectuals and economic elites understood indigeneity, and the effects of these understandings on people so labeled. The research entailed a discussion of racism and paternalism, a phenomenon that I found to be central to interethnic relations in Mexico and that was and still is understudied. I defined paternalism as a subtle form of discrimination that constructed racialized groups as lovable (as long as they stayed in their place), but also as fundamentally inferior. I found that those labeled indigenous at the Mexican border struggled for inclusion and the opportunity to move up the socioeconomic ladder. However, the powerful encouraged them to perform elite stereotypes of indigeneity, which kept them marginalized. Some of these preoccupations have accompanied me to this monograph. Like my previous book (Martínez Novo 2006), this one explores how the powerful conceive of indigeneity and how their ideas and related practices affect the lives of marginalized individuals and groups. Recurring topics are racism and other more subtle forms of discrimination.

I started conducting fieldwork in Ecuador in 2002. Some differences with my previous research drew my attention: although the state was overpresent in Mexico, it was relatively absent from the indigenous territories that I visited in Ecuador. Other nonindigenous actors were more salient—particularly the progressive Catholic Church and left-leaning intellectuals. These groups were also important in Mexico, but they were overshadowed by the presence and influence of government officials and state institutions. I started to investigate the development projects sponsored by nongovernmental actors in Ecuador, as well as the degree to which their goals harmonized or conflicted with indigenous expectations. Resonating with what I had previously found in Mexico, although the indigenous grassroots showed interest in inclusion and social mobility, leaders and their nonindigenous allies aimed to preserve native languages and cultures and keep this population relatively isolated as subsistence peasants. Later, I expanded my research into the study of intercultural bilingual education, a perfect setting to continue exploring interethnic relations. I noticed some tensions: indigenous people had achieved autonomy to manage their own system of education, but their schools received scant funding and the beneficiaries perceived them as a second-class option.

On the other hand, I was able to observe how indigenous people courageously conquered new spaces that had previously been closed to them. At FLACSO, the public research university where I worked for eight years, European cooperation agencies funded a graduate program for indigenous students from throughout Latin America. These students struggled to gain the acceptance of faculty, classmates, and the administration. Indigenous and Black students were successful in opening up this academic institution to a diverse student body and were able to graduate with advanced degrees. Their experiences are discussed in chapter 5.

The generalized perception at the time was one of a vibrant social movement struggle, increasing if reluctant societal inclusion, and new conquered spaces. In this context, I explored the ambiguities and tensions, advances and drawbacks of multicultural recognition under neoliberalization: some spaces were opened but not without great effort. Indigeneity was celebrated, but people and the institutions that served them remained underfunded and undervalued. Limited cultural recognition was privileged over greater equality. Advances and utopian experiments coexisted with the legacies of the past.

As I was enmeshed in the analysis of interethnic relations under neoliberal conditions, a radical change took place. Rafael Correa, a candidate who self-identified as leftist and Catholic, was elected in 2006. He was a college professor, and a good number of his early collaborators came from the very institution where I worked. Although I identify with the Left and come from a long line of radical and antifascist activists in Spain, Correa's movement did not convince me. Alianza País, Correa's party, decided not to present candidates for Congress because that institution represented for them the corrupt rule of political parties. Once in power, Correa dismissed the just elected Congress and called for new elections for a Constituent Assembly to rewrite the constitution. Correa's desire to reinforce executive power over checks and balances, and his social conservatism—antiabortion, ambiguously anti-LGBT, fond of aggressive masculinity—drove me away from this political movement even before Correa was first elected.

I also observed from early on the tensions in the regime's public performances of indigeneity. In Correa's first presidential inauguration in January 2007, he spoke the Kichwa language, wore an embroidered shirt with indigenous motifs, and chose a parish in an area populated by Kichwa-speaking peasants as the location for the event (Colloredo-Mansfeld, Mantilla, and Antrosio 2012). However, he did not interact with the locals as equals, and instead treated them as part of the background. In the launching of the regime's first development plan in the fall of 2007, government officials had mestizos in indigenous costume representing the indigenous nationalities of Ecuador. These performances posed a stark contrast to the struggles for inclusion and participation that I had witnessed before.

On the other hand, interesting developments were taking place at the time: creative environmental currents were part of the governing coalition, the 2007–2008 Constituent Assembly was vibrant with proposals for interculturalism, plurinationalism, affirmative action, the rights of nature, and the prohibition of labor subcontracting, among others. Correa and his inner circle struggled to control the Constituent Assembly and to limit what it could do. Declarations of plurinationalism, interculturalism, and the rights of nature made it to the constitutional text, but Kichwa and other native languages were not accepted on equal standing with Spanish; consultation with indigenous peoples regarding resource extraction was not made binding for the state; and indigenous territorial circumscriptions were set up in a way that made their creation very difficult. More important, the constitution centralized decision making in the executive and gave it absolute control over strategic sectors and nonrenewable resources.

Two years into Correa's rule, conflict started between the government and the Confederation of Indigenous Nationalities of Ecuador (CONAIE), the largest, nationwide indigenous organization. Beginning in January 2009, CONAIE demonstrated against drafts of mining and water laws that the communities had not been consulted on and that, according to CONAIE and other activists, would allow for the arrival of large-scale, open-pit mining and the privatization of water. Mining companies needed water in abundance and small-scale peasants were also thirsty for the resource and expected a progressive government to redistribute it. After the agrarian reforms of 1964 and 1973, large landowners had granted their laborers small plots that were typically located in the hills and poor in water. Meanwhile, hacienda owners had kept the best valley lands and hoarded the water.

Two months after the first protests, the government ended the autonomy with which indigenous organizations had managed intercultural bilingual education and drastically reduced the budget for indigenous development. Other dramatic events followed: Bosco Wisum, a Shuar teacher, was shot to death in demonstrations against the government in September 2009, and the Shuar leadership rather than the police were charged with the homicide. A Shuar radio station was threatened with closure for having called its audience to antigovernment demonstrations. President Correa scorned Marlon Santi, the head of CONAIE, on national television. Then, public prosecutors charged several indigenous leaders with the crimes of sabotage and terrorism, until hundreds of them were entangled in lengthy legal processes. Correa and other high government officials ridiculed indigenous customary law, which was recognized in 1998 and ratified in 2008, as a primitive practice. In 2014 the Supreme Court circumscribed indigenous law to cultural issues internal to communities and of lesser importance. The councils for indigenous and Afrodescendant development and for women, which previously had the rank of ministries and were tools for the participation of social movements in government, were closed and replaced by councils for equality whose members were selected by merit. The president, high government officials, and other members of the ruling party Alianza País continued making statements about indigenous leaders and organizations that would not have been considered politically correct in the previous period. The retrenchment in intercultural bilingual education policies, discussed in detail in chapter 4, was notorious, with most schools now teaching only in Spanish, indigenous teachers evaluated and then laid off, and community schools closed for alleged lack of quality. Affected by co-optation, division, and repression, indigenous organizations were in disarray, a process that is discussed at length in chapter 2.

In 2015, when demonstrations against the regime erupted in opposition to a proposal for permanent presidential reelection and changes to workers' social security, indigenous leaders were harshly repressed and communities in the areas of higher density of indigenous organization were militarized. A state of exception was declared in the southern Amazon where activists were resisting Chinese mining companies that had received government concessions. Not only were indigenous rights not moving forward, but the hard-won victories of the previous decades were now at risk, if not altogether gone. The environment of tolerance that had sent racism to a backseat, although it had definitely not ended it, transitioned toward a different milieu in which crude stereotypes were not only allowed but also celebrated. The book calls these multidimensional transformations "the undoing of multiculturalism."

As this was happening, the regime and its national and international supporters bragged about constitutional advances toward plurinationality, interculturalism, affirmative action, the rights of nature, and Sumak Kawsay or Buen Vivir (Good Living), a concept allegedly based on ancient Andean philosophy that became a central goal of development. Scholars, particularly at the international level, called Correa's regime decolonizing. More specifically, intellectuals praised Sumak Kawsay as proof that indigenous worldviews had finally made it into public policy. More sober critics justified the setbacks in indigenous rights with the argument that the government had prioritized ending poverty over collective rights, but that the fight against poverty was going to equally benefit the indigenous and Afro-Ecuadorian populations. A third group considered that the original project was groundbreaking and that the 2008 constitution was at the forefront of racial and environmental rights, but that a conservative inner circle had betrayed the revolution. As often happens in polarized political environments, those who were critical from the start were dismissed and labeled liberal or right-wingers. These intellectual debates are explored in depth in chapter 7. These events, tensions, and ambiguities, as well as the author's previous intellectual trajectory, inform the topics covered in this book: the rise and decline of indigenous rights in the transition from neoliberalization to the Correa regime.

Indigenous rights have retrenched not only in Ecuador but also throughout Latin America and globally, as the frontiers of extraction have moved forward in the context of the commodity boom of the first two decades of the 2000s. Here are some examples: Chile's Mapuche struggled against multinational forest companies, hydroelectric projects, and large landowners in their territories. The Chilean state has responded to indigenous resistance by militarizing Mapuche communities and charging and sentencing indigenous leaders under antiterrorism laws (Hale and Millamán 2018; Postero, Risor, and Prieto Montt 2018). Brazil's indigenous peoples have been displaced and some of their leaders assassinated in the context of the expansion of commercial agriculture and mining frontiers in the country's Amazon region (Farthing and Fabricant 2018). The Standing Rock Sioux of the United States courageously fought against the construction of the Dakota Access Pipeline that would move a half million barrels of oil a day beneath the Missouri River, the tribe's main source of drinking water. The Standing Rock movement confronted brutal police violence. Although the Obama administration ended up not approving the construction of the pipeline due to environmental concerns, President Trump issued an executive decree reversing the decision (Elbein 2017). The Dongria Kondh tribal people of Odisha, India, have mobilized against a bauxite mining operation run by the Vedanta Corporation of the United Kingdom. Despite the great damage that this kind of mining has done to vulnerable tribal peoples in India, the state of Odisha supported open-pit mining as one of its main strategies for development (Martínez Novo et al. 2018). Moreover, the Indian government proposed to roll back consent requirements for development projects that impact forest-dependent indigenous communities like the Kondh (Shakia and Gordon 2016). Under pressure from several governments (particularly Kenya, Tanzania, India, and Brazil), the World Bank relaxed its standards for indigenous protections in a revision to its indigenous people's policy in 2012 (Shakia and Gordon 2016). It was expected that the bank would broaden its indigenous policy after the UN adoption of the 2007 Declaration on the Rights of Indigenous Peoples. Instead, "free, prior, and informed consent" was watered down and substituted for the softer concept of "broad community support" in the revised guidelines. Some countries have also been able to opt out of prior consent if they feel that the policy is inconsistent with their national constitutions or that it may promote ethnic strife.

Indigenous peoples have become the main obstacle for the extraction of commodities, the prices of which boomed in the early 2000s. Because native groups were historically pushed out of the fertile valleys and into the less productive rain forests and mountain ranges, they inhabit the territories where most of the remaining strategic resources are located. This book shows that resource extraction impacts not only the areas and groups where the activity takes place but also collective rights at the national and international levels. States restrict indigenous autonomy and try to limit their political organization and cultural cohesion to curb resistance to extractivism.

In a special issue of the journal *Cultural Studies*, Laura Junka-Aikio and Catalina Cortés-Severino (2017) define extractivism as the current moment of dwindling resources, environmental degradation, and social and economic inequality that conveys a sense of urgency. The authors understand extractivism in its narrow sense as the mass-scale removal of nonrenewable resources such as oil, gas, and minerals. However, they also encourage scholars to think more broadly about extractivism, as a paradigm of severe exploitation characteristic of late capitalism. Researchers must reach beyond the immediate sites and effects of extraction and examine the wider ideologies, discourses, and practices, the cultures and worldviews, underpinning this activity. Imre Szeman (2017) adds that extractivism often takes place in the periphery and the countryside. Even though urban dwellers are highly dependent on the products of extraction, the geographic location of this activity away from urban settings may render it invisible to urbanites. Extraction may involve native peoples and remote territories, but an expanded view of the phenomenon affects all contemporary situations. Extractivism is a process that reshapes the natural and social environment and has consequences for those living close to the sites of extraction as well as for those far from these locations. This book focuses on the effects of extractivism beyond mines and wells, and particularly on the consequences of extractivism for national and international multicultural policies.

Racial Formations, Racism, and Paternalism

Neoliberalization and Correa's nationalist-extractivism produced particular configurations in the social construction of race and ethnicity and in the management of racialized populations. I follow the premise that race and ethnicity are socially constructed and historically fluid. The process of defining racial and ethnic groups is fraught with confusion, contradiction, and unintended consequences. Definitions and categories are created and contested from above and below, as state-imposed classifications face challenges by individuals and groups (Omi and Winant 2015). Thus, this book is not only concerned with indigenous movements and communities but also with the state, nongovernmental actors, and interethnic relations. For instance, chapter 3 analyzes the Ecuadorian state's changing definitions of ethnicity and race in the two conjunctures under study.

The book discusses not only the *indigenismo* of the Ecuadorian state but also the projects of Catholic missionaries, anthropologists, ethnolinguists, and other actors in the transition from neoliberalization to nationalist-extractivism. Like Joanne Rappaport (2005), this research conceptualizes indigenous movements as "intercultural utopias" shaped by indigenous peoples as well as by their allies. Indigenismo is understood widely as the policies for indigenous peoples produced by non-Indians, as non-Indians taking the role of mediators and "ventriloquists" for indigenous voices, and as the larger political realm of interethnic relations (Ramos 1998). The book argues that while some advocates have been vital for the rise of an indigenous movement and for the advancement of indigenous rights, other actors have sought to co-opt and weaken indigenous organizations, particularly those branches that have opposed resource extraction in their territories or have posed challenges to centralized governance.

I build on Michael Omi and Howard Winant's concept of racial formation, "the socio-historical process by which racial identities are created, lived out, transformed and destroyed" (Omi and Winant 2015, 109). Omi and Winant understand race as both a social-historical structure and a set of accumulated signifiers. Racial projects link structure and signification. "A racial project is simultaneously an interpretation, representation or explanation of racial identities and meanings and an effort to organize and distribute resources (economic, political, cultural) along particular racial lines" (Omi and Winant 2015, 125). Racial projects connect the cultural meanings of race with the ways in which social structures and everyday experiences are racially organized.

This book examines the role of government and nongovernmental actors in the creation and implementation of such racial projects. It then contrasts racial projects created from above with those of indigenous individuals, communities, and organizations. The book starts with an examination of the role of the state in race making and analyzes how official projects have shifted (or not) with historical conjunctures (see chapters 2 and 3). Chapter 4 discusses intercultural bilingual education, a space in which different actors and racial projects (state, intellectual, religious, and social movement) converge. It continues with the contribution of anthropologists to the making and unmaking of the Ecuadorian indigenous movement (chapter 5) and the role of missionaries in raising indigenous consciousness and political organization (chapter 6), and ends with an examination of subtle and more open forms of discrimination, another domain where state, intellectuals, and social actors converge (chapter 7).

Racism is often defined narrowly as racial hate, an approach that hinders the understanding of racial inequality (Omi and Winant 2015). Missing from this interpretation are the ideologies, policies, and practices that normalize racial domination. Omi and Winant argue that a racial project can be defined as racist if it reproduces structures of power based on racial signification and identities. On the other hand, an antiracist project is one that undoes or resists these structures. Therefore, hate does not need to be present for a project to be racist. Similarly, this book understands racism widely as the ideas and practices that sustain inequality on the basis of physical or cultural racialization. I am particularly concerned with paternalism and other forms of subtle discrimination, which communicate care and even love, but also uphold inequality. Chapter 7 examines ventriloquism, a practice through which the dominant speaks for, while also silencing, the subaltern. However, the book is also concerned with the reemergence of more virulent forms of discrimination, which it links to the intensification of extractivism, the erosion of democracy, and to white and mestizo backlash.

The Political Economy Approach and the Management of Diversity under Neoliberalism

This book explores forms of governance of the indigenous peoples of the Ecuadorian Andes and the Amazon by examining indigenous politics in the wider context of interethnic relations as well as through a historical lens that reaches back to roughly the 1970s. However, some chapters look farther back in history as needed to debunk the multiple layers of the past that help explain particular issues. The book builds on the political economy and cultural studies traditions as it aims to understand contemporary people's experiences within wider historical, socioeconomic, political, and geographic contexts (Grossberg 2006; Mintz 1985; Roseberry 1994; Wolf 2010 [1982]). Lawrence Grossberg calls this method "radical contextualism" and argues that the approach considers any event relationally, as a condensation of multiple determinations. The idea is to examine an issue by placing it in the big picture.

Grossberg notes that the practice of contextualism in cultural studies often involves an effort to critically examine a particular conjuncture. A conjuncture should not be understood simply as a slice of time or a period, but as a moment defined by the accumulation and condensation of contradictions (Grossberg 2006, 5). According to Grossberg, it is at the level of the conjuncture, and through a better understanding of the conjuncture, that knowledge can be most usefully articulated to political struggles and radical possibilities. The conjuncture examined in this book is the transition from neoliberal to economic-nationalist governance in first two decades of the twenty-first century. In each period there are important differences, but continuities as well. My purpose is to write a political history of the present (Grossberg 2006, 2). Citing Raymond Williams, Grossberg (2006, 5) encourages us to "get the balance right between the old and the new, the emergent, the dominant and the residual." An effective analysis of the conjuncture opens onto a multiplicity of overlapping contexts, of contexts operating at different scales, and what we might call embedded contexts (Grossberg 2006). For example, to understand race and ethnicity in the 2010 population census in chapter 3, I find it necessary to examine social movement struggles, the workings of the nationalist-extractivist state, the influences of multilateral organizations such as the United Nations as well as indigenous memories of colonial and republican census taking. The commitment to complexity, contingency, contestation, and multiplicity are central to this kind of analysis (Grossberg 2006).

The book analyzes how the neoliberal and nationalist-extractivist conjunctures led to a progressive deterioration of indigenous rights. Whereas several governments had a neoliberal orientation in Ecuador since the 1980s, the government of Rafael Correa (2007–2017) self-identified as and has been called postneoliberal (Lu, Valdivia, and Silva 2017). Correa undid some central tenets of neoliberalism: he enlarged and expanded the reach of the state, aimed to protect national production with tariffs and nationalist campaigns, and forbade precarious labor arrangements. This does not mean that the regime, as did others of the turn to the Left, transcended neoliberalism in any permanent or comprehensive way (Goodale and Postero 2013; Orta 2013). The expansion of the state was tied to the sales of Ecuadorian oil in the international market, progressive labor regulations were reversed once the prices of oil plunged, and some neoliberal cultural logics survived the shift (Orta 2013). Although the terms neoliberalism and postneoliberalism may seem technical, Ecuadorian citizens used the labels to convey their experiences: indigenous and other Ecuadorians perceived these conjunctures as sets of policies corresponding to two sharply differentiated time periods that transformed their lives in radical ways.

I prefer to use the term "nationalist-extractivism" rather than postneoliberalism to convey that neoliberalism was not permanently transcended or improved on under Correa's rule. However, it was not left intact either, but replaced by a different political economic model that was nationalist and geared toward reinforcing and protecting the state and the national economy. It was also extractivist because it depended almost exclusively on natural resource rents for its political and economic reproduction. From a political standpoint, it was a semiauthoritarian or hybrid regime, which kept a democratic facade, holding elections and respecting some basic rules of democracy, while also manipulating the public sphere and civil society (Conaghan 2017). I prefer the term "nationalist-extractivism" to Eduardo Gudynas's (2009) "progressive extractivism." In my view, the term "progressive" still reflects the ambivalence of some intellectuals toward the regimes in which they participated. "Progressive extractivism" glosses over the semiauthoritarian, nationalist tendencies, and only highlights the poor environmental choices. Nationalist-extractivism is not necessarily a new configuration because it takes many traits from the former import substitution, oil-fueled (if oil was available), and nationalist Latin American states of the early twentieth century.

The first conjuncture considered in this book is neoliberalism. I understand the concept as a set of policies and processes that give shape to a particular style of capitalism. Neoliberalism is typically associated with the retrenchment of the state, the privatization of sectors previously owned and managed by the state, the shrinking of social policies, particularly in education and health, or their privatization at the hands of nonstate actors such as nongovernmental organizations or faith-based organizations. Neoliberalism is also associated with the "flexibilization" of labor. The neoliberal labor structure relies on a small core of permanent workers and a growing periphery of temporary, part-time, and subcontracted labor (Harvey 1990). Globalization is a central tenet of neoliberalism, a practice that favors open borders, free trade, outsourcing, and exports (Harvey 2005). The logic under neoliberalism is the concentration of profits at the hands of a small elite and the dispossession of the majority as labor becomes cheaper, more precarious, and more difficult to organize, and as the social services and subsidies provided by the state diminish (Harvey 2005).

As David Harvey (2005) has noted, this process started first as a set of ideas that were elaborated in conservative think tanks and then tried in different parts of the world with varying levels of effectiveness and in uneven ways. Neoliberalism started to be implemented in the 1970s and spread throughout the world in the 1980s and 1990s. It started as a response to what elites perceived as the rigidities of Fordist capitalism and the welfare state, which were characterized by an inflexible organization of production, an organized full-time labor force that was able to capture a greater share of the profits, and a safety net of state services and subsidies. Of course, the core of laborers was mostly white and male, and other workers were excluded from these benefits.

In Latin America, neoliberalism did not arrive as a choice of the government or the majority of the population, but was mostly imposed by US-led multilateral organizations such as the International Monetary Fund (IMF) and the World Bank in the context of the debt crisis of the 1980s. Financial packages for indebted countries required undertaking structural adjustment measures and budget austerity. In this context, the size of the state was reduced, state enterprises were privatized, the budget for social services shrank, and state subsidies for first necessity products were eliminated or reduced. These general recipes were applied unevenly depending on the social struggles and balance of power in each country. For these reasons, some authors prefer to call these changes neoliberalization instead of neoliberalism, to emphasize their unevenness instead of reifying it (Peck, Theodore, and Brenner 2010). As structural adjustment was applied in different countries in Latin America, popular riots and uprisings took place. In the case of Ecuador, the vibrant indigenous movement of the 1990s has been interpreted as a reaction to structural adjustment measures (Zamosc 1994). Some structural adjustment recipes such as the elimination of the subsidies for oil and gas could not be implemented in Ecuador due to the recurrent uprisings of the indigenous movement and its allies.

Combining political economy with the work of Michel Foucault, other authors have understood neoliberalization as a political rationality that emerges as a form of governmentality (Brown 2003; Radcliffe 2015). Based on Foucault's thought, Wendy Brown defines governmentality as a process by which the state educates its subjects instead of only controlling or repressing them. In this way, governmentality is a "mode of governance encompassing, but not limited to the state, which produces subjects, forms of citizenship and behavior and a new organization of the social" (Brown 2003, 2).

Brown argues that neoliberalization reaches beyond material processes to the souls of citizens by extending and disseminating market values. Neoliberal political rationality submits the political sphere and every policy and action to considerations of profitability and cost–benefit. In this mindset, all human action is understood as rational, entrepreneurial action. The makers of neoliberalism did not understand these dispositions as being inherent to human nature, but as ideas that needed to be disseminated through institutional practices and rewards for enacting this vision. According to Brown, the imposition of neoliberal rationality has dire consequences for liberal democracy. Neoliberalism entails the erosion of oppositional political, moral, or subjective claims located outside of capitalist rationality, but inside liberal democracy. This book looks not only at neoliberal but also at nationalist-extractivist rationalities and governmentalities. It considers how neoliberalization and nationalist-extractivism structured individual and collective subjectivities and behaviors. It also discusses how elements of a neoliberal rationality were able to survive under Correa's rule, despite the fact that he rejected neoliberalism.

Omi and Winant (2015) associate neoliberalism in the United States with the racial ideology of color blindness, or the idea that race has become irrelevant. The civil rights movement accomplished partial reforms at a tremendous human cost. Omi and Winant argue that after these reforms, there was a conservative backlash that intended to resignify race in order to contain the social movement. Because open racism was no longer legitimate, the Right continued using stereotypes, but it did so through coded words and euphemisms. Then conservatives evolved toward the idea of "reverse racism," which held that racially inclusive policies were unfair to whites. The Right presented itself as having apprehended the true meaning of civil rights, that race should not matter. Color-blind approaches went beyond reverse racism in that they repudiated the very concept of race. This ideology fits well with neoliberalism due to its individualist emphasis. However, it clashes with the racist projects of neoliberalism such as anti-immigrant initiatives, racial profiling, mass incarceration, the disenfranchisement of voters, and the assault on welfare.

Color blindness is not the only racial project of neoliberalism. A shallow form of multiculturalism also pairs well with processes of neoliberalization. Multiculturalism consists of state and social reforms achieved as a result of the struggles of racialized populations. Similarly to the United States, in Latin America these gains eventually gave way to backlash. Conservatives accepted some symbolic and cultural recognition, while hindering deeper structural changes and the redistribution of resources. This strategy has been called "neoliberal multiculturalism" (Fraser 1996; Hale 2002, 2006; Martínez Novo 2006; Postero 2007). Indigenous activists were classified as those who were "permitted" because they stuck to shallow cultural and folkloric claims, the so-called *indio permitido* (a concept that Charles Hale borrowed from Silvia Rivera Cusicanqui), and those labeled "subversive" who were repressed or criminalized because they sought more profound socioeconomic changes. These strategies have allowed neoliberal multiculturalism to shape indigenous subjectivities.

For Ecuador's indigenous peoples, neoliberal forms of governance emphasized cultural recognition and provided token positions for leaders, while also precluding deeper socioeconomic transformations for communities and the grassroots. Indigenous organizations were given autonomy in domains such as education but they were not allocated enough funds to make it work well. Moreover, policies like Indigenous and Afro-Ecuadorian Peoples Development Project (PRODEPINE), designed and financed by the World Bank in collaboration with the Ecuadorian state, encouraged indigenous leaders to focus on short-term technical solutions and localized development projects while postponing more comprehensive agendas that would benefit the communities (Bretón 2005). In Ecuador, neoliberal multiculturalism produced disaffected indigenous grassroots—those for whom things had not gotten better—that were ready to support the nonindigenous project of Rafael Correa. Poor non-Indians who felt excluded from World Bank's ethnodevelopment and other multicultural perks were also eager to support Correa's project, particularly rural and provincial whites and mestizos.[1]

On the other hand, neoliberal forms of governance did bring some cultural recognition, delegitimized open racism in the public sphere, and encouraged participation and decentralization, which in some cases facilitated indigenous political organization and allowed activists to challenge the neoliberal status quo (Postero 2007). Multicultural policies opened spaces for indigenous individuals and allowed some youth to have access to higher education, factors that contributed to the advancement of this population.

Deepening the intellectual trend that articulates larger political economic processes with the making of subjectivities, recent work combines political economy with phenomenological approaches and examines how individuals experience wider processes at the intimate levels of emotions, affects, and the body (Gutiérrez Aguilar 2014; Krupa and Nugent 2015; Tapias 2015). These works not only connect the global with the local but also articulate different scales of analysis with the affects and sensations of individuals. As María Tapias (2015, 129) puts it, "through women's stories I seek to explore what neoliberalism 'felt like,' drawing upon their local knowledge of the body, emotions and sociality as these interacted in dialogic relationship with political, juridical and economic state structures." Similarly, this book explores how political economic processes shape the intimate fabric of civil society, affect people's everyday experiences, their subjectivities, desires, and fears. The authors cited above examined lived experiences under neoliberalization. This book expands the analysis to the study of individual experiences with nationalist-extractivism.

---

1. I use "whites and mestizos" or "white-mestizo" instead of just "mestizos" to highlight the diversity within the dominant group in Ecuador. Although "mestizo" is the term that Latin American states have promoted throughout the twentieth century, not all individuals in the racially dominant or unmarked strata of society identify or are identified with this term. Some still use "white" to refer to themselves and others. The term "white-mestizo" coined by Andrés Guerrero and then used by many other scholars in Ecuador calls attention to the social difference between an elite of European and landowning descent and the middle- and working-class strata of society.

From Postneoliberalism to Nationalist-Extractivism

The literature on postneoliberalism has focused on both the antineoliberal political turn in Latin America that led to the election of several left of center governments in the first decade of the 2000s, and the aftermath of the 2008 global economic crisis that gave rise to novel forms of social and political resistance, particularly in Europe, the United States, and North Africa (Castells 2012; Peck, Theodore, and Brenner 2010). As a result, a number of experiments attempting to rework the state, the economy, and civil society have been called postneoliberal (Elwood et al. 2017). Some states undertook redistributive projects and refused to cooperate with the austerity imperatives of multinational institutions. Social movements such as Occupy in the United States, Indignados in Spain, and Aganaktismenoi in Greece resisted austerity policies and have politicized inequality in novel ways (Castells 2012).

Postneoliberalism has been interpreted as a set of contradictory and reversible interventions that articulate change with vestiges of neoliberalism and with the previous legacies of liberalism and colonialism (Elwood et al. 2017). For these reasons, some authors prefer to call the phenomenon "neoliberalism interrupted" (Goodale and Postero 2013) or "semineoliberalism" (Orta 2013). Elwood argues that although Global South states have tried to implement changes to transcend neoliberalism, they have been locked in adverse positions vis-à-vis global capital and multilateral governance that have hindered these transformations. For instance, South Africa had all the conditions for the construction of a postneoliberal society: robust social movements, high levels of inequality, and a strong left-leaning leadership. However, these conditions did not allow this country to create a postneoliberal society, but rather what Patrick Bond has called a nationalist neoliberalism (Elwood et al. 2017). While keeping a radical nationalist discourse, Nelson Mandela was forced to accept multilaterally imposed structural adjustment measures that left South Africa in a situation of high inequality, poverty, and unemployment. Similarly, the return of the state in Latin America came with attempts at redistribution and the expansion of social programs as well as a position of noncooperation with transnational capital. However, these advances were paid for by a commodity-based extraction economy governed by global prices. Global South countries trying to overcome neoliberalism were confronted with two options: either bend to multilateral requirements in order to get financial aid, or become independent from the IMF and the World Bank by privileging resource extraction at a time of booming prices.

The crisis of neoliberalism arrived earlier in Latin America than in the Global North. Latin Americans protested the discontinuation of social welfare benefits, as well as poverty, inequality, and stagnant economic growth during the 1990s and in the first decade of the 2000s. Latin American social movements also questioned racial and ethnic discrimination (Escobar 2010). A central tenet of postneoliberalism in South America has been "bringing back the state"—a stronger state more present in all aspects of social, political, and economic life. Bringing back the state has been fraught with paradoxes. A stronger state has sometimes meant reasonable regulation, more social services, and greater redistribution, but also an excess of control over territory and society. Furthermore, authoritarian means of securing regime power in the face of social movement resistance have produced ambiguities that have systematically truncated its transformative potential.

In its early days, the Correa regime tried to build a postneoliberal state by strengthening public participation in strategic sectors of the economy, particularly oil, mining, and public services. The state renegotiated contracts with transnational companies, raised income and indirect taxes, and increased its efficiency in collecting them. It regulated the financial sector, asking the banks to repatriate capital held abroad and strengthening public and cooperative banks. Development planning attempted to prioritize internal development and selective import substitution industrialization over an export orientation. The regime protected national industry with tariffs on imports and a publicity campaign called "Ecuador First" that encouraged citizens to consume Ecuadorian products. Correa also sought to increase national sovereignty, ending an agreement that permitted a United States military base in Ecuador, and diversified its international relations, strengthening ties with China, other Latin American countries, and the Middle East. Furthermore, Correa's regime sought to push back neoliberalization through labor policies and redistribution. Forms of precarious labor were forbidden and all workers were expected to enjoy full-time, indefinite contracts and to be registered with the social security. State-led redistribution took several forms. The executive increased the minimum wage and assisted its poorest citizens through policies such as the Bonus for Human

Development (a conditional cash transfer), the Bonus for Housing, and the Dignity Electricity Tariff (F. Ramírez 2010).

Despite these efforts, the Correa regime did not succeed in diversifying the economy, instead continuing to depend and increasing its dependency on oil, raw materials, and agro-exports. Private investment was hindered by greater regulation and relatively high wages for the region due to a dollarized economy. In Ecuador's rentier economy, diversification of private investment was unlikely, given that abundant public rents from oil could be easily captured with less risk (Coronil 1997). The economy relied on publicly funded projects, particularly in strategic sectors and infrastructure. The expansion of extractive activities worsened environmental damage and exacerbated opposition by indigenous peoples and others living in extraction frontiers, as well as by environmentalists, key participants in the Correa government in the early years.

Building a more inclusive society was also constrained by middle- and upper-class control of key government positions. Structural reforms to redistribute non-oil wealth and the means of production, such as a comprehensive agrarian reform, were not undertaken (Radcliffe 2012). Redistributing some oil rents to the poor proved easier than tackling complex social, political, and structural change. Elites have profited from public investment through contracts with the state and subsidies on production, with the one hundred biggest banks, construction, commercial, industry, and agrobusinesses growing 50 percent more from 2007 to 2011 than they had in the previous years (Acosta 2013, 16). Elites resisted higher wages and state regulations, yet benefited greatly from public investment, growth of internal markets, and political stability. Furthermore, a professional middle-class captured state rents through high-paid consultancies, jobs in the public sector, and scholarships.

This process of rapid state formation could only continue while oil and commodities prices skyrocketed from rising Asian demand. With oil prices decreasing since 2014, the Ecuadorian state has continued relying on China as an investor and lender, but could not negotiate from a position of strength. Loans and concessions came at high interests and with disadvantageous terms. As oil prices continued plunging, Ecuador was not able to keep borrowing with its devalued hydrocarbon resources as collateral. With few resources to distribute, the political legitimacy of the regime eroded, state growth slowed, and the privatization of state enterprises and layoffs of public employees ensued (Acosta 2016; Petrich 2016). Dwindling state rents were accompanied by the resurgence of some neoliberal strategies. Desperate for private investment, the Correa government announced a proposal of law to bring "flexible" labor arrangements back (*La República*, February 6, 2016).

As state redistribution stalled, social control and repression increased. Building a stronger and bigger state based on extraction resulted in authoritarian tendencies and the wish to control autonomous social movements, particularly those like the indigenous movement that were able to threaten governability and/or the extraction of those resources on which the state's budget depended. This book examines the process of deterioration of multiculturalism in Ecuador, a trend that has been evident in recent years, but that has yet to be thoroughly studied. Anthropologists have criticized the shallowness of neoliberal multicultural policies and their inability to consistently raise the standard of living of indigenous populations (Hale 2002; Martínez Novo 2006; Postero 2007). However, the rise of nationalist, extraction-oriented governance in the period 2000–2015 shows that the state and oil and mining companies perceive even those limited understandings of collective rights typical of neoliberalism as an obstacle. On the other hand, the rentier petro state has been able to cut back on indigenous rights because the social movements were weakened and depoliticized in the previous neoliberal period.

Nationalist-Extractivism and Indigenous Rights

Turn to the Left governments in Latin America in the first decade of the 2000s not only rejected neoliberalism but also questioned the legacy of colonialism and the environmental crisis (Escobar 2010; Lander 2017; Postero 2017). Because these regimes originated in social movements—indigenous, Afrodescendant, environmental—instead of political parties, they combined the insights of socialism with those of the new social movements (Lander 2017). Scholars believed that the recognition of cultural diversity would come this time with the redistribution of resources (Hoffman French 2009; Postero 2007). However, growing dependence on resource extraction eventually thwarted the goals of expanding indigenous rights and preserving the natural environment (Lander 2017; Lu et al. 2017; Postero 2017). After a decade or more of rule by the Left in several South American countries, indigenous rights have not improved to the degree that scholars predicted, and in many cases have retrenched. An author sympathetic to the Hugo Chávez regime has argued that indigenous rights are the Achilles heel of the twentieth-first-century Latin American Left (Angosto Ferrández 2015).

Historically, the Latin American Left criticized development based on resource extraction because it depends on exports, transnational corporations dominate the sector, and labor conditions are poor. Leftists proposed avoiding dependency, diversifying production, and industrializing raw materials (Gudynas 2009). Despite this tradition, twenty-first century-Left governments continued to prioritize "extractivism," "a style of development based on the appropriation of nature that feeds a nondiversified production system and that depends on the international insertion of the country as a provider of raw materials" (Gudynas 2009, 188).[2] The Latin American Left not only continued with the extractivism of previous regimes but also intensified it, opening new frontiers and pursuing the mining of new commodities (Gudynas 2009).

However, there are differences between natural resource extraction under leftist regimes and the practices of the past or those of the countries that have not turned toward the Left. For this reason, Gudynas calls the extractivism of the twenty-first-century Left "neo-extractivism" or "progressive neo-extractivism." An important difference is that now the state has a more active role. On the other hand, the state still privileges an export orientation and accepts a subordinate position in the world market as an exporter of raw materials.

Left governments have been more effective in justifying resource extraction and in palliating the social unrest that it causes than their neoliberal counterparts. Through the renegotiation of contracts with transnational companies, higher taxation, and the preference for state companies, Latin American states have captured a larger share of the profits. Some of this money has been used for social assistance programs and conditional cash transfers to the poor, legitimating these governments as left-leaning (Gudynas 2009). Extraction has been justified as a way to end poverty and as a necessary sacrifice to achieve national development (Farthing and Fabricant 2018). However, the regimes still aimed to attain financial success and to make as much money as possible. Thus, the socioenvironmental impacts of

---

2. Translations in this book are the author's unless otherwise indicated.

extraction have remained the same or even worse than those produced by transnational companies (Farthing and Fabricant 2018; Gudynas 2009; Lu, Valdivia, and Silva 2016). Meanwhile, twenty-first-century Left governments have denied or minimized the social and environmental impacts of extraction, and its detractors have been depicted as having occult political agendas or as being manipulated by foreign powers (Gudynas 2009). Furthermore, this book argues that government officials with a trajectory in the Left have been able to work more effectively from within social movements to divide and repress them.

As these governments opened new frontiers and externalized the social and environmental costs of extraction, they clashed with organized social actors, particularly indigenous peoples (Farthing and Fabricant 2018; Gudynas 2009). Most states have accepted consultation with indigenous communities, but prior consultation has not been legislated as binding for the state, and most of the time consultations are not conducted. Extractivism has conditioned territorial organization, the assignation of protected areas, and the plans, or lack thereof, for agrarian reform. For instance, twenty-first-century Left countries have not implemented sweeping agrarian reforms, and have instead promoted land titling. Agrarian reform conflicts with extractivism, which benefits from land concentration in private hands. There is also pressure to open protected areas and natural parks to oil and mining prospecting (Angosto Ferrández 2015; Gudynas 2009; Lander 2017).

Another difference compared to previous forms of extractivism lies in geopolitics. Asian demand produced the boom in prices of commodities from roughly 2000 to 2011, which closely coincided with the turn to the Left in Latin America. In this context, China became the main customer for Latin America's raw materials as well as its main investor and lender. As Latin America exported raw materials to China, it imported manufactured goods from it. This commodity boom pushed the traditional boundaries of extractivism beyond hydrocarbons and mining to also include biofuels and other monocrops (Farthing and Fabricant 2018). We now examine some concrete examples of the conflict between the nationalist-extractivist state and indigenous people.

Flora Lu, Gabriela Valdivia, and Néstor Silva (2017) have conducted an ethnography on the relationship between the Waorani people of the Ecuadorian Amazon, the state, and oil companies under Correa's rule. The authors highlight the contradictions between national discourses and what happens on the ground. They acknowledge that oil extraction has intensified and that the government has used that money for social assistance programs, prioritizing the areas affected by resource extraction. One change is that formerly private oil companies conducted development projects directly in communities, often replacing an absent state. Under Correa, the regime has preferred to collect taxes from the companies and to take development into its own hands through a public institution called Ecuador Estratégico (Strategic Ecuador). The authors compare two Waorani communities, one that hosts a private transnational oil company and another managed by the state company Petroamazonas. After a thorough study of the health and social indicators and community perceptions, the authors conclude that the socioenvironmental impacts of the public company are worse. In addition, they find that the development work of Ecuador Estratégico has been inefficient, unsustainable, and disrespectful of Waorani culture.

Nancy Postero's *The Indigenous State* (2017) shows that for indigenous peoples important advances took place in Bolivia after the victory of Evo Morales, its first self-identifying indigenous president in 2005. The new constitution declared Bolivia communitarian and plurinational and decolonization became the main goal of the state. However, the constitution also subsumed local autonomy to centralized decision making. As Morales's political party Movimiento al Socialismo (MAS; Movement toward Socialism) consolidated in power, support for indigenous self-determination and autonomy waned. Resource extraction intensified under Morales and hydrocarbon contracts were renegotiated, allowing the state to capture a larger share of the profits. Those profits were redistributed as conditional cash transfers to the poor and the state also built infrastructure in their communities. Indigenous autonomy, Vivir Bien, and policies to palliate climate change contrasted with Morales's emphasis on resource extraction in such a way that discourses started to diverge from practices. As the state prioritized resource extraction, it continued to sacrifice indigenous people. Furthermore, resistance to extractivism was repressed through co-optation, police violence, and the silencing of opponents through the legal system (Postero 2017).

In contrast to the situation in Bolivia and Ecuador, the indigenous movement in Venezuela was weak and almost nonexistent before Chávez came to power there (Angosto Ferrández 2015). The Bolivarian state launched the movement. Chávez granted ample rights to indigenous people for the first time in the 1999 constitution, which declared the republic multiethnic and pluricultural and recognized indigenous forms of social organization and culture (Angosto Ferrández 2015; Lander 2017). However, the implementation of all these rights depended on the demarcation of indigenous territories, and territorial recognition has been minimal (Angosto Ferrández 2015; Lander 2017). The regime has promoted the creation of indigenous communal councils instead. According to Luis Fernando Angosto Ferrández, the indigenous population has agreed with the government that the priority is to bring socioeconomic and political enfranchisement rather than autonomy and self-government. Disagreeing with Angosto Ferrández, Edgardo Lander (2017) understands the requirement to create communal councils as a form of colonization because indigenous citizens are required to organize in the same way as the rest of the population to access public funds. In addition, if indigenous territories are not demarcated, the state can avoid prior consultation. Similarly, education in indigenous languages has not been implemented because it can only be implemented in indigenous territorial demarcations.

Resource extraction is the reason that the Venezuelan government has favored organization in communes and weak indigenous territorialization (Angosto Ferrández 2015; Lander 2017). The state did not want to recognize indigenous territories to avoid confronting cattle, logging, and mining interests. Lander (2017, 36) states: "To demarcate indigenous habitats would have posed important obstacles in the future to commercially exploit the abundant mineral reserves, like gold and coltan, that are located precisely in the territories that indigenous peoples currently inhabit." Coltan is a mineral used to make electronics and batteries for electric cars.

The regime entered into a deep economic and political crisis in 2013 with the collapse of the price of oil and the death of Chávez. As oil prices plunged, the response was not to look for alternatives to extraction, but to shift from oil to mining. In 2016, President Nicolás Maduro issued an executive decree dedicating 12 percent of the national territory to a mining block called Arco Minero del Orinoco (Orinoco Mining Arc). Maduro invited transnational companies to bid for concessions to conduct large-scale open-pit mining there. Several indigenous groups inhabiting the territory were not consulted. The government used the army to repress their protests. As an area of great biodiversity, the Orinoco regions is of immense importance to the planet's climate regulation.

Claudia Briones (2015) explores indigenista politics in Argentina during what she calls the neoliberal and "national-popular" periods. "National-popular" refers to the governments of Néstor Kirchner and Cristina Fernández de Kirchner (2003–2015), which were part of the left turn. Briones argues that the politics of recognition arrived in Argentina along with neoliberalization in the 1990s. A constitutional reform recognized indigenous peoples in order to elevate Argentina to international standards. However, there were few initiatives to implement this constitutional mandate. Argentine indigenous people experienced multiculturalism in association with other contradictory policies like the delegation of state responsibilities to third parties, the shift of responsibility to vulnerable populations, and the transformation of indigenous political leaders into managers of development projects. During the neoliberal period, indigenous people addressed the state confrontationally, criticizing its lack of political will to fulfill international treaties.

Changes took place during the governments of the Kirchners. In 2004 indigenous leaders became advisers to the National Institute of Indigenous Affairs. In 2006 a Directorate of First Peoples (*pueblos originarios*) and Natural Resources was created in the Ministry of Environment and some of the most critical Mapuche leaders participated in it. According to Briones, an unprecedented dialogue took place between indigenous movements and the state. However, the conflict between indigenous Argentineans and Cristina Fernández erupted in 2010 during the bicentennial celebrations. Native leaders organized a march to the presidential palace asking for historical reparations. Among other things they requested the right to prior, informed consultation, and the regulation of extractive industries. These demands were not presented in a confrontational manner, but as a dialogue with the executive and the president. Cristina retorted that not only indigenous people but everyone had been discriminated against, challenging the idea that indigenous people deserved special reparations. She also noted that rather than creating new state structures such as indigenous territories, it was better to reinforce the already existing communities. Cristina added that oil extraction needed to continue so that Argentina could avoid importing fuel. To counter indigenous demands asking the state to respect international treaties on indigenous rights, Fernández de Kirchner called the legislation "imperialist." After the impasse, there were evictions and deaths, and indigenous protests were criminalized.

To sum up, the governments that self-identified with the Left kept resource extraction as their main strategy for development and expanded it.

They did not improve the social and environmental costs of the activity. Adverse effects impacted indigenous peoples more than other groups. However, because these governments originated in the social movements, they also granted indigenous rights in paper and sponsored symbolic performances related to indigeneity, while making these rights difficult to implement or widening the gap between state discourses and practices. Due to resource extraction, these governments were cautious not to put into effect any rights that involved hard territoriality or self-government. Territorial demarcation and autonomy appeared in legislation and official declarations but they were weakly implemented or not applied at all. Moreover, none of these governments conducted a comprehensive agrarian reform. Cultural rights like intercultural bilingual education were also watered down because it would facilitate political consciousness and social movement cohesion. Light and folkloric versions of ethnic identity were preferred over hard and particularly territorialized autonomy. Meanwhile, social movements were co-opted, criminalized, repressed, and divided. Resource extraction limited indigenous rights in complex ways that go beyond pollution and the health effects that occur in the areas of extraction. This book is dedicated to exploring these wider impacts of extractivism.

Methodology

The book combines "studying up" the state, elites, and other influential individuals, with multisited ethnography in indigenous communities and with indigenous intellectuals, activists, and professionals (Marcus 1983; Nader 1969 Rappaport 2005; Shore and Nugent 2002). Studying up allows me to interrogate the cultures of power, to analyze the racism and paternalism of elites, and to be able to identify when powerful individuals or institutions use the symbols of indigeneity for their own purposes. When the cultures of power are not specifically interrogated, racism and paternalism might fall out of focus, and elite iterations of indigeneity might be taken for grassroots points of view. For instance, this perspective facilitates the analysis of ventriloquism, when non-Indians speak for indigenous people while also silencing their voices.

One problem ethnographers confront when they study up is that of access (Nader 1972; Shore and Nugent 2002). Political, economic, and intellectual elites might operate hidden from public view, be of difficult access, or not want to be studied. My former location in Ecuadorian academia for eight years allowed me to make contact with an array of sectors of Ecuadorian society leading to a "kaleidoscopic" understanding of indigenous issues (Canessa 2012). I was a professor at FLACSO, a public research university in the city of Quito, from which the main cadres of Correa's government came. This position gave me privileged access to spaces, individuals, and events that help contextualize indigenous experiences.

Studying up is combined with rigorous work in indigenous communities. I have done fieldwork for more than a decade in the Andes and the Amazon. I started working in 2002 in the parish of Zumbahua, located in the Cotopaxi province in the central highlands. Next I conducted fieldwork in communities near Cotacachi, in the northern highlands, and others close to Riobamba and Cañar, located in the central and southern highlands, respectively. In addition, I have worked extensively with the Shuar of the southeastern Amazonian province of Morona Santiago. I visited Shuar centers near the city of Macas in the Upano Valley as well as in the more remote region of Transkutukú. There, I visited the parish of Taisha, close to the border with Peru. I learned Kichwa, a dialect of Quechua, at the Catholic University of Ecuador and at the Tinkunakuy School of Kichwa Language and Culture and have continued practicing in communities and with indigenous teachers and friends.

Many students of national indigenous politics have had a highland-centric perspective, because Ecuadorian anthropology has been centered in the capital city of Quito (see chapter 5). On the other hand, many Amazonists do not study the highlands and typically do not consult that literature. However, the connections between highlands and lowlands in the Andes have been important since precolonial times (Arnold and Hastorf 2008; Muratorio 1991; Salomon 1986). As an exception, a few students of national indigenous politics have considered both the Andes and the Amazon (e.g., Lucero 2008; Postero 2017). By following a political economy perspective, I aim to place indigenous peoples in a wider geographic context and to look at connections, which explains my choice to examine indigenous politics in both regions.

Anthropologists do fieldwork in communities but less often have a national perspective or "study up" powerful non-Indian actors. Political scientists tend to have a comprehensive, state-centered perspective, but rarely speak a native language or spend significant time in communities. By combining the strengths of these approaches, this book seeks to make a fresh contribution to the study of indigenous politics and rights. I use qualitative and interpretative methodologies, reproducing the narratives and life histories of indigenous intellectuals and commoners as well as the experiences of their allies. I also interpret in-depth state events, performances, and documents (see also Postero 2017). The book also profits from archival work, particularly in chapter 4 on intercultural bilingual education, chapter 5 on Ecuadorian anthropology, and chapter 6 on the Salesian Missions. Chapter 4 also benefits from my collaborations with indigenous graduate students from FLACSO and other indigenous scholars. Specific methodologies used in each chapter will be detailed there.

Organization of the Book

Chapter 1 provides the historical and geographical background needed to make sense of the chapters that follow. It discusses the diverse nationalities that populate Ecuador, the colonial and postcolonial oppression of indigenous people, and the history of the indigenous movement.

Chapter 2 centers on the indigenista policies of Rafael Correa and contrasts the racial projects of the state under neoliberalism and Correa's nationalist-extractivism. State indigenismo is discussed in three contexts: the rise and decline of the indigenous movement, the contradictory legislation on indigenous rights under Correa's Citizens' Revolution, and the practices of government as reflected in everyday interactions between the government and indigenous citizens. The chapter argues that Correa's regime was characterized by a central contradiction: while claiming to recognize indigenous peoples and aiming to decolonize Ecuadorian society, the regime was also engaged in a process of state formation that demanded the centralization of decision making and a focus on the extraction of natural resources. The chapter shows that individual rights in the form of antidiscrimination and affirmative action measures have been prioritized over collective and territorial rights because the latter may hinder oil and mineral extraction as well as agroindustry.

Chapter 3 discusses how the Ecuadorian state has interpreted and measured ethnicity and race in the transition from neoliberalism to nationalist-extractivism. However, to comprehend these official understandings of race, the chapter reaches back to the first 1950 census and even farther back to colonial and nineteenth-century census taking. A paradox is the contrast between the importance of indigeneity in international and national perceptions of Ecuador, and the small number of indigenous people that repeatedly shows up in censuses since 1950. The chapter concludes that the state has had an interest in undercounting indigenous peoples to emphasize whiteness and modernity and to weaken a strong social movement. In addition, the indigenous population has not revealed itself for its own reasons: informed by colonial experiences, indigenous communities still associate censuses with taxes and forced labor recruitment.

A second line of inquiry in chapter 3 relates to changing constructions of ethnicity and race. In the 1950s, the Ecuadorian state focused on language, material culture, and occupation (who was a hacienda peon) to separate the indigenous from the mestizos, and eschewed the concept of race. In the 1980s and 1990s, in the context of increasing political mobilization by indigenous groups, Ecuadorian scholars defined indigeneity in relation to territory and political participation. More recently, the state has shifted to understandings of race of North American inspiration like hypodescent (the assignment of the children of a mixed union to the subordinate group) and self-definition. Interestingly, North American concepts of race have continued to inform Ecuadorian public policy under Rafael Correa who self-identifies as anti-imperialist.

On the basis of participant observation and interviews in rural schools in various regions of the country, chapter 4 explores the projects of indigenous communities and their nonindigenous allies in intercultural bilingual education. The indigenous individuals I interviewed perceived the school system as a tool to integrate themselves into mainstream society and move up the socioeconomic ladder. Their allies privileged the use of schools to preserve and enhance native language and culture and aimed to keep indigenous peasants relatively isolated to preserve their unique way of life.

The chapter discusses two periods of experimentation with intercultural education: the neoliberal period was characterized by the important role of nongovernment allies, localized experiences, and the tensions between ally-influenced and indigenous goals in indigenous education. In the nationalist-extractivist period, the state takes over education and discontinues indigenous and ally autonomy with dramatic consequences. The regime declares all education intercultural, but waters down the project. New standardized textbooks written in Spanish replace materials in native languages. Moreover, the Correa administration closes community schools and consolidates them in larger "schools of the millennium." The closure of community schools triggered a process of migration from the communities to cities that had important consequences for indigenous lives, identities, and politics.

Chapter 5 discusses the collaborations and estrangements of anthropologists and indigenous peoples from the 1970s to the Correa decade. Anthropologists and indigenous peoples are often understood as allies and collaborators. Although this assumption is certainly true, the story is more complex. Ecuadorian anthropology intended from its inception to be an applied discipline whose aim was to understand indigenous peasants' living conditions in order to change them. The ethnographic method was considered central to this aim because it helped ground what had previously been a highly abstract conversation. Scholars have argued that the 1970s Left emphasized class and did not understand the political potential of ethnicity. However, the chapter demonstrates that part of the Left mobilized ethnic identity as a tool to resist capitalism, a conceptualization that contributed to the agenda of the indigenous movement. The chapter then analyzes the depoliticization of academics during the neoliberal period (1980s and 1990s) due to their need to double as consultants in a moment of retrenchment of the state and budget cuts in higher education. On the other hand, many anthropologists collaborated with a vibrant indigenous movement.

Chapter 5 then discusses the co-optation of some academic contributions in the context of state centralization and the commodity boom in the first decades of the 2000s. Other scholars sided in this period with indigenous struggles and against extractivist development. Still others sought to write about less controversial issues to avoid political retaliation. The chapter concludes with an examination of the recent insertion of indigenous scholars in Ecuadorian academia and the problems that they have confronted due to structural racism.

Chapter 6 focuses on the interactions between Catholic Salesian missionaries and the Kichwa and Shuar of Ecuador. In the Amazon, the Salesians faced specific tensions: How would indigenous peoples respond to the shift of missionaries from encouraging cultural assimilation (from the end of nineteenth century to the 1960s) to promoting the preservation of native languages and forms of social organization (from the 1960s to the present)? How could missionaries encourage the Shuar—and convince themselves— to preserve a cultural tradition that had been characterized by internecine wars, violence, and the custom of polygyny? In the highlands, the Salesians started their work in the 1970s with Kichwa peasants who had just been released from servitude and granted some land through the agrarian reform. The missionaries did not need to confront their own contradictory legacy there, and it was easier to preserve an Andean tradition that they understood as characterized by reciprocity and solidarity. The challenge, however, was to encourage the formation of a self-sufficient peasantry in steep, badly eroded, tiny plots located at high altitude.

During the Correa decade, missionaries found themselves in a double bind: some allied with Correa whom they perceived as progressive and—more important—someone who was a lay Salesian missionary. On the other hand, as the conflict between the government and organized indigenous people picked up, Salesian priests working on the ground sided with the social movements and started to elaborate an environmentally and socially minded theology. The chapter analyzes how the Catholic Church transitioned from an assimilation approach to efforts to preserve indigenous cultures, and from a position that understood the environment as an object to be mastered by man to a theology invested in overcoming environmental degradation and poverty.

Chapter 7 analyzes two forms of discrimination against indigenous people, ventriloquism and open racism, and argues that a transition from paternalism to open intolerance has taken place in Ecuador in the context of nationalist-extractivism. Ventriloquism, when non-Indians speak for indigenous people, is analyzed through the Sumak Kawsay (Good Living) policies of the government of Rafael Correa. Open racism is examined by looking at government repression against indigenous leaders and communities and presidential speeches. The chapter contends that the state's ventriloquist and racist discourses and practices are equally rooted in the country's colonial past. These findings are then contrasted with the writings of scholars that have called the government of Correa decolonizing. The chapter examines the ways in which decolonial theorists informed and promoted Correa's policies and argues that decolonial scholars have been insufficiently self-critical and reflective of their own complicity with the state's repressive project vis-à-vis indigenous communities.

The conclusion analyzes two racial formations in Ecuador, the neoliberal and the nationalist-extractivist, and compares the second to what has happened in other countries that turned toward the Left in the first decade of the 2000s. The conclusion also offers a reflection on my intellectual trajectory and the advantages and disadvantages of the methodology.

CHAPTER 1

BEING INDIGENOUS IN ECUADOR

Ecuador is a country of amazing geographic and cultural diversity, great natural beauty, and considerable academic interest. It is crossed east to west by the equator, from which it takes its name, and north to south by the Andes Mountains. Altitudinal changes create ecozones where products ranging from tropical fruits to high-altitude, cold-climate tubers and cereals can be grown. Predating the Spanish conquest, the inhabitants of the Andes took advantage of this possibility, fostering social relations that allowed them to exchange products among ecological niches at different altitudes, a practice that peasants continue to this day (Murra 2017 [1969]). On the other hand, the Andes Mountains made communications relatively difficult and divided the country into regions with distinctive histories and identities.

The coastal lowlands have been linked to the world market and have produced world famous cocoa and bananas for export, among other commodities (Striffler 2001). Across the sea from the coast are the Galápagos Islands, well-known as the setting of Charles Darwin's nineteenth-century research on evolution and for their rare concentration of endemism and biodiversity. The Ecuadorian coast was densely populated in precolonial times and holds many archaeological treasures. It is also the center of much archaeological research. However, coastal indigenous peoples were largely displaced, exterminated, or assimilated after the conquest, except in the more remote areas of the coastal interior (Tsáchilas) or on the northern coastline (Chachi, Epera, and Awá). Thus, the coast is still home to a few indigenous nationalities as well as numerous indigenous migrants from the highlands who have arrived more recently seeking work as seasonal farmworkers, in construction, or informal commerce. At the end of the twentieth century some previously assimilated groups reinvigorated their indigenous identities (Bauer 2012).

It is important to note that Amerindians in Ecuador call themselves nationalities instead of tribes, a term that they find offensive. The word "nationality" conveys the idea that they speak a distinct language and have claims to a particular history and territory. Influenced by leftist intellectuals, indigenous organizations adopted the term "nationality" in the second half of the twentieth century. Purportedly, Ileana Almeida, an Ecuadorian ethnolinguist who studied in the Soviet Union, encouraged the indigenous movement to adopt the term "nationality," which she imported from the concept of oppressed nationalities of the Soviet Union.

The best-known of the nationalities of the coast are the Tsáchilas, whom the Spaniards called "colorados" because they died their hair and sometimes their bodies red with achiote (bixa orellana). The Tsáchilas are also known in Ecuador for having powerful shamans. The coast is also home to Afro-Ecuadorians. On the northern coast, many Afro-Ecuadorians descend from former escaped slaves from Colombia who created maroon communities. There was some slavery in Guayaquil and its surrounding area. Coastal peasants originate from a mixture of indigenous people, Afrodescendants, and European settlers and are called montubios (see chapter 3 for the history and politics of the term). The coast is also home to Euro-American settlers and an oligarchy enriched by the export–import trade (Chiriboga 1980; A. Guerrero 1980).

The highlands are also characterized by great biodiversity. The inter-Andean valleys are the most populated areas due to their temperate climate, relative freedom from tropical diseases, and agricultural fertility. This region was the center of the hacienda system during colonial and republican times. The hacienda system subjected the indigenous inhabitants of the land to serfdom and debt peonage, and restricted their freedom of movement. Indigenous workers were transferred with the property when it was sold, could not move from one hacienda to another due to the debts they incurred with the landowner, and the *hacendado* had legal jurisdiction over them. Although a nominal salary was assigned to farmworkers, they were rarely paid, wages were very low, and the landowner typically made small advances in seed and clothing called *suplidos* and *socorros* that left the workers structurally indebted. In addition, workers' menial wages shrank even more when the animals died or the products of the harvest were lost. Workers were physically punished in the hacienda's main square according to time-honored rituals that included whippings (A. Guerrero 1991; Lyons 2006). Although indigenous people were named Ecuadorian citizens when the country became independent from Spain in the early nineteenth century, they did not become active citizens until much later due to literacy and property requirements for voting (A. Guerrero 2010). Indigenous women and some men were also subjected to domestic servitude in the landowner's house on the hacienda or in their urban residence. Indigenous people remained serfs until the 1964 Agrarian Reform Law that abolished precarious labor relations. Illiterates voted for the first time with the return to democracy in 1979. To this day, the vote of illiterates is optional in a country where voting is mandatory, a legacy of past voter suppression.

Before Spanish colonization, the highlands were home to several ethnic groups who were briefly conquered by the Incas and who, although they originally spoke various languages, came to speak Kichwa, a dialect of Quechua, the language of the Incas (Salomon 1986). The highland Kichwa are divided into thirteen subgroups called "pueblos" in Spanish. Pueblos are commonly translated into English as "peoples" but the word rather means "towns." In Spanish the word "pueblo" means both people and town, an ambiguity that has created some confusion. These towns were colonial settlements or *reducciones* where indigenous people were concentrated to better control and tax them. In colonial times, wider indigenous solidarities were broken down into smaller town-based identities (A. Guerrero 2010). The towns spoke slightly different dialects of Kichwa and used distinctive clothing such as different poncho colors and decorations, a peculiar hat, or specific blouses or embroidery. The Spaniards encouraged these visual differences to be able to recognize indigenous individuals as members of a specific town for taxation purposes. Indian towns paid taxes, but Spaniards or "forasteros" (natives who moved from their original town to another or to the city) did not. The highlands and in particular the Chota-Mira valley are also home to Afro-Ecuadorians brought as slaves to the sugar cane plantations of the Jesuit priests. Euro-Ecuadorians and mestizos also inhabit the Ecuadorian highlands. As in the rest of Latin America, *mestizaje* is understood as an identity that blends Amerindian and European physical and cultural heritages. It is an ethnically white exclusionary identity that is closely identified with the dominant Spanish language, national culture, and cities (Colloredo-Mansfeld 2009, 10).

The Amazon or Oriente has a different history. It is a region of spectacular biological and cultural diversity as well. It is home to several indigenous nationalities that speak Kichwa and other languages. Among the larger nationalities are the Shuar and the Achuar, with whom this book is concerned (Descola 1986; Rubenstein 2002). Other nationalities are the lowland Kichwa, Waorani, Siona, Secoya, Cofán, and other smaller and reethnicized groups. The Amazon was colonized much more recently than the coast or the highlands due to its impenetrability, widespread tropical diseases, and warring native groups. However, the Amazon has not been as isolated as is frequently assumed. The region has experienced several commodity booms, including in gold, rubber, and more recently oil (Muratorio 1991). Missionaries have been central to the colonization of the Ecuadorian Oriente. They were Catholic in the Shuar south and Kichwa north and Evangelical Protestant among the more remote Waorani (Rival 2002). The region became more connected to the rest of the country when poor peasants from the highlands colonized it after the Agrarian Reform and Colonization Laws of 1964 and 1973, and after oil began to be massively extracted from the region in the 1970s. Modernizing Latin American states have conceived of the Amazon as an "empty" space for national expansion and as an escape valve for social tensions. The Amazon's oil reserves have become an immense source of wealth for funding state modernization projects (Lu, Valdivia, and Silva 2017).

Ecuadorian indigenous people with the assistance of their allies have resisted the hacienda system in the highlands as well as colonization and natural resource extraction in the Amazon. Starting in the 1930s and 1940s, indigenous peasants allied with the Communist Party to fight labor conditions on haciendas, serfdom, debt peonage, and cultural discrimination, and to request access to arable land (Becker 2008). The party created its Ecuadorian Federation of Indians (FEI) branch in the 1940s. The FEI's most prominent leader was Dolores Cacuango, a barely literate woman who nevertheless promoted indigenous education. The struggle for land was connected to the struggle for indigenous education because native people understood that literacy was required in order to gain access to the land through lengthy lawsuits that aimed to make agrarian reform laws effective. The Catholic Church became politicized after the Second Vatican Council (1962–1965) and also helped indigenous people to organize for access to the land and for intercultural bilingual education. Indigenous leaders formed by the Catholic Church created the first provincial branches of what would later become the Confederation of Indigenous Nationalities of Ecuador (CONAIE).

In the Amazon, the Salesians, a Catholic order, helped the Shuar create the Interprovincial Federation of Shuar Centers (FICSH) in 1964. The FICSH was founded to claim Shuar territory in order to stop the colonization process. It is important to note that the Agrarian Reform of 1964 liberated highland peasants from serfdom, forbade precarious labor relations, and gave them property title for their *huasipungos* or small plots that landowners had previously assigned to them only in usufruct. Public haciendas were also subdivided and distributed among their workers after the reform. However, for Amazonian peoples the Agrarian Reform had a totally different meaning. They still call it by its complete name: Agrarian Reform and Colonization Law. The law conceived of the Amazon as an empty space available for colonization aimed at decreasing social tensions in the highlands. The Shuar and their Catholic allies tried to counter this perception and practice. These efforts caused a process of sedentarization among the Shuar, who concentrated in towns called *centros* similar to the colonial *reducciones* (see chapter 6). The Shuar needed to demonstrate that their land was effectively occupied in order to avoid colonization by highland peasants. They had originally been semisedentary hunters, fishers, and gardeners.

In 1986 indigenous organizations from the Amazon, the highlands, and the coast created a unified federation, the Confederation of Indigenous Nationalities of Ecuador. The first president of the organization was Miguel Tankamash, a Shuar. CONAIE had a tiered, community based organization (Colloredo-Mansfeld 2009), starting from the communities and, in the case of the Shuar, the centers. These town administrations then joined second-tier organizations, which subsequently joined provincial, regional, and national confederations (Zamosc 1994). The original aims of CONAIE were the resolution of land conflicts in the highlands, the consolidation of indigenous territories in the Amazon, and intercultural bilingual education in both regions (Lucero 2008). Intercultural bilingual education was made official in 1988. In 1990 the indigenous movement organized a spectacular national uprising that made urban mestizos aware of the political power that indigenous people had amassed in the preceding decades (J. Almeida et al. 1993). After the uprising, periodic *levantamientos* (uprisings) every other year were able to halt some neoliberal reforms (F. Guerrero and Ospina 2003).

The attempts at neoliberalization in Ecuador started after an economic crisis caused by plunging oil prices and international indebtedness under President Osvaldo Hurtado (1981–1984). Afterward, different governments aimed to privatize lands and state enterprises and cut subsidies to basic products. However, the periodic uprisings of the indigenous movement, which became a vanguard for other antineoliberal urban social movements, hindered the implementation of the reforms. Leon Zamosc (1994) has interpreted the indigenous movement of Ecuador as a popular reaction to neoliberal reforms (see also F. Guerrero and Ospina 2003).

Indigenous activism and political influence made this social movement a target for co-optation. In the late 1990s, the World Bank designed a well-funded project called Indigenous and Afro-Ecuadorian Peoples Development Project (PRODEPINE), the multilateral institution's first experiment with ethnodevelopment. PRODEPINE, as well as the numerous nongovernmental organizations (NGOs) that proliferated in the country during the neoliberal era, encouraged indigenous leaders to become technicians focused on localized projects and abandon their previous more radical political agenda (Bretón 2005). Roberto Santana (2004) argued that CONAIE kept its antineoliberal discourse while simultaneously collaborating with neoliberal NGOs and multilateral organizations like the World Bank. Meanwhile, different adminstrations also worked to co-opt the indigenous movement to the point that CONAIE acquired quasi-state functions. CONAIE's activists became government officials in intercultural bilingual education, intercultural health, and other domains. They also joined state ranks when they were hired by the Council for the Development of the Nationalities and Peoples [or Towns] of Ecuador (CODENPE). CODENPE was a state organization specifically created to manage the PRODEPINE program's money. Its director, an indigenous leader, had a position equivalent to being the head of a ministry. As indigenous leaders became high government officials and state technicians, and as native intellectuals became tokens within neoliberal multiculturalism, they decreased the pressure for structural change in the communities they represented and became increasingly detached from their constituency.

Ten years after the consolidation of CONAIE, the indigenous movement in coalition with public-sector unions and urban social movements created Pachakutik, a political party. The party's name means "new beginning" in the Kichwa language (Becker 2011). Pachakutik was created in 1995, a year after CONAIE and its allies launched a successful struggle to defeat a referendum proposed by President Sixto Durán Ballén (1992–1996). The referendum aimed to launch a neoliberal land reform as well as other so-called modernization measures. From 1996 to 2006, Pachakutik was able to obtain 7–10 percent of the national vote and important provincial and local victories (Mijeski and Beck 2011). In 1996 Freddy Ehlers, a television producer, ran for president in alliance with Pachakutik. However, he lost to Abdalá Bucaram, a populist politician from the coast. In 1997, Bucaram was ousted by the indigenous and other urban movements and his successor, Fabián Alarcón, launched a Constituent Assembly. The 1998 Constitution recognized for the first time the multicultural and multiethnic nature of Ecuador and granted indigenous peoples collective rights.

In the year 2000, CONAIE participated with Colonel Lucio Gutierrez in a coup d'état against the recently elected president Jamil Mahuad in the context of a deep financial crisis, a huge migration diaspora, and the dollarization of the economy. The coup failed, but Mahuad was ousted and his vice president Gustavo Noboa was put in his place. In 2002, after having spent a few months in jail, Colonel Gutierrez, in alliance with Pachakutik, was elected president. Members of Pachakutik, including some indigenous leaders, were named heads of ministries such as Agriculture, Education, and Foreign Affairs. Gutierrez reserved for his party, Sociedad Patriótica, made up of former military and police personnel, key ministries such as Economy and Defense. A year after Gutierrez's investiture, the alliance between Sociedad Patriótica and Pachakutik broke down. Gutierrez tried to sign a Free Trade Agreement with the United States and continue the neoliberal policies of previous governments. Pachakutik and CONAIE were weakened by their participation in the 2000 coup and their subsequent alliance with Gutierrez (Zamosc 2007). The colonel was ousted in 2005, but this time the urban middle class rather than the indigenous movement was a decisive factor.

During this period of political turmoil and frequent ousting of presidents, various presidents tried to weaken the indigenous movement. Abdalá Bucaram allied with the evangelical indigenous organizations and some leaders to debilitate CONAIE. Gustavo Noboa conducted clientelism at the community level to try to bypass CONAIE's structures. Lucio Gutierrez tried similar tactics. Simultaneously, PRODEPINE distracted the indigenous leadership from seeking structural changes and encouraged them to become project managers. In addition, after the failed alliance with Gutierrez, Pachakutik decided to expel its mestizo advisers and encourage an Indianist, nationalist agenda. Both disaffected mestizo advisers and the indigenous grassroots, who had not seen enough change after ten years of neoliberal multiculturalism, gravitated toward the novel political project of Rafael Correa and his recently created political group Alianza País.

During the early years of indigenous mobilization, the issues at stake were land, labor conditions, and intercultural education in the highlands (Lucero 2008; Zamosc 1994), colonization, the creation of indigenous territories, and indigenous education in the Amazon (Erazo 2013). Environmental conflicts and the damage done by natural resource extraction became increasingly salient items on the agenda of the indigenous movement in the first decade of the 2000s. This interest coincided with the commodity boom and the subsequent expansion of the oil and mining frontiers. Environmental conflicts had been going on in some regions of Ecuador during the previous years, but they had yet to become the main issue for CONAIE.

An important conflict took place in the Amazon community of Sarayaku, which fought for many years to expel the Argentine oil company CGC from its territory. The Ecuadorian government had granted a concession to this company without the community's approval. Sarayaku resisted the company and eventually achieved its expulsion. When CGC left Sarayaku, it planted the territory with mines. Sarayaku sued the Ecuadorian state in the Inter-American Court of Human Rights (IACHR) for granting the territory to CGC without the prior consultation required by international law. The IACHR ruled in favor of Sarayaku in 2012. Marlon Santi, a native of Sarayaku who was politicized during this struggle became president of CONAIE in 2008. He was harassed and mocked by Correa's government on national television. In 2016 Santi became the president of Pachakutik. After a prolonged period of crisis of the indigenous movement since roughly 2004, Santi was able to repoliticize and further radicalize CONAIE on the basis of the struggle against extractivism and for water conservancy and redistribution.

Another emerging leader of CONAIE who grew out of the struggle against extractivism and for clean water is Carlos Pérez Guartambel. He later changed his first name to Yaku, meaning "water" in Kichwa. Pérez studied law at the University of Cuenca and made a political name for himself as the leader of the Union of Community Water Councils of Azuay, a province located in the southern highlands. In 2011 Pérez was charged with terrorism and sabotage for closing a road to protest a gold mining project in Quimsacocha, south of the city of Cuenca. The government had granted the project to the Canadian company Iamgold. Resistance to mining had built up in Quimsacocha since 2003. Guartambel was elected president of Ecuarunari (the branch of CONAIE for the highlands) in 2013. More recently, in the elections for provincial and local authorities of 2019, Pérez was chosen governor of the Azuay province.

A third emerging leader of CONAIE with an environmentalist curriculum is Marcelino Chumpí, who was chosen governor of the southern Amazon province of Morona Santiago in 2009 and reelected in 2014. Chumpí declared Morona Santiago an ecological province and forbade oil and mining concessions in all Shuar territories. The southern Amazon is an area threatened by new oil grants and large open-pit mining projects (Sacher 2017). The Ecuadorian army has confronted indigenous activists in this province to protect the mining companies.

Let's take a closer look at this conflict. In August 2016, the police and the military displaced between thirty and forty Shuar people from Nankints, a Shuar center. Law enforcement aimed to facilitate open-pit cooper mining by the company Explorcobres S.A., property of the Chinese Railways and Construction Company and Tongling. In November of the same year, the Shuar took the mining camp arguing that it was illegal because the Ecuadorian government had not conducted the prior consultation mandated by the constitution. The confrontation left several people wounded and a policeman dead. After the incident, Correa's government declared a state of exception in the Morona Santiago province and sent in tanks and helicopters. The police searched houses without judicial authorization and detained community leaders. Then the forces of order displaced several communities that were located in the Panantza-San Carlos mining area. The displaced were mostly women and children because the men had previously escaped. According to testimonies, the military entered the town shooting and planted the fields and houses with incendiary mines. Women and children crossed the jungle in the middle of the night trying to escape state repression. Two Shuar women gave birth in the jungle as they fled from the military. They did so with the help of other women and a small stick that they sharpened to cut the umbilical cord. As they reached safety, the women cried for their lost fields and domestic animals. They were also distressed because they had lost their old aluminum pots and pans and their kids' school supplies (Giménez 2017).

The president of the Shuar Federation, Agustín Wachapá, gave an eloquent statement against mining and called on the Shuar to defend their territory. Then the government searched the offices of the Shuar Federation and arrested Wachapá. His wife criticized the way he was arrested: he was thrown onto the floor, kicked, and mocked (Giménez 2017). President Correa declared to the press that the rebels were not ancestral peoples but dangerous armed groups. Government followers drew on old racist stereotypes that they distributed in social media. For instance, they called the Shuar "stinky Jivaros who smelled like rotten fish." The incident pushed back a decade or two of successful intercultural coexistence.

The price of copper multiplied fourfold at the beginning of the twenty-first century because of its scarcity and its importance to the modernization of developing countries. China buys 40 percent of world copper, which explains why it has sought an association with Ecuador to exploit one of the biggest reserves located in the so-called Cordillera del Cobre (Copper Mountain Range) in the southern Ecuadorian Amazon, which is home to the Shuar. The Shuar complain that open-pit mining will displace them, hoard and pollute their water, and make agriculture, cattle raising, hunting, and fishing impossible. Three Shuar anti-mining activists have died in unclear circumstances, and their cases have reached the Inter-American Court of Human Rights (Agencia Efe 2015).

In 2012 the Comptroller General's Office found several instances in which the Ecuadorian government had failed to comply with the law. It ordered the suspension of mining in Panantza-San Carlos, where Nankints was located. The report made clear that the project was carried out using dubious standards. For instance, the mine is close to water sources and mining in such areas is forbidden in Ecuador. The Panantza-San Carlos project is the second open-pit mining project in Ecuador. The other is Mirador, also located in the Copper Mountain Range and owned by the same public Chinese companies.

The Shuar have resisted these mining projects since 2006. At the time, they forced the Canadian company Lowell out of the area. Raul Ankuash, a leader of FICSH has argued that the Shuar nationality has always opposed mining, but that the companies have generated internal divisions in the organization. The Shuar Arutam People, an indigenous territorial organization, took the mining camp of the Canadian company and built the community of Nankints there. Mario Melo, a human rights lawyer who defends the Shuar Arutam People, argues that the land originally belonged to them. However, the Ecuadorian Agrarian Reform Institute unfairly allocated some of this land to mestizo peasants in the 1970s. These peasants sold the land to the mining companies, but the Shuar people do not consider the sale legitimate. For these reasons, the Shuar Arutam People filed a civil rights action against the Panantza-San Carlos project in March 2019 (Ponce Icaza 2019).

The prominence of these new environmentally minded leaders and grassroots movements attests to the centrality that the environmentalist and anti-extractivist agenda has acquired for the indigenous movement of Ecuador in the past two decades. This agenda has been able to repoliticize CONAIE and Pachakutik after a period of crisis and has confronted the organizations with the nationalist-extractivist regime of Rafael Correa. The anti-extraction agenda has also helped reconnect CONAIE's leadership to some of its grassroots constituency. This does not mean that CONAIE has abandoned other more traditional grievances like intercultural education or land struggles. The indigenous uprising of the fall of 2019 that forced President Lenin Moreno to reverse an attempt to cut subsidies to oil and gas demonstrates that subsistence issues still matter a great deal to indigenous organizations. We now turn to a closer examination of Correa's policies and the government's interactions with Ecuador's indigenous nationalities.

CHAPTER 2

DISPENSING AND CURTAILING RIGHTS THROUGH POLICY AND PRACTICE

The first formal investiture of Rafael Correa as president of Ecuador took place in Zumbahua, a rural parish inhabited by Kichwa-speaking peasants on January 15, 2007. This parish is located approximately 4,000 meters above sea level in the central highlands of Ecuador. Zumbahua is also the site of a mission of the Salesians, a Catholic order. Correa chose Zumbahua to show that his government favored indigenous people and the rural poor and to demonstrate a special commitment to these peoples. He had been a lay Salesian missionary for a year in this parish (see also chapter 6).

My husband, a sociologist friend, and I climbed at dawn with many other cars and buses from the provincial capital Latacunga to the high *páramo* of Zumbahua. When we arrived, the parish had the atmosphere of a carnival. Among the indigenous inhabitants of the parish, we found Ecuadorian intellectuals, artists, nongovernmental organization (NGO) activists, and foreign tourists. As we reached the town's main square we realized that the center of the square had been closed to the general public: only special guests, most of them non-Indians, were allowed inside. Interestingly, Correa was to speak at the heart of indigenous Ecuador, but the inhabitants of that parish, with the exception of the highest leadership, were not allowed into their own town's plaza. I spoke with three young

Kichwa sisters whom I knew from my earlier fieldwork in Zumbahua and asked them what they thought about their town's square being closed to them during the presidential inauguration. They answered with smiles on their faces, and proudly holding a newspaper that discussed the presidential investiture, that this was the first time a president had come to their town. Presidents Hugo Chávez of Venezuela and Evo Morales of Bolivia were among the important guests scheduled to speak that day. The presidents arrived by helicopter, amazing all present. Then the speeches started. Correa spoke last. He thanked the Salesian priests who sponsored his missionary activity in Zumbahua, and referred to his time as a lay missionary as his most important learning experience, even though he also held a PhD in economics from the University of Illinois at Urbana-Champaign. He uttered some sentences in the Kichwa language, which he claimed to have learned while living in Zumbahua. Although he was able to remember the names of several priests, he did not name a single indigenous person he met during that period. After Correa's speech, Rodrigo Guanotuña, the president of the parish council (*junta parroquial*), gave him the *vara* staff of office, a long stick typically made of silver and held in the hand that is used as a symbol of authority and has distinguished indigenous community presidents from colonial times. Guanotuña did not give a speech. The only indigenous person who briefly spoke at the ceremony was César Umajinga, a leader of the indigenous and peasant movement of Cotopaxi, a branch of the Confederation of Indigenous Nationalities of Ecuador (CONAIE). Why did Correa start his presidency in an indigenous community while also avoiding close contact with its indigenous inhabitants? Why would he use the indigenous language, but fail to remember indigenous individuals from the parish where he worked? And how did indigenous Ecuadorians react to these tensions between inclusion and exclusion?

Correa claimed to rule for the vulnerable and the dispossessed, and argued that he was radically changing the country through what the governing party, Alianza País, called a Citizens' Revolution. Initially, he sought the support of the indigenous movement for this transformation and emphasized the symbolic inclusion of indigenous peoples. This was important to succeeding in a country where the indigenous movement had become the most prominent political actor in the preceding decade (Colloredo-Mansfeld 2009; Pallares 2002; Zamosc 2007). Correa's party sponsored legal changes in the 2008 constitution that were aimed at expanding indigenous rights. In addition, the concept of Sumak Kawsay, Kichwa for good living, was to guide the development strategies of the regime as spelled out in its 2009–2013 national development plan (SENPLADES, Plan Nacional Para el Buen Vivir). Despite what seemed to be substantial advances in indigenous rights, CONAIE soon clashed with this government. The conflict erupted in January 2009 with indigenous demonstrations against a mining law that opened the way for large-scale mining, and a proposed water law that indigenous organizations did not perceive as redistributive of this important resource. The organizations argued that the proposed law cleared the way for the privatization of water because mining companies needed large quantities of this resource. Indigenous organizations then protested another decree that abolished their autonomy in the administration of intercultural bilingual education.

Charles Hale made an often-cited argument about the ethnic project of neoliberalism (Hale 2002, 2005). Based on his research in Central America, Hale argued that neoliberal governance of diversity includes the limited recognition of some cultural rights and the rejection of more radical proposals for socioeconomic change. The result is the creation of a dichotomy between recognized and unrecognized indigenous subjects that shapes indigenous subjectivities, co-opts indigenous movements, and marginalizes their most radical elements. If neoliberal institutions and governments have particular ways to administer ethnic diversity, is there a coherent racial project in nationalist-extractivist Ecuador? Does this project, if it exists, expand on or reverse neoliberal multicultural policies? And, how does this project relate to the ethnic policies of other turn to the Left countries?

Authors writing in the early years of the turn to the Left in Latin America tended to be optimistic regarding the policies of inclusion of indigenous and Afrodescendant peoples. In an article that surveys changes in Venezuela, Bolivia, and Ecuador, Arturo Escobar (2010) highlighted important transformations at the level of constitutions and plans of government that included a reversal of neoliberal policies, a renewal of democracy, and the inclusion of proposals of social movements that seek a society more inclusive of non-Western perspectives as well as a new relation to nature. When Nancy Postero wrote *Now We Are Citizens* (2007), she argued that the new moment of postmulticultural citizenship in Bolivia was characterized by a combination of the ethnic recognition and participation afforded during the neoliberal period with a struggle for greater redistribution of the nation's resources. Jan Hoffman French (2009), reflecting on the case of Brazil, agreed that postneoliberalism expanded neoliberal recognition and participation with more rights for indigenous and Afro-Brazilians, and also linked these rights to concrete resources. Luis Fernando Angosto Ferrández (2008) also highlighted the symbolic inclusion of indigenous peoples in the Bolivarian Republic of Venezuela. In addition, Chávez, who on occasion claimed to be indigenous, named the indigenous cacique Guaicaipuro a national hero, promoted indigenous names for important landmarks, and organized encounters of indigenous peoples whom the regime associated with national dignity and anti-imperialism.

However, scholars also had reservations early on regarding the ways these regimes were addressing indigenous peoples. Escobar (2010) saw a tendency toward the concentration of power in the state, and a continuation of traditional understandings of development based on the extraction of natural resources. He also perceived a tension between states trying to use the creative energies of social movements, and contrary tendencies to exclude social movements from government and to try to control them. Similarly, Angosto Ferrández (2008) argued that the ethnic policies of Venezuela were plagued by contradictions. While recognizing the right of indigenous peoples to organize according to their uses and customs, the Ministry of Indigenous Peoples marginalized autonomous indigenous organizations. Anthropologists working on Bolivia also noted some exclusions. Robert Albro (2010) pointed out that the constitutional focus on the Aymara, rural indigeneity, and collective rights excluded other ways of being indigenous—for instance, the experiences of urban indigenous people who use both collective and individual strategies. Andrew Canessa (2006) found that the ideology of the Morales regime, permeated by NGO understandings of indigeneity and by the use of indigeneity as a metaphor for radical politics, environmentalism, and nationalism, appealed more to urban cosmopolitans rather than reflecting the ways of rural people speaking an indigenous language and living in community.

In Correa's Ecuador some legal rights were expanded , but the legislation was contradictory, difficult to implement, or barely implemented. The regime appropriated indigenous symbols and demands but did not recognize indigenous peoples as actors. The neoliberal emphasis on participation was reversed and substituted for the mere socialization of decisions that had already been made. Finally, prejudices against indigenous peoples became legitimate again in the public sphere.

I build on scholarship that deals with the anthropology of the state (Cohen 1981; Coronil 1997; Das and Poole 2004; Sharma and Gupta 2006). I was present at several public events in which the Correa government presented itself to indigenous peoples, I observed sessions of the Constituent Assembly of 2007–2008, and I had access to some intellectuals of the regime. I complemented this ethnography of the nationalist-extractivist state with fieldwork in indigenous communities as well as work with indigenous intellectuals in Quito. In addition, I was able to participate in some events of environmentalist networks that work closely with the indigenous movement in Ecuador.

The Crisis of the Ecuadorian Indigenous Movement in the First Decade of the 2000s

The indigenous movement of Ecuador has been called the strongest in Latin America because it was able to unify organizations from the community to the national level and because its massive uprisings were able to deeply affect state policy (Pallares 2002; Yashar 2005; Zamosc 2007). However, when Rafael Correa's presidency began in 2007, this social movement was in relative decline. The crisis of CONAIE, which started around 2004, was multidimensional, and different authors emphasized different reasons for it (Ospina 2009). Many pointed to the indigenous movement's ill-conceived alliance with Colonel Gutierrez. Scholars criticized the lack of solid democratic values of the indigenous movement for participating in the coup (Zamosc 2007).

Some authors pointed out that the crisis of the indigenous movement could have been caused by its institutionalization and participation in politics (Ospina 2009; Van Cott 2009; Zamosc 2007). Leon Zamosc (2007) argues that the struggle to control the state led the indigenous movement to carry out some opportunistic moves, which caused it to lose legitimacy. Donna Lee Van Cott (2009) added that indigenous elected authorities might have been subjected to unrealistic expectations on the part of voters that were not fulfilled. Another explanation based on my own observations in indigenous communities, is the growing gap between the leaders and the grassroots. Some leaders became technocrats focused on national and international contexts, and to a certain degree they lost contact with the communities. In addition, the communities had not seen enough change at the grassroots level after more than a decade of uprisings and political participation. For example, in a visit to the Shuar Federation in Sucúa in February 2007, leaders were discussing the need for sophisticated information systems to map their territories, whereas ordinary people reported being concerned about endemic illnesses such as malaria as well as basic subsistence issues (field notes, February 2007). In the province of Chimborazo, Pancho Coro, a community activist, argued: "Here many people love Dr. Macas [a historic leader and the president of CONAIE] but the indigenous movement is finished. The leaders . . . they do business among themselves at the expense of the people. They sold themselves. Indigenous leaders are absorbed by the system. There is no leader willing to defend the poor" (interview, June 6, 2008). According to Luis Alberto Tuaza (2009), community members were tired of organizing and demonstrating without seeing clear results.

Rudi Colloredo-Mansfeld (2009) has argued that it is not homogeneous social composition, but class differentiation that has produced a powerful indigenous movement in Ecuador. He shows that middle-class indigenous individuals with more resources, education, contacts, and mobility are essential to explaining the organizational strength of this social movement. However, differential access to the benefits of identity politics may produce resentment and mutual alienation. Ethnicity is a strategy that has benefited indigenous leaders more than communities. This is because the politics of recognition and the "tokenism" associated with them during the period of neoliberalizaton created a few jobs for leaders while precluding greater structural transformations that might have reached indigenous communities.

The crisis of the indigenous movement in the first decade of the 2000s was reflected in electoral results. In the 2006 elections, Pachakutik ran with its own indigenous candidate, Luis Macas, in an attempt to replicate Evo Morales's 2005 victory in Bolivia. For this reason, Pachakutik did not accept running in alliance with Rafael Correa. However, Macas obtained less than 2 percent of the national vote (Báez and Bretón 2006) and only 25 percent of the indigenous vote (Van Cott 2009). Pachakutik's delegation to Congress decreased from eleven to six deputies.

The indigenous movement seems to have lost some of its relevance as an avant-garde of antineoliberal and radical struggles with the rise of Correa's project in 2006. For instance, Correa attracted a good number of intellectual collaborators of Pachakutik and CONAIE, further weakening the indigenous movement. According to Van Cott (2009), the indigenous movement needed to reassess the political scenario after the Left came to power. It was easier to be in the opposition of conservative governments than to deal with a left-of-center government that deprived the indigenous movement of wider political support. In addition, the turn of the indigenous movement inward toward a more restricted indigenous agenda after the expulsion of mestizos from Pachakutik did not help either. This happened after the failed alliance with Lucio Gutierrez caused indigenous activists to think that they had overstretched their movement. This strategy further deprived Pachakutik from mestizo and urban support. Many of these Pachakutik mestizos became important cadres in the Correa government; for example, Doris Solis was minister coordinator of politics in 2010–2011, Augusto Barrera was mayor of Quito for Alianza País for 2009–2014, and Virgilio Hernández was a key member of Alianza País at the National Assembly.

In a context in which the political effectiveness of the indigenous movement dwindled and the government of Rafael Correa claimed to stand for poor indigenous people and had resources to distribute, some medium-level indigenous leaders and community members gravitated, although ambivalently, toward this project, causing further divisions. The government distributed benefits to the population in the form of jobs, public works, and cash transfers. The best known cash transfers were the bonus for human development, which provided a small monthly subsidy to families that sent their children to school, the bonus for housing, and the programs *socio bosque* (partners for the forest, see chapter 6) and *socio páramo* (partners for the highlands) that subsidized communities that preserved their natural environment. Seeing benefits in allying with Correa, some successful Pachakutik provincial leaders like Mariano Curicama, governor of Chimborazo, and César Umajinga, governor or Cotopaxi, became close to Alianza País, Correa's political party, while continuing to be members of Pachakutik and CONAIE.

On June 6, 2008, President Correa spoke in the city of Riobamba. A number of indigenous people from different communities of Chimborazo had been mobilized and arrived in buses provided by the provincial government (controlled by Pachakutik) to listen to the president. Pancho Coro argued: "The governor [Curicama] tells the communities that they must receive the president [Correa]. Curicama has nothing to do with Pachakutik any more. Curicama already belongs to Correa. These things weaken the indigenous movement" (interview, June 6, 2008). People descending from the communities to see the president told me that they must go to listen to his speech. Otherwise their communities would fine them. One man argued: "The governor [Curicama] has said that if we do not go, we will lose the bonus for poverty [a cash transfer of US$35 a month at the time], and our water projects" (field notes, June 6, 2008). Manuel Agualsaca reported that he is unhappy with Correa because the cost of life has risen, which is why, in his view, CONAIE is opposing Correa. However, he said he must attend the president's speech for reasons of accountability (*rendir cuentas*) to the Ministry of Education, because he is a teacher. He must go listen to Correa because of the things he receives, even though he disagrees (interview with Agualsaca, field notes, June 6, 2008).

Such ambivalence touched the indigenous movement in intimate ways, setting kin against kin. For example, Marlon Santi, the former president of CONAIE, became a radical opponent of Correa's government and was harassed by government propaganda on television for opposing the government's natural resource policies. Meanwhile, his first cousin Carlos Viteri, at the time executive secretary of the Institute for Regional Ecodevelopment of the Ecuadorian Amazon (ECORAE), a government institution financed by oil company taxes, distributed subsidies to increase support for Correa's government among Amazonian peoples. Two delegates to the National Assembly accused Viteri of using ECORAE's public moneys for electoral ends (ecuadorenvivo.com, June 16, 2011). A Shuar assemblywoman, spoke at a February 2010 meeting of the Shuar Federation against government support for mining and oil companies and against the harassment of indigenous people by the government, and her brother, who was the government delegate for the Ministry of Culture in the province of Morona Santiago, was organizing a government-friendly counterdemonstration (field notes, January 20, 2010).

However, as the Citizens' Revolution consolidated and polarization increased, some of these ambivalent allies were increasingly marginalized from the ruling coalition. For example, the Shuar congresswoman's brother eventually had to leave his job at the Ministry of Culture. The comptroller of Correa's government ordered the impeachment of the Pachakutik governor César Umajinga in April 2012 under accusations of corruption. Umajinga had been among the strongest supporters of President Correa within Pachakutik. Alianza País mayors in the province of Cotopaxi and the indigenous vice-governor (an ex-Pachakutik who became a member of

Alianza País) ousted Umajinga before he even had time to appeal. Umajinga had lost favor with Correa's government when a referendum for greater executive control of the judiciary and the media was defeated in the province of Cotopaxi in May 2011 (*El Comercio*, June 13, 2012; *El Mercurio*, June 13, 2012; *El Universo*, May 29, 2012; *Hoy*, May 19, 2011).

The government's strategy fluctuated between promoting divisions within Pachakutik and CONAIE and conducting open confrontation with this movement. I documented that entire families who had a Pachakutik member among their ranks lost their jobs in the public sector (fieldwork notes, December 2012). This strategy shaped subjectivities. The message was that ambivalence or outright opposition would not be tolerated. This strategy constructed indigenous people not as actors who might give their support at a given time but with whom the government must negotiate at another time, but as obedient subjects. In addition, the fluctuations between co-opting and dividing and repression had the effect of creating confusion and further weakening the movement.

Advances and Ambiguities in Indigenous Rights in the 2008 Constitution

The 2008 constitution meant some advances in indigenous rights over the 1998 constitution. However, due to tensions in the ruling coalition, some points were kept intentionally ambiguous and some advances were not possible. The Constituent Assembly of 2008 debated whether Ecuador should become plurinational or intercultural. Plurinationalism was associated with autonomy, the redistribution of resources, and indigenous representation in different state institutions (Monica Chuji, interview by author, April 2008). Interculturalism referred to the right to be different, antidiscrimination measures, and inclusion in the nation (Pedro de la Cruz, interview by author, April 2008). After some debate, a consensus was reached in the governing party Alianza País, and both terms, "plurinationalism" and "interculturalism," were adopted in the constitution. However, some of the demands associated with these terms were watered down. Plurinationalism was accepted, but in other sections the constitution emphasized the unity and predominance of the central state. The sovereignty of the state supersedes territorial autonomy, and the special representation of indigenous nationalities beyond regular elected representation was not accepted.

To understand how these decisions were made, it is important to take into account how the Constitutional Assembly was organized. The governmental movement achieved an absolute majority in the Constitutional Assembly (72 out of 130 seats). Soon after the election, the institution was criticized for the lack of autonomy of its members vis-à-vis the presidency and the executive. For instance, when indigenous organizations pressed for the recognition of the plurinational state, the assembly delegated work on the topic to the ministers and secretaries of the executive branch. Thus, the presidency formulated the core element of the policy (Ortiz Lemos 2015).

On the other hand, the government's priority was to show that the social movements had contributed their proposals to the new constitution. For this purpose, the Constituent Assembly created the Unit of Social Participation (UPS). This institution coordinated the interaction between civil society organizations and the assembly. However, two issues prevented the proposals of social movements from influencing the constitutional text: UPS only allowed those groups that were friendly to the government to participate in discussions. Sometimes these were governmentally sponsored groups that had been organized for electoral purposes and were presented to the public as social movements. Moreover, UPS was unable to process the huge quantity of demands received from civil society groups. In this way, the procedure seemed participatory, but was tightly controlled by the executive. In addition, the social movements saw themselves as participants and accepted highly controversial items that they might not have accepted otherwise (Ortiz Lemos 2015).

Another issue that created tensions in the governing coalition was whether to declare Kichwa an official language on equal standing with Spanish. Many deputies to the Constituent Assembly wished to do so, but the final consensus reached by Correa's party was to retain Spanish as the only official language and to declare Kichwa and Shuar as "languages of intercultural communication." The reasons given by the governing party for keeping Kichwa inferior in relation to Spanish were: Kichwa is an oral language; it is not a national language; it would be very costly to implement making Kichwa an official language; the imposition of Kichwa on the coast would generate resentment; and it would be better for the population to learn English (DINEIB 2008).

Antidiscrimination and affirmative action were important advances in the 2008 constitution and in the secondary legislation developed afterward.

Antidiscrimination principles appear throughout the constitutional text and have been further developed in Presidential Decree 60, issued September 28, 2009 (Correa 2009). Presidential Decree 60 declares: "The state will try to achieve (*procurará*) the hiring of Afro-Ecuadorians, indigenous, and montubios [mestizo peasants from the coast] in all its institutions in a proportion that will be not less than their participation in the total population". This decree, however, was not thoroughly implemented (Observatorio sobre discriminación racial y exclusión étnica 2012). One of the few experiences of implementation was the hiring of twenty indigenous, eleven Afro-Ecuadorians, and ten montubios as low-level diplomats by the Ministry of Foreign Affairs in 2012. In the case of indigenous applicants, the applications were processed through FENOCIN (National Federation of Peasant, Indigenous, and Black Organizations), and other groups friendly to the government, including some branches of CONAIE that allied with the regime (applicant, personal communication, August 2012). This strategy strengthened these alternative organizations and branches showing that those who supported the regime had resources to distribute, and it further weakened and divided CONAIE. Candidates underwent a personal interview in which they were asked their political affiliation and their thoughts about Correa's regime. According to one candidate, those who were not sponsored by an organization friendly to the government did not get the job (interview by author, December 19, 2012).

The question of indigenous territories and control of nonrenewable natural resources remains a problematic and ambiguous arena in the constitutional text. Indigenous territories (*circunscripciones territoriales indígenas*) are included in the text. However, these circumscriptions do not pertain to the regular territorial organization of the state. To generate an indigenous territory, interested groups were to base their petition and carry out a referendum in the divisions of the state that already exist as decentralized units such as parishes (*parroquias*), counties (*cantones*), and provinces (Constitución 2008, 158). A problem with this method is that the current divisions of the state are based on the distribution of the mestizo population. Typically, indigenous populations are located on the margins of these divisions, the center of which is the mestizo parish or town. This would make the official approval of indigenous territories very difficult (Julián Larrea, personal communication, September 2009). The Organic Code of Territorial Organization, Autonomy, and Decentralization (COOTAD), the secondary legislation issued in October 2010 elaborated on the issue and retained this difficulty. The 2008 constitution and COOTAD seem to make possible the formation of indigenous territories with state budgets, a step beyond the mere recognition of the neoliberal period. However, by requiring circumscriptions to be equal to traditional divisions of the state or additions of these (i.e., a group of parishes or provinces), no new rights are effectively granted. From 2007 to 2014, not even one new indigenous territory was created (García 2014).

Furthermore, it is clear in the constitutional text that nonrenewable natural resources belong to the central state. The chart of indigenous rights in the constitution establishes that communities should be consulted when their territories or rights are affected, but it is not clear whether this requirement is binding for the state. Alianza País did not accept unambiguous binding consultation for indigenous peoples in the constitution (Gina Chávez, assistant to a constituent deputy, personal communication, April 11, 2008). Environmentalists and supporters of indigenous rights lost this battle, but they introduced an ambiguity in the constitutional text that they tried to use in favor of the communities. The constitution establishes that Ecuador would respect all international treaties regarding indigenous and human rights. That includes the 2007 United Nations Declaration on the Rights of Indigenous Peoples, which mandates that the consent of indigenous communities is needed in order to extract natural resources from their territories (Alberto Acosta, personal communication, April 10, 2008).

State Practices for Managing Diversity

An important conflict pertained to the system of intercultural bilingual education (see also chapter 4). In February 2009 (right after CONAIE demonstrated against the mining law published on January 29, 2009), the Correa government abolished the autonomy of indigenous organizations to elect authorities to the National Directorate of Intercultural Bilingual Education or to decide on educational policies through Executive Decree 1585. This decree established that the minister of education would manage the intercultural bilingual system according to national public policies. All authorities in this system would be freely nominated or removed by the minister. This meant a significant change and regression for indigenous organizations because they had been able to elect the system's authorities, to design the curriculum and educational policies, and to hire its teachers since 1988. This decision, which contradicts the concept of plurinationality declared in the 2008 constitution, caused great discontent in the indigenous movement. It is important to note that many of the movement's cadres are bilingual teachers. The intercultural bilingual system is also one of the main sources of employment for indigenous professionals in a very discriminatory labor market. Furthermore, the autonomy of the intercultural bilingual system of Ecuador was unique in Latin America (Abram 2004).

Several reasons were given for this change that went against the idea of autonomy implied by the declaration of the plurinational state. According to the Ministry of Education, intercultural bilingual education had been delegated to indigenous organizations in the context of the neoliberal retrenchment of the state. For this reason, bilingual education had become the booty of a handful of corrupt leaders who had used the system for their own profit, "politiziced" it, and were the cause of the serious quality problems in the system. The ministry also accused CONAIE of being "racist," because they had monopolized intercultural education for the sake of indigenous organizations, had taught children about indigenous struggles, and had not included mestizos (Ministerio de Educación del Ecuador 2009).

On March 31, 2011, a new Organic Law of Intercultural Education (LOEI) was issued. This law refers not only to the education of indigenous people but also to the whole educational system, which now becomes intercultural in its totality. For example, the law establishes that the state is obliged to "progressively include in the curriculum the study of at least one ancestral language as well as the systematic study of non-official national realities, histories, and local knowledge" (LOEI, Title I, Article 5, letter l).

A separate system of intercultural bilingual education persists, but it becomes part of the Ministry of Education and the minister remains its main authority. A Plurinational Council has advisory and accountability functions. It is made up of several representatives of the executive and one representative per indigenous nationality. These representatives, however, are not chosen by the nationalities according to their customs, but selected through processes defined by the Council of Citizen Participation and Social Control, a technocratic institution close to the executive.

A section of the LOEI forbids teachers to paralyze education or carry out political proselytism in school, an article probably directed to the powerful

Maoist UNE (National Teachers' Union) and to CONAIE, the two organizations that have controlled the public education system in Ecuador and have often protested against different governments.

The law contains several tensions: (1) a centralization of decision making in the executive that assumes the responsibility for the implementation of interculturalism throughout society; (2) an appropriation of interculturalism for the nation and a blurring of the meaning of the term at the expense of interculturalism as a specific political project of indigenous peoples; (3) a criminalization of protest within the educational system, one of the most politically active sectors of civil society in Ecuador; and (4) the use of the word "ancestral" throughout the law to refer to indigenous language and culture, relegating indigenous knowledge to the past in classical indigenista fashion.

A Kichwa linguist, who is an authority in the intercultural bilingual system in the province of Imbabura and a member of FENOCIN, interprets the law in the following way. He appreciates several positive aspects of the law. For the first time, the whole educational system becomes intercultural and it is now based on the indigenous concept of "good living." Moreover, a general educational law in the country has a whole section spelling out the importance of intercultural bilingual education. He praises the requirement of including the teaching of ancestral languages, knowledge, and history in the curriculum. As a linguist, he is also happy with the creation of an Institute of Ancestral Languages, although he believes it may divide indigenous professionals because they have already begun fighting to capture positions in the newly created institute. He acknowledges that the government has assumed the debate on interculturalism and that the earlier intercultural bilingual system has been absorbed by the larger system, formerly called "Hispano" (meaning nonindigenous) and now called "of intercultural education." According to the interviewee this has happened because of the failure of the previous intercultural bilingual system and its indigenous teachers and administrators to carry out the required pedagogical revolution. Finally, he notes that the most troubling part of the law to teachers in the Imbabura province is the section on evaluation and accountability that can affect their employment. He thinks that the pedagogical change should have been carried out progressively, through training, instead of through an "evaluation hunt" (*cacería evaluadora*) (interview, July 27, 2012).

This interview shows the effects of the law on indigenous people: it recognizes their political project but appropriates it for the state and for mestizo society due to the alleged inability of indigenous professionals to carry it out efficiently. Indigenous peoples are recipients and not shapers of intercultural policies. The law creates some jobs for professionals that are seen as an opportunity, but it also has the ability to punish through a nonnegotiated evaluation process. The law tries to shape a particular kind of indigenous subjectivity, one that sees mestizos as the appropriate thinkers and agents and the indigenous as recipients, unable to design and implement policies autonomously.

Another indigenous intellectual, an anthropologist and member of the Cañari Kichwa people, a teacher in an intercultural bilingual school in Cañar, and a longtime member of CONAIE, has a different opinion. When I asked him what he thought of the LOEI he answered:

> With all sincerity, I must respond that I do not like that law. I say this not because I am against Officialism [Correa's government], but because this is a law that does not respond to the real needs of Ecuador. Let me tell you the process of creation of this law. By request of the actors of the system of intercultural bilingual education, there was a process of prelegislative consultation. In this process, by consensus, we requested that intercultural bilingual education be considered an autonomous system from the administrative, technical, and financial points of view. This proposal was not taken into account. The government argued that prelegislative consultation with indigenous people is not binding. It is unbelievable the way they have treated us. Well, the term "intercultural" was created by academics, but we appropriated it in intercultural bilingual education, trying to dialogue, trying to look for mutual respect by the peoples who live together. However, today that term has been appropriated by Officialism as a political symbol. For me, "interculturalidad" is not an abstract term. It is concrete.
>
> Ninety percent of the teachers do not agree with this system being implemented in Ecuador. The only ones who agree are those who have become part of Officialism, because one of the strategies of this system has been to divide and destabilize the organized social systems, and to divide the indigenous movement with even greater strength. Many leaders have been bought in exchange for jobs. (Interview, July 29, 2012)

In December 2012 I visited the intercultural bilingual high school in the province of Cañar where the interviewee teaches. In contrast to the recent past when educated indigenous teachers led the institution, a mestizo woman with a lower level of education was directing the school. Another indigenous teacher in the province of Chimborazo with an MA level of education told me that the director of his intercultural school was now a mestizo who had not yet completed his BA (interview by author, December 22, 2012). The human capital painstakingly built during the indigenous movement's period of strength was now unacknowledged and underused.

Another source of conflict between the government and indigenous organizations is the administration of natural resources such as oil, minerals, and water. This is an additional domain in which indigenous movements have lost autonomy. Large-scale mining is a recent activity in Ecuador. The first mining law was issued in 1991. By 2007, 2.8 million hectares had been granted to mining companies. Half of that area was for the extraction of metals, an extremely polluting activity (Amnesty International 2012). In November 2008, Correa's government presented the project of the mining law to the National Assembly. Despite a constitutional requirement stating that indigenous peoples should be consulted when their rights or territories are affected, their organizations were not adequately engaged in the design of this law. The law opened the path for the development of large-scale mining in Ecuador. President Correa promoted the law arguing that it facilitated "responsible mining" by giving the state greater control over the activity (Amnesty International 2012). A conflict developed between the state, which wanted to promote large-scale mining, and indigenous organizations, which argued that mining would lead to violations of their human rights. This situation resulted in protests at the end of 2008 and beginning of 2009. Despite these conflicts, the law was approved in January 2009 (Amnesty International 2012).

Kurt Weyland (2009) differentiates two kinds of political styles in those governments that turned toward the Left in Latin America beginning in the late 1990s. One group of governments were more blunt and radical in both their political discourse and policies. Others were more moderate, although they sought to implement social policies and carry out some redistribution. According to Weyland, the governments that allowed themselves to be more radical were those that possessed large deposits of nonrenewable natural resources, particularly Venezuela, Bolivia, and Ecuador. As governments struggle to extract more nonrenewable resources to be able to sustain social policies, they enter into conflict with indigenous movements. Paradoxically, damage to indigenous territories and communities was carried out or allowed to happen to fuel the small programs that allowed the government to remain quite popular within and outside indigenous communities. The result was the fragmentation of indigenous social movements between those who resisted forcefully and those happy with the policies of redistribution.

Anthony Bebbington and Denise Humphreys Bebbington (2011) argued that extractive activities expanded aggressively in Andean-Amazonian countries in the first decade of the 2000s. Extractive industries opened new frontiers and deepened their work in already exploited areas. The authors noted that neoliberal and postneoliberal governments responded in similar ways to this wave of global expansion of extractive activities: governments desperately needed and took advantage of the profits generated by these activities, and claimed that they used the revenues to improve the standard of living of the national population. They also confronted social movements in frontier areas with increasing intolerance and in some cases with violence, and tended to criminalize and stigmatize those who opposed extraction. In this context, indigenous rights and autonomy, even of the more restricted kind, seemed to directly threaten this intensified extractivism.

The regression in autonomy for the control of intercultural bilingual education, territories, and natural resources was accompanied by a strong campaign to delegitimize the indigenous leadership in presidential speeches, by intellectuals who were close to the government, and in government-owned media. For example, President Correa asserted: "What legitimacy does CONAIE have? . . . We, the majority must decide how we want to organize and how we want to live. And a few stone throwers should not impose their will. Thirteen million Ecuadorians should rise against these troglodyte attitudes that want to keep our country in the past. . . . What CONAIE does is not resistance; it is aggression" (quoted in Amnesty International 2012, 21). A document by Erika Sylva Charvet, the minister of culture, and Rafael Quintero Lopez, the undersecretary of the Ministry of Foreign Affairs, both of whom are recognized social scientists, claimed that since 2009 CONAIE had been attempting to conspire against President Correa and the constituent process in alliance with the extreme Right and with financial aid from US institutions that seek to destabilize the Latin American Left. According to the authors the indigenous movement and the teachers' union were part of a corporatist Left that defended private interests, had abandoned the struggle for social reform, and was useful to neoliberalism (Quintero Lopez and Sylva Charvet 2010). In the state-owned newspaper *El Telégrafo* (June 13, 2010), the opinion writer Guido Calderón argued that the ancestral cultures of Ecuador lack a historical contribution: "They are only characterized by a rosary of complaints and resentments. . . . I see neither their historical nor their contemporary contribution. Their actions are limited to threats, social disruption, and the exhibition of permanent violence. . . . They want us to accept their barbarism by force as part of our lives. Even more, they expect our laws to lie below their brutal indigenous law. A bunch of leaders addicted to substances do not create cultures and even less ancestral cultures" (Calderón 2010). Was this a backlash against indigenous people by resentful mestizos who had only unwillingly remained silent and accepted the respect required by the recognition policies of neoliberal multiculturalism? Unfortunately, after listening to presidential speeches, individuals like Calderón felt it was legitimate to expose points of view such as those reproduced above. Paradoxically, some of the most severe critics of the indigenous movement were intellectuals like Sylva who not so long ago were advocates of the indigenous movement and wrote influential pieces on it. Similarly to the Guatemalan mestizos studied by Charles Hale (2006), the racism of some mestizos in Ecuador survived the period of expansion of the indigenous movement and government recognition of indigenous rights. During that period, racism remained relatively hidden because its public iteration became politically incorrect and reproachable. However, resonating with the Guatemalan case, racism would reappear as soon as mestizos perceived that their material interests were threatened. This occult racism resurfaced fast when a "progressive" government legitimized mestizo prejudices again.

In a 2012 report on the criminalization of the right to protest in Ecuador, Amnesty International argued that the climate of hostility created by the public statements of the president and other authorities against the indigenous movement had the effect of making more difficult the work of those who defended human rights and legitimating aggressions against them by private interests.

The report also demonstrated that the government used the legal system to discourage protest. After antigovernment protests, public prosecutors accused indigenous and peasant leaders of crimes such as terrorism, sabotage, and obstruction of public roads. Many of these accusations were abandoned for lack of proof, but the trials were long and costly and had the effect of discouraging leaders and communities to voice their views. Finally, when social leaders accused mining and oil companies of threats and physical aggression, the state did not investigate them (Amnesty International 2012). In this regard, the former president of CONAIE Luis Macas has argued:

> There's a political motivation for the government's assault on the indigenous movement in the current moment. It's not that the government simply wants to get rid of the Indians, or that it's racism for racism sake. No. The objective is to liquidate the indigenous movement in this country, to dismantle and destroy this movement. Why? Because the indigenous movement is the principal social and political actor in the country that has struggled against the economic model. . . . And this project of development is rooted in the exploitation of natural resources. We, the indigenous movement, which has an emphatically different conceptualization of Mother Nature, are saying no. So, clearly, it's got to liquidate our movement. It's got to sweep aside all the social movements that stand in the way of its development model, starting above all with the indigenous movement. (Webber 2010, 9)

The Racial Project of Nationalist-Extractivism

The indigenous movement of Ecuador confronted a project of state formation in a moment of relative organizational weakness. The government allowed for some apparent legal advances in indigenous rights, and indigeneity was symbolically important. However, these principles were plagued by tensions between centralization and autonomy, used to co-opt and divide, or barely implemented. One reason for this was that the government was originally constituted by different currents: one current was environmentalist, for indigenous rights, and participatory, and a second current was centralist and extractivist. Unfortunately, the second current gained strength at the expense of the first. In addition, the first more radical current was in charge of producing government discourse, whereas the second, also called pragmatic, had a more prominent role in the practices of government.

What is the ethnic project of the nationalist-extractivist regime in Ecuador? There was recognition of indigenous people but it was contradictory or barely implemented. Moreover, counterdiscourses stigmatized indigenous peoples, particularly those who tried to maintain an autonomous voice. Regarding policies of redistribution, some were based on ethnicity, such as government positions at institutions of service to indigenous peoples or limited positions based on affirmative action in the Ministry of Foreign Affairs. Other policies of redistribution were universal, such as the bonus for human development and other cash transfers to the poor. However, the data indicate that these resources were used to strengthen support for the government, and to divide and co-opt indigenous organizations. Indigenous people feared the withdrawal of these funds if they did not show faith in the government. From this point of view, the ethnic project of this government was not different from that of neoliberalism: the government offered limited symbolic recognition and some targeted redistribution that disciplined indigenous people and separated "permitted Indians" from recalcitrant ones. In Ecuador, the nationalist-extractivist state expected uncritical support. The state carried some socioeconomic transformations, but it was not willing to negotiate them with autonomous social actors.

On the other hand, the nationalist-extractivist project was not characterized by the promotion of the kinds of tolerance that permeated earlier neoliberal attitudes. Recalcitrant Indians were criminalized through the legal system and harshly stigmatized in discourses, which contributed to raising the levels of prejudice and even violence against indigenous people in Ecuadorian society. From this perspective, there was a reversal in relation to the "neoliberal multicultural" moment. Neoliberalism also promoted levels of decentralization, autonomy, and participation that were retrenched during the Correa decade.

Another reversal was the appropriation of the agendas and symbols of indigenous movements, the blurring and stretching of their meaning, and the exclusion of indigenous people from the symbolics of indigeneity and from the management of policies that affect their lives. The intercultural policies of this government were not negotiated with collective actors; technocrats devised them for passive recipients. We witnessed a regression from a participatory kind of indigenismo that originated in the 1970s and was typical of the neoliberal period, to the kind of paternalist indigenismo that characterized an earlier period of strong states, populist regimes, and import substitution industrialization that dominated roughly from the 1930s to the 1970s. This paternalist indigenismo was accompanied by a symbolic construction of the mestizo as the embodiment of the nation and as the active subject.

The indigenista agenda of the government was also plagued by contradictions and ambiguities: rights were granted but the process of obtaining them was tortuous, as in the case of titling indigenous territories. Calls for autonomy and rights in the constitution clashed with its centralizing and authoritarian tendencies. Interculturalism was promoted but mestizos appropriated and managed it. These ambiguities created a confused terrain, one that allowed those inside and outside who wished to believe in the multicultural policies of the government to deny a regression in rights. This confusion also affected indigenous movements that showed ambivalence toward this government and seemed to lack a clear line of reaction (see also chapter 6).

How does the policy toward diversity of the Correa decade compare to that of other twenty-first-century-Left regimes? A focus on the extraction of natural resources also limits indigenous rights in Bolivia (Postero 2017), where the Morales government faced opposition from indigenous organizations in the areas of extraction. The centralizing tendencies of a strong state are also present in Venezuela, where indigenous autonomy was rescinded to organize people from above (Angosto Ferrández 2008). As in Ecuador, state appropriation of ethnic symbols and agendas leads to the exclusion of alternative forms of indigenous organization and subjectivity in Bolivia and Venezuela (Albro 2010; Angosto Ferrández 2008; Canessa 2006; Postero 2017). However, the construction of indigenous citizens as passive recipients of policy seems to be more extreme in Ecuador. In Bolivia, the government originated in social movements whereas in Ecuador the president and many influential government officials were middle-class, white-mestizo intellectuals and technocrats. Venezuela had opportunities for participation, even if orchestrated from above, that did not exist in Ecuador. To sum up, a combination of technocratic paternalism, intolerance, and outright repression shaped the ethnic policies of nationalist-extractivist Ecuador.

CHAPTER 3

THE MINIMIZATION OF INDIGENOUS NUMBERS AND THE FRAGMENTATION OF CIVIL SOCIETY

This chapter discusses how the Ecuadorian state has interpreted and measured ethnicity and race in the transition from neoliberalization to Correa's nationalist-extractivist regime. However, to better understand state views on social classification, the chapter reaches back to the first 1950 census and even farther back to colonial and nineteenth-century population counts. Population censuses and census debates are excellent windows into exploring racial formations as well as articulations between state racial projects and those of other social actors. The chapter examines the degree to which nationalist-extractivist views of race and ethnicity departed from those of the neoliberal period. It also shows how Correa used the census to delegitimize and weaken the indigenous movement and to play identity-based groups against each other.

The history of ethnic statistics in Ecuador is intriguing because of the contrast between the importance of indigenous struggles and indigeneity in the national and international perception of the country, and the smaller number of indigenous population that repeatedly shows up in censuses since the first national census was conducted in 1950. A long-term debate centers on the multiple reasons for undercounting the indigenous population. In contrast, the Afro-Ecuadorian population has more recently shifted from its historical invisibility in the eyes of the state to becoming a sizable part of the population according to official statistics (de la Torre 2002; Rahier 1998, 2012; Whitten 1981; Whitten and Quiroga 1998). The montubio group, made up of rural mestizos from the Ecuadorian coast, has become politicized as an ethnic movement and joined official statistical counts in 2010 (Bauer 2012; Pallares 2007; Roitman 2009). In the context of the Confederation of Indigenous Nationalities of Ecuador's opposition to government development policies, and Afro-Ecuadorian and montubio leaders' choice to work with the state, it has been convenient for the regime to present smaller indigenous numbers in the census while rendering the other two groups visible (Bauer 2012; de la Torre and Antón Sánchez 2012).

A second and related argument developed in this chapter is the shift in Ecuadorian official statistics since approximately 2000 from ways to read social difference based on language, culture, occupation, territorial, and organizational affiliation inspired by early twentieth-century Latin American intellectual traditions, to understandings of race based on an individual's self-definition, and to hypodescent, a North American–inspired concept.[1] This shift went hand in hand with the consolidation of neoliberalism in Ecuador. Interestingly, some of these understandings continued under Rafael Correa, a president who features antineoliberal and anti-imperialist rhetoric.

The census is understood here as political and is studied as a manifestation of the state in its ideological, institutional, and practical dimensions (Angosto Ferrández and Kradolfer 2012; Clark 1998; Nobles 2000). The chapter explores the ambiguous meanings and uses of statistics as power-ridden sources of information for the administration of populations (Foucault 2006 [1991]; Scott 1998), as ideological devices to legitimize particular state projects (Clark 1998), and as institutions that shape racial categories and affect citizenship rights (Nobles 2000).

An understanding of census taking is complicated by the ambiguities that characterize statistical data and their uses. Statistics appeared at the end of the eighteenth century simultaneously with the idea of the "art of government" (Foucault 2006 [1991]). The art of government was understood at the time as something different from sovereignty, which was associated with the particular interests and goals of the ruler. In contrast, statistics helped

---

1. In societies where racial or ethnic groups are arranged hierarchically, hypodescent is the assignment of the child of a mixed union to the subordinate group.

construct the idea of the population as an aggregate. The population then became the target of modern forms of government that claimed to operate for the common good. Statistics also became a technology to know the population in order to administer and shape it. Thus, statistics is key in the construction of the public function of the state and is also a technique for the administration and manipulation of the public. One of the ambiguities of statistical data is that they are understood simultaneously as ideology (a deformation of reality) and knowledge (a truth that has practical applications). Instead of a falsification, statistics have rather been interpreted as a simplification of reality for the purposes of state legibility and control (Scott 1998). However, when paired with the power of state institutions, these simplified representations have the ability to remake reality because the state has the capacity to treat people according to its own schemata. Finally, different populations throughout history have resisted becoming legible to the state, as they have understood the articulations between legibility, control, and the extraction of surplus (Scott 1998).

The state is elusive and ambiguous. This is because the state, like a mask, hides something that should not be uncovered if it is to keep its legitimacy and stay in control: this hidden reality beneath the mask is the appropriation of what is public for private ends as well as illegitimate forms of domination (Abrams 2006 [1988]). The state is better grasped as an idea, a projection that legitimizes domination in the name of the common good. In addition, the state can be studied as a system of institutions that are the producers of the idea of the state. Censuses belong to the domain of the "state idea." They are key ideological devices that help legitimate state elites as those who pursue common goals. On the other hand, we must study the census bureau ethnographically as the institution that produces these ideological representations.

This work uses census documents and data not so much to learn about the population as to understand the cultural and political assumptions of those who produced the census (Clark 1998). The categories of social identity used in censuses can be linked to projects of national development and to the ways in which the state conceives of the national population. The categories used in data collection reveal concepts of society and personhood. Furthermore, we can learn about technologies of rule by studying the documentation that states generate about the population (Clark 1998). Therefore, a study of census taking is an ethnography of the state.

Scholars have discussed more specifically the connections between national censuses and race and ethnicity with a focus on Latin America. Melissa Nobles's (2000) comparative study of censuses in the United States and Brazil critically examines the construction of race categories in and through national censuses. Nobles shows the connections between concepts of race, censuses, and citizenship rights: censuses shape racial discourse that then affects public policies. Policies for their part establish who has or lacks certain rights. In response to these uses of censuses by states, individuals and groups seek to alter the terms of racial discourse to advance their own political goals.

It is important to historicize and contextualize the practice of census taking—to locate it within the conjuncture—to better show its political nature (Angosto Ferrández and Kradolfer 2012). National censuses and their use of racial and ethnic categories have gone through several stages in Latin America. The first censuses were conducted by liberal states engaged in processes of state formation, modernization, and institutionalization. A second stage took place in the context of nationalist regimes that promoted the assimilation of indigenous and Afro-Ecuadorian groups through the concepts of mestizaje and whitening. In this second stage, Latin American governments understood ethnic classifications in terms of culture to avoid the scientific racism that dominated early twentieth-century Europe as well as the juridical distinctions between groups that characterized colonial Latin America. Starting in the 1970s, processes of decolonization, civil rights movements, indigenous movements, and a turn toward critical social science positioned the recognition of diversity instead of assimilation as the progressive goal in a third stage of census taking. The context was also favorable for participatory agendas for indigenous and other marginalized groups.

A more recent milestone in ethnic statistics has been the United Nations World Conference against Racism that took place in Durban, South Africa, in September 2001. There, the UN denounced the lack of data disaggregated by race and ethnicity and encouraged states to produce this information to fight discrimination (Angosto Ferrández and Kradolfer 2012; Antón Sánchez and del Popolo 2008). These global processes of affirmation of diversity were reinforced by the multicultural constitutionalism of the 1990s in Latin America (Van Cott 2005). Self-identification was originally proposed by indigenous groups and international organizations as a way for indigenous peoples to control their own self-definition instead of leaving it to states (Angosto Ferrández and Kradolfer 2012).

However, we need to further reflect on the consequences of self-identification. Self-identification is associated with group recognition and collective rights. On the other hand, this indicator highlights the individual and the subjective over the collective character of identities. It also understands identities as constructed from below instead of as power-charged identifications. It can also be a changing indicator that depends on how individuals would like to self-identify at particular conjunctures. Another tension in self-identification is that many states do not seem to trust the indicator and use additional markers believed to be objective, such as language, to measure identities (Angosto Ferrández and Kradolfer 2012). Interestingly, in Ecuador self-identification has not resulted in larger indigenous numbers.

The sources used in writing this chapter are varied, relying on secondary literature discussing Ecuadorian censuses, consultancy reports, writings by government officials involved in census taking, interviews with government officials and indigenous and Afrodescendant intellectuals who have participated in census taking, interviews with indigenous intellectuals not working for statistics institutions, and journalistic pieces.

Contextualizing Ethnic Social Movements in Contemporary Ecuador

The historical strength of the indigenous movement of Ecuador, its oppositional politics, and its relative crisis in the first decade of the 2000s, help explain the state's interest in undercounting indigenous people as well as the official insistence that indigenous people are a minority. The history of this social movement is discussed in chapter 1.

The Afrodescendant population of Ecuador has been historically concentrated in the northern province of Esmeraldas, where free Blacks established maroon communities in the sixteenth century, and in the Chota-Mira valley, where Africans were brought as slaves in colonial times to work on the sugarcane plantations of the Jesuit priests. Norman Whitten (1986 [1974]) and Ronald Stutzman (1974) show that the Afro-Ecuadorian population of Esmeraldas and Valle del Chota were not organized on the basis of their identity in the 1960s and 1970s. Some prominent Black intellectuals joined the Marxist Left and preferred to emphasize class solidarity (de la Torre 2002). In the 1980s, the progressive Catholic Church, and more specifically the Comboni Missionaries working within the Afro Pastoral, encouraged the formation of identity-based organizations among the Black population. The work of the Comboni Missionaries with Black catechists and activists produced a number of regional and thematic Black organizations that tended to emphasize cultural rather than socioeconomic struggles. At the end of the 1990s, the Inter-American Development Bank and the World Bank provided funds to further strengthen these organizations. Catherine Walsh (2012) argues that, similarly to what happened to the indigenous movement, the investment of the Inter-American Development Bank and the World Bank in Afro-Ecuadorian organizations contributed to their focus on a technical agenda rather than a long-term or radical political agenda. Experts on Afro-Ecuadorians argue that this social movement has shifted from invisibility during the period of monocultural mestizaje to state corporatism and co-optation during the neoliberal and nationalist-extractivist periods (de la Torre and Antón Sánchez 2012; Rahier 2012; Walsh 2012). Carlos de la Torre and Jhon Antón Sánchez (2012) note that Afro-Ecuadorian leaders have focused on a cultural agenda that has alienated other Afrodescendant people who have not felt represented by this movement and have continued to organize as part of the poor. Furthermore, the Afro-Ecuadorian movement has been weak and fragmented along regional lines. Due to this history, Afro-Ecuadorian leaders have chosen a nonconfrontational strategy, and have instead requested incorporation into the state (de la Torre and Antón Sánchez 2012). They have achieved some improvements in race relations such as affirmative action, albeit poorly implemented, and antidiscrimination policies as well as positions for themselves in the high echelons of the state (Rahier 2012). Meanwhile, the claims of poor urban Afrodescendants and rural Black communities struggling against land grabs by palm oil and other companies have been underemphasized (Walsh 2012).

The rural inhabitants of the Ecuadorian coast make up a third group called montubio that was incorporated into official statistics in 2010. At the beginning of the twentieth century, the writers of the Guayaquil group discussed montubio identity in works of social realism intended to expose issues of poverty and rural–urban migration (de la Cuadra and Robles 1996; Roitman 2009). The Guayaquil group was a literary movement of the Ecuadorian coast in the 1930s and 1940s. Their works of fiction aimed to convey social realism as well as the inequalities and injustices that took place in Ecuador at the time. Five writers were part of this movement: Joaquín Gallegos Lara, Enrique Gil Gilbert, Demetrio Aguilera Malta, José de la Cuadra, and Alfredo Pareja Diezcanseco. In their early twentieth-century writings, montubios were described as mixed race peasants of Indian and African descent "with drops of white blood" (Roitman 2009, 118). However, the radicalism of the Guayaquil group was an exception. There was a stronger twentieth-century literary tradition that portrayed a folkloric montubio identity in order to promote coastal regionalism (Pallares 2007; Roitman 2009). In the same vein, the economic and intellectual elites of Guayaquil sponsored montubio festivals and research in the 1990s to provide a popular basis for their regional project (Estrada 1996). Montubios were historically organized in peasant unions along class lines or in communes (Bauer 2012; Pallares 2007). At the end of the 1990s, some montubios identified as indigenous Manta-Wankavilka in an attempt to tap into the funds of the World Bank and international nongovernmental organizations specifically intended for ethnic groups and due to their marginalization as poor mestizos (Bauer 2012). However, the Confederation of Indigenous Nationalities of Ecuador (CONAIE) did not accept reethnicized Manta-Wankavilka or montubios easily into their organization (Pallares 2007). In this context, a montubio group originating in a peasant union staged a hunger strike to pressure President Gustavo Noboa (2000–2003) to recognize them as an official ethnicity. The president did so in an executive decree in 2001. The 2008 constitution confirmed the legal status of montubios as a people. Similarly to Afro-Ecuadorians, montubio organizations have worked with the state rather than confronting it (Pallares 2007). Pallares (2007) suggests some explanations for this: even in the more radical social realist tradition of the Guayaquil group, montubios were never described as revolutionary actors and their folklorization was a stronger tendency. Montubios have not belonged to a single political party, but to several parties, some of them populist, such as Partido Roldosista Ecuatoriano. As soon as they became an organized ethnic group, montubios were incorporated into the state through the Council for the Development of the Montubio People of the Coast (CODEPMOC). Although the montubio group Montubio Corporation of the Coast (Corporación Montubia del Litoral) launched a more radical political agenda to solve rural poverty, the stronger organization, the Montubio Solidarity Movement (Movimiento Montubio Solidaridad) that has controlled CODEPMOC, has tended to focus on short-term technical development goals (Pallares 2007).

Ethnic Identities as Reflected in Population Censuses and Census Debates

During the mid-twentieth century, a period of indigenous struggles for access to land and for better labor conditions within the hacienda system, observers believed that indigenous people constituted a third to half of the Ecuadorian population (Clark 1998). This perception may have originated in a 1942 estimate of the National Directorate of Statistics of Ecuador, which calculated that the population of Ecuador was 39 percent Indian (Clark 1998), or in earlier nineteenth-century lists of indigenous taxpayers that estimated the indigenous population of the highlands to be 46 percent (F. Guerrero 2005). However, the proportion of speakers of indigenous languages registered by the first national census of 1950 was much lower, only 16.3 percent (Clark 1998). Scholars argue that indigenous peoples were undercounted in the 1950 census because of lack of access to some areas of the national territory such as the Amazon, indigenous resistance to being counted, the fact that urban bilinguals were not counted as Indians, and the state's desire to represent Ecuador as more urban and mestizo than it really was (Clark 1998; Prieto 2004). Indigenous uprisings against the 1950 census occurred because indigenous peoples associated it with the colonial goals of taxation and forced labor recruitment (Clark 1998; Prieto 2004).

Between the 1960s and the 1980s, Ecuadorian censuses did not include questions on ethnicity or race due to a desire to integrate Indians into the nation and to the emergence of projects of mestizaje. After a decade of intense indigenous organizing in the 1980s, the 1990 census again included a question on the languages spoken by the population. Once more, only 3.84 percent reported speaking an indigenous language (INEC, 1990 population census processed by ECLA/CELADE 2003–2007). This census was taken a few months after a nationwide indigenous uprising paralyzed the country. The 1990 census results were challenged because indigenous organizations boycotted it (F. Guerrero 2005). Despite existing data of the censuses of 1950 and 1990 on speakers of indigenous languages, the Ecuadorian state failed to convince Ecuadorians and foreign observers alike that indigenous people were few. Observers continued to consider the higher estimates as correct (Clark 1998; Lucero 2008; Yashar 2005).

When the 2001 census, for the first time, used self-identification to determine ethnic and racial categories in the country, only 6.83 percent of Ecuadorians identified as indigenous. In 2010, 7 percent of Ecuadorians claimed an indigenous identity through self-identification. Why did self-identification not increase indigenous numbers? Yet self-identification seems to have benefited other ethnic groups. With the relative strength of the Afro-Ecuadorian movement in the late 1990s, this population becomes visible in official statistics. In 2001, 4.9 percent of the population self-identified as Afro-Ecuadorian, but in 2010 the share increased to 7.2 percent, 0.2 percentage points higher than those who identified as indigenous in the same year. These numbers are most intriguing for an Andean country long perceived as a nation with a sizable indigenous population. Furthermore, the montubio group was added as an ethnic category to the population census in 2010, and more citizens identified with it than with the indigenous group. UN, ECLA (Economic Commission for Latin America), and Ecuadorian experts argue that statistics disaggregated by ethnicity are a way to empower ethnic groups and to fight against their discrimination in society (Angosto Ferrández and Kradolfer 2012; Antón Sánchez and del Popolo 2008). But is this always the case? In Ecuador, ethnic statistics seem to have empowered some groups while disempowering others. Alternatively, statistics may have disempowered all groups by causing them to compete against each other.

Table 3.1 summarizes the evolution of ethnic statistics in Ecuador from 1950 to 2010 and spells out the criteria used in each census to classify the population. The Ecuadorian state has changed its way to count ethnic groups over time. In the 1950 census, the state did not count people by race for fear of revolts, and under the influence of Latin American indigenista discussions. The Ecuadorian state wanted to distance itself from both colonial censuses that counted by race in order to tax and recruit Indians and from early twentieth-century European scientific racism (Prieto 2004). The census identified indigenous people using culture (language and material culture) as well as socioeconomic occupation (who was a hacienda laborer) as the markers (Prieto 2004). In 1990 language was the trait that defined being indigenous. However, scholars believed that indigenous numbers were too low in both censuses and felt the need to recalculate the indigenous population combining the data from the 1950 and 1990 censuses with additional

TABLE 3.1. Percentages of the population of Ecuador according to race and ethnicity in population censuses

Population censuses	How is ethnicity/race counted?	Indigenous	Afro-Ecuadorians	Montubios	Mestizos	Whites
1950	Language	16.3				
1962	Not counted					
1974	Not counted					
1982	Not counted					
1990	Language	3.84				
2001	Self-identification	6.83	Total: 4.97 Black: 2.23 Mulatto: 2.74		77.42	10.46
2010	Self-identification	7.0	7.2	7.4	71.9	6.1

Source: Compiled on the basis of sources cited in this chapter.

criteria such as living in a territory defined as indigenous and participating in a community or organization (F. Guerrero 2005; Knapp 1987; Ramón 1994; Sánchez Parga 1996; Zamosc 1995). Besides language, territory and participation in indigenous institutions were the traits privileged in Latin American indigenista discussions led by Mexican intellectuals (Martínez Novo 2006).

In contrast, the concepts adopted after the 2001 census are hypodescent for the Afrodescendant population (the idea that the offspring of a mixed union are automatically assigned to the subordinate group), an emphasis on race instead of culture, and an individualized understanding of ethnic difference that is not historically grounded or power-aware. The 2001 census was the first to use self-identification; it also had another question about language. The self-identification question was: "Do you consider yourself indigenous, Black (Afro-Ecuadorian), mestizo, mulatto, white, or other?" Respondents of the indigenous option were asked to name a nationality or people with which they identified, but were not provided specific choices. The options in the self-identification question made direct reference to race (Black, white, indigenous, mixed [mestizo and mulatto]). The concept of race, a notion that the Ecuadorian state had not used since the colonial period, was reintroduced in the first decade of 2000 under the influence of international organizations such as the Inter-American Development Bank (IDB) and the United Nations. According to an indigenous census specialist, the questions of the 2001 census came directly from the IDB (Luis Fernando Pijal, interview with author, July 15, 2014). Interestingly, race arrived in close association with self-identification, thus making this change appear to be a progressive step toward recognition. The first time race and self-identification were used together was in 2000 in a survey to measure indicators of childhood and households (Encuesta de Medición de Indicadores de la Niñez y de los Hogares), a poll that was intended as rehearsal for the 2001 census. This poll was possible "thanks to the auspices of several international organizations," among them the UN Children's Fund, UN Population Fund, UN Development Programme, and the IDB (F. Guerrero 2005, 20).

It is no wonder that the way the self-identification question was formulated as well as its methodology caused a heated debate. F. Guerrero notes that the public emphasized that it was more appropriate to ask about "culture" than "race." According to Guerrero, the 2001 census avoided asking about "culture" to avert the danger that those sympathetic to the indigenous cause would identify as indigenous. It is important to note that this census was carried out only a year after the attempted coup d'état of Colonel Gutierrez in alliance with CONAIE that resulted in ousting President Jamil Mahuad. The interim president Gustavo Noboa may have had good reason to undercount indigenous people in the 2001 census. In addition, the public claimed that the interviewers were poorly trained and that many had classified people instead of asking them to define themselves (F. Guerrero 2005). This might have been a way for low-level government officials to maintain control over classification instead of surrendering it to individual citizens, as the methodology of self-identification required. Another shortcoming of the methodology criticized at the time was that the head of household identified all members of the family instead each member being asked to self-identify. This patriarchal legacy of the first population census of 1950 continues to this day (Clark 1998). Even the way the census was written implied that others would identify some people. For example, those who were less than one year old were expected to self-identify with one race or ethnic group. This seems to raise a contradiction between the idea of individual self-identification and the way the state identified people in practice.

Estimates of the indigenous population at the time were much higher than what the census portrayed: in several publications and public speeches, CONAIE argued that 35 percent of the population was indigenous; the

IDB estimated without explaining how the number was calculated that indigenous and Afro-Ecuadorians made up 25 percent of the population in 1999; and the World Bank calculated the indigenous population as 10.4 percent at the end of the 1990s in its proposal for the Program for the Development of Indigenous and Black Peoples (F. Guerrero 2005). It was widely believed that the 2001 census underestimated the indigenous population. However, public debates hesitated between the idea of an undercount and the idea that the data indicated a deep process of acculturation of the indigenous population (Luis Alberto Tuaza, interview by author, January 2014).

In the 2001 census, for the first time, national statistics took into account the Afro-Ecuadorian population, which had been statistically invisible until then. The emphasis of earlier censuses on cultural traits such as language and the avoidance of references to race may have contributed to the statistical invisibility of Afro-Ecuadorians. The lack of an organized Afro-Ecuadorian movement until the late 1990s may be another factor of invisibility. To calculate the Afro-Ecuadorian population, Blacks or Afro-Ecuadorians (placed together in one category) and mulattoes were combined, making up 4.97 percent of the population. We should note that this strategy resonates with North American ideas of hypodescent as a mixed person, a mulatto, is added to the subordinate category (Black or Afro-Ecuadorian) (Nobles 2000). It is reasonable to ask: If the mulatto category had been omitted from the 2001 census, would self-identified mulattoes have chosen Black or white? According to Latin American constructions of race favoring whitening and hyperdescent (the assignment of the child of a mixed union to the group considered to be socially dominant), it is very possible that this population would opt to identify as white if the mulatto category were not available (Wade 1997).

According to Nobles (2000), hypodescent was adopted in the United States at the beginning of the twentieth century and was first popularized in the 1930 US census. The idea originated in earlier definitions of racial membership in the legal systems of southern states and was devised to avoid racial ambiguities in order to maintain segregation under the Jim Crow laws (Nobles 2000). Although Latin American ideas of gradation and whitening certainly suggest the racist concept of white supremacy (Stutzman 1981), statistics officials and social movements should also examine the origins and implications of hypodescent before adopting it uncritically. Furthermore, using the same logic, the mestizo population should have been added to the indigenous population to increase indigenous numbers, but this did not happen. Hypo- and hyperdescent were used strategically to increase the numbers of Afro-Ecuadorians while decreasing the numbers of indigenous people. Interestingly, something different happened in Bolivia's 2001 census. There the category mestizo was omitted and people who felt that their identity was partially indigenous were encouraged to identify as indigenous (Schavelzon 2014). This happened in the context of indigenous mobilization and political empowerment.

The novelty of the 2010 census in Ecuador was the participation, following United Nations recommendations, of ethnic social movements and government officials working in development institutions for Afro-Ecuadorians, indigenous, and montubios in the design of census questions and in the self-identification campaign. The designers of the 2010 census took into account some of the criticisms of the 2001 census: the self-identification question gave greater weight to culture this time, although race was still a factor. The question was: "How do you identify according to your culture and customs?" And the options were: (1) indigenous, (2) Afro-Ecuadorian or Afrodescendant, (3) Black, (4) mulatto, (5) montubio, (6) mestizo, (7) white, or (8) other. Taking into account the options, "race" was still important despite the polite reference to "culture and customs" in the question. Although some options such as Afro-Ecuadorian and montubio seemed to refer to ethnicity, both terms also have racial connotations. After the struggle of the Afro-Ecuadorian movement to emphasize its character as an ethnic group and not a "race," the option Afro-Ecuadorian or Afrodescendant, which in 2001 appeared in parentheses after "Black," was presented separately this time (Jhon Antón Sánchez, personal communication, January 2014). In addition, those who chose the indigenous option were passed on to several choices of peoples and nationalities, a change that emphasized their language (the concept of nationality is based on speaking a distinct language) and culture over a generic indigenous identity.

The concepts of race and ethnicity cannot be neatly distinguished theoretically. In the nineteenth and early twentieth centuries, race implied phenotype classification but phenotypes were associated with psychological and cultural characteristics. On the other hand, ethnicity and culture have been used as euphemisms for race when the term lost legitimacy after the atrocities committed during World War II (Wade 1997). However, for social movements in Ecuador it is important to emphasize culture or ethnicity rather than race. In the eyes of the Afro-Ecuadorian movement for instance, culture and ethnicity suggest historical advances toward inclusion, whereas race refers back to colonial oppression and slavery (Jhon Antón Sánchez, interview, January 2014). Culture or ethnicity may very well be a euphemism for race, but social movements regard the euphemism as necessary when tackling this sensitive issue.

The debut of the montubio category in the 2010 census deserves further comment. Karem Roitman (2009) criticized the 2001 census for conflating many meanings under the category mestizo, a highland label, which made up 77.7 percent of the population. She suggested that mestizo had been privileged over coastal categories such as montubios or cholos. The inclusion of montubios may signal that statistics officials have been aware of the academic critiques of the previous census. More likely, however, officials included the montubio category for political reasons. The political potential of montubios may have influenced the state decision to recognize them as a people. They constitute a sizable portion of the population (7.4 percent according to the 2010 census) and many of them reside in the provinces of Manabí and Guayas, which are densely populated and thus key to winning elections. In the 1990s, montubios attempted to ally with CONAIE; some of them were undergoing a process of reindigenization (Bauer 2012). Although the montubio identity was promoted by the elites of Guayaquil who have opposed President Correa, the president managed to achieve political support among montubios through his control of state resources and his ability to co-opt local leaders. The creation of this category may have had the political effect of weakening the indigenous movement by separating a group in the process of reindigenization from it. Moreover, given the opposition of the indigenous movement to the extraction-based and other development policies of the Correa government, indigenous demographic weight was now balanced by that of Afro-Ecuadorians and montubios, two groups whose leaders have tended to work with and support the government.

The distribution of ethnic groups in the 2010 census is intriguing: according to the data, montubios represent 7.4 percent of the population, Afro-Ecuadorians 7.2 percent, indigenous peoples 7 percent, mestizos 71.9 percent, and whites 6.1 percent. Observers have expressed suspicion about the "perfect" distribution and gradation of minority groups because each makes up approximately 7 percent of the population, and indigenous people are the weakest minority (interview with SENPLADES [National

Secretariat for Planning and Development] government official by author, January 2014). The second census to ask the population about their ethnic self-affiliation seems to have finally fixed ethnic groups in the public imagination as comparable minorities. To accept the indigenous group as a minority among others has been possible in the context of a crisis of the indigenous movement and of Correa's verbal attacks against its leaders. This is far from the majority or half of the population that CONAIE claimed to represent in the 1990s. This public representation of ethnicity has had the effect of delegitimizing the claims and the resistance of indigenous movements, and of strengthening presidential claims that a minority should not impose its will over the country's majority. For example, President Correa said in the context of an indigenous demonstration against a water law proposal that in CONAIE's opinion would concentrate and privatize this resource: "We are more, we are many more. And here, as in any democracy, an absolute minority that is abusive, arrogant, and made up of stone throwers will not rule. The majority will rule, fellow countrymen" (Correa's speech in Plaza Grande, Wednesday, July 2, 2014). This discourse also has an effect on dominant conceptualizations of who represents the nation and who is marginal to it. This is an excellent example of the census bureau as a race-making institution that has important effects on citizenship rights (Nobles 2000).

Regarding the white category, in 2001, I witnessed discussions among Quito upper- and upper-middle classes concerning whether they should identify as whites or mestizos. In these informal conversations, men tended to prefer the white category, while women were more inclined toward mestizo. From these exchanges, I gathered that to identify as white was considered arrogant, a characteristic that would better fit men than women because women saw modesty as an important female virtue. In 2010 some editorial pieces in the press may have reflected private conversations between upper- and middle classes, stating that the correct census answer was mestizo instead of white. For example, Susana Klinkicht argued: "In the 2001 census, many chose the 'white' response in a country where almost everybody should feel mestizo." The white option was again considered arrogant, and almost a rejection of Ecuadorian nationality, insofar as whiteness has foreign or "foreign wannabe" connotations. The white category decreased from 10.46 percent in 2001 to 6.1 percent in 2010. This may be in part because of the campaign stating that mestizo was the right answer. Another reason is that a number of montubios had self-identified as white in 2001 (interview of Pijal by author, July 15, 2014).

Identities in the 2010 Census according to Statistics Officials Representing Ethnic Groups

Afro-Ecuadorian Expert Perspectives

Antón Sánchez (2014) analyzes the 2010 census from the point of view of the Afro-Ecuadorian movement. He self-identifies as Afrodescendant and, although he is originally from Colombia, he has worked with the Afro-Ecuadorian movement for a number of years. His published PhD dissertation (Antón Sánchez 2011) discusses the history of this social movement. Antón Sánchez has worked for the Ecuadorian statistics bureau since 2004, when he joined the System of Social Indicators of Ecuador (SIISE). Later he joined the National Statistics Commission for Indigenous and Afro-Ecuadorian Peoples (CONEPIA). This commission, created in 2007, allowed for the participation of civil society in the design and promotion of ethnic statistics. Government officials with a focus on indigenous and Afrodescendant development, scholars, representatives of ethnic social movements, and United Nations Population Fund experts discussed the design and methodology of ethnic statistics within CONEPIA. Representatives of the montubio people joined CONEPIA later through their state development institution CODEPMOC (Chisaguano 2012).

In a study by Antón Sánchez and Fabiana del Popolo (2008) for the Economic Commission for Latin America and the Caribbean and the European Commission, the authors criticize previous census rounds for privileging the indigenous over the Afrodescendant population. The authors considered it important to make the Afrodescendant population statistically visible in order to study the articulations between race and poverty, as well as to compensate this population for the legacy of slavery. For Antón Sánchez (2014), being counted is an opportunity for empowerment and for the achievement of citizens' rights. He connects the use of self-identification in the census with article 21 of the 2008 Ecuadorian Constitution, which reads: "People have the right to create and preserve their own cultural identity and to decide about their belonging to one or several cultural communities" (Constitution of the Republic of Ecuador, chapter 2, section 4, article 21).

Interestingly, this way of conceiving identities is subjective, based exclusively on personal choice, and unconnected to history, power relations, or even phenotype constraints. According to Antón Sánchez, the introduction of self-identification in the census had the effect of strengthening the process of organization of the peoples and nationalities. The demand for statistical visibility originated for him in the peoples and their organizations, and the state, through its statistical institutions, has made efforts to respond to these demands.

An important debate for Afro-Ecuadorians has been whether racial or cultural criteria should be used. In the 2001 census, racial and ethnic criteria were combined in a single option, the Black (Afro-Ecuadorian) option. Another option was mulatto, which was sociracial. Antón Sánchez notes that the Afro-Ecuadorian movement preferred to emphasize ethnicity over race. The Afro-Ecuadorian movement had requested from the 2007–2008 Constituent Assembly that the Black category be eliminated and substituted for Afro-Ecuadorian, a concept that for them referred to history, culture, and identity instead of race. Whereas only the term "Afro-Ecuadorian" was used in the constitution, the Afro-Ecuadorian movement did not achieve the elimination of Black from the census. However, it was successful in getting the option Afro-Ecuadorian separated from the options Black and mulatto. Statistics specialists retained the categories Black and mulatto with the argument that Afrodescendants still identify with them. CONEPIA and the Corporation of Afro-Ecuadorian Development (CODAE, a state institution) promoted identification with the Afro-Ecuadorian option. The Afro-Ecuadorian movement believed that the concept of Afrodescendant overcame discrimination and allowed integration, in contrast to Black, which reminded them of colonialism and racism. Interestingly, Afro-Ecuadorians combined interpretations of difference based on the Latin American tradition—such as deemphasizing race, focusing on culture, and seeking integration—with North American ideas of hypodescent such as adding mulattoes to Blacks and calling all of them Afrodescendants. Intellectual traditions were used strategically according to the movement's goals.

Jean M. Rahier (2013) has noted that Black culture in Ecuador does not originate in Africa but is an original creation of the new world that is syncretic and has many European elements. Nevertheless, the Afro-Ecuadorian movement has highlighted Africa as the source of their identity. The Comboni Catholic Missionaries, who were important for the emergence of this social movement, emphasized the African origins of Black American culture and taught this to the leaders in readings and workshops. Later Afro-Ecuadorian leaders attended international workshops, where they met other Afrodescendant leaders, and have reinforced a diasporic identification.

Regarding census results, Antón Sánchez notes that the self-identification of Afro-Ecuadorians increased significantly from 4.9 percent to 7.2 percent, whereas indigenous peoples only increased 0.2 percent, a proportion that is not statistically significant. Antón Sánchez explains this difference in terms of the importance that each social movement attributes to being represented in the census. Another reason is the kind of campaign that each organization chose. For Afro-Ecuadorians, visibility was important in order to be able to claim resources and public policies from the state. Additionally, Afro-Ecuadorians recognized the connections between census numbers and newly created affirmative action laws (Antón Sánchez, personal communication, December 2012).

Why would indigenous peoples not be interested in the same things? One reason could be the historical indigenous distrust of censuses that originates in their use for taxation and recruitment in colonial and early republican times. This distrust remains alive in indigenous communities, as explained in the sections below. For instance, the Kichwa statistics expert Luis Fernando Pijal, who participated in CONEPIA, argues that when indigenous people are counted, "they think that they owe something" (i.e., that they will have to pay a tax) (interview with author, July 15, 2014). In contrast, Afro-Ecuadorians had been statistically invisible and had thus not been taxed or recruited on the basis of population statistics. Another reason may be differing concepts of social movement strategies. The Afro-Ecuadorian movement, which has been weaker and more loosely organized, has focused on making demands of the state (de la Torre and Antón Sánchez 2012). Showing numbers in the census is important for requesting rights from the state. In contrast, the indigenous movement has focused more on staging demonstrations in the streets to show its organizational strength. Antón Sánchez notes that Afro-Ecuadorian organizations chose to use television ads for the campaign to promote self-identification. Indigenous organizations, on the other hand, preferred a community- and organization-oriented campaign with workshops and *chaskis* (delegates who would take the information to the organizations and communities). According to Antón Sánchez, as the census results show, the television campaign was more successful.

CODAE had greater political weight than indigenous or montubio organizations when the 2010 census was being discussed. For instance, montubios protested because indigenous peoples had two possible entries in the census, by language and self-identification; Afro-Ecuadorians had another two, by ethnic identity and socioracial identity; and montubios had only one entry (Antón Sánchez, personal communication, January 2014). This is an example of how census categories and the process of census taking produced competition between ethnic groups.

Indigenous Expert Perspectives

One of the indigenous professionals who participated in CONEPIA is Silverio Chisaguano Maliquinga. He is a native of the province of Cotopaxi and has a BA from the Central University of Ecuador and an MA from FLACSO (the Latin American Faculty for the Social Sciences, a public research university). He is a member of the Ecuadorian Federation of Protestant Evangelical Indigenous Peoples (FEINE). FEINE has had an ambiguous relationship with Correa's government, which it has generally supported but, on occasion, has criticized with regard to policies toward agrarian and water rights issues. It is interesting to note that the experts representing social movements in CONEPIA tend to be from those organizations or branches that are friendlier to Correa's government.

Like Antón Sánchez, Chisaguano Maliquinga (2012) connects the need to produce ethnic statistics to the pressure of indigenous peoples to obtain their collective rights as spelled out in the 2008 Constitution. He also associates the production of ethnic statistics to United Nations and other international legislation that defend indigenous rights. Finally, he connects the need for statistics disaggregated by ethnicity to the new affirmative action laws spelled out in article 11 of the 2008 Constitution. Similarly to Antón Sánchez, Chisaguano Maliquinga accepts the understanding of identity in article 21 of the constitution, which describes the right to create and preserve a cultural identity as a matter of individual choice. He recognizes the legitimacy of indigenous, Afro-Ecuadorian, and montubio peoples on the basis of their official recognition in the constitution, and accepts the possibility that other peoples may organize politically and be recognized in the future. Thus, he seems to accept the legitimacy of self-definition instead of promoting a historically grounded, power-aware concept of ethnicity.

On the other hand, challenging interpretations of the data that present the indigenous population as a minority, Chisaguano Maliquinga's strategy is to add the Afro-Ecuadorian and montubio populations to the number of indigenous individuals to produce a proportion of 21.61 percent for the nationalities and peoples.

Chisaguano Maliquinga explains the different methods used in the campaign to encourage people to self-identify with an ethnic group. We should note that on the website www.autoidentificate.com, which was part of the official campaign, no efforts were made to promote the self-identification of whites or mestizos, but only of indigenous, Afro-Ecuadorians, and montubios. White and mestizo identities are still largely understood as unmarked by the intercultural and plurinational state. Alternatively, given widespread tendencies to "identify up" in Latin America due to an ideology of whitening, the state may have encouraged people to identify in the subordinate categories.

CONEPIA conducted its campaign by phone. Chisaguano Maliquinga also notes the use of television and radio spots. He dislikes television because of its high costs and because many indigenous families do not own a television. Phones are also problematic because many indigenous homes do not have a line. He prefers the radio, which is less expensive, has greater reach among the indigenous and rural populations, and has been used historically by the indigenous movement (see chapter 4). In addition, CONEPIA used events featuring popular artists and folkloric dances to promote self-identification. Chisaguano Maliquinga criticizes these events for being too expensive. The promotion strategy he prefers is the use of territorially based promoters who work with social organizations. He also likes workshops for leaders and common people, during which the importance of self-identification is explained to them. If leaders are aware of the importance of self-identification, they will take these ideas to their organizations and constituencies, magnifying the impact at a lower cost and with an organizational twist. Chisaguano Maliquinga notes that the campaign was financed primarily by international organizations, which contradicts his own previous argument about the grassroots origins of the demand for statistics disaggregated by race and ethnicity. This expert also suggests that indigenous organizations should explain the importance of ethnic statistics to their constituencies and that international cooperation should require social actors to use ethnic statistics in their proposals for development funds as a strategy to teach the leadership about the importance of these data. This statement contrasts again with the argument that disaggregated statistics are a grassroots demand. We can also read between the lines that resistance against disaggregated statistics is to be expected from the indigenous population.

A second indigenous expert working for CONEPIA in processing the 2010 census is Luis Fernando Pijal, a Kichwa speaker from the Lake San Pablo area close to Otavalo. He has a BA in business from the Central University and an MA in rural development from Centro Superior de Investigaciones Científicas (Spanish National Research Council). Pijal worked for the National Institute of Statistics and Censuses (INEC) from 2008 to 2011. Later he got a job at the Council for the Development of the Nationalities and Peoples of Ecuador (CODENPE), and more recently in 2013 he became a low-level diplomat in the Ministry of Foreign Relations within an affirmative action initiative.

Pijal (2014) agrees on the connection between statistics disaggregated by ethnicity and the struggle for a more egalitarian society. He emphasizes the role of CONEPIA not only as the designer of the concepts and methodology in the census but also as an institution that processes data and makes it available to the indigenous peoples and nationalities. Similarly to Chisaguano Maliquinga, Pijal adds indigenous peoples to Afro-Ecuadorians and montubios to reach the proportion of 21.6 percent of indigenous peoples and nationalities. This suggests possible alliances between social movements. In fact, Afro-Ecuadorians and peasants from the coast had allied in the past with indigenous struggles. Another strategy to challenge the statistical minoritization of indigenous people is to focus on the absolute growth of the indigenous population, which is 22.6 percent, instead of its relative growth, which is only 0.2 percent.

A topic of interest for Pijal is the demographic distribution of the different nationalities. He notes that the Kichwa nationality dominates demographically making up 71.7 percent of the indigenous population. The Shuar population follows with 7.83 percent. It is interesting that 14.24 percent of indigenous people do not know to which nationality or people they belong. Half of these are urban dwellers who self-identify as indigenous. It is possible that part of the indigenous population, or even the interviewers who were filling out the forms, might have felt confused by the technical terms used to name peoples and nationalities on census forms. Terms such as "panzaleo" or "puruhá," which refer to archaeological cultures, are not in everyday use even for the members of these groups. Another possibility is that some of those who are urban and do not know their nationality might be indigenous people who became mestizo and are undergoing a more recent process of reethnicization (Fine-Dare 2007).

Regarding the indigenous language, Pijal notes that 34.5 percent of indigenous people are monolingual in a native language, and most monolinguals tend to live in the Amazon. This number seems high based on my ethnographic experience in the highlands and the southern Amazon of Ecuador. It is rare to find a monolingual even in isolated places like the Taisha parish located in a remote Amazon area close to the Peruvian border. The only monolinguals I have found are elderly people who still understand and speak some Spanish. Younger generations tend to be bilingual or speak Spanish only. Perhaps the high number of monolinguals represented in the census arises from confusion when answering the question about being monolingual in a native language and speaking it. On the other hand, 32.6 percent of self-identified indigenous speak only Spanish, and 28.5 percent are bilingual in Spanish and an indigenous language. This data resonates with the debate on acculturation and culture loss that took place after the 2001 census (F. Guerrero 2005).

In an interview with the author (January 2014), another indigenous professional working for CONEPIA who wished to remain anonymous added that the data in the census do not reveal the real number of indigenous people in Ecuador. He thinks that indigenous people do not identify as such for several reasons, the most important ones being the loss of cultural identity and the high degree of discrimination. These are connected for the interviewee because discrimination generates processes of identity loss. The official thinks that the census questions and the campaign were well-formulated and conducted, but that the campaign lacked sufficient funds. He believes it is important disaggregate statistics by ethnicity because it makes ethnic diversity visible, it shows who people are, where they live, how they live, and reveals the social inequalities that still exist in Ecuador. When asked why the Ecuadorian state is interested in disaggregating statistics by ethnicity, he answers: "There are many reasons: for example, to formulate a political strategy for this sector of the population. And also to identify where they are. . . . Or, perhaps to design public policies to overcome inequality." It is interesting that the reason ranked third in importance is the official reason justifying the need for ethnic statistics. Regarding the role of indigenous organizations in the census process, he argues that they participated in the statistical process and contributed experts to the campaign. However, he also notes that some leaders resisted the census because they are not interested in having the real number of indigenous people known (interview of indigenous government official with author, January 13, 2014).

Unfortunately, the participation of civil society seems to have ended after the 2010 census. CONEPIA was closed when the director of INEC was replaced (interview with Pijal by author, July 15, 2014). In addition, the institutions for development of indigenous, Afro-Ecuadorian and montubio peoples were closed and substituted for by a Consejo de la Igualdad (Equality Council) whose members are not chosen by the social movements as the members of CODENPE and CODAE were, but are selected on the basis of merits by the Council of Citizen Participation and Social Control, an institution close to the executive (Redacción política, "Asamblea aprobó la ley de Consejos de la Igualdad," *El Comercio.com*, accessed July 24, 2013).

Responses to the 2010 Census by Indigenous Intellectuals and Communities

I interviewed five indigenous intellectuals who are in contact with communities as teachers or leaders regarding the 2001 and the 2010 census in January 2014. These interviews provide feedback on the perception of the census process by indigenous intellectuals not working for the census bureau, and living in indigenous communities.

None of the interviewees states that 7 percent accurately represents the size of the indigenous population in Ecuador. Moreover, all interviewees except one strongly reject this number. One argues: "I think we indigenous people are more. It is true that there has been more migration in recent years, but even in cities we find visible indigenous populations as well as different community experiences." In contrast, another interviewee from the Amazon province of Morona Santiago argues that the methodology of the 2001 census was criticized by indigenous organizations and that it has been greatly improved in 2010. He notes the participation of indigenous organizations in the design of the 2010 census, the noticeable campaign for self-identification, and an increased emphasis on culture, customs, and identification with a particular nationality, instead of on a generic indigenous label. He argues that in his province the share of those who self-identified as indigenous has increased significantly—from 41.2 percent in 2001 to 48.4 percent in 2010. This interviewee indicates that there might have been regional differences in how the census was promoted and conducted. It is important to note that the Shuar prefer to identify with their nationality and culture and reject a generic indigenous identity. Therefore, the phrasing of the question with a focus on culture and nationality instead of race in 2010 might have been important to increased self-identification in the southern Amazon.

The interviewees, including the leader from the Amazon, note several reasons that explain why the indigenous population might have been undercounted in the census. Similarly to the indigenous statistician, they point toward discrimination and its associated effects as encouraging people to shed or hide their indigenous identity. An interviewee argues: "Some people decided not to self-identify because they do not know how to speak Kichwa, they do not wear an indigenous outfit, they are ashamed, they live in the city, and not in the countryside." Another interviewee says: "Perhaps some decided not to identify because being indigenous is not an advantage—on the contrary, it is a disadvantage." Some of the interviewees note an increase in discrimination and a fear of being identified as indigenous under Correa's government due to the regime's conflict with the indigenous movement. An interviewee states: "Even though the Ecuadorian state is supposed to be plurinational and intercultural, the main problem is racism. There was a healthy pride in being indigenous in the 1990s, whereas today racism is flourishing." Another interviewee claims: "Ecuador is undergoing a process of de-Indianization or acculturation because ethnic and cultural identity are not functional to the political goals of the Correa government and even less so for globalization." This interviewee refers to the indigenous movement's opposition to the mining and oil extraction policies of the government and the regime's alliance with mining and oil interests. In this sense, being indigenous, meaning being in opposition to extractivism, is not convenient either for the government or for transnational economic interests. A third interviewee argues: "In the 1990s, the political participation of indigenous peoples raised their self-esteem in terms of recognizing themselves and self-identifying as indigenous. In 2010, with the tension between the government and indigenous organizations and with presidential challenges to the indigenous leader class . . . this could be a reason why some people are not identifying as indigenous. They are scared of losing government subsidies."

According to the interviewees, methodology is another factor that explains the undercount of the indigenous population. All interviewees agreed that the interviewers sent to indigenous homes in 2010 were mestizo teachers or students from the provincial capital of their indigenous region. In my ethnographic experience as well as in the literature on internal colonialism, the level of discrimination is higher in provincial capitals of indigenous regions than in large cities that are more immersed in the global ideology of multiculturalism or in smaller communities where mestizos interact intimately and on a daily basis with indigenous people (Aguirre Beltrán 1967; Burgos 1997 [1970]; González Casanova 2006; Villavicencio 1973). In contrast, in 2001 the interviewers were indigenous. An interviewee argues that when the interviewer is mestizo, it can have several effects on the data: on the one hand there is a linguistic difference with the interviewed population, and the interviewer may not be able to clarify the questions in the interviewee's native language. Second, indigenous people may be afraid or ashamed to choose an indigenous self-identification and convey it to a member of the dominant ethnic group. The third effect is the tendency for mestizos to respond for indigenous people. This tendency is historically grounded in a colonial past when indigenous peoples were legally defined as minors, could not represent themselves, and had to be represented by mestizo advocates (A. Guerrero 1994). This third problem happened to some interviewees even though they are educated indigenous intellectuals. It is probably more frequent when the interviewer is counting peasant populations. One interviewee stated: "In some communities the interviewers did not ask the question. In our home, for example, the interviewer did not ask the self-identification question. We asked: 'Where is the question about what we consider ourselves to be?' He responded: 'I believe that you must already consider yourselves to be mestizos [*creo que ustedes han de considerarse ya como mestizos*].' We responded: 'No, we are indigenous.'" Another interviewee had a similar experience: the interviewer filled in the response without asking. In this second case, the indigenous interviewee was upset about the omission, but was less assertive and did not ask the interviewer to change the response. Other interviewees had a different experience and were asked about ethnic self-identification.

In another case, an indigenous family was not interviewed at all because they did not follow government instructions to stay at their "main home" on the day of the census. They are native to an indigenous community but have moved to the provincial capital. When census takers arrived, the family requested to be interviewed in their community of origin, but census takers argued that they were only authorized to count people at their main address. Thus, the mobility of this population from communities to cities or their double residence may account for some undercounting.

Another methodological problem that affected the data is that, despite instructions to census takers printed on the forms that they are to individually interview each family member, they typically interview only the head of the household. Thus, the father would choose the identity of all family members. The effects of this methodological problem are uncertain, however. On the one hand, if we accept that women tend to preserve ethnic identity more than men do, this may have raised the number of mestizos (de la Cadena 2012). On the other hand, the father may have identified younger generations as indigenous. Had these generations been asked, they might have identified as mestizos. This is consistent with the analysis of the 2001 census by Fernando Guerrero (2005), who indicates that there are intergenerational processes of acculturation.

Most interviewees also point out that the official campaign for self-identification was weak and insufficient. One interviewee said, "It is a known fact that there was not enough training of census takers. The training of respondents was even weaker." The interviewee from the Amazon argues that the campaign presented in television spots and posters was noticeable, but was geared toward urban rather than rural areas since rural inhabitants may not have had a television, and posters were placed in provincial cities rather than in remote rural areas. This could explain why the campaign was more successful among Afro-Ecuadorians, as this population is more urban than the indigenous population. According to the 2001 census, the indigenous population was 82 percent rural and 18 percent urban. The Afro-Ecuadorian population was 68.7 percent urban and 31.3 percent rural.

According to interviewees, indigenous people may also be suspicious of the government's intentions and its uses of census data. They do not believe that the government uses the census data to redistribute wealth or to create better public policies. On the contrary, they still think that the government might want to appropriate their property, use the data to control them, or use it to argue that indigenous people constitute a minority that should not have the same say as the majority. One interviewee argues:

> In a state like ours, which we understand as plurinational and intercultural, it is necessary to have clear percentages regarding ethnicity. However, this process should be geared toward recognizing the rights of indigenous peoples and promoting their participation in the state. Ecuador has a law of affirmative action to guarantee the presence of indigenous and Afro-Ecuadorian peoples in the state. But we have to consider whether this law is being implemented. I can say by personal experience that to be indigenous in Ecuador is to be a disadvantaged citizen. I believe that the state wants to know the real percentage of the indigenous and Afrodescendant populations, but it does not want to create public policies toward this sector of the population, or to guarantee their true participation in the state and in democratization processes.

Another interviewee argues: "The results of the census have been and continue to be used in a perverse way. Like suggesting that indigenous peoples are a minority. Therefore, a minority can not make decisions and impose its will over the majority, even if the minority is an ancestral people." The same interviewee claims that when talking informally about the census in his community he heard sentences such as: "Who would be coming to count us? What is the government up to? They say that they are giving us more resources. They have always said this and then, there is nothing! An old lady added, 'I hope they do not take our little lands. What intention could they have?'" One interviewee expresses a similar point of view when asked why the government is interested in statistics disaggregated by ethnicity. He says the reason is "to create and apply public policies according to its own interests and against those of the peoples and nationalities. The government is using ethnic statistics to close spaces that allow the ethnic and cultural development of the peoples and nationalities that share the Ecuadorian soil." The interviewee from the Amazon adds: "A quantitative assessment of the percentage of the indigenous population yields precise information about the demographic map of Ecuador, which helps those who formulate public policies to make decisions. However, the risk is that the government uses these data for its own interests, particularly to reinforce the discourse that in a democracy a minority cannot impose its will over a majority."

Susana Klinkicht (2010) in an editorial piece published in *Hoy* before the 2010 census was taken states: "The indigenous and Afro-Ecuadorian population has reasonably argued about the political aspect of this question [of ethnic self-identification]. This is relevant in their debate with the president's office that attempts to minimize their presence." According to Klinkicht, suspicions regarding the intentions of the government when counting the population are not only found among the indigenous population. She adds: "The insecurity regarding the political project of the current government has created gossip and rumors that do not make things easier. People fear expropriations, taxes, and inappropriate use of the data, even more so when the census asks about name, last name, age, and place of residence. Fear is a factor that could have an impact on results."

These suspicions regarding censuses should be read in the long-term context of a state that has not been redistributive and that has used population counts to extract surplus and labor from the population. Colonial censuses were used for the purposes of taxing and recruiting the indigenous population (F. Guerrero 2005). In local censuses conducted at the beginning of the twentieth century it was reported that the population hid from enumerators (Clark 1998). When the 1950 census was taken, there were attacks on census takers and an uprising in the province of Chimborazo that President Galo Plaza had to put down in person. Indigenous leaders showed President Plaza a document exonerating them from taxes dating from the times of the Liberal Revolution to explain why they were resisting the census (Prieto 2004).

When asked about the point of view of indigenous organizations regarding the past two censuses, an interviewee stated: "In 2001 the indigenous movement challenged the low percentage of indigenous self-identification. In the pastoral work of the Riobamba dioceses, we expressed discontent with the census results. The data were then interpreted as a consequence of the acculturation process and the migratory phenomenon. In 2010 indigenous organizations and other social groups did not debate the census results." Perhaps the crisis and fragmentation of the indigenous movement in the first decade of the 2000s, the electoral defeat of 2006, or the fact that a second census based on self-identification continued to show small indigenous numbers, encouraged the organizations not to question the census results publicly and to accept their portrayal as a minority.

On the other hand, another interviewee claims that indigenous organizations criticized the political use of census results to question indigenous rights and to call indigenous people a minority. A third interviewee argues that indigenous organizations have challenged the census because of the lack of an adequate campaign and because census takers lacked adequate training. The Shuar interviewee has a different opinion: "In the province of Morona Santiago we are the majority and this is a technical tool for the authorities elected by popular vote who are in their majority Shuar and belong to the Pachakutik movement. They invest in the people who are in need, the majority of whom are indigenous."

Race, Ethnicity, and Poverty

A rationale that the Ecuadorian state has provided for disaggregating statistics by ethnic group is that it allows the determination of connections between ethnic adscription and poverty as well as the detection of discrimination. The main idea that F. Guerrero's (2005) analysis of the 2001 census conveys is that although indigenous peoples were able to become political actors and to achieve legal recognition of their collective rights during the decade of the 1990s, their socioeconomic status did not improve accordingly. Guerrero explains the persistence of indigenous poverty in terms of the limitations of the agrarian reform: indigenous people were only able to acquire a little land of bad quality without enough water for irrigation. Moreover, they had insufficient access to education, lacked adequate housing and health services, had low compensation for their work compared to that of other citizens, experienced persistent discrimination, and had to migrate to supplement their income.

Guerrero notes a great transformation in social indicators in Ecuador from 1950 to 2001. For example, child mortality decreased from 140 per thousand to 29.2 per thousand. However, when these indicators are disaggregated by urban and rural location and by ethnicity, inequality becomes evident. For instance, child mortality among indigenous people was still 59.3 per thousand in 2001. Among Afro-Ecuadorians the same indicator was 29.3 per thousand, only 0.1 higher than the national rate. Education statistics also show racial inequality. The rate of illiteracy was 9 percent for the nation, 28.1 percent for indigenous people, 40 percent for indigenous women, and 10.3 percent for Afro-Ecuadorians in 2001. It is noticeable that the poverty indicators for Afro-Ecuadorians, although higher than the national mean, are much closer to the national rates than those for indigenous people. According to Mauricio León Guzmán (2003), the explanation for this difference is that most indigenous people are rural, whereas most Afro-Ecuadorians are urban. The 2001 census indicates that the indigenous population is 82 percent rural and 18 percent urban. The Afro-Ecuadorian population is 68.7 percent urban and 31.3 percent rural.

Regardless of differences among ethnic groups, the poverty rates for indigenous people and Afro-Ecuadorians are higher than for the rest of the nation. The indicator that Guerrero privileges is "unsatisfied basic needs" (NBI), which takes into account not only income but also housing, infrastructure, and services. According to the 2001 census, 61.6 percent of Ecuadorians live in poverty using the NBI indicator, whereas 87.8 percent of indigenous and 72.5 percent of Afro-Ecuadorians are poor. If the white and mestizo population is disaggregated from the rest, its rate of poverty is 59 percent.

Discussions of ethnicity, race, and poverty became particularly controversial after the 2010 census was processed and the results were publicized in 2012. One of debates concerned which indicator for poverty should be used. Let's take a closer look at the implications of the particular indicators: "unsatisfied basic needs" is the measurement that experts and the Andean Community prefer because they consider it a "hard" indicator for poverty. It "defines a home as poor when it has severe deprivations in access to education, health, nutrition, housing, urban services, and employment" (SIISE 2014). Differently from an income-based indicator, NBI measures standard of living reached over time as well as access to services that depend not only on cash, such as sewerage or roads. The method of measuring poverty by income or consumption takes into account a threshold calculated on the basis of the cash needed by a family to buy a basket of goods and services that satisfies basic needs like food, housing, clothing, education, and health. The NBI method is more difficult to measure and expresses long-term changes, thus varying at a slower pace than the income indicator. The income method, on the other hand, is more sensitive to short-term changes (SIISE, www.siise.gob.ec, accessed January 27, 2014). Table 3.2 shows the rates of poverty by NBI in the 2001 and 2010 censuses according first to F. Guerrero (2005) and second to the SIISE website accessed in January 2014.

According to the official data of the Correa government, poverty has been substantially reduced in Ecuador. However, this reduction varies by ethnic group. Mestizos with a reduction of 15.7 percentage points is the

TABLE 3.2. Percentage of poverty by unsatisfied basic needs in 2001 and 2010

Group by self-identification	Poverty 2001*	Poverty 2001**	Poverty 2010**
Indigenous	87.8	94.1	88.0
Montubio			83.6
Afrodescendant	72.5	80.9	69.8
Mestizo	59.0	70.8	55.1
White		56.2	46.3
Total	61.6	71.4	60.1

Sources: Compiled on the basis of data by the authors cited in the table.
*F. Guerrero (2005).
**SIISE (2014).

group with the greatest reduction in poverty. Afro-Ecuadorians have seen their poverty reduced by 11.1 percentage points, slightly below the national rate, which is 11.3 percentage points. The poverty of indigenous people has been reduced by 6.1 percentage points. This finding is significant in a context in which the indigenous movement opposed Rafael Correa's government. A government that claims to support social justice and to sponsor decolonization should have considered it a priority to reduce the poverty of the indigenous population, the poorest ethnic group in Ecuador. However, the data show that the government does not seem to have prioritized the reduction of poverty among indigenous people in its public policies. This may explain indigenous skepticism regarding the links between ethnic statistics and redistribution.

Furthermore, the data on poverty by NBI in the 2001 census that the SIISE released on its website in 2013 is not the same as the data of the authors Fernando Guerrero (2005) and Mauricio León Guzmán (2003) in their previous analyses of the 2001 census. According to Guerrero (2005), the proportion of indigenous people who were poor by the NBI indicator in 2001 was 87.8 percent and not 94.1 percent as SIISE reports on its official website today. If this is compared to the share of indigenous poverty by NBI in 2010, which is 88 percent, indigenous poverty has actually increased by 0.2 percentage points instead of decreasing! The share of Afro-Ecuadorian poverty was 72.5 percent in Guerrero's study for the 2001 census, instead of the 80.9 percent that the official site shows today. Thus, compared to 69.8 percent in 2010, the poverty of Afro-Ecuadorians decreased by only 2.7

percentage points, instead of 11.1. The total for Ecuador in Guerrero's study was 61.6 percent instead of the official figure shown today for 2001—71.4 percent. This means that comparing Guerrero's data to 60.1 percent as the website shows for 2010, poverty has been reduced by 1.5 percentage points, instead of 11.3.

The author asked a statistics specialist how it was possible for today's official data on poverty by NBI for the 2001 census to differ from the data that appears in studies that were written after the 2001 census. The specialist answered that the government recalculated the data on poverty and extreme poverty by NBI for the 2001 census in 2012. After the 2010 census results were known, the data on poverty caused a great deal of controversy. The results were not published until the end of 2012. Before that, the government used the indicator of poverty by income and consumption, which was more sensitive to short-term changes and supported President Correa's argument that poverty had been substantially reduced (interview by author with statistics official, January 2014).

These findings are significant because Correa claimed that the reduction of poverty was his most important political achievement. This debate took place under circumstances in which the government was being criticized for its focus on the extraction of natural resources, its repression of indigenous, social, and environmental activists, its prosecution of journalists, and its repression of freedom of expression and association in the country. All these drawbacks in civil and political rights were justified as a trade-off to control the political opposition and to enable the implementation of bold policies to reduce poverty and inequality. For instance, in an interview with President Correa during his trip to Spain to receive a doctorate honoris causa at the University of Barcelona for his poverty reduction policies, the journalist Guillermo Altares contrasted Correa's success in the fight against poverty with the lack of freedom of expression and the weak protections for the environment in Ecuador. Correa responded, "We are the champions in Latin America in the reduction of inequality" (Altares 2014). The lower estimate of reduction in indigenous poverty according to government indicators, or the rise in indigenous poverty if we use the pre-2012 data, in a context of confrontation between the government and CONAIE, begs many questions. This is particularly worrisome because the government claimed to have prioritized overcoming the legacy of colonialism.

On the other hand, an indigenous intellectual not working for the statistics bureau believes that indigenous poverty may have been overstated in the 2010 census. In our interview, he argued:

> Poverty continues to be a problem in indigenous communities. However, I do not agree with the percentage of indigenous poor presented in 2012. I think that even those involved in agricultural tasks have improved their income level. In the conversations that I have had in Colta and Guamote, they claim to have improved their agrarian production because the national and provincial governments have constructed irrigation canals. The younger population that has migrated to Quito, Guayaquil, and Cuenca has also increased their income substantially. Even those working in the informal sector have been able to achieve considerable gains.

Indigenous people might have hidden their economic gains to avoid being taxed after the state counted them.

Changing Racial Formations in Population Censuses

Population censuses offer a window for looking at how the Ecuadorian state has interpreted and reorganized difference in the transition from neoliberalization to nationalist-extractivism. To better grasp the continuities and changes in racial formations in this particular situation, it is also important to consider longer-term racialization processes. In the colonial and early republican eras, the Ecuadorian state separated Indians from non-Indians for the purpose of taxing the Indians and recruiting them for forced, unpaid labor. The legacy of these practices continues to this day in the form of reasonable indigenous mistrust of state intentions when counting by race. Basically, the idea that the goal of the census is to redistribute wealth does not seem to have held in Ecuador. Indigenous and other people still associate the census with the extraction of surplus, of unpaid labor, or with state control over the population.

In the first population census of 1950, the Ecuadorian state decided to avoid racial classifications for fear of revolts, to distinguish itself from the colonial state, and because it was under the influence of Latin American debates that tried to eschew scientific racism. Ethnicity was measured based on language, material culture, and socioeconomic characteristics. From the 1960s to the 1980s, both race and ethnicity were avoided in population censuses in the context of projects of mestizaje and so as to integrate indigenous people into the nation. This happened as the Ecuadorian state conducted structural transformations such as the Agrarian Reforms and the electoral modification that gave the vote to illiterates in 1979. In the Ecuadorian experience, democratization and redistribution of resources to ethnic groups took place without the need for statistics disaggregated by ethnicity.

In the 1980s and 1990s, in the context of indigenous organization and struggles, identities became politicized. The preferred official way to understand ethnicity in this period continued to be language, but living in a territory defined as indigenous as well as political affiliation with communities and peasant organizations were markers that scholars used to recalculate indigenous numbers on the basis of census data. However, the debates of the time show the tensions between the revitalization of identities and processes of hiding and shedding identity that have to be understood in the context of persistent discrimination and processes of rural–urban migration.

The year 2001 marks the introduction of a package of official understandings of social difference associated with the consolidation of neoliberal multiculturalism and the import of North American concepts of race into Ecuador. Race was reintroduced and it displaced previous Latin American understandings of difference as cultural, socioeconomic, territorial, and political. Whitening (a form of hyperdescent) and gradation were substituted by hypodescent for those of African origins, but not for those of mixed indigenous and European ancestry. An emphasis on race instead of culture was reported to lower the number of those labeled as indigenous. On the other hand, hypodescent increased the numbers of those labeled as Afrodescendants, a minority that was able to counterbalance the indigenous movement. A greater emphasis on the population of African descent also resonated with dominant North American understandings of race as a white–Black issue. The combination of the decrease of indigenous numbers and the higher visibility of other minorities that were friendlier to the government was a technique of rule that started in this period.

Indigenous struggles against neoliberalization and extractivism were delegitimized because indigenous people were represented as a minority among others. It was not necessary to render indigenous or Afrodescendants invisible to maintain mestizo domination. The state was able to recognize these ethnic groups while also portraying them as minorities that are not central to the nation. This is one way in which census constructions of race affected citizenship rights in Ecuador (Nobles 2000).

Race and minoritization strategies went hand by hand with the methodology of self-identification, a move that made the change seem progressive. Although self-identification was originally an indigenous demand to prevent the state from defining who is indigenous, the technique also fits well with the individualism promoted by neoliberal rationality (Brown 2003). Self-identification makes identity seem the result of a personal choice disengaged from historical or power dynamics. Moreover, self-identification has been more an idea to legitimize the state than an actual practice, as census takers continued to use their own judgment to identify others. Furthermore, the 2001 census unveiled the dark side of neoliberal multiculturalism for the first time. Indigenous peoples had struggled and been recognized politically, but they continued to live in conditions of socioeconomic marginalization (F. Guerrero 2005). In 2001 we have statistics disaggregated by race without further redistribution, as neoliberal policies intensified social inequalities.

Interestingly, this differs from what happened in Bolivia when the 2001 census was taken in the midst of popular mobilizations against the privatization of water and for state control over natural resources. There, a majority of Bolivians (62 percent) identified as indigenous (Schavelzon 2014). This result was linked to the political conjuncture of popular and indigenous struggles, but also to how the census was designed. The mestizo category was not included as an option. Therefore, those who had some relation to indigeneity were encouraged to identify as indigenous. Also, in the Bolivian census (question 29), Afro-Bolivians and peasants were conceptualized as part of the peoples and nationalities. Thus, those who might have identified as mestizo, Afrodescendant, and indigenous were aggregated to the indigenous and originary groups (Schavelzon 2014). This resembles the strategy of the indigenous statistics specialists in Ecuador who calculated the peoples and nationalities at 21 percent by adding the indigenous, the Afro-Ecuadorians, and the montubios. However, Ecuadorian indigenous statisticians did not add the mestizos into the mix. It seems that in Ecuador, mestizo continued to be seen as a dominant category similar to white. In fact, the category white-mestizo is often used in Ecuador based on the influence of the sociologist Andrés Guerrero.

We observe changes and continuities in racial formations in the 2010 census, which corresponds to the period of nationalist-extractivism examined in this book (2007–2017). The minoritization of indigenous people continues and intensifies, as does the enhanced visibility of other minorities friendly to the regime (Afro-Ecuadorians and montubios). This strategy legitimizes a project of state formation based on extractivism as well as the fragmentation and repression of organized civil society. Those who protest and those negatively affected by state development projects constitute a minority among others who cannot decide for the majority or stop its progress. President Correa often used this discourse in his weekly speeches to demonstrate who represents the nation and who is marginal to it. Despite Correa's anti-imperialist rhetoric, some understandings of difference in the neoliberal period such as hypodescent for Afrodescendants and an individualistic conceptualization of race continued. The latter is endorsed in the article of the 2008 constitution that allows Ecuadorians to "freely" create or choose their belonging to one of several identity-based communities.

In Bolivia the indigenous state of Evo Morales also confronted highland and lowland indigenous groups that struggled for greater autonomy and against extractivism (Schavelzon 2014). However, the conflict was not portrayed in this case as a struggle between an unmarked mestizo majority and a violent indigenous minority. Salvador Schavelzon (2014) argues that a generic indigeneity now positioned at the center of the state confronted other more specific forms of being indigenous. The role that the census plays to legitimate the public function of the state, which claims to govern for the common good while actually pursuing particular interests, becomes clear in these two examples (Abrams 2006 [1988]; Foucault 2006 [1991]). These facts also demonstrate how censuses are shaped by specific projects of national development (Clark 1998).

Returning to the analysis of the 2010 Ecuadorian census, although some emphasis on race continued and international statisticians insisted on its relevance, there was a shift to a cultural understanding of difference with a focus on ethnic categories, a preamble to the census question emphasizing "culture and customs," and greater stress on indigenous nationality on the basis of language instead of a generic (racial) indigenous identity. This shows that international organizations and the state cannot impose categories at will but that these need to be negotiated with civil society. Censuses, like the state itself, mediate between social groups with unequal power (Abrams 1988; Nobles 2000).

Another continuity with the earlier period of neoliberalization is the use of self-identification. This methodology continues to be an idea more than a consistent practice. In addition, there is a reversal in relation to 2001 regarding who the census takers are. If interviewers were indigenous during the period of multicultural neoliberalism, they tend to be mestizo and urban under nationalist-extractivism. This increases fear about identifying as indigenous as well as the ventriloquism of interviewers. Another reversal is an increase in discrimination and an attack on indigenous movements and their leaders, which boosts fears about identifying as indigenous, because this identification is associated with opposition to the government. The process of acculturation triggered by prejudice continues and intensifies.

These reversals in multicultural attitudes and tolerance go hand by hand with "progressive" steps such as self-identification and the participation of civil society in census design, promotion, and processing. Again, this methodology legitimizes the information obtained in the census process, which minimizes the numbers of the indigenous, increases the visibility of other groups, and depoliticizes identity struggles by understanding identity as a matter of individual choice. However, civic participation is orchestrated from above favoring the contribution of government-friendly organizations and individuals in census taking and promotion. Furthermore, both CONEPIA and the state institutions for the development of indigenous, Afro-Ecuadorian, and montubio people were eventually closed. So the continuing participation of ethnic civil society in future censuses is now in question.

In the nationalist-extractivist period the data on poverty and ethnicity/race are the most controversial. The government recalculates and manipulates indicators in order to demonstrate a substantive reduction of poverty, a decrease that justifies government attacks against the environment and civil society. However, even when using the official numbers, the data show the persistence of indigenous and rural poverty under the rule of a government claiming to decolonize the nation.

CHAPTER 4

CREATING AND DISMANTLING INTERCULTURAL BILINGUAL EDUCATION

This chapter first examines why and how intercultural bilingual education (EIB) for indigenous people began in Ecuador in the second half of the twentieth century, and how it functioned during the neoliberal period from roughly the 1980s until 2007. The purpose is to analyze the significance and reach of EIB, as well as its tensions and contradictions, in order to set the stage for a subsequent discussion of how the system was dismantled under President Rafael Correa.

The Achievements and Tensions of Intercultural Education under Neoliberalism

A close look at the origins of EIB shows tensions between two goals: to provide an education for indigenous peoples where there was none before, and to make available schooling that is relevant to indigenous linguistic and cultural identity. These goals may seem complementary, but they can also produce contradictions: the first might call for a school system that imparts mainstream knowledge to those who are excluded, whereas the second perceives education as a space for the reproduction of a distinct language and culture. Other tensions explored in this chapter are those between a liberating, democratic pedagogy and the continuation of authoritarian or simply dull ways to teach. A third friction involves a contrast between an education system aimed at questioning all forms of oppression and one that continues the exclusion and sexual exploitation of indigenous girls in intercultural schools.

Some of these tensions can be attributed to neoliberal multiculturalism, which brought limited cultural recognition and autonomy to the indigenous education system without allocating enough resources to make it work well. This partly explains the gap between EIB discourses and their uneven implementation on the ground (Cortina 2014; López 2014). Other frictions can be attributed to the different agendas of the multiple actors that created EIB, some wanting access to formal mainstream education while others aimed to preserve indigenous traditions. Finally, some contradictions originate in the contrast between the radical political agenda of EIB and the forces of inertia.

The impulse to take into account indigenous culture in educational institutions originates in the struggles of indigenous movements and their collaboration with their nonindigenous allies (e.g., religious groups, political activists, development workers, and intellectuals) (Rappaport 2005). According to accounts of indigenous movements in Latin America in general and more specifically in Ecuador, one of the most important demands of these movements has been the preservation of cultural distinctiveness and the promotion of alternative ways of knowing (Sieder 2002; Warren and Jackson 2003; Yashar 2005). So far, the mechanism for achieving this goal has been EIB. As Nancy Postero and Leon Zamosc state, "a key demand from all groups is the recognition of cultural difference and its corollary, the need for protection of indigenous culture. . . . For most indigenous groups the implementation of bilingual intercultural education policies is a keystone of the new citizenship" (2004, 15). In another survey of the bibliography on indigenous movements in Latin America, Jean Jackson and Kay Warren (2005) agree that cultural and historical recovery is the first step toward reaching other goals, such as self-determination and autonomy. Because indigenous movements are understood as "new social movements" based on cultural identity, the preservation and enrichment of such an identity should presumably be a central point in their agendas.

However, a closer ethnographic look at indigenous communities and their practical approach to education shows—as Andrew Canessa (2004) and Denise Arnold and Juan de Dios Yapita (2006) have argued for Bolivia, María Elena García (2005) for Peru, Michael Uzendoski (2009) for the Ecuadorian Amazon, and Carmen Martínez Novo (2006) for Mexico—that there are differences between the cultural project of the indigenous movement and how it is understood and implemented in practice at the community level. For example, despite official statements by the leadership of indigenous movements about linguistic and cultural preservation and reinforcement, indigenous parents demand that their children be educated in Spanish and, specifically, that they be taught reading and writing in that language (García 2005; Martínez Novo 2006). Scholars have also observed that intercultural teachers spend most of their time teaching Spanish literacy and basic conventional mathematics operations (Canessa 2004; Martínez Novo 2006). Paradoxically, in the daily practices of the intercultural school system little importance is given to teaching academic subjects in native languages, the wisdom of elders, and non-Western systems of recording and transmitting knowledge orally as well as through the use of textiles. Before the conquest, the Inca and other native groups used textiles to tell stories and record information (Arnold and Yapita 2006). As a result, Western approaches to knowledge, such as literacy and Western content are typically taught to indigenous children (Arnold and Yapita 2006; Canessa 2004; Uzendoski 2009). Official intercultural education discourse and indigenous leaders argue for the teaching of indigenous knowledge, but parents and children demand mainstream content, and teachers struggle to provide this knowledge to their students while also asserting publicly that they are preserving the group's culture. This analysis demonstrates that the struggle to infuse indigenous or Western knowledge into intercultural education signals a gap between the leaders and grassroots of the indigenous movement in their understanding of the role of formal education, and it also illuminates the different goals of nonindigenous allies and indigenous communities. Whereas allies and leaders seek to preserve indigenous traditions, commoners seek an education that trains them for the modern world, that is adapted to their schedules and life circumstances, and that also protects them from discrimination. The chapter further discusses the survival of indigenous knowledge in the form of oral narrative and elder wisdom outside of formal educational institutions—in the family and community spaces. It then compares intercultural elementary education with the status of indigenous knowledges in higher education.

The chapter also examines gender relations and gender discrimination within intercultural bilingual education in the southern Ecuadorian Amazon. The topic of gender inequality among indigenous peoples has been silenced by indigenous organizations that feared internal divisions, and whose leaders were mostly men (Luykx 2000; Muratorio 2000). Similarly, scholars and actors of EIB have avoided publicly discussing gender oppression in indigenous settings for fear of stigmatizing indigenous people or not sufficiently valuing their traditions, or because Andean gender relations are understood as complementary and free of hierarchies and oppression. Influenced by the association of gender inequality with capitalism in the work of Friedrich Engels, Marxist feminists have held that gender oppression among indigenous peoples is a result of the colonial encounter. However, Blanca Muratorio (2000) conducted archival research on the topic among the Kichwas of the northern Ecuadorian Amazon and found that violence was both a part of traditional gender relations and a result of contact. Similarly, Aurolyn Luykx (2000) noted that instances of oppression of women in indigenous communities are too numerous and diverse to be explained only in terms of colonial influence.

Luyxk proposes examining critically gender discrimination in intercultural education for several reasons: (1) because it has not been thoroughly examined, as most actors of bilingual education are experts on interculturalism but not on gender, and because actors and intellectuals in EIB have perceived gender analysis as an external imposition of funding agencies; (2) because experts have prioritized valorizing indigenous cultures and have avoided criticizing them; (3) because the point of view of dominant individuals within a particular tradition should not be taken as the worldview of the whole group; and (4) because forms of oppression should be questioned in all cultures without imposing a particular point of view on others; and people should be open to learning from other cultures to criticize their own. Regina Cortina (2014, 18) adds, "We do not have enough research of how EIB is affecting the education of indigenous girls and whether it is contributing to greater gender equality."

The research presented in this chapter is the product of my collaboration with four indigenous academics and activists, some of whom were involved in the indigenous movement. Some of the data were gathered as part of a larger project that started in 2007 on race and citizenship in the educational system of Ecuador. The research was conducted in forty-four schools in the highlands, on the coast, and in the Amazon (Martínez Novo and de la Torre 2010). The data relevant to intercultural bilingual education, which constituted only one section of the larger study, were gathered by the author and three indigenous researchers Kar Atamaint, Juan Illicachi, and Raúl Cevallos Calapi in the province of Morona Santiago, inhabited by the Shuar people who speak Shuar Chicham and Spanish, and in the northern and central highlands of Ecuador, where people who identify as indigenous speak Kichwa and Spanish. A total of twelve indigenous languages are spoken in Ecuador, but only Shuar and Kichwa, which are the languages with the largest number of speakers, are included in this analysis. In addition, the chapter analyzes data from interviews carried out by Luis Alberto Tuaza in collaboration with the author on oral traditions in the province of Chimborazo (Tuaza 2010). The interviews are used with Tuaza's permission and the analysis is mine. Tuaza has published his own analysis of the interviews elsewhere (Tuaza 2017).

Given the contrast between discourses and practices, it was important to look beyond official documents and the recorded statements of leaders, nongovernmental organizations, and teachers to assess the educational system. Thus, the research discussed here emphasized fieldwork in schools and observations of daily practices inside and outside the classroom. The researchers wrote ethnographic descriptions and carried out open-ended interviews with actors of the educational system such as administrators, teachers, parents, and students.

The History of Indigenous Education in Ecuador

It is important to understand why and how indigenous education started in order to debunk some of the tensions of EIB during the neoliberal multicultural period. Struggles to advance socioeconomically and related political organizing have been linked to attempts to open educational opportunities for the indigenous population. As Arnold and Yapita (2006) have shown for Bolivia, the struggle of indigenous communities for their rights to land made them aware of the importance of achieving literacy to enable them to fight the necessary legal battles without the help of intermediaries. Similarly, a study on the origins of EIB in the Ecuadorian highlands (Martínez Novo 2004) showed that peasants struggling for the implementation of agrarian reform laws found it necessary to open schools and achieve literacy so that they could litigate with the Ecuadorian state as well as apply for its development and credit programs. As Veena Das and Deborah Poole (2004) have argued, the state is very much about the need to prepare and understand written documents, a domain from which Andean peoples have been historically excluded (Arnold and Yapita 2006; Ramón 1991).

The following example illustrates the connections between literacy and the struggle for land. Rafael Pérez Anrango, an indigenous activist from the Imbabura province, showed me the house on the hacienda that his organization had seized after a decades-long struggle and that was later transformed into a communal house. I asked him: "So what concrete actions did you carry out to take this hacienda?" I was thinking that he would respond by telling me about arriving at the hacienda house at night, taking the administrator hostage, occupying hacienda lands, and so on. However, he simply responded, "We went to Quito and started a lawsuit."

On that occasion, Rafael Pérez Anrango made me aware of a book he had written, *Tierra comunitaria de Tunibamba por fin eres nuestra* (Communitarian Land of Tunibamba You Are Ours At Last) (Pérez Anrango 2007), in which he narrates the long struggle of his community for the land of this hacienda. The following excerpt from Pérez Anrango's account shows that reading and writing play a central role in indigenous activism:

> Segundo Olmedo Flores, a member of the community, gives us his testimony of how the struggle for the recovery of community land started: "The struggle to recover community land started in 1978. A lawyer from the city of Latacunga gave me a book explaining the Agrarian Reform Law. And I started to read, and I found that the law favored the possibility of legally taking a hacienda located contiguous to an indigenous community" (76). . . . The alternative that we took was to struggle through the law for the recovery of Tunibamba's community land (78). . . . Besides, we analyzed that by law and history these lands belonged to us, and thus, it is legitimate for us to struggle for them through the law (79). . . . How did we find out that long ago these community lands belonged to our ancestors? Because there are documents, and between so many arguments this is a very truthful one (80). . . . My dream of making the commitment to struggle for the poor became a reality in that assembly, because when I was a child, I read the word of God in Kichwa, and I thought that one day I will be an adult and then I would help my community to overcome the situation of injustice (102–103). . . . To carry out this struggle, I did not have

any formal education or adequate knowledge, and, on top of that, I was scared to talk with the authorities in Quito (104). . . . One night I had a dream. I was close to hacienda Tunibamba, exactly across the road, and a voice could be heard, and that voice asked me to write on the walls of the hacienda these words: We must struggle for the liberation of the poor. And I did, I wrote just this (106).

Reading and writing were the means to reach awareness about injustice as well as the privileged tools to end it. Beyond the obvious practical uses of literacy to litigate with the state, this account also assigns strong spiritual powers to reading and writing, and connects these activities to the domains of religion and the supernatural. Reading and writing must have had a very powerful character for those excluded from achieving these skills. The connection between literacy and religion may also originate in the reliance of liberation theology on literacy and the Bible to teach religion to the grassroots (see Lyons 2006). Liberation theology was an important influence in the struggle of the community of Tunibamba narrated by Pérez Anrango (2007, 118–121).

Historically, indigenous people who did not know how to read and write used local lawyers, colloquially called *tinterillos*, to help them in their legal struggles with the state and landowners (Becker 2012a). But learning how to read and write would certainly give peasants a greater awareness of the political context and an enhanced ability to fight back. In the case discussed here, some members of the community were able to read and write (others signed the petition for the hacienda land with their fingerprints, a practice required for those who did not know how to write [Pérez Anrango 2007, 83]), but the community also used a socialist lawyer and a woman who worked for the progressive Catholic Church as intermediaries in their legal struggles. Pérez Anrango's narrative describes the struggle of his community as an exchange of paperwork between the community and different offices of the state over almost two decades.

The distance between what I expected when I first spoke with Pérez Anrango, an extralegal direct action of occupation of the hacienda, and what had taken place, a tortuous legal intervention, teaches us about the importance of documents, literacy, and writing in the struggles of social movements. We are also able to grasp how the state, understood as a continuous circulation of paperwork (Das and Poole 2004), can certainly be

CREATING & DISMANTLING INTERCULTURAL BILINGUAL EDUCATION

FIGURE 4.1. The author and Rafael Pérez Anrango looking at the lands of former hacienda Tunibamba, June 26, 2008. Photo by Mónica Bustamante at the request of the author.

threatening to those who have been excluded from access to formal education in the dominant language.

A review of the historical records indicating how bilingual education started in some regions of Ecuador elucidates another reason for the need for EIB: to create opportunities for schooling where none were previously available (Martínez Novo 2004). Despite the existence of republican laws created after the formation of the Ecuadorian Republic in 1830, which required the education of Indians, the majority of indigenous peoples were excluded from even basic literacy until the 1960s and 1970s.

In 1833 a presidential decree established that a school for Indians be set up in each *parroquia* (parish). The same decree assigned a few scholarships for indigenous students to attend a prestigious seminary in Quito. However, the indigenous communities themselves, instead of the Ecuadorian state, were expected to provide the funds required for indigenous education (Yánez Cossío 1996). Meanwhile, the education of indigenous peoples of the Amazon was delegated to the Catholic missions. The first Ecuadorian president, Juan José Flores, divided the Amazon into four provinces and requested that the pope create missionary vicariates that would be in charge of the administration, provision of infrastructure, education, and health in the Amazonian provinces of Ecuador. In 1895 the liberal government of President Eloy Alfaro established that "there should be special schools for Indians, so that they can exercise their rights and duties as citizens." Similarly, the law stated: "In all agrarian estates with more than twenty Indians registered, the master should send Indian children to the nearest school until they are fourteen years old. If there were no schools nearby, the master should provide one for free on his own land" (Yanez Cossío 1996, 75). Despite these noble intentions, the law was barely implemented. Moreover, as Andrés Guerrero (2000) has shown, the Ecuadorian state delegated its duties to third parties such as landowners who, with some illustrious exceptions, were not interested in their peons' learning how to read and write. As noted above, in the early republican period, the education of indigenous peoples was also delegated to the indigenous communities that were responsible for funding it, or to the Catholic Church. In this way, the state could have progressive educational laws without investing the corresponding economic resources and administrative efforts. As stated in the 1895 Executive Decree, lack of educational opportunities for indigenous peoples in Ecuador has also meant exclusion from citizenship, because those who could not read and write in Spanish were not able to vote or be elected until 1979, with the expansion of suffrage following the return to democratic rule. Before that date and during periods of democratic rule, there was a literacy requirement to vote. To the present day, the vote of illiterates is optional in Ecuador, reflecting past literacy requirements for citizenship, whereas the vote of the literate population is mandatory.

The Law of Education of 1938, strongly influenced by Mexican indigenismo, emphasized the incorporation of diverse human groups into the national culture. During this period, the government of Ecuador created schools for the education of indigenous teachers, but according to Consuelo Yánez Cossío (1996), nonindigenous students took advantage of this educational opportunity instead. In the 1960s and 1970s, indigenous education was still associated with adult education and the teaching of literacy, with an emphasis on the assimilation of indigenous peoples. This tendency changed in the 1980s with the rise of the indigenous movement and the return of the country to democracy, and during the progressive governments of Presidents

Jaime Roldós Aguilera (1979–1981) and Osvaldo Hurtado (1981–1983). During this period there was an emphasis on the revalorization of native cultures, literacy in native languages, and indigenous rights. Bilingual and bicultural education became official in 1981 in the regions where the indigenous peoples constituted a majority, and new schools for indigenous teachers were created. In 1984 the Ecuadorian government made an agreement with the German Agency for International Cooperation to further enhance EIB.

However, progressive educational laws and policies have often been only imperfectly implemented in Ecuador. Most indigenous peoples remained illiterate until well into the twentieth century due to state negligence and the opposition of the landowning class. This was illustrated by the fact that pioneer educational experiences for indigenous peasants started as clandestine schools sponsored by the Communist Party and its Ecuadorian Federation of Indians branch in the 1940s. Despite these early efforts, by the late 1960s, approximately 70 percent of indigenous men and 95 percent of indigenous women remained illiterate in some regions (Martínez Novo 2004).

Additional reasons for creating an intercultural bilingual system involved the struggle to combat discrimination against indigenous children in mainstream schools. The few indigenous activists and intellectuals who went through the mainstream educational system in the 1960s and 1970s had traumatic experiences (Burgos 1977 [1970]; de la Torre 1996, 2000). For this reason, they later sought to create alternative spaces free from white and mestizo discrimination and violence. Before that was possible, as Carlos de la Torre (1996) has described, racial hierarchies were brutally inscribed in the bodies and minds of young indigenous men and women. For example, indigenous students were physically punished, made to sit in the back, and taught that indigenous people were suitable for agricultural work but not for intellectual endeavors (see also Juan Illicachi's interview in chapter 6).

During the second half of the twentieth century, the political Left, the progressive Catholic Church, and Protestant missionaries, as well as development agencies and some intellectuals, particularly ethnolinguists, sponsored regional educational institutions and school systems for indigenous peoples (Yánez Cossío 1996). All these regional experiences were later consolidated by the state under the management of the National Directorate of Intercultural Bilingual Education (DINEIB) after its creation in 1988. In addition, all rural schools in areas with an indigenous population majority were transferred to the intercultural bilingual system and all the teachers in them were relocated, regardless of whether they were indigenous or mestizo, and whether or not they were bilingual in Spanish and the native language of the area. In Ecuador, once the intercultural system of education was created, the previous mainstream system was renamed Hispanic, meaning based on Spanish language and culture and not indigenous. The Ecuadorian state agreed to allow indigenous organizations to manage the intercultural bilingual education system autonomously; this was a unique move in Latin America but it also followed long-term Ecuadorian traditions of delegation of state functions to nonstate actors.

This history created some tensions between preexisting systems managed by religious or other actors and the new management by indigenous organizations. Some legal loopholes produced a lack of clarity about who was in charge of what. Another tension was related to the mestizo teachers who were transferred into the intercultural system. Indigenous professionals of EIB argue that some, but not all, of these teachers were hostile to EIB (Cevallos 2007; Illicachi 2007). One reason for this hostility was that some mestizo teachers who now had to answer to indigenous administrators as their bosses resented the reversal of colonial racial hierarchies that placed mestizos above Indians. Another reason for hostility was that being involved in the education of Indians was considered lower status compared to educating nonindigenous children. A third reason was that transferred mestizo teachers tended to live in larger towns or provincial cities, and being assigned to intercultural education meant waking up earlier in the morning and transporting themselves to an indigenous community to teach (Illicachi 2007). An additional problem was that many of them were not fluent in the native language of the children they were teaching.

The diversity of regional experiences made the system a heterogeneous one, reflective of different influences. For example, the System of Indigenous Schools of the Cotopaxi Province (SEIC) led by Father José Manangón, a radical indigenous priest inspired by liberation theology and Paulo Freire's (2000 [1968]) *Pedagogy of the Oppressed*, was characterized by a participatory pedagogy adapted to the social and environmental surroundings of the students. Unfortunately, in other regions of Ecuador the pedagogy used in intercultural classrooms remained teacher-centered and based on rote learning because the early agents of schooling were less progressive. It is thus important to take into account these different origins and histories and not to homogenize the educational system.

As previously documented (Martínez Novo 2004), there were tensions between the understandings of religious and other educational activists about what it meant to create an indigenous education, and the demands of the rural population that benefited from these educational opportunities. Educational activists emphasized training in agricultural techniques, intercultural pedagogy, and classes in indigenous language and culture. Indigenous peasants were aware of the limits of smallholder agriculture based on tiny, eroded, and unproductive plots located at high altitude in the case of the highlands as well as the restrictions of low-paid employment in rural teaching. Therefore, these indigenous peasants demanded an education that would be useful in the "modern" urbanized world and would ideally include training in subjects such as English, technology, tourism, accounting, mechanics, and other "modern" or urban professions.

The main motivation to create EIB was the possibility for its beneficiaries to achieve socioeconomic mobility and inclusion through the waging of legal battles in the language of the state and the acquisition of skills that would allow them to become active citizens. Another motivation was access to education, the main tool for the unprivileged to achieve social mobility. The school was perceived as a mechanism for acquiring the mainstream knowledge that would make socioeconomic inclusion feasible for rural indigenous populations. However, the only way to achieve these goals was with the help of activists, religious leaders, nongovernmental organizations, and intellectuals who valued these populations and their traditions and wanted to preserve and reinforce indigenous culture and languages. In the neoliberal period, indigenous peasants had to rely even more on nongovernmental activists as the state reduced its social policies and retrenched.

This relationship between activists and the more practical goals of deprived populations explains some of the tensions in the implementation of the intercultural bilingual school in the neoliberal period. As Joanne Rappaport (2005) has shown for Colombia, regional leaders and collaborators differ from local teachers in their vision of intercultural bilingual education. Local teachers tend to privilege the political objectives of the communities, as they are more sophisticated politically than academically. Rappaport notes that the communities selected the teachers because they were political activists, and not for their academic credentials. Teachers understood the school as a center for political organizing, and tried to empower students with the skills and knowledge to address injustices (Rappaport 2005). Interethnic relations, a reflection on cultural differences, and pedagogical objectives were more important to regional leaders and their collaborators than they were to local teachers.

Appropriation of Mainstream Knowledge versus Linguistic and Cultural Preservation in Intercultural Education

Despite their discourses on the importance of cultural and linguistic preservation, even the leadership of the indigenous movement was not convinced by what it advocated. One of the most shocking findings of my study done in collaboration with indigenous intellectuals was that most indigenous people continued to perceive bilingual education as second class. Few leaders or teachers sent their children to bilingual schools and most favored white-mestizo Hispanic institutions in provincial capitals (see also Cevallos 2007; Illicachi 2007). Sometimes, having enough money to pay for the bus to the nearest city, better uniforms, and more school supplies and books, made the difference between going to a rural intercultural school or an urban Hispanic school.

If the leadership of the indigenous movement shied away from bilingual education it is not surprising that many indigenous people did not want their children to be a part of it. Indigenous communities claimed that they did not want an education in Kichwa because they already knew the language. Instead, they wanted their children to learn foreign languages that were seen as more useful in a globalized economy, as well as computer applications, which were correctly perceived as the necessary preparation for the modern world. Many indigenous merchants from Otavalo who traveled to Europe and the United States to sell their crafts or interacted with tourists at home perceived the acquisition of a foreign language as a necessity, not a luxury. In contrast to resource-deprived rural bilingual schools, urban schools offered classes in English, computer studies, music, physical education, and art. The Ministry of Education did not cover the salaries of English and computer studies teachers in the neoliberal period, but in urban Hispanic schools parents agreed to pay a little extra to get training in the areas deemed fundamental but not yet a part of the official curriculum. In many of the interviews with indigenous parents and children in the northern and central highlands as well as the southern Amazon, indigenous parents emphasized the lack of training in English and computer technology as reasons to rate Hispanic education higher than EIB (Cevallos 2007; Illicachi 2007; Martínez Novo and de la Torre 2010). Not surprisingly, the number of students in bilingual schools in the Imbabura province decreased. Whereas 11,500 children were enrolled in 1989, 10,795 were enrolled in 2006. According to the Provincial Directorate of Intercultural Bilingual Education (DIPEIB) administrator Raúl Cevallos (2007), "Seventy percent of rural indigenous children in the Cotacachi area attend urban Hispanic schools."

Furthermore, Kichwa and other indigenous languages did not experience the revival and prestige promised by the promoters of EIB. In the Otavalo and Cotacachi areas where an indigenous middle class and indigenous entrepreneurs ruled cities together with indigenous mayors in the early 2000s, an indigenous language revival would have been expected. However, as Marleen Haboud (2004) and Gina Maldonado (2004) have shown, many young indigenous peoples no longer spoke Kichwa.

The decline in the use of indigenous languages, even in areas politically and economically dominated by indigenous peoples, was due not only to the population's preference for Hispanic schools but also to the fact that education in the intercultural bilingual system was not conducted in native languages as it should have, according to the official guidelines for intercultural bilingual education (Modelo del Sistema de Educación Intercultural Bilingue), approved by the Ministry of Education in 1993 (Ministerio de Educación y Cultura 1993). On the contrary, all education took place in Spanish, and native language was only a special class that typically happened for an hour once or twice a week.

In some native-language lessons, words in the native language were taught but Spanish was the language of the class, particularly in the Shuar region of the southern Amazon. As is well-known, mixing languages is less effective than immersion in the language to be taught and it may create confusion between languages for children. Furthermore, native languages were often used to introduce Western concepts such as the national anthem, Western tales, or Western divisions of time such as the months of the year or days of the week. This strategy mimicked earlier missionary practices of using native languages for purposes of evangelization and teaching the Bible.

The cultural component was even less developed than the bilingual component of EIB. As Uzendoski (2009) pointed out in regard to the Napo-Kichwa of the northern Amazon, the knowledge of elders was not given enough importance and it was rarely used in intercultural bilingual classrooms. Uzendoski (2009) and Arnold and Yapita (2006) have also argued that non-Western methods of recording and transmitting knowledge, such as rock engraving and textiles, were not taken into account in intercultural bilingual systems, which remained exclusively focused on Western forms of literacy. There were differences among regional systems, however. Intercultural schools in Imbabura occasionally invited elder *yachaks* (wise men) to talk to students, particularly during periods of holiday celebrations. However, we did not document similar practices in the Shuar schools of the Amazon or in schools in the central highlands.

Paradoxically, the teaching of language and culture was the central reason stated for needing an intercultural bilingual system, but something not perceived as important by most teachers, parents, and students. See, for example, this quote from an interview with a Shuar mother of the southern Ecuadorian Amazon who is proud to be part of the indigenous movement:

> Of course, I identify as Shuar. Wherever I go I say: "I am Shuar, I am from the Amazon, I am Ecuadorian." And people look at me with surprise. However, it is also unfair that today's schools teach only Shuar. How can children learn if they don't teach them good Spanish? When we went to school we had well-prepared teachers from Quito and Guayaquil. At least thanks to those teachers we learned to speak good Spanish. We want to get education for our children. Because we do not have good education, we get delinquency. They [the Salesians] taught us well. They taught us how to do things, how to cook, how to greet people, how to eat properly, how to use the broom . . . But, today schools don't teach children good manners. That is why I say that there is a lot of corruption. There is corruption in our own race. (Interview by author, February 19, 2006)

Here, the interviewee seems to criticize both the transfer of the school system from the missionaries to indigenous organizations and the shift in approach from assimilation to linguistic and cultural survival. The quote might very well be interpreted as internalized prejudice, as the interviewee rejects indigenous teachers (as opposed to well-educated mestizo teachers from the main cities of Ecuador) as instructors for her children. However, the quote also reflects how communities perceive the role of schools: their function is to help children deal with national society. This woman does not perceive her request that schools teach mainstream knowledge (Spanish and "good manners") as a contradiction to her pride in her Shuar heritage and support of the indigenous movement.

Interestingly, the interviewee complains that all instruction is provided in Shuar, but our observations in the schools of the Shuar region where she lives contradict this assertion. We observed that Shuar schools taught all subjects in Spanish, whereas Shuar Chicham constituted the content only of a class taught sporadically, and in fact often in Spanish with only a few Shuar words. We did not find a single school where Shuar was the main language of instruction, not even in Taisha, a relatively isolated community in Transkutukú, close to the border with Peru. The woman may be taking the official discourse of leaders and teachers at face value, or her comment may be interpreted as normative: students should be taught in Spanish, not Shuar.

Another reason for the lack of emphasis on language and culture is related to the insufficient number of teachers trained in those areas. Bilingual education was understaffed because different national governments did not create new positions in the intercultural system. In addition, Kichwa language teachers continued to receive less recognition than Spanish language teachers in Hispanic schools and, according to some teachers, they also received less pedagogical training (Cevallos 2007; Illicachi 2007; interviews with teachers by author 2007). For example, Juan Illicachi (2007, 9) noted: "People believe that in order to teach Kichwa it is not necessary to study. It is enough to be an Indian. The Kichwa language is understood as being only of and for the Indians. . . . To teach the Spanish language you need to study for a minimum of four years. To teach Kichwa [educational authorities] do not expect teachers to receive any training." Raúl Cevallos (2007, 3) interviews a teacher who adds: "We are failing in EIB because the majority of us are Hispanic and we have not received enough training in how to use bilingual [Kichwa–Spanish] texts."

Many rural mestizo teachers were reassigned to indigenous bilingual schools without receiving enough guidance on indigenous languages and culture. In Imbabura's bilingual educational institutions, for example, out of 511 teachers only 20 percent spoke the indigenous language (Cevallos 2007). Some mestizo teachers complained that they had to teach under the supervision of indigenous authorities. The pedagogy of some mestizo teachers within the intercultural system seemed to reproduce deeply entrenched prejudices against indigenous peoples, which questions whether the bilingual system was able to create a prejudice-free environment as Canessa (2004) also questioned in the case of Bolivia.

Classroom Practices and Pedagogy

The SEIC is an example of alternative pedagogies (Martínez Novo 2004). Building on theories of popular education and the ideas of Paulo Freire, teachers used the student's previous experiences and natural surroundings to impart locally relevant knowledge. For example, educators used seeds or agricultural products to teach math in the early grades. Teachers listened to the students' interests and taught content adapted to their needs. Administrators adjusted the school calendar to student work and agricultural schedules so that they could complete the appropriate grade level. Teaching techniques were interactive and participatory. The same was not the case in other intercultural bilingual schools.

In many intercultural schools, pedagogy continued to emphasize rote learning. Teachers very rarely used textbooks or interactive teaching materials, which were sometimes available in rural schools thanks to the help of nongovernmental organizations (the government seldom provided anything more than the initial infrastructure and teachers' salaries). The most common pedagogical technique was to use the blackboard to write information that children then copied and memorized. For example, we observed a computer class in an intercultural bilingual school in the southern Amazon where children did not have access to a computer. High school students had to write and memorize sentences such as "the mouse is located to the right side of the computer." This was not particular to intercultural bilingual education, but a more general problem of the educational system for the rural poor in Ecuador. This anecdote also attested to the desperate attempts of indigenous peoples to integrate themselves into modernity and technology, even in the absence of the essential resources. Arnold and Yapita (2006) have interpreted this emphasis on memorization and recitation, which also plagues the intercultural bilingual system in Bolivia, as a way to cover up the fact that both teachers and children are barely literate. The authors also argue that these practices draw on long-term Andean traditions of oral recitation grounded in both pre-Hispanic and colonial times.

Teachers were occasionally trained in new pedagogical techniques.

FIGURE 4.2. Classroom in the System of Indigenous Schools of Cotopaxi, a service managed by the Salesian Order, July 17, 2002. Photo by the author.

FIGURE 4.3. Classroom in a community of the Zumbahua parish, Cotopaxi, July 17, 2002. Photo by the author.

FIGURE 4.4. Celebrating the Ecuadorian flag in a classroom in Morona Santiago, southern Amazon, February 20, 2006. Photo by the author.

However, they seemed to perceive these workshops as opportunities to collect certificates that would help them move up in their teaching career, and not as experiences they could implement in the classroom (interviews with teachers by author, 2007).

We found two central problems affecting many schools in the intercultural bilingual system: the scarce time dedicated to effective teaching and the fact that teachers rarely used lesson plans. According to our field observations, children were receiving a maximum of two hours of effective teaching from Monday to Thursday, which is a maximum of eight hours a week. Typically, after a lesson of one and a half or two hours, children were sent to the schoolyard and classes rarely resumed. Most Fridays, teachers received training or, if they lived far away, they just did not come to school. Children, however, spent long hours rehearsing nationalistic parades in the schoolyard, inspired by the military training of the teachers in what was at the time an autonomous system controlled by the indigenous organizations. In addition, according to our field observations, many schools did not properly fulfill the official teaching schedule. For example, we found teachers to be on vacation and schools closed a month before the official date for the end of the school year.

Our fieldwork also revealed that many teachers improvised and had no lesson plans. For example, in one school we observed a teacher giving the very same lesson on both Monday and the following Friday. Most of the time, teachers seemed to be improvising the lesson of the day. Again, these problems were not particular to intercultural bilingual education, but characterized the whole public educational system, particularly rural schools.

Discipline, planning, and the completion of schedules seemed to greatly improve in cases in which the Catholic Church oversaw the intercultural bilingual school system, for example, in SEIC and in some public-mission schools (*escuelas fisco-misionales*) in the southern Amazon. This is why many indigenous parents preferred church control over indigenous autonomy.

Indigenous Knowledge outside of the School

Although indigenous knowledge, languages, and cultural traditions were not sufficiently taught in Ecuadorian intercultural bilingual schools, the example of Kichwa community pedagogy discussed below demonstrates that indigenous language and indigenous knowledge in the form of oral tradition still play an important role in the education of indigenous children and continue to be reproduced (Tuaza 2017). However, this native knowledge in its more complex form is still located in the community and was not successfully conveyed to EIB during the neoliberal multicultural period.

Luis Alberto Tuaza and I interviewed Petrona Pilamunga Duchi, better known as Mama Pitu, who is a wise woman and well-respected elder in the province of Chimborazo. We were interested in recovering the many folktales she remembers and uses to educate the youth in her community. She lived in Cicalpito, an indigenous community of Cantón Colta. Until recently, Mama Pitu was a peasant who owned small plots near her community, cultivated the land, and raised domestic animals. However, her experience was also deeply linked to the hacienda system, in which she worked when she was younger, and to subsistence agriculture—industrial agriculture and rural–urban migration. Her family members migrated to the coast since the times of the hacienda to work on sugar or banana plantations that exported their production to the world market. Mama Pitu's relatives also traveled periodically to Guayaquil, where they worked as informal vendors to supplement their meager incomes as peons and, after the 1964 and 1973 agrarian reforms, as subsistence peasants. Her children currently live in Quito and that is why she migrated to the capital city when she became too old to live on her own.

Mama Pitu was highly respected by community children and youth who often came to her house to hear her tales. These stories did not represent a pristine pre-Hispanic, indigenous peasant community: characters in Mama Pitu's tales lived on haciendas and migrated to the coast to sell their wares. Hacienda owners and their wives were often described as benign characters, whereas hacienda overseers (*mayordomos*) were evil characters. Overseers physically punished peasants and, according to Mama Pitu, lied to their bosses who were ignorant of the mistreatment that workers suffered. Hacienda owners typically fostered paternalistic relationships with their peons (A. Guerrero 1991). Characters in Mama Pitu's tales also migrated and found unimaginable riches in their travels. On their way to the coast they found God in the shape of a tall, white man whom they called *tayta amito* (Father the Little Master), a common idiom to refer to God in this region. God would punish peasants for their greed when they migrated, having left their own lands uncared for.

An interesting feature of Mama Pitu's tales involves the roles of humans and animals. When humans did something that Pitu considered morally wrong, they became animals, and evil animals such as the condor disguised themselves as wealthy humans to deceive peasant women into marrying them. For example, a wife who complained to her husband that they were not having enough sex, discovered that every night he mutated into a bull and escaped to the lake to have sexual relations with cows. A landowning lady who did not want to have relations with her husband left the house and had sexual relations with a horse, and so on. The tales were moral stories intended to teach that it is important to care for one's partner within the family in order to avoid becoming animallike.

Interestingly, the boundaries between human and animal were blurred, and characters were able to move easily from one state to the other. This resonates with Eduardo Viveiros de Castro's (2000) discussion of Amerindian perspectivism, a worldview in which humans, animals, and spirits share a common human condition but take on different natural shapes while perceiving the world from a human perspective. However, in contrast to Viveiros de Castro's description of perspectivism—where changes in bodily nature and point of view do not seem related to morality or they indicate a superior form of spirituality such as when the shaman becomes a jaguar—Pitu's tales describe a change of status from human to animal or from animal to human seemingly as the result of a moral failure. Mama Pitu seemed to be teaching children and youngsters what it takes to become fully human, for example, to take care of one's partner or one's land and to avoid leaving the land abandoned so as to travel in search of the perceived amazing riches of migration, all in order to avoid falling into animalism. Children and youngsters enjoyed these tales and laughed a lot, as the stories had many humorous elements.

The kind of knowledge produced and preserved by Pitu resists an essentialist characterization and cannot be understood in opposition to Western knowledge or modernity. Pitu did not discuss her "indigenous" wisdom in opposition to modern life, nor did she intend to contrast the two types of learning. Her teachings included historical lessons about the hacienda system as well as more contemporary warnings about the opportunities and dangers of migration and the fate of subsistence agriculture in such a situation. The teachings were therefore both native and modern. The tales were not only stories of resistance and decolonization but also teachings about paternalism, the goodness of some masters, and the evils of others (see Scheper-Hugues 1992, for a discussion of paternalism, good bosses, and bad bosses). They were more like an expression of popular culture, full of contradictions, including the historical experiences of the group, their views of what it means to be human, and the relation of villagers to other than human beings, as well as their forms of accommodation and resistance to different systems of oppression. We are dealing here with complex manifestations of indigenous and peasant worldviews. This is a good example of what Rappaport (2005) has called interculturalism from below, a set of ideas that integrates knowledge of the outside world from a native perspective and includes relations between human cultures as well as interactions with the nonhuman and spiritual realms.

Unfortunately, this important source of knowledge did not find a successful and complete articulation in the EIB school system. Although EIB aimed to incorporate precisely this kind of knowledge into the formal education system, our observations in schools in three regions of Ecuador showed that elders were not invited often or taken seriously by the EIB school system, and did not have a permanent or steady role in school pedagogies.

One reason this knowledge was not fully incorporated was that elders lacked formal education titles, which caused bureaucratic difficulties in regard to including them in regular pedagogical activities. In addition, on the few occasions when we observed elders being invited to school activities—for example, in a school in Cotachachi, Imbabura—the kind of knowledge they were asked to impart was folkloric, focused on indigenous festivities like Inti Raymi, or the traditional Andean celebration of the sun. Complex accounts, such as one produced by Mama Pitu that inserts indigenous experiences within modernity and includes strategies of both resistance and accommodation, may challenge the essentialist sensitivities of some activists and teachers, as well as their nonindigenous allies.

Tensions in Intercultural Higher Education under Neoliberalism

In his work *Educación Superior e Interculturalidad*, Luis Fernando Cuji Llugna (2011) found some of the same tensions in intercultural higher education. Cuji Llugna studied two universities that self-identified as intercultural: (1) the Cotopaxi Academic Program (PAC), founded by Catholic Salesian missionaries to provide higher education to indigenous peasants in the central highlands of Ecuador; and (2) the Intercultural University of Indigenous Nationalities and Peoples (UINPI), created and sponsored by the Confederation of Indigenous Nationalities of Ecuador (CONAIE) and the Scientific Institute of Indigenous Cultures (ICCI), a nonprofit organization founded by CONAIE's ex-president, Luis Macas.

Cuji Llugna argues that interculturalism became an empty signifier understood and used by different actors in diverse ways within these higher education institutions. He asserts that because many actors, particularly the students, were not aware of academic discussions of interculturalism, they tended to use previous understandings of difference based on ideas of race, mestizaje (racial and cultural mixture), and Catholicism, among other currents of thought. For example, both professors and students tended to understand interculturalism as the interaction between people of different phenotypes, as a mixture of race and culture that gives way to mestizaje, and as loving your brothers as you love yourself. Because academic discussions of interculturalism did not typically occur among teachers and students in these institutions, they tended to draw on everyday understandings of difference that came from earlier discourses diffused by the state or other actors. The problem with this, according to Cuji Llugna, was that everyday prejudices and stereotypes continued to be passed on even within these intercultural settings.

Similarly, Martínez Novo listened as education specialists and national indigenous leaders discussed interculturalism in elementary and secondary schools. One leader defined the concept as "mestizos sharing their power with indigenous people and as the search for interaction in equality." This is exactly what the local teachers were striving for when they understood education as a political endeavor intended to strengthen the social movements and their political struggles for land and inclusion. However, the concept of interculturalism was seldom used explicitly in a school setting by teachers or children. This resonates with what Rappaport (2005) found in Colombia, where regional leaders and their collaborators discussed interculturalism, but local teachers and communities were unaware of the term. Rappaport argues that interculturalism in Colombian EIB consisted in seeking to create horizontal relationships and integrating Western knowledge for the purposes of indigenous peoples and within a native perspective. This is different from US multiculturalism, which is understood as tolerance for minorities and minority participation in representative democracy (Rappaport 2005).

Another important point made by Cuji Llugna is that the more an intercultural university became institutionalized, the less indigenous it became. He found that *comunidades de aprendizaje* (learning communities) as practiced by UINPI, produced the most interesting experiences of interculturalism in these universities. In learning communities everyone in the community participated in teaching and learning regardless of whether they had an academic title. Indigenous knowledge had a prominent role within this experience. However, because of their characteristics, learning communities were not able to provide academic degrees and gave only certificates, diminishing their usefulness for students who wished to obtain a degree in order to find a job.

The more that intercultural universities became institutionalized and responded to the requirements of national higher education boards in order to be allowed by the state to operate, the more they became like other universities, albeit poorer in terms of resources and infrastructure. The professors needed to have academic degrees, and many of them were mestizos, even though indigenous professionals with degrees were also available. This raises the question of whether intercultural administrators preferred mestizo professionals. In addition, as the universities became institutionalized, the knowledge and curriculum became more conventional and more similar to those of other universities, but they still had fewer resources, and their professors worked under more precarious labor contracts.

An important feature of these universities is that they provided access to education for indigenous and other rural people. They were cheaper than conventional universities and, more important, they only required student attendance on weekends or during vacations. According to Cuji Llugna, who conducted a survey with a number of students at these two universities, the majority of respondents had tried to enroll in a conventional university but lacked money and time, and had to work, and thus found the intercultural institutions more compatible with their busy lives. Cuji Llugna wrote that the students of these intercultural universities, indigenous or not, demanded that they become more like conventional universities that teach practical knowledge, have more infrastructure, and provide a better quality of education. What they liked about these intercultural institutions is that they protected the students from discrimination, were less expensive,, and enabled students to work while they studied.

With regard to culture and language, Cuji Llugna indicated that what passed as indigenous knowledge in these institutions was often elitist, not practical enough for the students, and sometimes discriminatory. For example, some teachers of indigenous knowledge at UINPI were urban mestizos, trained in conventional universities and disciplines. When they taught indigenous knowledge, they assumed previous conventional knowledge that the students of these universities often did not have, making "indigenous" teachings incomprehensible to them. In other instances, students did not see the practical use of some of the so-called Andean knowledge and technologies. For example, they speculated about how they could use Andean mathematics to measure a plot of land or build a house. This is another way that these teachings were elitist in Cuji Llugna's view. Finally, some urban mestizo professors used the writings of other non- Indians (for example, Josef Estermann's *Filosofía Andina* [Andean Philosophy], which Cuji Llugna found to be very influential in intercultural universities in Ecuador) to teach indigenous students about Andean issues (Estermann 1998). In private, students disagreed with their professors' teachings on Andean identity, but classroom power relations forced them to accept the outside definitions of what it means to be indigenous, which exoticized indigenous peoples and relegated their culture to the past.

Similar to what happens in elementary intercultural education, in higher intercultural education, native languages were not the medium of instruction, but were instead the content of specific language classes that were often conducted in Spanish. Furthermore, Cuji Llugna found that mestizo professors and mestizo students continued to be the leaders in intercultural classrooms, thus reproducing everyday racial hierarchies. However, the author argues, the institutions have not thought about this or sufficiently discussed the topic. When the issue of racism was raised, administrators made references to "reverse racism," or to discrimination against mestizos by Indians.

Therefore, similar to the elementary intercultural education system, in Ecuador's intercultural higher education institutions, students demanded mainstream practical knowledge without racism, at a lower cost, and adapted to the availability of time of those who work. The administrators of these systems were committed to providing indigenous knowledge, but they did so using constructions of indigeneity by urban mestizos, which were not free of prejudices and stereotypes and were then taught to indigenous students. According to Cuji Llugna, this was a worrisome form of symbolic violence because stereotypes were imposed on students while simultaneously pretending to recognize their experiences.

Intercultural Education and Gender among the Shuar of the Ecuadorian Amazon

The Shuar are an indigenous group located in the southern Ecuadorian Amazon and across the border with Peru. According to the 2010 population census, about 80,000 Shuar make up approximately 8 percent of the indigenous population of Ecuador, constituting the second largest linguistic group after the Kichwa. Until a few decades ago, the Shuar were hunters and gatherers, lived in disperse habitats, and were organized through kinship lineages (Rubenstein 2005). Rafael Karsten (1935) and other anthropologists thereafter wrote about their warfare habits as well as their custom of shrinking the heads of dead enemies in order to curb their spiritual power. Since the end of the nineteenth century, Catholic Salesian missionaries have colonized the Shuar.

Formal Western education for Shuar children began during the 1940s in boarding schools founded by the missionaries. There, the Salesians worked to transform Shuar gender relations according to Western Christian morals. More specifically, they questioned polygyny, arranged marriages for very young girls, and sexual freedom, among other aspects of Shuar gender relations and sexuality. The Shuar intellectual José Vicente Jintiach (1976) claimed that sexual repression and lack of personal freedom were the most difficult aspects of missionary education for Shuar children and youth. On the other hand, Jintiach appreciated the opportunity to have access to Western-style formal education.

The Shuar Intercultural Bilingual Radio Education System (SERBISH) was launched by the Interprovincial Federation of Shuar Centers with help from the missionaries in 1972 as part of a comprehensive political and organizational strategy to educate a population that was dispersed throughout the rainforest (see chapter 7). The missionaries also controlled "Hispanic" education in the region, which is public and missional (*fisco-misional*) because the Ecuadorian state has delegated the provision of education to the Catholic Church in frontier regions. The Shuar complained that even though the missionaries managed both systems, Hispanic education had better infrastructure and resources.

The Salesians promoted the inclusion of girls in the school system. Originally, girls were placed in female-only boarding schools. Sometimes, the integration of Shuar girls in Western education was forced: a woman stated that when she was a child she was abducted by a Salesian nun and placed in a mission boarding school and was never able to see her parents again (interview, February 2006). This was part of a strategy of forced cultural change that has been used in other colonial contexts (Rubenstein 2005). In other instances, Shuar parents brought children to mission schools so they would be able to prosper and become brokers between Shuar and Ecuadorian society (Rubenstein 2005). In the boarding schools, the Salesian priests and nuns planned student marriages to promote a monogamous Christian union between persons of adequate age by Western standards (Muratorio 1992; Rubenstein 2005). More recently, public-missional schools have become coed "because in real life men and women share spaces in today's world and our students should be prepared to behave correctly in such a situation," (interview with Mother M., director of a coed missionary school in Sucúa, February 2006).

Despite mission efforts to integrate Shuar women into formal Western education, the situation was not one of equality in the first decade of the 2000s. According to a study by José Pozo (2005), a medical doctor interested in social issues who resides in the region, 62 percent of the Shuar who are illiterate are women. When women completed elementary education, very few proceeded to high school. Men constituted 73 percent of Shuar high school graduates and 93 percent of Shuar college graduates. In an assembly of Shuar organizations, Dr. Pozo gathered some possible explanations for this lack of gender parity in education: women did not continue their education because they married very young. In addition, even though college scholarships were available for men and women, few women took advantage of them because they did not have a high school diploma. The migration of women to work as domestic servants in the highlands or in oil-producing regions in the northern Amazon also helped explain these statistics. Dr. Pozo's study proposed that Shuar women receive scholarships to complete high school, and that family planning campaigns be carried out among Shuar girls. The Intercultural Shuar and Achuar School System supervisor, Manuel Mashinkiash, added that there were discriminatory aspects that originated in Shuar family culture: "In some cases, parents still think that women should cultivate the garden, take care of the children, and perform other domestic tasks. Therefore, some parents decide not to send their daughters to school. In contrast, the males are encouraged to study" (interview, February 2006).

Another form of discrimination that we found in the intercultural bilingual system in Morona Santiago was the stigmatization of pregnant girls and their expulsion from the school system, while the men who impregnated them were not punished at all. This issue was not associated with traditional gender relations but with the missionaries' imposition of Catholic morals in missionary schools. Article 74 of the internal regulation manual of the Shuar Intercultural Bilingual Radio Education System,, as intercultural bilingual education is still called in the region despite the fact that the radio is not used to teach anymore, states: "In addition to the reasons contemplated in Education Law, the following will be considered reasons for a student's expulsion: 'becoming pregnant while in school . . . , being an accomplice or author of a proven crime, behaving immorally and showing a lack of respect for educational authority'" (SERBISH 2000, 61). The manual was last revised in 2000 and was still in use at the time of this fieldwork. The stated reason for judging a pregnant girl and a delinquent in the same way was that both were a bad moral example for the community. The stigmatization of pregnant girls, not only by educational institutions but also by parents and the community, is reflected in a quote by the supervisor Manuel Mashinkiash (interview by author, February 2006):

> Regarding the issue of pregnancies, I authorized a girl to stay in school. I authorized her, but then the parents of other school children had a meeting and decided to expel her. I sent a notification stating, "No, she has to stay." I mean, if there would be a decision by the girl's parents that they are going to support her baby, I would agree that the girl should be separated from her studies, but if she was to assume the responsibility, the care of the baby and everything, why should we deprive her of an education? Then they told me that my position was not pedagogical, that it was a scandal against ethics and morals.... Somebody in the community told me: "Then, Mr. supervisor even the worst criminal would be able to come to our schools." I responded: "I would accept the very Devil as soon as he complies with the norms."

This quote shows that Catholic morals are part of the everyday life and worldview of many Shuar after a century of missionary work in the region. On the other hand, the supervisor thought that the exclusion of pregnant girls from education was a threat to their ability to support themselves and their children in the future. It is interesting that the supervisor did not argue that becoming pregnant is not a moral crime, or that the girl should not be deprived of her constitutional right to education. Instead, his argument was a practical one. His reference to the devil is an example of the fine sense of humor of the Shuar.

Another problem we encountered during our fieldwork in the schools of the province of Morona Santiago was sexual harassment and, more important, unpunished sexual abuse and rape of young girls. These problems affected Shuar girls in intercultural bilingual schools as well as in Hispanic schools, and were also a general predicament of the Ecuadorian education system (*El Comercio*, Feburary 21, 2006, 19). In the province of Morona Santiago, the debate on sexual harassment and sexual abuse in schools increased after a campaign on the Rights of Children and Adolescents conducted by UNICEF. A Shuar female adolescent who was harassed by a teacher claimed that she became aware that she could denounce the abuse after she was trained in the rights of children (interview, February 2006).

Similarly, an intercultural educational authority (interview, February 2006) noted: "In the Code of Childhood and Adolescence the concepts are very clear. However, we should also update our system. I mean, because the code contains topics that are very complicated for teachers regarding the sexual harassment of female students."

Discussing sexual harassment with several educational authorities, we realized that what they were calling harassment were instead two cases of rape of students by teachers. We were able to document the cases after an interview with Carlos Zabala (interview, February 2006), the lawyer for the Provincial Directorate of Intercultural Bilingual Education in Morona Santiago. Zabala was working on the accusations of the girls' families against the teachers. One of the cases took place in the community of Chinimpi, in the county of Palora located in the northern Upano Valley close to the borderline with the province of Pastaza. The other case happened in the community of Caputna, in the county of Santiago, in the Upano Valley south of Macas, the provincial capital. Interestingly, both cases occurred in urbanized areas and not in the more remote sections of the province deep in the rainforest. One case involved the rape of a ten-year-old girl by a teacher in the school facility and during school hours. According to the lawyer, the teacher sent the other students to play outside while he committed the crime. One of the teachers had been accused of this kind of crime before. According to Zabala, for several reasons, neither of the teachers was punished. According to Ecuadorian Education Law, a professional defense commission must investigate sexual abuse by a teacher. However, such a commission did not exist for intercultural bilingual education. In the Palora case, the teacher's responsibility for the act could not be demonstrated, even though the girl accused him. When the girl refused to go to school, the teacher was transferred to another school. In addition, her parents lacked the economic resources to pursue the case. The Santiago case was closed because the legal process was conducted inappropriately. In both cases, the rape of very young girls (approximately ten years old) was treated as an administrative fault by the intercultural bilingual system. Although the girls' accusations were public documents, we could not get access to the documents. the government officials of the Provincial Directorate of Intercultural Bilingual Education of Morona Santiago dragged their feet to prevent us from learning more. According to Zabala, rape and harassment cases, including those resulting in pregnancy, ended in impunity due to the lack of economic means of the victim's families. They typically reached agreements with the offenders. For example, one family forgave the offense in exchange for two cows and a horse. Zabala also noted that it was common for twelve-year-old girls to marry the teacher when a case of rape ended in pregnancy.

We were able to document another case of sexual harassment and discrimination against a Shuar girl in a public-missional Hispanic high school in the city of Macas (interview, February 2006). The girl had great academic and leadership credentials and decided to run for president of the student council. She told us that the teachers resisted the idea that a "little Shuar girl" (*shuarita*) would be the class president, and encouraged students not to vote for her. The school psychologist also encouraged her to withdraw her candidacy, arguing that losing would affect her psychologically. The girl remained in the competition and was able to win despite the opposition of teachers and administrators. She was very proud of her achievements, but then was humiliated in front of the whole class by a teacher who touched her in public. After the incident, the teacher kept harassing her and calling her on the phone. The teacher also called the student "an exotic beauty" in public. The girl decided to denounce the behavior to the school authorities. Those in charge asked her to use the Catholic value of forgiveness and to forget about the issue. She was forced to continue in the same teacher's class. The girl reported that the situation had affected her grades, as she could not concentrate. In addition, she started to doubt the Christian values she had been taught in school. Although other girls accused the same teacher of sexual harassment, he was not sanctioned. We asked the girl whether the fact that she was Shuar might have affected the behavior of the teacher or the negligence of the school authorities. She was not aware that ethnicity would make a difference in her case, as the teacher also harassed non-Shuar girls. However, she stated that the sexual offender might perceive Shuar girls as more vulnerable and less likely to protest.

Rape and harassment were not limited to intercultural bilingual education or to Hispanic education in the Amazon region. According to Rocío Rosero, a feminist and director of the National Women's Commission, when teachers abuse students "processes do not work. They use legal excuses to avoid being sanctioned. Accusations are hidden and the educational authorities do not help to make them transparent. A study carried out in 2000 by the National Women's Commission [of Ecuador] revealed resistance on the part of teachers and educational authorities who want to treat this topic [of sexual abuse] as an administrative fault and not as a felony" (*El Comercio*, February 21 2006, 19).

This situation continued in the following two decades. A study conducted by UNICEF, World Vision, and the Ecuadorian Ministry of Education in 2017 found that 23 percent of students in Ecuadorian schools had suffered sexual harassment and that teachers committed 51 percent of the abuses (Unidad de investigación, *El Telégrafo*, December 11, 2017). The Spanish newspaper *El País* announced that nine hundred cases of harassment had been denounced in Ecuadorian schools between 2014 and 2017. In addition, one hundred cases of abuse occurred in a single school in Guayaquil, and five of them were considered rapes (España 2017). The issue became so salient that President Lenín Moreno (in office since 2017) decided to investigate the whole national public and private educational systems of Ecuador for cases of sexual harassment. Moreno also consulted voters in a referendum on February 4, 2018, on whether they supported eliminating statutes of limitations for cases of sexual abuse against children and adolescents. In this referendum, 73.53 percent voted affirmatively.[1]

Although we encountered a problem that was general to the Ecuadorian education system, it was troubling that this took place in intercultural bilingual education, because the system had been aimed toward the liberation of indigenous children and toward questioning all forms of inequality and exclusion.

I have laid out the contributions and drawbacks of intercultural bilingual education in Ecuador from its creation to the neoliberal period. The next section explains how and why the system was dismantled during the Correa decade.

Dismantling Intercultural Education

The first significant transformation was the elimination of the autonomy of the intercultural bilingual system through Executive Decree 1585 in February 2009, a change ratified later in the Organic Law of Intercultural

---

1. See El Universo, "Consulta 2018: Resultados a Nivel Nacional. Preguntas del Referéndum," https://www.eluniverso.com/resultados-consulta-popular-2018-ecuador (accessed June 18, 2018).

Education (LOEI) of 2011. Interestingly, indigenous people lost their educational autonomy only a few days after CONAIE demonstrated against a new Mining Law that allowed for the expansion of large-scale mining. Moreover, the executive retrieved all the funding from the account of the Council for the Development of the Indigenous Nationalities and Peoples of Ecuador (CODENPE). CODENPE's secretary, Lourdes Tibán, argued that a high authority had subtracted the money in retaliation for CONAIE's participation in the protests (Ecuador Inmediato January 21, 2009).

Executive Decree 1585 stated that the minister of education would be in charge of teaching and administration hires, curriculum design, and the production of educational materials. As noted in chapter 3, indigenous organizations were formerly responsible for these activities. According to a statement by the Ministry of Education, the Ecuadorian state had delegated intercultural education to a corporative group (CONAIE) in the context of the retrenchment of the state during the neoliberal period. CONAIE had monopolized intercultural education and was responsible for the system's lack of quality and for politicizing and corrupting it. Both the Executive Decree and LOEI required the creation of a Council of Nationalities to guide intercultural education policies. However, this council had only advisory capacities and indigenous organizations did not elect its members. Instead, they were selected based on merit by the Council of Citizen Participation and Social Control, an institution close to the executive. Thus, indigenous peoples lost their autonomy and their educational agency and became mere recipients of policies.

LOEI eliminated the difference between the mainstream education system, formerly called Hispanic (*hispano*), and the intercultural bilingual system intended for indigenous people. The law labeled the whole system "intercultural," but the concept of interculturalism was only vaguely defined in the law. In the LOEI interculturalism is "the egalitarian coexistence and interaction that promotes unity in diversity, mutual appreciation among persons, nationalities, and peoples in the national and international contexts" (LOEI 2011, title IV, chapter 2, article 79, p. 30). Thus, interculturalism shifted from being a political project of indigenous organizations to being a vague declaration that includes both the national and the international contexts.

In a study of discrimination and citizenship in the Ecuadorian education system, Martínez Novo and de la Torre (2010) found that elite private schools in Quito often interpreted interculturalism as a celebration of the cuisines and customs of European countries and the United States, an understanding that resonates with the definition of interculturalism in LOEI.. Raúl Vallejo, the minister of education at the time the law was issued, had previously been the principal of one of these private schools.

According to LOEI, interculturalism also involves teaching "ancestral" languages and "nonofficial" histories and cultures (LOEI 2011, title II, chapter 2, article 6, letter l, p. 12). While Correa was the president, this requirement was not implemented in the schools previously defined as Hispanic or in private schools. In addition, intercultural bilingual schools stopped teaching native languages and content.

The first thing that happened after the elimination of the autonomy of the intercultural bilingual system was a replacement of administrators and other educational authorities. The historic indigenous leaders who populated DINEIB and the DIPEIBs were replaced with younger professionals sympathetic to the regime. In an intercultural high school, a mestizo woman who had a BA replaced the indigenous principal who held an MA degree. The government paid severance to a number of professionals who had been cadres in the indigenous movement to encourage them to retire. Then it hired younger professionals without much political experience. Government control of hiring in intercultural education had a strongly adverse effect on the indigenous movement. A position as a bilingual teacher is one of the few jobs open to indigenous professionals in a racist labor market. While the indigenous movement lost its ability to provide employment to its constituency, the control of educational positions gave the regime political clout.

The intercultural curriculum and textbooks also underwent changes. The books and educational materials in Kichwa and other native languages that were developed in previous decades by indigenous intellectuals with the help of allies such as the progressive Catholic Church, the German Agency for International Cooperation, anthropologists, and ethnolinguists were replaced with standardized materials in Spanish. The struggles of indigenous organizations and the history of indigenous uprisings, which had been highlighted in the previous materials, were now erased from the textbooks.

When I interviewed the director of intercultural education in zone 6, which included Azuay, Cañar, and Morona Santiago in July 2015, the official stated that the ministry of education was preparing materials in native languages, but that these were not available yet. Intercultural bilingual schools had operated for seven years with Spanish-only texts (interview by the author, July 22, 2015). However, as a strategy of resistance, some teachers kept copies of the previous textbooks and continued to use them in their classrooms. A characteristic of the Correa regime was to start from zero and avoid building on previous experience. This showed an authoritarian attitude, as the regime did not recognize the contributions of its predecessors.

The Closure of Community Schools

The most dramatic change that took place during Correa's presidency was the closure of community schools and the relocation of their students to larger "axis schools" (*escuelas eje*) each of which served from 500 to 1,000 students. The paradigmatic example of an axis school is the "school of the millennium" (*escuela del milenio*) that features cutting-edge infrastructure and technologies. In the context of the territorial reorganization of the school system, the regime decided to cut the number of schools from 19,023 to 5,189. There were plans to close up to 13,000 schools by 2017 (Mena and Terán 2014). The schools closed were those with a single teacher for all grades as well as schools with several teachers that had less than 25 students per teacher. The majority of these schools were located in indigenous and other rural communities. President Correa justified the closing of community schools by claiming that they were "little schools of poverty" (*escuelitas de la pobreza*) and that in order to promote educational quality it was necessary to consolidate them.

Observers described the process as brutal. The government used a "surprise" strategy: The district director called the teachers, parents, and students to a meeting. There he communicated that the school would be closing. Then the official asked students and their parents to transport the student's desk to the consolidated school, which could be located one to two hours away on foot. Most did move their desks this way. Later the government used more subtle strategies such as sending government officials from the Ministry of Education to convince parents of the disadvantages of community schools and the advantages of consolidated schools (Mena and Terán 2014).

The closure of community schools carried multiple profound consequences. The link between the school and the community had been one of the pillars of intercultural bilingual education. The origin of EIB was political because it questioned colonialism and forced assimilation, sought to preserve and reinforce indigenous language and culture, and to promote access to education for those excluded (Cortina 2014; Martínez Novo 2004). Historically, EIB was meant to strengthen indigenous political organization by encouraging critical consciousness and educating leaders who were then able to claim access to land and territory as well as to achieve other socioeconomic and political objectives (Arnold and Yapita 2006; CRIC 2009). The indigenous movement of Ecuador was organized from the community level up because the colonial state had fragmented wider indigenous polities and identities (Abercrombie 2001). The colonial state allowed indigenous leadership and social organization only at the community level. These were the *pueblos de indios* (Indian Towns) that were created in the colonial period through resettlement and were ruled indirectly through indigenous chiefs or *kurakas*. Therefore, the connection between the school and the community in the indigenous world means the school's grounding in the political. In addition, the community–school connection allows for the participation of parents and authorities (Cortina 2014). Furthermore, the link between school and community permits exchanges with elders and other wise people, connecting education to indigenous language and culture, which in the colonial context also took refuge in the communities (Martínez Novo 2014; CRIC 2009). Separating EIB from communities thus meant making education less political, separating it from the native language and culture, and rendering it less participatory.

The liberation theologian and pioneer of indigenous education in Ecuador Father José Manangón noted that the creation of community schools was a way to decolonize education because it allowed indigenous people to avoid traveling to the mestizo parishes and county (*canton*) centers where the first rural schools were located. Indigenous people had been mistreated and discriminated against in these white-mestizo spaces. According to Manangón, the school strengthened the community and grounded the population in the countryside in the 1970s, at a time of strong rural–urban migration (José Manangón, interview with author, July 30, 2015).

Single-teacher community schools might not be the best educational option, but they are also not synonymous with educational failure, as President Correa asserted. For instance, Luis Alberto Tuaza, one of the first indigenous PhDs and college professors in Ecuador (interviewed in chapter 5) studied in one of these single-teacher schools. For Tuaza, having a school in his community was essential to determining his future. It would otherwise have been impossible for him to study given his family's economic situation (Luis Alberto Tuaza, interview with author, July 16, 2015).

After school consolidation, students had to walk two hours or more by foot from where they lived to the new school. The authorities claimed that they would provide transportation, but this did not happen in most cases (Manangón, interview by author, July 30, 2015). Children had to walk through rugged Andean and Amazon terrains, crossing roads, rivers, and overcoming other difficult obstacles. Apart from being tiring, this was also dangerous for young children. Some children paid truckers to take them closer to the consolidated school. The customary payment for an informal ride was fifty cents, which is a high price for already precarious family economies (Manangón, interview with author, July 30, 2015). The alternative for many families was to send their kids, or to move the whole family, to the provincial capital or to Quito where they had relatives. This accelerated an already strong process of internal migration.

The closure of a school produces a fast decline of communities. School consolidation encourages migration to provincial capitals and to Quito, leaving the communities empty of youth and children. The transfer of teachers to the consolidated schools, often located in larger mestizo towns, deprives the communities of an intellectual and political leader. In addition, the role of the school as a social, cultural, organizational, and political center is lost.

A similar process of school consolidation that took place in the United States during the twentieth century offers some useful lessons. The literature suggests that the effects of school consolidation were more political than pedagogical or administrative. Thomas Lyson (2002) argued in a study of school consolidation in upstate New York that small town schools played multiple roles. Besides providing education, they were social and cultural centers and symbols of the vitality and identity of the community where they were located. Viable towns had a school, and those that were dying lacked one. Lyson asserts that school consolidation took place based on the belief that the quality and efficiency of education would improve in larger schools. However, pedagogical research has questioned the concept that larger size implies more academic achievements. For instance, the best universities in the United States advertise the small size of their classes and the small number of students per teacher as proof of educational quality. Larger schools do not affect education quality and school consolidation negatively affects rural communities. Because the schools are social and cultural centers, this kind of sociability declines or disappears when the institution closes. According to Lyson, the closure of the school affects the kind of civic life that roots the population to a place.

Alan DeYoung and Craig Howley (1990), in a study of school consolidation in West Virginia, agree that schools are places where people build their social reality and democratic culture. Although school consolidation was justified in terms of costs and efficiency, the reasons for consolidation were political, linked to the imposition of visions of national development aimed at replacing local political logics. Similarly, Randall Sell and Larry Leistritz (1997), in a study of the consequences of school consolidation in North Dakota, argue that participation in community organizations declined in the communities that lost a school. In addition, these communities were deprived of a source of employment and the presence of professionals. The small businesses in communities that lost a school declined or disappeared.

In Ecuador, some communities reacted against school consolidation. Teachers, parents, and students forcefully rejected this process. Father Manangón even proposed returning to an education in the margins of the state such as the one that existed in the 1960s and 1970s in rural Ecuador. According to the religious leader, the Ministry of Education did not allocate any resources to the schools that refused consolidation (interview with the author, July 30, 2015). The reopening of community schools was one goal of the protestors in the antigovernment demonstrations of August 2015.

Anticommunity Policies and Their Links to Extractivism

According to Father Manangón, the community and the kind of Andean thought that it allows challenge capitalist logics. In Manangón's own words, "the community is the pebble in the shoe of capitalist development." As noted above, the community was also the basis of the political organization of the Ecuadorian indigenous movement that opposed neoliberal reforms, contributed to ousting two presidents, and challenged the extractivist policies of the Correa regime. In addition, Manangón argued that accelerated migration from communities to cities opened up land for lumber, mining, and oil companies.

The challenges that communities faced during Correa's presidency were

FIGURE 4.5. Law enforcement arrives in the community of Saraguro in August 2015. Photo from Colectivo de Investigación/Acción Psicosocial, "Informe preliminar sobre las estrategias estatales de control social y represión en el marco del paro nacional en Ecuador, 13–23 Agosto 2015," Quito, August 2015, accessed May 20, 2020, https://investigacionpsicosocial.files.wordpress.com/2016/06/informe-estrategias-estatales-de-control-y-represic3b3n-social-durante-el-paro-nacional-y-las-marchas-indc3adgenas.pdf. Original source *Diario la Hora*.

not limited to school consolidation. On September 30, 2015, Ecuadorian law enforcement collaborated with the security forces of the Chinese mining company ECSA to brutally displace a neighborhood in Tundayme, a Shuar center located in the southern Ecuadorian Amazon. The government had granted ECSA the right to exploit an open-pit mine in Tundayme. A report on large-scale mining in Ecuador states: "Recently, the population has experienced, physically and symbolically, the process of land grabbing by ECSA. A year ago, ECSA-Tongling-CRCC [the Chinese state railroad company] ordered the destruction of the church and the school of the San Marcos neighborhood, which the community had built through *minka* collective labor. The testimonies speak to the psychological impact of the demolition" (Sacher et al. 2015, 18). This quote exemplifies the collaboration of the Ecuadorian state with a mining company, the fact that the community endangers this alliance, and the connection between the destruction of the school, and in this case also of the chapel, with the displacement of *comuneros* to open up lands for extractive activities.

The confrontation of the government with indigenous communities as

CREATING & DISMANTLING INTERCULTURAL BILINGUAL EDUCATION   143

FIGURE 4.6. The first school of the millennium in Zumbahua with its walls painted with Andean motifs. Photo by the Ministry of Planning of Ecuador, accessed October 4 2017, https://www.planificacion.gob.ec/wp-content/uploads/downloads/2013/05/Proyectos-de-Inversión-Pública-en-Cotopaxi.pdf.

political units was also shown in the repression of antigovernment demonstrations in August 2015. As a response to indigenous protest throughout the country, the government militarized the community of Saraguro located in the Loja province, in the southern highlands. The army burst into homes and beat up people including the elderly and pregnant women. The military then arrested twenty-nine people and charged them with terrorism and sabotage. Saraguro is the community of birth of important indigenous leaders like Luis Macas, twice the president of CONAIE, and Salvador Quishpe, the former governor of the province of Zamora Chinchipe and an environmental activist. Other indigenous communities perceived the militarization of Saraguro and the violation of the human rights of is population as a threat.

Despite the existence of policies that threatened communities, when I visited the offices of the ministry of education for Zone 6, which includes the provinces of Azuay, Cañar, and Morona Santiago and that are located in the city of Cuenca, a government official explained that the Ministry of Education had great interest in recovering the spirit and culture of the community through its intercultural policies (interview with author, July 2015). I asked how the ministry would recover the spirit of the community if it had closed community schools and the consolidated schools tended to be located in larger mestizo centers. The government official patiently explained that, although some consolidated schools might be located in larger population centers, there were plans to build infrastructure modeled after community houses and the ministry hoped to have communities and little animals painted on the walls of the consolidated schools. The indigenous movement has called this strategy "the folklorization of identity."

Axis and Millennial Schools

The axis and millennial schools are not ready to receive the students from the indigenous communities and to provide them with an education that is relevant and sensitive to their culture. For instance, at the millennium school in Zumbahua, Cotopaxi (which was the first one created) indigenous attire was not accepted in the classroom. Students were required to use Western-style uniforms only. The indigenous movement had struggled in the 1990s for the right to wear indigenous clothing and hairstyles in schools and other public spaces, and this was not only accepted but also encouraged in intercultural community schools.

Millennium schools are massive schools with a large number of children per classroom and teacher. These schools teach a standardized curriculum in Spanish. It is interesting that the Correa regime understood large class size and standardization as signs of educational quality, when elite institutions worldwide advertise personalized attention, a low rate of students per teacher, and curriculum and major offerings tailored to the individual student. The Correa regime's understanding of modernity resonated with the Ford factory's manufacturing standardized products for the mass market, a strategy typical of the early twentieth century. Perhaps the regime preferred the "Fordist" model of education to a neoliberal one that privileges production in small batches for specialized market niches to pump up consumption (Harvey 1990).

Millennium schools feature brand-new infrastructure and technologies such as digital blackboards, computer centers, and a virtual library. Despite these efforts, in a visit to the millennium Jatun Kuraka School of Otavalo, the ex-minister of education Rosa María Torres discovered that teachers did not know how to use digital boards because they had not been trained in this technology. Torres (2013) argued that Correa's model of education privileged infrastructure and technology rather than pedagogical innovation and teacher training. In addition, Torres discovered that security problems had a dire effect on the use of technology in the classroom. Thieves broke into the Jatun Kuraka School and stole some computers, after which the rest of the machines were stored in a secure warehouse out of the reach of students and teachers.

The Cacique Tumbalá School located in the parish of Zumbahua is another example of the regime's peculiar understanding of modernity. The government built the first millennium school on the site of the old Hispanic school of the parish, a mestizo town surrounded by indigenous communities. The Hispanic school occupied a former hacienda house, as Zumbahua was formerly a large hacienda property of the Augustinian order and later of the government's social security department (Weismantel 1998). The hacienda house, despite the bad memories it might have for peasants, was an iconic building. It was completely demolished to build the new millennial school. In this way, the regime destroyed what belonged to the past to build anew, using standardized models. Its understanding of modernity was antiquated: historic buildings were typically torn down to build anew in the 1960s and 1970s. Since the 1980s, the tendency has been toward the preservation of historic centers. The building of new standardized structures also benefited the companies that enjoyed public concessions. Interestingly, the Correa government gave the concession for building the millennial schools to the Chinese Railroad and Construction Company (CRCC), the same that was in charge of open-pit mining and hydroelectric infrastructure building in several areas of the country (Rodriguez Cruz 2018).

The naming of the millennium schools is also revealing: "Jatun Kuraka," the millennium school in Otavalo means Great Chief in Kichwa, and "Cacique Tumbalá," the school located in Zumbahua also refers to a male chief. On the other hand, the Bosco Wisuma School, located in the Sevilla don Bosco parish in the province of Morona Santiago, takes its name from a Shuar teacher killed in the 2009 antigovernment demonstrations. The government charged the Shuar leadership with the teacher's death. Ironically, the regime appropriated the memory of Wisum to name its millennium school. According to a Shuar witness, the government built a little house for the widow and the four children who survived Wisum, and the family lives under threats and is forbidden to talk or give interviews (interview by author with witness, July 8, 2015).

An additional problem of axis schools is a lack of bilingual teachers. Indigenous bilingual teachers from the closed community schools were expected to transfer to consolidated schools. However, the government decided to require all public school teachers to pass standardized tests. These were multiple-choice exams inspired by those used for admission to North American universities (SAT, Scholastic Assessment Tests). The exam was administered in Spanish, unless its purpose was accreditation to teach a native language, it was based on urban culture, and it was administered by computer and Internet (teacher focus group, Latacunga, August 2015). The test did not take into account the particular cultural, linguistic, and socioeconomic characteristics of rural teachers. As an older female indigenous teacher noted, some teachers are not accustomed to using computers or the Internet (teacher focus group, August 2015). If the teacher fails the test twice, she loses her employment. The Correa regime argued that standardized tests promoted meritocracy and educational quality. However, they excluded indigenous and other rural teachers, particularly women. The result was a sharp reduction in the available number of intercultural bilingual teachers. This was a big problem because bilingual teachers were already scarce before testing was implemented.

The system of evaluation of rural teachers was so bizarre that, in order to get a promotion, a rural teacher had to take 330 credit hours at the National Education University (UNAE), a flagship institution of the Correa regime, or at a college rated category A or B, which were elite colleges located in large urban centers. In addition, teachers were required to have a title recognized by the state, to pass the standardized exam discussed above with a grade of at least seven out of ten, and to publish articles in peer-reviewed academic journals (Mena and Terán 2014).

Despite the reduced number of intercultural bilingual teachers, the Ministry of Education still required that intercultural schools teach between ten and five hours a week of native language. The number of hours decreased as grades advanced, demonstrating the regime's assimilation perspective. It also required intercultural schools to teach ethnomathematics, ethnoscience, ethnohistory, intercultural aesthetics, and intercultural physical education. Instead of reinforcing intercultural education, these strong requirements have weakened it. Intercultural bilingual teachers do not feel prepared to teach these subjects, which were not part of the curriculum of UNAE at the time of this fieldwork. After school consolidation took place, and given the difficulties of fulfilling these requirements and the few intercultural bilingual teachers available, principals preferred to register their schools as Hispanic to avoid problems (Mena and Terán 2014).

Furthermore, the Intercultural University of Indigenous Nationalities and Peoples Amawtay Wasi lost its accreditation after evaluation by the Council for the Evaluation, Accreditation, and Assessment of the Quality of Higher Education (CEAACES) (see chapter 5). The main reason to close Amawtay Wasi was lack of educational quality (Figueroa 2015). When Amawtay Wasi was created it was registered as a private university. Had its founders registered it as public, it would have lost its indigenous character because of the strict regulations on how public universities were to be run. Amawtay Wasi then applied several times for public funds to strengthen its programs, but these were denied because it was defined as a private university (Mato 2014). Thus, Amawtay Wasi had a precarious existence. CEAACES evaluated the indigenous university, it did so as it would any other private college. CEAACES inquired about the number of professors with a PhD and how many of them were working full-time, about the university's infrastructure, the number of volumes in the library, and even the quality of the cafeteria and parking spaces (most indigenous people do not own a car and only use public transportation). An institution created by marginalized people with limited support was evaluated in the same terms as those used to assess the University of San Francisco, a United States–inspired liberal arts college for elite youth. The anthropologist Jose Antonio Figueroa, who led the evaluation committee, argued that Amawtay Wasi was exploiting professors by not offering dignified working conditions and it was cheating students by providing an education of lesser quality (Figueroa 2015). The Correa regime closed Amawtay Wasi stating that the government aimed to promote educational equity. However, it did so by closing the educational alternatives for indigenous people.

Achievements, Challenges, and Resistance in Intercultural Bilingual Education

Intercultural bilingual education was an important achievement of indigenous organizations. It provided a formal education for people who had been deprived of it for centuries, which allowed them to become more effective in claiming their rights to land and a better standard of living and in dealing with the state and national society. It also allowed them to become citizens, as they had been excluded from citizenship on the basis of literacy requirements. It aimed to protect indigenous people from the widespread discrimination and violence that they encountered in mainstream schools, although intercultural education under neoliberalism was not always fully effective in this regard. Many mestizo teachers were transferred to indigenous education without enough training and some continued discriminating against indigenous children. In intercultural elementary and higher education, mestizo teachers were sometimes preferred over their indigenous peers, which kept the racial order intact. Another reason that education could not protect indigenous children and youth from discrimination was that it lacked sufficient funding and thus languished as a second-class system.

The system of intercultural education in Ecuador was unique in Latin America in that it allowed indigenous organizations to hire teachers, decide on the curriculum, and manage education autonomously. Indigenous people were recognized and were able to participate in the policies that affected them, but they did not get enough resources to implement their designs effectively. Tensions in indigenous education affected how well it was able to preserve and reinforce indigenous culture and language; these problems were due to foundational disagreements on whether the system was intended to teach mainstream knowledge for indigenous purposes or to preserve a distinctive way of life. However, it did offer an essential service to a deprived people: it provided education where there was none, allowed for flexible schedules adapted to peasant and temporary migrant needs, and, even if discrimination remained in the system, it protected indigenous children from greater violence. This violence included physical punishment, insults and humiliations that did not take place to the same degree in intercultural schools (see interview with Juan Illicachi in chapter 5).

Some tensions in intercultural education are due to differences among the social participants interacting in the system. The findings suggest that the perspective of indigenous leaders and their nonindigenous allies differs from those of indigenous parents and students. Since the 1960s and 1970s, nonindigenous allies promoted an education based on cultural preservation as a form of respect for indigenous populations and as a well-meaning desire to preserve their cultural heritage. The implementation of these ideas has been uneven, though. For instance, not enough teachers were trained in bilingualism and intercultural pedagogies and sometimes lacked sufficient teaching materials. Those in charge of implementing EIB, community teachers, have not been convinced about the goal of linguistic and cultural preservation. The grassroots have demanded inclusion through literacy in languages and topics of power and the state such as Spanish, math, and later, English and computers. The leaders of indigenous social movements have been located painfully in the middle: they have adopted the discourses of allies in order to get support and funding, but as people originating from marginalized and excluded sectors, they have also been aware of the importance of education as an avenue for social mobility and respect. This explains the contradictions between indigenous leaders' public discourses and their private statements and practices. Most of the impulse for cultural recovery seems to come from outsiders, whereas insiders request access to mainstream forms of knowledge. As Denise Arnold and Christine Hastorf (2008) have shown, since preconquest times indigenous groups in the Andes have believed in the pertinence of the appropriation of power, wisdom, and traditions of other groups. This assimilation of the energies and proposals of others has been an important component of their own Andean tradition.

However, this does not mean that indigenous knowledge and language have no role in the communities. It is mostly Westerners who perceive mainstream ideas and indigeneity as oppositional, particularly because Western thought tends to assign indigeneity to the past or to the margins. In my experience, Andean and Amazonian individuals often perceive Western and indigenous forms of knowledge as complementary and not mutually exclusive. Both domains are appreciated as important sources of wisdom that an individual use to live life more fully. Complex renditions of indigenous knowledge such as Mama Pitu's clearly show indigenous peoples' experiences inserted into modernity. Mama Pitu's tales, however, may not be popular among activists and their nonindigenous allies because they are not necessarily heroic tales of resistance to colonization, but also accounts of accommodation, survival, and the acceptance of paternalism. A combination of factors could conspire to preclude this interesting compendium from being successfully articulated into formal education, including that her tales may not being always be heroic and her credentials may not have bureaucratic validation for work within the formal education system. Bureaucracy, a creation of the state, seems not to be open to horizontal intercultural conversations. It has been produced by a particular culture, the dominant one, and it creates procedural difficulties for the subaltern to be empowered.

Other tensions in the system in the neoliberal period were caused by the contrast between an innovative pedagogical proposal for the liberation of the oppressed and the forces of inertia. Intercultural schools did try to implement liberating pedagogies and were effective in doing so in a few cases. However, most teachers tended to replicate what they had learned as students and continued to use teacher-centered approaches such as recitation and memorization. In regard to gender, important efforts were made to educate girls, professionalize them, and provide for their specific needs as students. But inertia also involved the reproduction of gender discrimination and abuse. A critical assessment of gender issues in intercultural bilingual education is needed. It is necessary to break the taboo that precludes scholars and activists from denouncing gender oppression in indigenous contexts. However, it is also important to note that some authorities and teachers, such as the supervisor interviewed in this chapter, courageously opposed and denounced abuse.

In any case, we must not generalize about gender inequality in intercultural bilingual education in Ecuador. Intercultural bilingual education originates in multiple experiences and within different regional contexts. For instance, in my fieldwork in Cotopaxi at SEIC (Martínez Novo 2004) the missionaries favored the education of women, even against the community's wishes. Furthermore, the Salesians facilitated the ability of women who were mothers of small children to study, allowing them to come to class with their children and organizing childcare. Although sexual education and family planning were not addressed in this school system due to Catholic precepts, receiving an education helped Cotopaxi's indigenous women gain access to their reproductive rights. Similarly, the education of women was pursued in the southern Amazon and some administrators fought the exclusion of pregnant girls and against sexual abuse. Some discriminatory situations for indigenous girls can be interpreted as originating in the internal dynamics of the indigenous community, such as family resistance to educating girls, incidences of early marriages and pregnancies, and the patriarchal organization of a society of hunters and warriors that used to practice polygyny and in which violence against women has been present historically (Descola 1996). Other situations that discriminate against girls are due to the process of colonization by the Catholic missions.

What does the chapter reveal about the Correa government's relationship with Ecuador's indigenous people? First, although the 2008 constitution declares Ecuador an intercultural and plurinational state, important advances from the previous period were dismantled without making additional efforts toward improved intercultural coexistence. On the contrary, neoliberal multiculturalism was replaced by the return of a monocultural and assimilation-oriented racial project: intercultural bilingual education was largely dismantled at the elementary and higher levels, all education took place in Spanish, its designers were urban mestizo technocrats, and it was largely recentralized in mestizo parishes and county capitals.

The Correa regime continued using indigeneity, but its use of the concept was as superficial as the axis schools decorated with community and rural motifs. The regime desired indigeneity as a declaration and a decoration, as mere folklore or aesthetics, to gain political legitimacy in front of progressive national, international, and provincial audiences. However, the use of indigeneity did not entail a dialogue with the nationalities and peoples, it did not involve their participation, and it was used at the same time that the regime displaced *comuneros* and reinforced other dynamics that marginalized them.

The state became an agent of forced modernization. Previous experiences, actors, and even historic buildings were disregarded and demolished. On the other hand, it was an "old-fashioned" understanding of modernity that went back to a Fordist past of mass production and consumption. This process resonated with the shift toward import-substitution industrialization and economic nationalism (although with limited success as the government remained dependent on selling hydrocarbons abroad). Rather than constructing a novel form of socialism, Correa seemingly returned to a combination of the import-substitution and monocultural-assimilation model that had characterized Latin America in the first three quarters of the twentieth century.

This process of forced modernization and state formation was funded with income from nonrenewable natural resource extraction, particularly oil and large-scale mining. It was also financed by high interest loans from China in exchange for allowing Chinese companies to expand in Ecuador. As José Manangón argued, organized indigenous people were the pebble in the shoe of the regime's development model. Indigenous people were encouraged to move out of their territories and relocate in cities that alienated them from their culture, a process that does not sound very innovative. The closing of community schools was also an attack on indigenous political power and territorial rootedness: the decline of the community and outmigration from it also meant political demobilization in the indigenous context. Other strategies such as co-optation, the fragmentation of social organizations, and repression accompanied the attack on the communities as discussed in chapter 2.

However, these processes did not take place without a struggle. The social actors who gave birth to multiculturalism such as the indigenous movement, the progressive Catholic Church, environmentalists, some intellectuals, and others resisted. However, they did so in the context of a strengthened executive, lack of checks and balances, the criminalization and repression of social protest, and a lack of freedom of association and expression. Chapters 5 and 6 discuss how Correa's regime affected the allies of the indigenous movement.

After President Lenin Moreno was elected in May 2017, he aimed to dialogue with the indigenous movement. Despite belonging to Correa's political party, Alianza País, Moreno and his minister of education Fander Falconí tried to undo some of the policies of the previous government. Moreno reopened the indigenous university and there was talk of reopening community schools. However, it is not easy to return to the previous situation. Community schools had been closed for several years. Without maintenance, the buildings quickly deteriorated. In addition, the population had already moved to the provincial capitals and to Quito. A return to the multicultural state presents many challenges, but that of course depends on the vitality of social movements.

CHAPTER 5

ANTHROPOLOGY AND INDIGENOUS PEOPLES

Collaborations and Estrangements

This chapter discusses the relationships of anthropologists with indigenous peoples and the state, as well as the anthropological perspectives on indigeneity and rural issues. It analyzes how the understandings and projects of anthropologists contributed to shaping Ecuador's racial formations. It takes a political economy approach to intellectual production by looking at the material construction of culture (Grossberg 2006; Williams 1978). In doing so, the chapter considers how different conjunctures affected the circumstances under which Ecuadorian anthropologists were able to practice their profession. It also looks at the role of institutions in the creation of anthropological knowledge.

The chapter distinguishes three stages of anthropological production: (1) the origins and institutionalization of the discipline in the context of debates about the agrarian reform and the fate of the indigenous peasantry in what Ecuadorian anthropologists interpreted at the time as a transition from feudalism to capitalism; (2) the way in which anthropologists worked with an emergent indigenous movement under neoliberalization. The neoliberal period was characterized by the appearance of ethnic organizations, political and economic instability, a weak state, and the precariousness of academic work; and (3) the production of anthropological knowledge under the nationalist-extractivist regime of Rafael Correa. Scholars profited from a strong state and increasing investment in research and education, but they also suffered from limitations to their freedom of expression as well as attacks of the government on organized civil society. Although the political economic context is deemed fundamental, the chapter also highlights the agency of individuals who were able to make choices under particular sets of circumstances.

The relationship between anthropologists and indigenous peoples has been described in the past decades as one of collaboration but with some tensions (Briones 2015; Field and Rappaport 2011; Ramos 1990, 2007). Anthropologists are generally discussed as advocates who sometimes have to take a step back when indigenous groups take politics into their own hands or write self-ethnographies (Ramos 2007). It seems as if the colonial origins of the discipline are a thing of the past. The story is more complex, however. In Ecuador, anthropologists have been advocates and activists of, and have collaborated closely with, the indigenous movement, but a few have also worked for transnational companies and the state to co-opt, weaken, divide, and demobilize ethnic movements. Academics have sometimes done so because they needed a job. In other instances, they have acted out of the convictions of their own normative visions or nationalist projects.

The chapter ends by narrating the life histories of two indigenous intellectuals who have been able to attain PhD degrees and full-time academic jobs. Florencia Mallon (2011) has argued that indigenous intellectuals have not been able to fully join Latin American academia due to pervasive discrimination. This also holds true for Ecuador, but things are starting to change. The academics discussed below were able to find openings in the neoliberal and nationalist-extractivist conjunctures and racial formations and to fully join Ecuadorian academia. However, their inclusion has been precarious and conflict-ridden.

In Ecuador, the process of neoliberalization that took place from the 1980s to the mid-2000s was characterized by political, economic, and institutional instability. In *Ethnography in Unstable Places*, the US anthropologist Carol Greenhouse (2002) claims that research carried out under conditions of dramatic change allows us to question reifications of state and society because structures cease to be a given. Large-scale systems are revealed to be fragile amalgams of improvisatory arenas and expanded agency, and social projects and understandings that would otherwise be latent in society are able to surface. Thus, instability allows for more productive theorization and expands opportunities for thinking reflexively about both ethics and ethnographic methods as ethnographers become implicated in the situations about which they write.

Greenhouse, however, looks at instability from the standpoint of the relative stability of the researcher in the academia of the North—reducing the principle of "instability," in addition to the opportunities described above, to the risk and danger that anthropologists experience under the conditions of ethnographic fieldwork. The fieldwork trip, however, implies a situation of relative impermanence: no matter how long she is in "the field," the ethnographer is there as an outsider who will eventually leave and whose livelihood and permanent security does not depend on what happens in the field. Thus, what Greenhouse's book does not consider is how the related questions of "conjuncture" and "instability" shape research and writing done by academics located in "unstable places."

Ecuadorian social scientists, for instance, have complained, "The conjuncture can eat you up." Things change so rapidly that a study or interpretation may be obsolete in a few days. This vertiginous course of events can present problems as well as opportunities for academic reflection. Basically, sometimes there is not enough time to reflect on the events. In addition, scholars feel pressured to change topics of study according to the conjuncture, sacrificing long-term academic reflection. Esteban Krotz (2006, 50–51) notes that in Latin America the researcher and the group under study are affected by the same social crises. However, the epistemological value of this common experience is not always clear: it may facilitate comprehension and empathy. Yet the researcher may also be tempted to use an essayer's style, to excessively politicize the debate, or to "confuse" anthropology with social work.

On the other hand, periods of intense change and the scholar's insertion into the social fabric may allow for more relevant research agendas. As Arturo Escobar (2006, 12) has noted: "U.S. based Latin Americanist academic fields have treated Latin America largely as an object of study, even if many of its practitioners have done so from a political perspective and have built a practice of solidarity along the way. In contrast, critical perspectives arising from Latin America have been as a whole more prone to foreground radical political questions and positions."

After a long period of economic and political instability, the commodity boom of the 2000s brought with it political stability and a stronger, better-funded, yet semiauthoritarian state (Conaghan 2016; de la Torre and Ortiz Lemos 2016). Before becoming president, Correa was an academic. In the context of the reinforcement of the public sector and increasing investment in education, the regime allocated more resources for long-term, basic research. On the other hand, academics suffered in an environment that repressed and manipulated the social movements with which they worked. The chapter analyzes how a peculiar combination of semiauthoritarian rule and economic bonanza shaped what anthropologists were able or willing to write as well as their relations to social movements.

Ecuadorian anthropology is defined as scholarship written from within Ecuadorian institutions either by Ecuadorian nationals or foreigners who reside and work in Ecuador. Occasionally, this chapter also includes experts who are not Ecuador-based, but who have strong relations to the country. For a number of reasons, silence often surrounds this production. Reviews of the literature written in the North Atlantic often do not take the Ecuadorian authors into account, which leads these scholars to complain that they are treated as mere informants or field assistants by colleagues who adopt their ideas, but for the most part do not quote their works or add their name to publications. Similarly, Ecuadorian anthropology tends to be more open toward the outside, to new things coming from abroad, than it is to the idea of engaging the national tradition. This tendency may be explained by a combination of factors including the intellectual dependency that results from the colonial legacy, fear of conflict and its consequences for one's academic career, and the "politicization" of the universities in the 1970s and 1980s. During these decades, academics were not conceived of as intellectuals but as party members who were understood either as allies who should not be questioned or as opponents who needed to be ignored (Francisco Rhon, interview, August 14, 2006).[1]

This situation of invisibility might have changed somewhat in the mid-2000s. The commodity boom provided abundant public funds that allowed scholars to travel to international conferences and conduct academic training in the North. In addition, the meritocratic standards of the Correa regime required Ecuadorian academics to publish abroad. Thus, Ecuadorian anthropology gained international visibility.

---

1. Some of the same reasons have been used to explain the "conspiracy of silence" that surrounds Ecuadorian literary works from this time period (Arcos Cabrera 2005).

Its emphasis on politically engaged and applied work adds interest to a revision of Ecuadorian anthropological writings because of their important social impact. In reviewing anthropology-making institutions and anthropologists in Ecuador, I learned that the same two actors interacting with indigenous peasants and contributing to their political organization were also the ones producing anthropological knowledge: namely, the Catholic Church and the political Left. In addition, the boundaries between these two groups were often blurred by actors who worked together in the field and shared academic spaces. Thus, a review of the anthropological literature produced in Ecuador provides important clues about the debates of the Ecuadorian Left as well as the influence of religious ideas and practices. The applied character of Ecuadorian anthropology also has a darker side, as anthropologists have used their knowledge for the sake of private companies or the state to negotiate with, weaken, and co-opt popular groups.

Ecuadorian anthropology has received many influences from abroad and the resulting cosmopolitan character is an interesting value in itself. Some Ecuadorian anthropologists studied in North America or have been influenced by anthropologists who work in the United States and Canada and conduct research in Ecuador. Other anthropologists have studied in Europe, particularly France and Germany, and more recently in Spain. Similarly, French, German, Spanish, and other European anthropologists have done research in Ecuador. On occasion, foreign anthropologists have provided the opportunities for Ecuadorian academics to study at US and European institutions.

Latin American scholars and ideas have been equally influential. An old and strong relationship exists between Mexican and Ecuadorian indigenismo (Regalado 2010). Moisés Sáenz, one of the fathers of Mexican indigenismo, traveled to Ecuador in the 1930s to study the situation of Andean Indians. Sáenz advised the Ecuadorian Constituent Assembly of 1937–1938 and contributed to the design of the 1937 Law of Communes that resonated with Mexican revolutionary legislation on the *ejido*, a self-regulated peasant community based on collective ownership of the land. Later, Mexican indigenismo shaped the work of Misión Andina (1950s–1970s), a development program led by the United Nations and the International Labor Organization in collaboration with the Ecuadorian government (Bretón 2001; Prieto 2017). These influences and relationships encouraged a number of Ecuadorian anthropologists to study in Mexico. Before the institutionalization of the discipline in Ecuador, anthropologists like Alfredo Costales, Hugo Burgos, and Gladys Villavicencio received graduate degrees in that country. Burgos and Villavicencio studied for their MAs with Gonzalo Aguirre Beltrán and brought the paradigm of interethnic relations to Ecuador, the first model to address racism in a systematic way. Burgos then went on to earn his PhD at the University of Illinois, Urbana-Champaign in the United States. Later generations studied at Universidad Iberoamericana in Mexico City where they learned ethnohistory, Marxist peasant studies, and the critical anthropology of decolonization and indigenous liberation. Some of these anthropologists were the founders of the first anthropology department at the Pontifical Catholic University of Ecuador (PUCE) (F. García 2014a).

Other anthropologists, particularly those working for the Andean Center for Popular Activism (CAAP) were influenced by Peruvian and Bolivian scholarship. Finally, in the late 1970s and early 1980s, there was an important presence of political exiles escaping the military dictatorships of Argentina and Chile. Eduardo Archetti of Argentina was particularly influential. He taught at PUCE and conducted studies in the Ecuadorian highlands that have become classics, such as his work on the guinea pig as an object of ritual consumption and indigenous knowledge (Archetti 1997).

According to Krotz (2006), the emergence of the discipline of anthropology in the Global South was the result of a process of colonial and neocolonial diffusion. North Atlantic anthropologists who studied the societies of the South raised interest in the discipline as they trained assistants and gave talks on their investigations. Sometimes they provided opportunities for their trainees to attend programs and universities in the North. These interests raised by metropolitan anthropologists eventually led to the creation of museums, programs, and academic communities in the South (Krotz 2006). The newly created anthropological communities did not merely copy the ideas developed in the North, but also selected and adapted them to their national traditions and sociopolitical conjunctures.

A process similar to what Krotz describes above took place in Ecuador. For instance, John Murra trained Aníbal Buitrón, the first professional anthropologist, and gave him the opportunity to study at the University of Chicago. However, this chapter also argues that the institutionalization of anthropology in Ecuador was not just a process of colonial diffusion, but also responded to national needs and debates. In addition, the anthropological influences in Ecuador were not only from the North Atlantic, but firmly grounded in South–South relations.

The methodology of this chapter consists in interviews with Ecuadorian anthropologists, a selective analysis of their texts, life histories, and my experiences as a member of Ecuadorian academia for eight years. Being an outsider and then becoming an insider in Ecuadorian academia taught me how different the social processes appear from insider perspective, particularly because the researcher is affected personally by the very issues she is studying. An insider position also gave me greater access to the informal and formal spaces of academic discussion. Moreover, I learned about the difficulties of doing research and writing under conditions of political and economic instability. On the other hand, the insider position also brought limitations: my participation in a particular academic institution located in the capital city circumscribed my understanding of Ecuadorian anthropology. My aim is to seriously engage with an intellectual production that might be considered marginal, not only because it is an anthropology of the South but also because Ecuador is a smaller country. Ecuadorian intellectuals, however, have written pieces that have transformed their world substantially; they have also undertaken important public roles (Briones 2015; Jimeno 2008).

The Roots of Ecuadorian Anthropology

As happened in other countries in Latin America, during the nineteenth and early twentieth centuries there were passionate debates (among white-mestizos) on the position that indigenous people should assume in the newly created Ecuadorian republic. At the end of the eighteenth century, the Jesuit Juan de Velasco argued that indigenous people were the precursors of Ecuadorian nationhood. The influential archaeologist and historian Jacinto Jijón y Caamaño (1890–1950) disagreed, claiming that Ecuadorian Indians were incapable of civilization and in need of tutors such as the landowners and the Catholic Church (Moreno Yánez 1992; Prieto 2004). In the first decades of the twentieth century, Pío Jaramillo Alvarado argued that the *ayllu* or Andean community might be useful for assimilating Indians into the nation as corporations, instead of individual citizens (Jaramillo 1922). At the time, indigenous people were not yet active citizens who could vote and participate in politics. This did not take place in Ecuador until the return of democracy in 1979. Jaramillo influenced the drafting of the 1937 Law of Communes, aimed at integrating peasants into the state as self-governing corporations. The communes, inspired in the Mexican revolutionary *ejido*, resonated with the colonial indigenous communities, which were self-governing units characterized by collective landownership.

Aníbal Buitrón was the first Ecuadorian to obtain a formal anthropology degree. The Andeanist ethnohistorian John Murra granted Buitrón a scholarship to study at the University of Chicago (Andrés Guerrero, interview, February 2006). Buitrón's most important work is *The Awakening Valley* written with John Collier Jr. of Cornell University (Buitrón and Collier 1971 [1949]). The book is an illustrated monograph about indigenous life in Otavalo. Buitrón wrote the text and Collier, a pioneer in visual anthropology, took the photographs. Buitrón, an Otavalan mestizo whose father was a local authority, was equally influenced by Latin American indigenismo and British structural-functionalism. Inspired by indigenismo, one of the goals of *The Awakening Valley* was to propose that Ecuadorian indigenous peoples were able to progress and successfully integrate into the Ecuadorian nation. According to Buitrón, indigenous peasants should preserve some of their traditions, while transforming others that might hinder their progress toward modernity. Following the tenets of functionalism, Buitrón and Collier emphasized the cohesiveness and harmonious nature of Otavalan culture. They discussed in detail Otavalan agricultural techniques, their market orientation, textile traditions, and other customs. Buitrón praised the industriousness of Otavaleños and contrasted their effective agricultural techniques with the absenteeism and extensive agriculture of the white landowners, eliciting the need for an agrarian reform. Buitrón was the first to discuss discrimination in the market and public spaces, and by local authorities. He denounced the treatment of indigenous people in Otavalo, who still inherited debts, worked on haciendas as quasi-slaves, and were constantly abused by the authorities.

Many Ecuadorian anthropologists after Buitrón have focused on the indigenous peasantries of the Andean highlands. This fact is not unrelated to the centralism of Ecuadorian academia and the heavy concentration of universities and nongovernmental organizations (NGOS) in the highland capital city of Quito. There is an important archaeological tradition on the Ecuadorian coast at the Center for Archaeological and Anthropological Studies of the Polytechnic School of the Coast (Escuela Superior Politécnica del Litoral). Interest in the Amazonian region only grew slowly within Ecuadorian academia after the 1970s. One cause was the historical and cultural research stimulated by evangelization. Among other influences were the foreign Amazonists teaching temporarily at Ecuadorian institutions. In addition, the Ecuadorian state became increasingly invested in the Amazon or Oriente in the 1970s due to the colonization that accompanied the process of agrarian reform and the first exploitation of oil resources.

Following the creation in 1972 of the Catholic University's Department of Anthropology, Quito has remained the institutional center for Ecuadorian sociocultural anthropology. According to Andrés Guerrero (interview by author, January 20, 2006), the impetus behind the new anthropology department originated in a meeting of progressive Jesuits whose concern for the plight of Ecuador's highland peasants was at least partly inspired by the Vatican II Council (1962–1965) and the Conference of Latin American Bishops in Medellín (1968). Francisco Rhon (interview by author, August 14, 2006) added that progressive groups supported the creation of an anthropology department because they felt the need to promote empirically grounded scholarship that would transcend the rigid, theoretically oriented explanations of orthodox Marxism. Originally, the department had three research lines. One, inspired by leftist politics and the agrarian reform, focused on peasant issues and sociopolitical change. A second line responded to the religious character of the university and researched the popular manifestations of Catholicism. A third current, inspired by the work of John Murra and Frank Salomon, focused on ethnohistory (F. García 2011).

By this time (1972), the debate on the agrarian reform process (which had begun in 1964) was at its peak. In this context, the applied and politically engaged aspects of Ecuadorian anthropology were reinforced. Researchers in anthropology and other social sciences asked themselves what would happen to peasants after the reform and how this population would transition to capitalism from what scholars understood as precapitalist formations. Would they become successful capitalist farmers and improve their standard of living? Would they become proletarians or semiproletarians? What role could state-led development play in bettering the lives of Ecuador's peasant population? These questions were framed within a Latin American wide debate, the *campesinista-descampesinista* debate, which discussed how peasants would adapt to emerging capitalist modes of production (Chiriboga 1988; Seligman 2008). The answers to these questions had consequences for the revolutionary strategies of leftist parties; the discussion involved whether the Left should focus its political strategies on urban proletarians or on the countryside and peasants. The research lines of the newly formed anthropology department of the Catholic University were closely connected to these debates (F. García 1980). Influenced by the work of the Russian agrarian economist Alexander Chayanov (who had been translated into Spanish by the Argentine exile and then Ecuadorian resident, Eduardo Archetti), anthropologists at the Catholic University asked how reciprocity, kinship, and communal labor allowed for peasant survival during the colonial and hacienda periods and encouraged contemporary peasant resistance to capitalism. Others worried about the extent to which capitalism was in fact eroding these traditional cultural strategies.

Other anthropologists at the Catholic University focused on popular religion through collective fieldwork on religious rituals, particularly in the highlands (Rueda 1982). Much of this work was inspired by liberation theology and the Catholic Church's unprecedented acceptance—following Vatican II—of popular religion as a legitimate spiritual form. Another influence was the Barbados conference of 1971, which emphasized the importance of non-Western cultural elements for evangelization. A third source was Clifford Geertz's symbolic anthropology, which led Marco Vinicio Rueda and his disciples to privilege the analysis of symbols and ritual events.

The Salesian order also played an important role in the development of Ecuadorian anthropology. Starting in the late nineteenth century the Ecuadorian government granted the Salesians the authority to "civilize and Christianize the Shuar" in Ecuador's southeastern lowlands and, in the process, to ensure Ecuadorian presence along the highly contested border with Peru (Audiovisuales Don Bosco, *Misiones en el Oriente* n.d.; Botasso 1986; Rubenstein 2005). The original goal of the Salesians was to transform Shuar culture into the Western Christian model. A first step was to compile information on Shuar language, myths, and customs (Pelizzaro 1990). However, by the mid-twentieth century, the Salesians had begun to reflect on the importance of preserving an indigenous culture that was increasingly threatened by the colonization of Amazonian regions following the 1964 Agrarian Reform and Colonization Law. The missionaries inspired a process of organization that resulted in the formation in 1964 of one of the first modern indigenous organizations in Latin America: the Interprovincial Federation of Shuar Centers (FICSH). According to the

Salesian narrative, they were pioneers in promoting the Catholic Church's awareness of cultural and ethnic diversity at the first (1971) Barbados conference (J. Botasso, FLACSO Conference 2005; J. Manangón, personal communication, August 18, 2002).

In 1975 the Salesians started to publish their own research, along with writings by mestizo and indigenous intellectuals, and translations of foreign works in the collection *Mundo Shuar* (Shuar World). In 1980, stimulated by the growth of the indigenous movement and the implementation of bilingual-bicultural education, the order expanded the collection with a series titled *Mundo Andino* (Andean World). In 1983, they unified both collections in a publishing house named Abya Yala, which is the most important publisher of anthropological research in Ecuador. From its foundation, the main goal of Abya Yala was to promote respect for indigenous peoples and cultural diversity among non-Indians in Ecuador, while also providing materials to indigenous communities to promote better self-understanding and self-reflection (Audiovisuales Don Bosco, Abya Yala, n.d.; Cucurella 2005).

In 1987 the Salesians, led by Father Juan Botasso, founded the school of applied anthropology. Applied anthropology was used in the nineteenth and twentieth centuries to better administer colonized groups, particularly those colonized by the British (Kuper 1973). However, in the 1960s, critical anthropologists, among them liberation theology priests, proposed using anthropology to advocate for indigenous organizations and to help them with their development plans. Specifically, the school of applied anthropology was founded to encourage mission personnel to take cultural factors into account in their evangelization and human development strategies. The Salesians have also been pioneers in allowing access to higher education to indigenous, Afro-Ecuadorian, and other underrepresented students at their Salesian Polytechnic University (Universidad Politécnica Salesiana) founded in 1994.

The Latin American Faculty of Social Sciences (FLACSO) in Ecuador has also provided Ecuadorians and foreigners with graduate degrees in Andean history, Amazonian studies, and anthropology and has been a meeting place for scholars from Latin America, Europe, and North America. FLACSO is an international system of research and graduate training in the social sciences created in 1957 with the aim of developing the kind of Latin American thought that would formulate development proposals for the region. Similar to the other institutions mentioned above, the idea of applied and politically engaged social science was present since its inception. The international system of FLACSO first started in Chile but that center had to close after the coup d'état of General Pinochet. The centers in Mexico and Ecuador were founded in 1975 to give asylum to Chilean and later Argentinean academics escaping dictatorships. The anthropology department, which was opened in the early 1990s, had few permanent professors and was mainly based on the teaching of invited professors from North America, Europe, and other Latin American countries. Among them were Europeans such as Penelope Harvey, Olivia Harris, Joan Pujadas, Philippe Descola, and Anne Christine Taylor, academics working in North America such as Deborah Poole, Ruth Behar, Joanne Rappaport, William Roseberry, Blanca Muratorio, and James Fernández, and Latin Americans such as Guillermo de la Peña. This was a list of cutting-edge scholars many of whom were examples of critical thought and some of whom were women. According to the director of the program at the time, Xavier Izko, classes and conference papers given by women scholars was unusual at the time in Ecuador, and was only made possible by the fact that FLACSO's director, Amparo Menéndez Carrión, was a woman (personal communication). A few prominent Ecuadorian scholars like Andrés Guerrero and Diego Quiroga were also hired at FLACSO.

The history of FLACSO and the list of invited scholars attest to a characteristic of Ecuadorian academia that it still retains: its cosmopolitanism and the tendency to look abroad for inspiration, a trend that could also be read as intellectual dependency. Preference for foreign over national scholarship was not only intellectually and politically questionable but also entailed high institutional costs. Faced with a mounting financial crisis, FLACSO was forced to emphasize the sorts of applied research that could attract external funding. Universidad Andina Simón Bolívar is a graduate school and think thank similar to FLACSO. Universidad Andina has developed intellectual leadership in cultural studies and the education of Afro-Ecuadorians.

The role of the state has been weaker than the role of religious orders in the promotion of anthropological scholarship up to the first decade of the 2000s. However, in the 1970s thanks to money originating in the first oil boom and in the context of a nationalist military dictatorship, there was considerable funding for cultural matters. According to Andrés Guerrero (interview January 20, 2006) the Central Bank of Ecuador was a very important sponsor of archaeology, and the Development Fund for Rural and Marginal Areas (FODERUMA), which also depended on the Central Bank, employed many anthropologists in development programs. In addition, the Central Bank created the Otavalan Institute of Anthropology (Instituto Otavaleño de Antropología), an institution that sponsored archaeological and anthropological research linked to museums and also published monographs. According to Francisco Rhon (interview, August 14, 2006), most anthropologists who worked for the state through FODERUMA carried out narrowly focused consulting jobs that did not have an important intellectual impact other than allowing researchers' subsistence.

Nongovernmental organizations have also been sites for the production of anthropological knowledge. Older NGOs such as CAAP and the Center for Planning and Social Studies (Centro de Planificación y Estudios Sociales), for example, started their work in the 1970s in the context of radical political struggles that required independent research. Many others appeared in the following decades, particularly in the 1990s, a period when there was an NGO boom in Ecuador and throughout Latin America in the context of neoliberal agendas that sought a reduction in the state's role. The lack of long-term positions for social scientists within state agencies and universities together with the scarcity of research and development funding led scholars to create these nongovernmental centers to provide jobs for themselves. The pressure to seek private funds for research, however, has often resulted in the imposition of external theoretical and empirical agendas and the proliferation of short-term, narrowly focused and quickly written case studies.

However, some of the older centers like CAAP have resisted these trends sponsoring independent and critical academic research. CAAP has produced anthropological knowledge and development work for more than thirty years and publishes one of the most established journals in the social sciences in Ecuador: *Ecuador Debate*. This institution started in 1975 under the leadership of Francisco Rhon who is still its director. CAAP carried out peasant organizing, development programs, and research simultaneously, providing the ideal environment for the kind of engaged, applied anthropology that was common in the period. CAAP promoted important *campesinista* (and some *descampesinista*) scholarship and brought debates to Ecuador on the Andean community and Andeanness (*lo Andino*) inspired in Peruvian and Bolivian debates (CAAP 1981, 1984).

Ecuadorian Anthropology and Debates within the Left

Transitions to Capitalism and Modernization

Many scholars believed that the agrarian reforms of 1964 and 1973 would result in a transition toward capitalism and the formation of new peasant sectors. Marxists and other scholars had understood large properties in the highlands as feudal since they relied on servile labor until the 1964 reform. Similarly, relatively independent peasant communities were assumed to possess a logic different from capitalism that the agrarian reforms and the process of modernization were starting to break (Chiriboga 1988). Some researchers thought that contact with capitalism would cause the disintegration and proletarianization of the peasant community, meaning that peasants would lose their lands and sell their labor to large farms and in cities (L. Martínez 1984). Others noticed complex processes of semiproletarianization and recampesinization taking place in the Ecuadorian countryside. According to these authors, peasants would keep their lands but also sell their work seasonally and reinvest their wages in the small plots that they owned (Farga and Almeida 1981). Rural–urban migration was seen as the main mechanism of contact with capitalism and the principal source of destruction of these peasant/indigenous cultures of resistance (Sánchez Parga 2002).

The subject of a related debate was the transition of large agrarian properties. The large properties of the coast had been perceived as capitalist since the late nineteenth century because they exported cocoa and later bananas and other products to the world market (Chiriboga 1980; A. Guerrero 1980; Striffler 2001). In contrast, highland haciendas produced for the national market using nonwage labor arrangements. Despite the fact that the highland hacienda has been described as feudal, Andrés Guerrero (1983) showed that landowners thought and acted as capitalists when they marketed hacienda products and imported agrarian technology. However, labor relationships within haciendas were not based on salaries, but on customary rights and duties that subordinated workers to landowners while also preserving some of their pre-Hispanic indigenous customs (A. Guerrero 1991).

While European and North American structuralists and cultural ecologists had described the Amazonian peoples as relatively isolated,

Ecuadorian anthropologists scrutinized these same societies for evidence of historical colonization, state domination, and the penetration of oil and timber companies. As Alcida Rita Ramos (1990) has noted, Latin American anthropology has been more interested in studying interethnic relations than its foreign counterparts because its projects have been more political, but also because Latin American anthropologists have faced work and financial constraints that have not allowed them to spend prolonged periods of time among indigenous peoples and learn their languages.

The Debate on Culture, Discrimination, and Resistance

It has become commonsense to argue that the 1970s Latin American Left was characterized by a class-based approach with little sensitivity for the political potential of culture and ethnicity. However, Ecuadorian debates on culture and its role in the political organization of peasants challenge these widely held assumptions. Some authors such as Hugo Burgos (1997 [1970])—a progressive indigenist who was not part of the militant Left— Diego Iturralde (1980), and Gladys Villavicencio (1973), all of whom studied in Mexico, interpreted ethnic differences as a legacy of colonialism, internal colonialism, landowner and state domination. Burgos analyzes some central aspects of what is often understood as indigenous culture and demonstrates how these traits facilitated peasant domination. One example is the *minga* (communal work) used by the Incas, the Spaniards, hacendados, and the state to extract free labor from peasants for public works. Syncretic religious rituals were also a mechanism for the exploitation of the peasants when local elites and the traditional Church extracted economic profits from them through the rental of public spaces, costumes, religious objects and other necessities, and the sale of food and alcohol. Peasants were so indebted after these celebrations that they were forced to mortgage or sell their land to local elites. This argument contrasts with that of Rueda (1982), who understood peasant religious festivals as a factor of cultural resistance to colonization and creativity.

Likewise, Villavicencio (1973) observed during her fieldwork in Otavalo that local mestizos encouraged Otavaleños to keep the traditional indigenous dress and hairstyle as well as to remain monolingual in Kichwa to produce a clearly distinguishable group that they could exploit and discriminate against. Otavaleños who were able to speak Spanish or adopted a mestizo appearance were perceived as uppity and unmanageable (*alzados*) and were not hired in mestizo businesses. However, Villavicencio also noticed that an indigenous upwardly mobile group composed of the owners of textile workshops was reinforcing ethnic pride and perhaps starting to form an indigenous nationality as a strategy to fight discrimination, a conclusion that was forcibly rejected by more established indigenists like Gonzalo Rubio Orbe (1973). Although some earlier indigenista authors (e.g., Buitrón and Collier 1971 [1949]) had previously addressed the topic, Burgos's and Villavicencio's vivid descriptions of discrimination in the markets, public spaces, and public and private institutions of mestizo cities were among the first detailed analyses of racism in Ecuador.

Researchers at CAAP, meanwhile, set out to rescue cultural differences for leftist politics by emphasizing the historical traditions and strategies for resistance that characterized the Andean community (CAAP 1981, 1984). CAAP's focus on the community had several sources of inspiration, including cultural anthropologists' models of Andean reciprocity and solidarity, John Murra's model of vertical control of a maximum of ecological niches, José Carlos Mariátegui's and Chayanov's notion of "the peasant commune . . . as the cell to form a future communist society" (Roseberry 1989, 176), and the Catholic idea of base communities (A. Guerrero interview, January 20, 2006). This harmonic view of the community was not only an interpretation of reality but also an integral part of CAAP's political project and development work. For instance, CAAP encouraged peasants to put into practice the very strategies of solidarity that were supposed to characterize them previously. The views of father José Manangón, discussed in chapter 4, were influenced by the work of CAAP as this NGO worked closely with the Catholic Church.

Ethnolinguists formed another group on the Left that has been influential for the reinforcement of a social movement with an ethnic and cultural agenda, particularly because they designed and helped implement bilingual education, an institution that, as discussed above, is key to understand the political strength and organizational efficiency of the indigenous movement. Ethnolinguists were based in the Department of Linguistics at PUCE, in a program founded, according to Francisco Rhon (interview, August 14, 2006), as a counterweight to the influence of the Protestant Summer Institute of Linguistics. The ethnolinguist José Yánez (interview, May 5, 2006) argues that when the indigenous movement and some academics close to it like himself still sponsored class-based politics, ethnolinguists such as Consuelo Yánez and Ruth Moya were already promoting an ethnicity-centered agenda. Consuelo Yánez, for example, designed intercultural bilingual schools and developed Quichua grammars, textbooks, and other materials, some of which are still in use. Ruth Moya and her sister Alba worked on written materials for bilingual education and established the first degree in Andean linguistics for indigenous students at the University of Cuenca, providing a good number of intellectuals with access to higher education for the first time, and forming cadres who later implemented intercultural bilingual education in different regions of the country (Moya 1981). Another important ethnolinguist, Ileana Almeida (1996), who studied linguistics in the Soviet Union, imported the Stalinist concept of oppressed nationalities, a concept that was adopted by the Confederation of Indigenous Nationalities of Ecuador (CONAIE) under her influence.

The focus of José Yánez's (1988) *Yo declaro con franqueza: Cashnami causashcanchic* (I Truthfully Declare: This Is How We Have Lived) is somewhat different. His book discusses the oral history of a hacienda in Pesillo, Cayambe. Yánez emphasizes the political significance of collaborative research for raising peasant consciousness and promoting grassroots organization, as well as for learning about peasant historical rebellions, unionization processes, and political resistance to the hacienda system.

Gender and Ethnicity

Studies of gender in indigenous contexts focused first on the role of female labor in peasant economies. These studies emphasized the flexibility of labor roles as well as the dignity of women's status in indigenous communities (A. Martínez 1998; Poeschel 1986). On the other hand, the seminal work of Kristi Anne Stolen (1987) generated reflection in Ecuador on the oppression and violence suffered by peasant women in the highlands. This violence was characterized by José Sánchez Parga (1990) as a way to restore Andean harmony and as an Andean tradition of ritual fight linked to the Pan-Andean *tinkuy*. Since then, the debate on gender and ethnicity has continued to focus on whether indigenous societies are egalitarian from a gender point of view, or unequal and characterized by violence toward women. This debate is not, of course, restricted to Ecuador, but reaches across the Andean countries (see Harris 2008).

Often, the violence and oppression against Amazonian and Andean women has been interpreted as a Western or capitalist influence that has disrupted traditional gender relations that have been described as harmonious. Blanca Muratorio (2001) challenged this widely held assumption. Using archival and oral sources, she showed that gender violence among the Napo-Kichwas of the Ecuadorian Amazon has roots internal to the culture and also of colonial origin.

The discourse of gender complementarity, which is also part of the official self-description of indigenous organizations, justifies indigenous women's privileging of ethnic discrimination over gender oppression and their lack of common agendas with the white-mestizo and urban-centered feminist movement (Prieto 1998; Prieto et al. 2005). On the other hand, it has been argued that indigenous societies are hierarchical from a gender point of view and that indigenous women benefit from espousing a feminist agenda and adding to it, as would feminists whose movement was to become more inclusive (Prieto 1998; Prieto et al. 2005). Following up on this debate, Manuela L. Picq (2012) notes that Ecuadorian indigenous women were able to push forward ethnic and gender agendas in the debates of the 2008 Constituent Assembly. Whereas the recognition of indigenous customary law was an important milestone in the democratization of the Andean region, it also includes features that discriminate against indigenous women. Picq shows that indigenous women supported the inclusion of customary law in the constitution, while also lobbying for women's rights and parity within the indigenous justice systems.

Mercedes Prieto (2017) has focused instead on the relationships of indigenous women with the state and the development apparatus in the early twentieth century. Prieto shows that indigenous women played key roles in development because the state identified them as the actors more likely to transform and lead their communities. On the other hand, the state attempted to restrict native women to their domestic roles.

To sum up, anthropology started in Ecuador with the aim to better understand and tackle the challenges brought about by the agrarian reform and what was understood as a transition from feudalism and traditional peasant subsistence to capitalism. The diffusion of the discipline from the Global North played a role, but it was not the determining factor for anthropology's institutionalization. Differently from other Latin American countries, Ecuadorian anthropology was not driven by the state, but by the political agendas of the Left and the progressive Catholic Church.

Ecuadorian scholars debated the role that ethnicity was to play within the social transformations they were witnessing. Whereas some thought that ethnic markers worked to the disadvantage of those so labeled, others saw the Andean community and its traditions of solidarity as tools to resist oppressive structures. Likewise, those writing about gender and ethnicity disagreed on whether to understand Andean culture as intrinsically egalitarian or to see it as being crisscrossed by gender violence. They also disagreed on the origins of gender discrimination. Recognizing that gender inequalities also characterize indigenous culture has been important to allowing indigenous women to claim ethnic recognition while also working toward gender equality.

Ecuadorian Anthropology and the Indigenous Movement in the Neoliberal Period

Beginning in the mid-1980s, Ecuadorian anthropologists—influenced by their own activism with indigenous people and by an international academic turn toward the study of popular resistance—had begun to study the history and forms of indigenous protest (Bustamante 1988; Moreno Yánez 1985; Prieto 1980; Ramón 1987; Yánez 1988). The fact that many authors failed to fully comprehend the importance of the powerful organizational machinery that was in the making can be attributed, on the one hand, to the indigenous peasants' politically strategic (and historically justified) silence about their political activities, and on the other, to the role of the Catholic Church in the early indigenous organizations (Martínez Novo 2004; Rubenstein 2005). Many academics were anticlerical and dismissed the activities of the Church as reinforcing the status quo. In contrast, Father Juan Botasso (1986) was well aware from early on that strong political organizations based on indigenous identity were imminent.

After the first nationwide indigenous uprising in 1990, and following the recurrent mobilizations of the indigenous movement, a number of books and articles were published. These studies reflected an important characteristic of social sciences in Ecuador: many were studies of the conjuncture. One of the first books written by anthropologists after the 1990 indigenous uprising challenged traditional indigenista policies of assimilation, while also criticizing the Left for not having given enough importance to identity politics (Moreno Yánez and Figueroa 1992). Two influential collective works written right after the 1990 uprising are *Indios: una reflexión sobre el levantamiento indígena de 1990* (Indians: A reflection on the indigenous uprising in 1990) (Cornejo 1991) and *Sismo étnico en el Ecuador* (The ethnic earthquake in Ecuador) (Almeida et al. 1993). *Indios* brought scholars working on indigenous issues together with social actors such as indigenous activists, landowners, and the military; *Sismo étnico* also featured academic analyses by both white/mestizo and indigenous intellectuals. A decade later, Fernando Guerrero and Pablo Ospina (2003) focused on indigenous mobilizations as reactions to neoliberalization. The authors, however, also noted the collaboration of the indigenous movement with what they characterized as neoliberal governments and institutions since the movement's debut in party politics in 1995. Other authors have focused on particular aspects of indigenous struggles such as the search for the recognition of indigenous legal systems (F. García 2002). While documenting a wide array of indigenous legal procedures, some of these works reflect a romantic view of the community and fail to be sufficiently critical when indigenous legal practices collide with human rights.

Anthropologists working as consultants for (or otherwise funded by) international agencies have done much of the work on the indigenous movement since 1990. Most of this work has supported the movement even in moments of crisis or when it has made mistakes (for example, when it supported the 2000 coup d'état and entered into an alliance with Colonel Lucio Gutierrez). In fact, some of these scholars were themselves advisers to the movement or they collaborated closely with it in consulting or development work. This close collaboration made it difficult for some authors to acquire a critical position with respect to the indigenous movement, especially because scholars often required the approval of indigenous organizations to obtain funding from international organizations for consulting or development work.

Roberto Santana and Víctor Bretón made substantial critiques of the indigenous movement. Santana (2004), who teaches in France, drew on his long-term work on Ecuadorian indigenous politics to describe how the movement's organizational "fetishism" (excessive focus on political organization) prevented it from developing a coherent political project. Bretón (2001, 2005), who teaches in Spain, showed that development projects and particularly the World Bank's Indigenous and Afro-Ecuadorian Peoples

Development Project (PRODEPINE)—which has been widely embraced by the indigenous movement—failed to improve indigenous peoples' lives, and led to the political demobilization of a once radical movement. Bretón's work contributed to the indigenous movement's rejection of the second phase of PRODEPINE. Some critiques also arrived from the Catholic Church. Father Miguel Angel Cabodevilla (2004) of the Aguarico Vicariate, wrote a moving and passionate book about the genocide of what he calls the "hidden peoples"—indigenous groups neighboring the more numerous Huaorani and who maintain little contact with Ecuadorian society. Cabodevilla argued that oil and timber companies were encouraging the Huaorani Indians who led the Organización de la Nacionalidad Huaorani del Ecuador (a branch of the Confederation of Nationalities of the Ecuadorian Amazon and CONAIE), to exterminate these other peoples. Father Cabodevilla was ethically involved in protecting the human rights of "hidden" peoples who, paradoxically, were legally represented before the Ecuadorian state by the very organization that was contributing to annihilating them.

Indigenous Scholars under Neoliberalism

Although since the nineteenth century every Ecuadorian has enjoyed a constitutional right to elementary education (Ramón 1991), in practice most indigenous peoples were functionally illiterate and excluded from public education until at least the 1970s. The educational efforts of the Communist Party, which opened clandestine schools for indigenous peasants in the 1940s, the work of the progressive Catholic Church, and the struggles of indigenous activists and organizations themselves allowed for the formation of a group of indigenous intellectuals. These intellectuals started acquiring literacy, high school diplomas, higher education, and more recently, access to graduate education, mostly through international grants. In the 1990s indigenous people started participating in academic conferences as students, speakers, and audiences.

During the neoliberal period, most indigenous intellectuals found jobs in politics or intercultural bureaucracies, and remained underrepresented or absent from full-time academic positions. As a result, they did not publish as much as their white-mestizo counterparts, a problem that was often noted at meetings of the indigenous movement (Kar Atamaint, personal communication). Despite the history of difficulties and exclusion, indigenous authors were able to publish some of their works. They took two main approaches: some challenged essentialism and stereotypes and presented indigenous peoples as modern individuals, whereas others drew on strategic essentialism and employed white-mestizo stereotypes in order to make political claims.

In the 1970s, the Salesians started publishing the work of Shuar intellectuals in the collection *Mundo Shuar*. José Vicente Jintiach, a historic leader of the Shuar Federation and one of the first to access higher education at the Pontifical Catholic University of Ecuador, published his reflections on the difficult adjustments facing the Shuar youth who entered Salesian boarding schools (Jintiach 1976). Jintiach's book portrays the Shuar as a people fully integrated into and fond of modernity, who enjoyed the few films they had access to in Sucúa and the music of the Beatles. As is typical of the egalitarian Shuar culture, Jintiach was very critical of the Salesians' authority. According to the author, Shuar adolescents found the lack of personal liberty and the sexual repression they encountered in the boarding schools particularly painful. However, Jintiach unambiguously recognized how important it was for the Shuar to be educated in the dominant culture. Another work that questions essentialism and presents indigenous peoples as fully integrated into modernity is Gina Maldonado's (2004) *Comerciantes y viajeros: de la imagen etnoarqueológica de "lo indígena" al imaginario del kichwa otavalo "universal"* (Merchants and Travelers: From the Ethnoarchaeological Image of "the Indigenous" to the Imaginary of the "Universal" Kichwa Otavalo). Maldonado, who obtained her MA in anthropology at FLACSO Ecuador, draws on interviews with young Otavaleños who are business people and travelers to question the anthropological image of Otavaleños as a people "frozen in the past." Instead, she argues that Otavaleños are themselves struggling to define what it means to be indigenous within modernity and globalization.

Differently from Jintiach and Maldonado, a book by another anthropology MA from FLACSO, Raúl Ilaquiche (2004), represents indigenous culture as fixed since pre-Hispanic times, and argues that such a move is necessary in order to legitimize the claims of the indigenous movement to legal autonomy (a right recognized for the first time in the 1998 constitution). Ilaquiche is uncritical of the tensions between indigenous justice and human rights, which form one of the most important bottlenecks for the implementation of indigenous legal systems.

To sum up, the neoliberal period is characterized by a weak state and lack of economic resources that has led scholars to work in consultancies—mostly funded by international cooperation or multilateral organizations—and to focus on the conjuncture. The period, however, is one of strength of the indigenous movement, which becomes a sponsor of scholarship with the international funds that are allocated to its problematic. This situation produced collaborations between anthropologists and indigenous activists but also hindered Ecuadorian anthropologists' ability to take a position of critical distance. Indigenous people started joining the public sphere in this period thanks to international grants, but with limitations. Most jobs for them were in politics and intercultural bureaucracies and, thus, their academic production was necessarily limited. Their production can be sorted into works that challenge stereotypes and works that use strategic essentialism for political purposes.

Anthropologists and Social Movements during Correa's Presidency

Anthropologists' Perceptions and Insights on the Crisis of the Indigenous Movement

Ecuadorian anthropologists recognized that the indigenous movement became weaker during the Correa decade and they had an insider's perspective on this decline, as some of them were advisers or consultants to the social movement (Interviews with Fernando García, July 28, 2015; Pablo Ospina, July 10, 2015; personal communication with Marcelo Córdoba, July 2, 2015). An effective government strategy, anthropologists noted, was to asphyxiate indigenous organizations financially. Paradoxically, this happened during a period of economic boom. As noted above, foreign and national NGOs had been an important source of funding and support for the indigenous movement and its academic allies, but their help decreased after 2011. Correa's government regulated the financial operations and development work of foreign and national NGOs in order to control development money as well as the ability of civil society to resist the regime (Chiriboga 2014; Conaghan 2017). Executive Decree 812 issued in 2011 required foreign NGOs to register with the government, submit all projects for approval, and align their plans with the government's development priorities. The decree forbade all foreign NGO personnel and their families to join activities deemed political

(Conaghan 2017). It also forbade international NGOs to channel funds from bilateral or multilateral sources, closing an important source of funding over which the government now established a monopoly (Chiriboga 2014; Conaghan 2017). In addition, the Correa regime canceled the deductions for private businesses that donated to NGOs and civil organizations, forcing national NGOs to downsize and reduce programming (Chiriboga 2014). Moreover, Decree 16, directed at national civil organizations, established that the executive could close organizations that engaged in political activities reserved for political parties or endangered public policies or national security (Conaghan 2017).

In addition to these financial regulations and juridical insecurity, the post-2008 global economic crisis reduced the funds that donor countries had available for the purpose of international cooperation. These countries redirected their development efforts to the poorest recipients. At the same time, some Latin American countries, including Ecuador, were reclassified as being of middle income due to the commodities boom of the 2000s, and were no longer a priority for international cooperation (Chiriboga 2014). Moreover, Spain, which was the main donor to Ecuadorian NGOs and social movements and made up 18 percent of Ecuador's international cooperation money, was hit particularly hard by the crisis and sharply reduced its international impact (Chiriboga 2014).

As a consequence of this juridical insecurity and financial squeeze, international assistance to Ecuador's NGOs decreased by half in 2014 compared to what it was in 2011–2013 (Conaghan 2017). Moreover, donor countries such as the United States, Switzerland, and the Netherlands ended their cooperation with Ecuador, as did important institutions such as the German Konrad Adenauer Foundation (Conaghan 2017). The US Agency for International Development pulled out in 2013 because the Ecuadorian government did not renew its programs or allowed new start-up activities. Konrad Adenauer closed in opposition to Decree 16 and increasing government control over NGOs (Conaghan 2017). In addition, the Pachamama Foundation, an NGO that supported environmentalist and indigenous causes, was forced to close in 2013 under Decree 16 for having engaged in politics and opposing a round of oil concessions. In 2009, the Correa government tried to close Acción Ecológica, the oldest and most important environmentalist NGO collaborating closely with the indigenous movement. However, the order was reversed due to international and national pressure. Most of this cooperative funding had addressed environmentalist and social movement causes (Chiriboga 2014). The regime controlled other sources of income for indigenous activists as well. As discussed in chapter 4, the government ended the autonomy of the intercultural bilingual education system. This move terminated indigenous organizations' control of intercultural education jobs and consultancies, which reverted to the Ministry of Education.

Furthermore, the 2010 territorial law, the Organic Code of Territorial Organization, Autonomy, and Decentralization (COOTAD) did not recognize the indigenous community, the backbone of the indigenous movement, as a fundamental unit of the state with the right to a budget allocation. The parishes, which are the mestizo towns surrounded by indigenous communities, were recognized instead. Parish mestizos and parish councils were politically and economically empowered under Correa and became an important social base of the regime (Marcelo Córdoba, conversation with author July 2, 2015).

As the autonomous indigenous movement dwindled and lost control over sources of funding and jobs, academics sometimes helped the regime to create parallel organizations that did receive funding and state support. The creation of social organizations from above is a common strategy of semiauthoritarian regimes for the manipulation of civil society (Conaghan 2017; Ortiz Lemos 2015). In 2014, the National Federation of Peasant, Indigenous and Black Organizations took a leading role in bringing indigenous groups together to create a progovernment group called Indigenous Alliance for the Citizen's Revolution (Alianza Indígena para la Revolución Ciudadana). The Ministry of Peoples asked a foreign social scientist and expert on the African diaspora who was a grantee of the Prometeo Program to help create the National Council for Afro-Ecuadorian Unity (Consejo Nacional de la Unidad Afro-Ecuatoriana) (García, interview with author, July 28, 2015).[2] According to an anthropologist, the parallel social organizations were "made of paper" and very fragile. If government funding ended, they would stop working (García, interview with author, July 28, 2015).

Despite this situation, some leaders of CONAIE, *comuneros* from the areas affected by natural resource extraction, schoolteachers affected by the changes in intercultural education, and peasants unhappy with the lack of

---

2. The Prometeo Program brought recognized scholars to Ecuador for a year or more under excellent economic conditions to foster research collaborations.

a comprehensive land and water reform resisted the regime. The anthropologist Fernando García saw the struggle of indigenous organizations to counter the efforts of the Correa government to divide and co-opt them. For example, Marcelino Chumpí, a Shuar leader affiliated with Pachakutik, was able to win the elections in Morona Santiago and became the province's governor in 2009. Chumpí opposed oil drilling and open-pit mining in his province. Alianza País made an effort to divide the Shuar organization FICSH. Correa's party distributed computers, boat motors, and chickens to the membership of the organization. As a result a group from FICSH broke away and started to support the president. The government also invested a large amount of money for public works in this region of the southern Amazon. Correa himself traveled to the area several times to speak to the Shuar. Despite Alianza País's efforts to win over the province, Chumpí was reelected in 2014.

Although indigenous autonomous legal systems were recognized in the 1998 and 2008 constitutions, the Correa government struggled to limit their scope. A 2014 sentence of the Constitutional Court circumscribed indigenous justice to minor, internal conflicts that strictly relate to identity and culture. Coordination between indigenous and mainstream systems of justice had been a bottleneck of legal pluralism. The anthropologist Fernando García, an expert on indigenous customary law, was put in charge of creating a new law of coordination between indigenous and ordinary justice for the National Assembly. The Pachakutik assemblywoman Lourdes Tibán presented the draft of the law to the assembly. However, the document did not even reach a second debate because Alianza País boycotted it. According to the anthropologist, the slogan of Alianza País at the National Assembly was "nothing for the Indians" (García, interview with author, July 28, 2015). The Correa regime's encroachment on the indigenous movement was multifaceted, systematic, and highly effective and also affected the social movement's academic allies.

Intellectual Turns under Semiauthoritarian Rule

Despite this situation, with the exception of Luis Alberto Tuaza (2011), Ecuadorian anthropologists have not written a comprehensive account of the crisis of the indigenous movement or the difficulties it has faced under Correa's rule. Those who are concerned with indigenous rights are working on environmental conflicts and extractivism. They tend to define extractivism in its narrow sense as the mass-scale industrial extraction of nonrenewable natural resources such as oil, gas, and minerals (Junka-Aikio and Cortés Severino 2017).

On the basis of Eduardo Gudynas's ideas, the anthropologist Ivette Vallejo (2014) explains how the "new extractivism" of left-leaning governments differs from previous forms of exploitation of nature. Turn to the Left governments still rely on and expand export-oriented primary economies. The difference between Left policies and neoliberal ones is that in Left policies the state, instead of private companies, controls the process. Moreover, extraction-oriented policies are justified by a socialist rhetoric of national interest and overcoming poverty. Instead of working with transnational companies from the capitalist North, the government prioritizes state companies of socialist or what they call "progressive" countries, particularly China. Instead of having the oil companies negotiate their social responsibility policies and their local development programs directly with the affected communities, the government collects taxes and centralizes the development programs. The government claims to have left behind the clientelism of the oil companies and the dependence of the population on the NGOs, while increasing the population's dependence on—and gratitude to—the regime. These policies have created divisions in Amazon grassroots organizations according to Vallejo's research. Some leaders hope to access the economic benefits arising from oil and to be able to control the environmental impacts. Others are afraid of the pollution, decrease in agricultural production, fishing, and hunting, and the illnesses caused by these industrial operations.

Other authors highlight the contradictions between the environmental and pro-indigenous rhetoric of the regime and its parallel discourses and policies of extractivism and forced modernization (Espinosa Andrade 2017; Uzendoski 2018,). Michael Uzendoski shows how a leftist regime uses the discourse of Sumak Kawsay (Good Living) to project a progressive image, while also promoting extractivism and capitalist modernization. In Amazonia, according to Uzendoski, "Good Living" is the label for a series of emblematic government development projects that create a moral debt that then justifies extraction. Uzendoski shows how the state is intertwined with and inseparable from private companies. He also discusses the ways in which the state micromanages populations through specialized branches of the executive, "decentralized" local governments, and the parish councils, while leaving out autonomous indigenous communities and organizations.

Now with more funding for basic research and working in an environment that is not open to critical views, some authors have chosen to investigate seemingly less contentious topics. A number of anthropologists continued with, or turned toward, historical research. During the past decade, Ecuador has experienced a noticeable boom in historical studies. Growth in the field of ethnohistory builds on a tradition that goes back to the origins of Ecuadorian anthropology. However, some anthropologists have turned to history due to shrinking NGO funding and programming. In the previous period, NGOs and international cooperation had funded ethnographic research on current issues. In addition, during the Correa decade, government interest and funding were available for the kind of work that Eduardo Kingman Garcés calls "the reactivation of memory." Ministries, particularly the Secretary of Culture and Heritage, and municipal governments were interested in promoting work on cultural history (Kingman Garcés and Muratorio 2014). This strategy made sense to a nationalistic regime that was interested in rethinking the nation's historical narrative. On the other hand, anthropologists argue that doing ethnohistory is a way to engage in political arguments without being captured by the conjuncture (Teodoro Bustamante, interview with author, August 5, 2015). Avoiding the conjuncture became possible due to greater institutionalization and abundant funds for research.

An example is Kingman Garcés and Muratorio's (2014) *Los trajines callejeros: memoria y vida cotidiana, Quito, siglos XIX–XX* (Street Hustle: Memory and Daily Life in Quito in the Nineteenth–Twentieth Centuries). The authors write about popular material and intangible culture in Quito from the late nineteenth to the twentieth century. The Municipal Government of Quito, the Institute of Patrimony, and the City Museum sponsored the publication. UNESCO's interest in intangible cultural heritage gave visibility to the study. The book seeks to investigate popular memories and identities through a careful examination of the material culture, testimonies, and ephemera of the urban poor, whom the authors describe as having strong roots in the indigenous world.

The authors emphasize the value, beauty, and right to exist of a culture that Quito's elite has not sufficiently appreciated and that seems to be waning with modernization. The work is political in the sense that it seeks to counter the processes of displacement of the urban poor from the historic center of Quito by arguing that these groups are the shapers of the city's rich traditions. Quito's municipal elites had tried to displace these groups, which they perceived as dirty and backward, from the capital's touristic core and replace them with a folkloric, sanitized rendering of culture.

Kingman Garcés shows what is specific to postcolonial cities, challenging the interpretation that Latin American cities are islands of modernity and Western culture. He claims that Quito was—and is—an agrarian and indigenous city. The elite based its rents and identity on the hacienda system. Popular groups fluctuated between the countryside and the city, and Quito depended on the colonial relationship with the indigenous communities in its periphery that provided most urban services. Kingman Garcés argues that the city was a space of interaction between ethnic groups where the ethnic frontiers became blurred without being dissolved. In a chapter that discusses a union of construction workers, he shows that class and race cannot be easily disentangled in the city. Construction, street vending, street cleaning, and other humble occupations have been historically constructed as "Indian" work.

Another shift that occurred during the Correa decade is Ecuadorian anthropologists' adoption of the "ontologies" paradigm (Kohn 2015). Similarly to ethnohistory, this paradigm is ingrained in Ecuador's anthropological tradition. One of the pioneers of the ontologies approach is Philippe Descola (1986), an Amazonist and disciple of Claude Lévi-Strauss who conducted fieldwork among the Achuar of the Ecuadorian Amazon in the 1980s. A more recent reference is Eduardo Kohn (2013), who has worked with the Kichwa of the northern Ecuadorian Amazon. Kohn's grandparents migrated to Ecuador from Italy and the Czech Republic to escape Nazism. However, Kohn grew up in the United States and studied at the University of Wisconsin–Madison with the Ecuadorianist ethnohistorian Frank Salomon.

The ontologies paradigm questions the Western separation between nature and culture on the basis of how other cultures understand the relationships between humans and nonhumans. The paradigm also aims to study ways of being beyond the human (Kohn 2015). The adoption of this paradigm has allowed Ecuadorian authors to focus on environmental issues that are central to the current conjuncture, while also avoiding an explicit political position. Although the ontologies paradigm promotes appreciation for the various entanglements between humans, nonhumans, and natural features, which is a political pursuit under the current environmental crisis, it is also highly philosophical and unconcerned with specific political struggles.

Alexandra Martínez (2007), however, adopts the paradigm for reasons that are more immediate. She argues that questioning the dichotomy between nature and culture strengthens the claims of the indigenous movement and that such an approach is useful in improving Ecuador's public policies. Similarly, Vallejo (2014) in her study of Correa's neo-extractivist approach, contrasts government practices with the ontologies of Amazonian people who do not perceive a division between nature and culture and have sociability networks that include people as well as nonhumans and natural features such as mountains and rivers. Bustamante (interview with author August 5, 2015), on the other hand, questions the uncritical way in which some Ecuadorian authors have adopted the ontologies paradigm. According to the anthropologist, the adoption of the approach has facilitated an abstract and essentialist perspective that does not allow engagement with current problems.

The ontologies paradigm, which understands nonhumans and natural items as capable of subjectivity and agency, influenced the adoption of the rights of nature in the 2008 Constitution of Ecuador via the advice of social scientists, particularly Eduardo Gudynas. Ecuador was the first nation in the world to make nature, independently of the human beings who inhabit it, a subject of rights. This approach, however, raises some questions: How will nature's subjectivity and agency operate within the mainstream legal system? If nature—or nonhumans—cannot represent themselves, who is going to represent them and speak for them when specific challenges arise?

In a dialogue between anthropologists and the Shuar and Achuar nations organized in 2018 by Shuar and Achuar politicians, activists, and intellectuals with the support of the French Institute of Andean Studies, Philippe Descola noted that neither humans nor nonhumans but only the relations between them should be the subjects of protection. He also suggested that ontological autonomy must be translated into political and juridical autonomy. The anthropologist added that if a policy gives rights to nature, that policy must also provide the concrete means to implement those rights. Humans should not be the origin of all rights, Descola continued, but only the representatives of a multitude of natures.

Anthropologists and the Manipulation of Civil Society

Ecuadorian anthropologists acknowledge that some colleagues have collaborated with Correa's regime for the purpose of containing the social movements. According to Bustamante (interview with author, August 5, 2015), those who had jobs in academia were able to remain somewhat independent, but the government controlled the rest of the jobs and consultancies for anthropologists, particularly after the contraction of NGO and international cooperation funding and programming. The anthropologists who worked for the government had two options: to try to work as technicians in their own nonpolitical projects or to become politicized. According to the anthropologist, those who tried to work on purely academic or technical projects were not successful in the long run. He provided the following example: "Let's say that they are working on a grammar of the Záparo language for the Ministry of Patrimony and they only want to work on that project. However, eventually they will be asked to provide people for a progovernment demonstration or to distribute resources among the people they are working with. Purely technical work is not possible" (Bustamante, interview with author, August 5, 2015).

Anthropologists who became politicized perceived those who did not support the regime as enemies. Government-affiliated anthropologists had two sources of power: they controlled public contracts and the access to data and information. They used government contracts to co-opt their peers. A way to silence those who were not affiliated with the government was to deny them the economic resources and the information to do research. Anthropologists working for the regime did not openly debate with the opposition, because debating was a way to recognize them and give them importance. A strategy was to listen to the arguments of the opposition and then challenge those arguments with the government's own propaganda machinery without acknowledging the source (Bustamante, interview with author August 5, 2015).

Tighter government controls of civil organizations as well as political polarization produced the closing of the Association of Anthropologists, Archaeologists, and Linguists of Pichincha, the only one operating in Ecuador. Executive Decree 16 required social organizations to have a certain amount of capital (US$4,000) and to deal with much bureaucracy to keep an organization open. Since this was an association run by volunteers, the legislation made it too burdensome to keep it open. On the other hand, anthropologists were unable to have a single voice because they were divided over their support—or lack thereof—for Correa's government (Bustamante, interview with author, August 5, 2015; Córdoba, conversation with author, July 2, 2015).

An anthropologist argued that intellectual repression was typically indirect. He noted, "You are not told what to research or what to write. However, those who criticize the government face the risk of losing their jobs" (anonymous interview with author, July 8, 2015). A journal issue that was critical of the government's higher education policies was not published. To justify their decision, the editorial board argued that the editor of the special issue did not have a PhD. The editorial assistant of the journal lost her job (Pablo Ospina, interview with author, July 10, 2015). These kinds of indirect repression may be typical of a hybrid regime that maintains the appearance of freedom of expression while also controlling what can be said in the public sphere (Conaghan 2017; Ortiz Lemos 2015).

The regime used the expertise of anthropologists to reverse some previous gains of the indigenous movement as well as to justify the reversal. The anthropologist José Antonio Figueroa played a leading role in the closing of the Intercultural University of Indigenous Nationalities and Peoples (UINPI). As a member of the Council for the Evaluation, Accreditation, and Assessment of the Quality of Higher Education (CEAACES), Figueroa was in charge of applying the fourteenth mandate of the 2007–2008 Constituent Assembly, which required the evaluation of institutions of higher education and the closing of those that did not pass. The fourteenth mandate was originally issued to protect students from failing, for-profit "neoliberal" universities. However, the legislation was also instrumental in closing the only indigenous-owned and-operated university.

In order to evaluate UINPI and the pedagogical institutes that trained indigenous teachers for the intercultural bilingual education system, Figueroa hired the Kichwa PhDs Armando Muyulema and Luis Alberto Tuaza, among other indigenous professionals. These academics were in charge of creating the criteria for the evaluation and writing of the questions in Kichwa. However, Tuaza stated in an interview that the professionals were not told the purpose of the evaluation and that they did not have real decision-making power (Tuaza, interview by author, July 16, 2015). Both academics eventually disagreed with and left CEAACES , but their temporary participation was used to claim that the evaluation had been culturally sensitive (Figueroa 2015). CEAACES ordered the closing of UINPI in October 2013. The reasons given in the act of suspension were: that the state was interested in guaranteeing the quality of education for students; that the knowledge of UINPI students was deficient; and that UINPI did not represent the whole Kichwa and Shuar nationalities, but only a small, corporatist group.[3]

In a book chapter justifying the closing of the indigenous university and his participation in it, Figueroa (2015) claims that UINPI had used ideas of cultural difference based on the writings of Walter Mignolo and Catherine Walsh to justify its pedagogical deficiencies as well as its exploitation of teachers and students. Mignolo (2003) and Walsh (2007) had argued that UINPI embodied nothing less than the epistemic autonomy of indigenous peoples and the end of intellectual colonialism.

Figueroa highlighted instead the importance of the intercultural alliances that had taken place in Ecuador since the Liberal Revolution of 1895: the alliances between indigenous people and socialists and communists in the 1930s and 1940s as well as the indigenous-mestizo alliances that led to the creation of the Pachakutik Party. Figueroa claimed that mestizaje was not only a Creole project but also an indigenous one. The anthropologist added that an emphasis on differences and the corporatist appropriation of the gains of indigenous peoples by a small group of leaders could only deepen processes of social exclusion. He asserted that interculturalism permeated the whole project of twenty-first-century socialism, and was very important to it. However, the government understood interculturalism as an empty space of encounter between the groups. The intercultural project of the regime, as Figueroa explains it, seems to be a continuation of the previous project of mestizaje. Encounter between groups is encouraged, but it takes place under the leadership of mestizos. Interestingly, in his previous book on the first indigenous uprising, Figueroa had criticized the state agenda of assimilation of native peoples (Moreno Yánez and Figueroa 1992).

Mestizo anthropologists were witnesses to the weakening of the indigenous movement during the Correa decade, but have not yet written a comprehensive account. Critical anthropologists have focused instead on

---

3. Consejo de Educación Superior, República del Ecuador, Acta resolutiva sesión extraordinaria, no. 12, November 4, 2013.

localized environmental conflicts and on how these affect indigenous peoples. Charles Hale, Pamela Cala, and Leith Mullings (2017) have argued that we are witnessing the emergence of a new racial formation in Latin America, characterized by the retrenchment of indigenous rights and underpinned by extractivism and white mestizo backlash. In this context, the authors suggest, indigenous struggles become localized and national-level struggles lose their previous relevance. Perhaps the work of Ecuadorian anthropologists resonates with this shift toward more localized environmental struggles. Meanwhile, other anthropologists have chosen to work on less controversial historical or ontological topics. Whereas anthropologists have been advocates of indigenous peoples, they have also used their expertise to weaken indigenous movements and their rights. The section also shows that the Correa regime has had a comprehensive strategy to silence academics and civil society on the basis of financial control and the cultivation of an apparent freedom of expression, while critical views are punished with lack of funding, lack of access to information, and professional harassment. Meanwhile progovernment or neutral scholarly positions have been rewarded with public funding and recognition.

Indigenous Anthropologists in the Transition from Neoliberalism to Nationalist-Extractivism

Paradoxically, despite the crisis of the indigenous movement and the further retrenchment of indigenous rights during the Correa decade, a few indigenous academics were able to find full-time positions in Ecuadorian universities. They also enjoyed the time and opportunity to publish, which was a rare prospect during the neoliberal period. Interestingly, the opening did not happen because of affirmative action or antidiscrimination policies, but due to Correa's attachment to the concept of meritocracy.

The government required all universities to have as many professors as possible with PhD degrees, so the institutions could pass evaluations under the fourteenth mandate and avoid closure. However, many universities did not have enough professors with an advanced degree, particularly in the provinces. A few indigenous intellectuals had been able to complete their PhDs with funding and educational opportunities that had become available in the previous neoliberal period.

I will tell the story and discuss the publications of two PhDs: Juan

Illicachi and Luis Alberto Tuaza. Interestingly, both were able to obtain positions at Universidad Nacional de Chimborazo (UNACH), in Riobamba. Riobamba is a provincial capital located in an area of high density of indigenous population. The hiring of the two Kichwa professors was possible thanks to the government's requirement as well as the intervention of Lexinton Cepeda, an open-minded associate dean. However, the positions they were offered were not permanent but based only on yearly contracts. Juan Illicachi (interview with author, July 15, 2015) and Luis Alberto Tuaza (interview with author, July 16, 2015) narrate their experiences in studying for a PhD, finding an academic position, surviving in a mostly hostile academic world, and navigating the political intricacies of Correa's presidency.

Illicachi was born in Puesetus Grande, an indigenous community in the parish of Flores, province of Chimborazo. He migrated to the provincial capital, Riobamba, when he was twelve. He says that he felt like a foreigner in the capital city because he spoke "poor" Spanish. He decided to study to gain respect, overcome trauma, and avoid discrimination. After pursuing an elementary education, a high school diploma, and a BA in the city of Riobamba, Illicachi was able to secure a grant from the Belgian cooperation to study for his MA at FLACSO, Quito. He provided letters of recommendation from CONAIE, ECUARUNARI (the branch of CONAIE for the highlands), and the bishop of Riobamba. He had previously been a catechist with the Catholic liberation theology movement in Chimborazo. Under the leadership of Monsignor Leonidas Proaño, also called the Bishop of the Indians, liberation theology was particularly strong in that province (see Lyons 2006). FLACSO professors taught him not only to be a teacher but also how to become a researcher, and Illicachi claims to have been transformed by the experience. He explains the tensions that he confronted when he did work on the relations between indigenous Catholics and Protestants in Chimborazo, research that he describes as a self-ethnography.

> I faced some problems when I did research. I forgot I was doing research and became a participant. That happened to me when I was doing fieldwork for my MA thesis. There are limitations when you do research from an insider's point of view. An American researcher and I were conducting fieldwork at the same time. She did not have access to the official documents. I did. However, I forgot the role of the researcher. The comrades (*compañeros*) hindered her research. I did not find opposition to mine. When I was recording they

> understood that I was recording to be able to listen again. When she recorded she was questioned: Why are you recording? They did not pay attention to my notebook. They thought I was the secretary of the organization. They asked her: Why are you writing? When I used the camera, doing that did not call attention upon me. But they would ask my research companion: Who will benefit from that picture? I conducted self-ethnography researching my own culture. I do not have experience with another culture. The mestizo does research as the dominant one. She looks at indigenous people as research subjects. I did research from a horizontal position. Sometimes I felt less. The past weighs on me. However, an academic title raises my self-esteem somewhat. The past created me as an inferior subject. My language, my clothing were useless.

Thus, Illicachi had greater access and insights than a foreign researcher, but he also struggled with his positionality in the field as well as self-esteem issues.

Illicachi argues that discrimination at FLACSO was not like the frontal racism that he had previously confronted in Riobamba. When he was a child, local mestizos told him: "You are coming from the countryside. Go to take care of the goats." At FLACSO racism was more subtle: "Some teachers thought that an Indian could not read [Michel] Foucault or [Pierre] Bourdieu. They thought that these authors were for mestizos. They believed that the Indian has a simple mind and not the complex system of thought of mestizos. They thought that the Indian should focus only on his own culture, not on Western thought. They said that if we do so, we are becoming too Western." After finishing his MA and thesis at FLACSO, Illicachi applied to a PhD program in anthropology at the Center for Advanced Studies and Research in Social Anthropology (CIESAS), Mexico City. It was difficult for him to get a visa because Mexico typically stops migrants from South America on their way to the United States. However, the Church of Riombamba helped him secure the visa from the Mexican Consulate. At CIESAS, the well-known Professor Aída Hernandez Castillo became his adviser and friend. He was able to complete his doctoral dissertation and graduate in a timely manner. Illicachi then joined the faculty at UNACH in Riobamba:

> When I applied for a job at UNACH they said: "He graduated in Mexico...," but then they retorted: "How can an Indian go to a conference wearing a

poncho? They are going to call us "runach" instead of UNACH."[4] Perhaps what they want is to acculturate us. An indigenous PhD is bad for the university. When I attend a faculty meeting we are required to wear a uniform. The uniform is a single-color suit. There is no way to wear a different outfit. To teach in a poncho is unacceptable to them. So the intention is to acculturate. However, we should not generalize. There are people at UNACH who are very conscious of the intercultural reality. There are people who are more open, people who have a past in the Church and the organizations, who combine being in academia with political activism. Many teachers at UNACH are from parishes in indigenous areas such as Colta, Cajabamba, and Alausí. They grew up in an environment of discrimination. Their ancestors were the *chicheros* [mestizo cantina owners] who lent money to the indigenous *comuneros*. So they try to reproduce the same power relations at the university. There are moments when racism comes to the surface at UNACH. When I went to FLACSO wearing my poncho they would treat me with respect. When I wear my poncho at UNACH, they say: "This is not the countryside. This is the university." At FLACSO they are more dedicated to research. At UNACH they do not worry that much about research, but about how you are dressed. They say: "Tomorrow you should wear such and such color." If you go to the University of San Francisco [a private liberal arts college], they wear jeans. The professors there are very informal. Is it worth it to struggle to be able to wear your poncho? Sometimes yes, sometimes not.

Illicachi states that when he and Luis Alberto Tuaza joined UNACH, it represented a success for all indigenous people. However, Ecuadorian universities are not yet ready for an indigenous person to be a professor, in his view. I asked Illicachi whether he also had problems with the students. He responded:

No, I have not had any problems with the students. With them, I openly identify as indigenous. I tell them that I am from the countryside, that I was a teacher there. I see many students in my classes who are ashamed of speaking Kichwa. I had previously met three female students who used to wear their *anacos* [indigenous-style skirt]. However, they do not wear their anacos at

---

4. "Runach" refers to the Kichwa word "runa," which means "human being." When used by white-mestizos, the word is pejorative and instead means Indian.

UNACH. They come in jeans. Few people arrive at UNACH with an anaco. We must inquire what kinds of discrimination they have encountered. For my family, it is a source of pride to abandon the anaco and to abandon the Kichwa language. They say: "Why does your daughter go to school with an anaco? You are not just anyone, you are a professor. Your daughter should stop wearing the anaco." They think that Kichwa is not good and that our indigenous clothing is not good. If we become prosperous, we must forget.

Illicachi notes that he had a mixed reception at UNACH: there was resistance to his arrival, but they also valued him. This is because he has a PhD and has published a book with a university press and several scholarly journal articles. He did not encounter racism when publishing, Illicachi claims, except for the fact that he has to follow Western writing conventions. But there is more discrimination at the university. Illicachi aims to teach with responsibility and to write with quality: "They must respect us, not because we are indigenous, but because we are intellectuals and researchers. But they must respect us as indigenous too!" Illicachi thinks that indigenous people have two options: the political option and the intellectual one. But whatever option they take, in order to eschew discrimination, Indians have to perform with higher quality. "We are not responsible for the present and future of only one individual, but of a whole people. The mestizo functions as an individual. The Indian functions in plural."

As noted above, the position that was originally offered to Illicachi was temporary. He wished to apply for a permanent position when one became available at UNACH. However, even though he had a PhD from a prestigious institution in Mexico, and enough publications to be tenured at a US institution, he was told he did not fulfill the requirements to apply for a tenure-track position. UNACH required an applicant to have directed a considerable number of MA theses in order to be a candidate. This requirement ensures that only those who have already had a job in a postgraduate institution can apply. Furthermore, Illicachi added: "The application was very expensive. It was necessary to spend up to US$250 in notarizations. I decided not to apply due to the costs. In addition, I did not fulfill all the requirements. I decided to wait until I had all the requirements before applying." The Polytechnic Salesian University published Juan Illicachi's dissertation as a book titled *Diálogos del catolicismo y protestantismo indígena en Chimborazo* (Dialogues between indigenous Catholics and Protestants in Chimborazo; Illicachi 2014). Using Foucault's theory—a theory he was previously told he would not be able to understand—Illicachi shows how religious groups contribute to shaping indigenous identities. On the other hand, indigenous Chimboracenses indigenize or, as Illicachi puts it, "runacize" the churches. The relationship between the churches and the indigenous population is crisscrossed by tensions: The congregations encourage the formation of critical subjects, but they also teach indigenous people to be docile toward God and the religious hierarchies. The churches promote indigenous culture and Runa autonomy, but they also bring in foreign understandings of progress and modernity. Religious groups open new spaces for women, but they also teach them to be submissive to their husbands.

According to Illicachi, there are similarities and differences between the Catholic and evangelical groups: both promote indigenous identity and the Kichwa language and have similar educational and cultural projects and comparable rituals. However, evangelicals helped indigenous people to become independent from the alliance between landowners and the traditional Catholic Church. In addition, evangelical pastors are indigenous, in contrast to Catholic priests, the majority of whom continue to be white or mestizo. Illicachi adds that evangelicals tend to be more horizontal and democratic than Catholics. In this way, the author, himself a Catholic catechist, encourages open-mindedness and appreciation of evangelicals among Catholics, in an attempt to avoid the acrimonious religious divisions that affect indigenous communities. He also uses the comparison between religious groups to advance some critiques of liberation and inculturation theologies.

Illicachi highlights the political impact of religion in Chimborazo. Both indigenous Catholic and indigenous protestant social movements have created political parties. Catholic liberation theology collaborated in the creation of CONAIE. The Ecuadorian Federation of Protestant Evangelical Indigenous Peoples (FEINE) is a social movement made up of indigenous evangelical protestants. CONAIE contributed to the founding of the Pachakutik Party, and FEINE formed Amawtay Yuyay, an evangelical political party. As both movements and parties defend indigenous interests and culture, Illicachi urges them to build alliances and engage in dialogues. He argues that even though these political movements are indigenous and confessional, they are not closed to mestizos or indigenous people from the other religious affiliation. Illicachi makes an interesting contribution because in the bibliography about CONAIE the links between the movement and the Catholic Church are seldom noted or analyzed in depth (Becker 2011; Colloredo-Mansfeld 2009; Lucero 2008). In addition, academics often perceive indigenous evangelicals as nonpolitical. Illicachi challenges these assumptions, and shows the importance of religion for indigenous political organization. However, for Illicachi, religion is not a force external to the indigenous world, but something that indigenous people shape in alliance with their white and mestizo allies.

The methodology of Illicachi's book is persuasive. As an indigenous, a Catholic, and a member of the indigenous movement of Chimborazo, Illicachi conducts a self-ethnography and explores his own intersecting identities. He questions the power relations between the interviewer and the interviewee as well as the colonial roots of anthropology. Illicachi also prioritizes his political compromise with the Kichwa people by healing wounds and avoiding unnecessary religious divisions. In addition, he questions the power relations within the churches. Being a Catholic, he is more critical of the Catholic Church than evangelism. His interviews are conducted in Kichwa and his participant observation also takes place in that language. He tries to focus his interviews not only on the most visible leaders, as anthropologists often do, but also on regular people. In 2018, Illicachi became the president of the Intercultural University of Indigenous Nationalities and Peoples that was reopened under President Lenín Moreno.

Luis Alberto Tuaza, from Rumicruz, another indigenous community in Chimborazo, was able to overcome many difficulties to complete a PhD and become a professor under a yearly contract at UNACH. Tuaza studied in a single-teacher school in his community with sixty other students at six different grade levels. The Ministry of Education paid the teacher's salary and the community provided the building, which at the time was a little house with a straw roof. To have a school in the community was important, he argued. It was nearby and the students could speak among themselves and with the teacher in their native language, Kichwa. The classes were held in Spanish until 1988, when the school joined the intercultural bilingual system. When Tuaza finished his elementary education, only one high school was in the vicinity. "The high school had two specialties: agriculture and aquaculture. It also taught about irrigation projects. We indigenous people had only those options. If we wanted to study something else, we had to go to Riobamba. There were no roads at the time, so we had to walk for one kilometer and a half to be able to take the bus toward Riobamba.

My parents brought the materials to build this house on their own backs. So I had to study agriculture, and I liked it."

After finishing high school, it was a challenge for Tuaza to continue studying, especially when his mother died and he became an orphan.

> Before her death, my mother was part of the pastoral work of Monsignor Proaño in Riobamba. She used to host missionaries at home. A Laurita nun befriended her. The nun thought that I should join the seminary and study social sciences. At the time, the Church gave a small scholarship of 3,000 sucres to Kichwa students. In exchange, we had to work for the dioceses. I went to the seminary in the city of Cuenca. I could study and I had the opportunity to attend the university. My grandmother had had a bad experience with the old priests, so she advised me not to waste my time with them.
>
> That is how my passion for studying was born. Without the support of the Church it would have been very difficult for me to study. The Laurita nuns corrected my writing and taught me public speaking. I suffered at the university because I was placed with students from schools like Colegio Borja and Asunción. But thanks to the support of Father Fernando Vega, I was able to succeed. I earned the same grades as the students from the best private schools. I spent seven years studying philosophy and theology in Cuenca and had a special sensitivity toward the indigenous world. Monsignor Alberto Luna encouraged me to dedicate myself to indigenous people and to the poor.

After graduating with a degree in theology, Tuaza became a priest in Riobamba. Later he decided to pursue a graduate degree. He found FLACSO through a Google search, took the entrance exam, and requested a loan from the government to pay the tuition. He was not aware that FLACSO had scholarships, and he did not have enough money for room and board in Quito:

> I did not have money for lodging or food, and Quito was very expensive. I asked the Laurita nuns if I could live with them at their hospice in the Tejar neighborhood of Quito. I slept on a mattress on the floor with the market porters. Then a priest hosted me at his house. In return, I worked at a retirement home. I made US$20 in alms, which was enough for photocopies. On the weekends, I returned to Riobamba to work with Father Modesto Arrieta and in that way I made a little extra money to cover my expenses. I was able

to complete my MA and write my thesis. It was about the indigenous party Pachakutik. I had a romantic perception of the indigenous movement at the time.

After graduating with an MA, Tuaza worked as a priest in the parish of Columbe in his native province of Chimborazo. During that time he became skeptical of the indigenous movement, development organizations, and the progressive Catholic Church. He realized that the communities were quite disconnected from these institutions. When he attended meetings and mingas (collective work parties) and collaborated on public works he realized that the NGOs, the indigenous organizations, and the Church had lost authority over the communities. He noticed that these institutions had abused the free labor of *comuneros* (see Tuaza 2011). "The community became open to the evangelical world, a fact that was not well-received by the dioceses. Evangelical Indians also needed support to get organized politically. I saw the need to work with the evangelical world. However, after six months, I was sanctioned because I was working outside of the lines of the Indigenous Pastoral. Then, I decided to continue studying for my PhD and FLACSO accepted me." Eventually, Tuaza left the Catholic Church and became an Episcopalian priest. More recently, he has also left the Episcopal Church to form his own indigenous church.

Like Illicachi, Tuaza enjoyed his time at FLACSO. He liked doing research and writing and meeting with other researchers. In addition, from 2009 to 2011 he was able to live on the research consultancies that he did for several professors. Tuaza notes that FLACSO helped him overcome the fear of racism and find his place in the religious world. "FLACSO helped me overcome racism. Thanks to academia, I have been able to find my space in the religious world. My pastoral work is the result of my academic reflection. I learned what Monsignor Proaño used to say, that we need organization and to build communities. Without organization we cannot take care of our needs. Due to the absenteeism of the state, we indigenous people have survived out of our collective work." Once he finished his PhD, Tuaza looked for academic work, but instead, he had several offers to work for the Correa government:

> I was asked to become a consultant for the Ministry of Politics under Minister Doris Solís [a mestizo woman and former member of Pachakutik]. They paid

US$2,500 a month. I worked there for only three days. My job was to read the newspapers and evaluate what they were saying about the government. Then I was expected to prepare counterarguments. I did not like it. There was a tendency toward lying and exaggerating the data. I rejected this proposal. Then, CEAACES hired me. They paid US$2,000 a month. I was asked to write evaluation questions for the social sciences. I was also in charge of evaluations of the intercultural pedagogical institutes [the schools that educated the intercultural bilingual teachers]. I created the questions in Kichwa. They did not explain to me the reasons for the evaluation. They said that it was to strengthen the institutes. But in reality it was a strategy to close the institutes. All the decisions were made by the white-mestizos of the regime. We were only peons. Once I realized that we were peons, I left that job. Later, CEAACES wanted to hire me to evaluate the indigenous university Amawtay Wasi [which they also planned to close]. They paid US$3,700 a month. I decided to continue teaching instead of earning the enmity of the indigenous organizations.

Then Tuaza joined the faculty at UNACH on a yearly contract like Illicachi. When a permanent position became available, he applied. He had a PhD and numerous publications, including two books, a manuscript about to be published, and several scholarly journal articles and book chapters. As happened to Illicachi, he was not successful. He explains:

I had the opportunity to join UNACH in Riobamba. The associate dean, Lexinton Cepeda was interested in hiring me. I was hired in a temporary position, though. Then they posted a permanent position. I had many publications but they were worthless there. I had all the requirements they listed. They argued that the copy of my identification was not properly notarized and sealed. I appealed because I had enclosed another copy that was notarized. They accepted the second copy, but declared that the position would remain vacant because one of the members of the tribunal did not have an MA, and was not qualified to judge me. Then I applied to another position to teach state theory at the Law School. They were looking for a scientist with research experience. Two of the judges did not arrive at the tribunal and again the administration declared that the position would remain vacant. There is little space for me at the university, but I still enjoy my pastoral commitment. It is important to make the communities visible. Paradoxically, UNACH ended up giving me a medal for educational merit.

When Tuaza first joined UNACH, he went to fill out the paperwork with the department's secretary. He found that his name had been changed to Luis Alberto Torres. He told the secretary: "Miss, there is a mistake here. My name is not Torres, but Tuaza. Could you please change it?" The secretary responded: "No worries. I just changed your name to Torres on purpose. No Tuaza can be a doctor here." Then Tuaza kindly requested to be changed back to his original family name. The secretary was just being "nice" and "doing him a favor" by upgrading him to mestizo.

Tuaza's PhD dissertation, published as a book by FLACSO (Tuaza 2011), analyzes the organizational crisis of the indigenous movement from the perspective of the grassroots. While working as a priest in Chimborazo, Tuaza noticed a contrast between the glorious organizational past of the area—about which he read in the pastoral reports of the 1980s and 1990s— and what he called the "organizational exhaustion" of the present. The grassroots' loss of interest in political participation had led to the decreased influence of the indigenous movement in the national political arena. To understand this, Tuaza used Sidney Tarrow's theory of social movements, and particularly his concept of "collective action cycles" (Tarrow 2004).

Given his rapport with indigenous communities and his deep knowledge of the Kichwa language, Tuaza was able to write an interesting critique of the bibliography on the emergence of the indigenous movement (Becker 2006; García 2006; Guerrero 1993). He argues that the bibliography praises the achievements of indigenous organizations, but fails to attain a wider perspective on the indigenous world. According to Tuaza, most authors have privileged the political over the economic, which is of greater concern to the indigenous communities. In addition, many studies only recover the voices of leaders, while eschewing the points of views of regular folks.

In contrast, Tuaza argues that the perceptions of the grassroots explain the decline of this social movement. According to Tuaza, the communities think that the leaders have asked for too much collaboration and have provided few tangible results in return. In the late 1990s and early 2000s, few public works have been started or completed, and the leaders have not proposed any innovative ideas. In addition, concepts used by the leadership such as plurinationalism and interculturalism have not been adequately explained to or socialized among the grassroots. Historic leaders stick to their positions and do not allow enough space for the young to participate. Moreover, leaders seldom consult the grassroots when they make a deal.

For these varied reasons, community members do not want to participate in the social movement, according to Tuaza. If they collaborate, it is mostly out of fear because they are fined or their water and electricity services are suspended. Commoners also complain that even the elderly or the dispossessed are forced to work in mingas or pay a fine, as leaders do not take into account personal hardship.

Another problem highlighted by Tuaza is that the *cabildos*, the traditional ruling bodies of communities, have lost much of their power. Historically, cabildos solved family conflicts, distributed communal land, and applied justice. Today, they have lost most of these functions. Development organizations have multiplied and have competed for the collaboration of comuneros, thus weakening the cabildo. The creation of parish councils also weakened cabildos, as the mestizo parishes became brokers with the central government and made the decisions for the communities. Another factor that explains the weakening of indigenous organizations is migration. The communities, which were the backbone of the indigenous movement, lie empty.

At the national level, Tuaza finds that the organizations have not fulfilled the expectations of the grassroots. The leaders have focused on political participation and on reaching public positions, and have focused less on the economic concerns of commoners. In addition, the leaders have concentrated on rural issues, while the grassroots do not necessarily live in the countryside or work only in agriculture. Temporary and permanent mobility are important realities for the grassroots. Therefore, according to Tuaza, a crisis of credibility of the leaders impairs their ability to mobilize commoners.

Tuaza's book is methodologically strong. His interdisciplinary approach combines anthropology with the insights of history and political science. He proposes a holistic view of the indigenous world, avoiding the separation between politics, the economy, and the cultural aspects. Tuaza recovers the voices of the grassroots through a combination of interviews, participant observation, and use of the archives of the Catholic Church and development organizations. Most of his interviews and observations take place in the Kichwa language. His long-term participation in the communities as a religious authority gives him great rapport. In addition, he had privileged access to the archives of the Catholic Church. Finally, Tuaza highlights the importance of listening and projecting a humble attitude.

The next book of this prolific author (Tuaza 2017) expands on one of the aspects that he found important in his first monograph: community culture as expressed in the teachings of an elderly wise woman, the Mama Pitu discussed in chapter 4 of this book. The book is bilingual in Kichwa and Spanish and penetrates deeper into the indigenous worldview through the author's analysis of oral narratives. Tuaza's perspective on indigenous culture is not static: He conveys an indigenous reading of history, modernity, and the relation of Runas to nonhumans. Like other Ecuadorian anthropologists, Tuaza seems to be shifting toward the ontologies paradigm. However, he does so on the basis of his deep knowledge of the Kichwa world.

Looking at the life histories and academic work of these indigenous authors and others we find some common patterns: the strength of liberation theology in Chimborazo explains their trajectories that were initially propelled by the Church. We turn to the role of the Church in the indigenous world in chapter 6. Multicultural funding and support originating in international cooperation during the neoliberal period allowed some to receive advanced degrees. They endured crude racism, but also enjoyed the support of some people in their native province. They felt more supported, although they also suffered from what they interpret as more subtle discrimination in the cosmopolitan universities of the capital city. When they returned to their native province, they were able to get jobs thanks to the meritocratic policies of the Correa regime. However, there are limits to meritocracy, as the jobs they can find are based on renewable contracts and they are not able to get permanent positions. Furthermore, the university strongly encourages them to become mestizos and acculturate in order to be able to conduct professional work. When they decide to retain an indigenous identity, they meet with hostility. These findings attest to the openings and limitations that the racial formations of neoliberalization and nationalist-extractivism offered to indigenous intellectuals.

Their academic work is enriched by a level of rapport and access greater than that of mestizo or foreign researchers. Thanks to this, they are able to raise important questions and discuss nuances that non-Indian authors may not be able to grasp. Indigenous academics are interested in mastering Western theories to show that they are as capable as white mestizos while also adding to them their knowledge of the indigenous world. Both authors are worried about religious divisions that may weaken and divide indigenous political movements, a topic that, while also addressed by nonindigenous authors, is not as fundamental to us. The politics of indigenous scholars in relation to the Correa government are somewhat ambiguous. While focusing on indigenous politics, Illicachi chooses not to speak directly about the national conjuncture. Tuaza is more direct, but struggles with the attempts of the government to co-opt him and his academic arguments.

Anthropological collaborations and racial formations

This chapter has looked at the intellectual production of Ecuadorian anthropologists on indigenous issues and their relation to indigenous peoples and the state, and has considered three conjunctures in which three different racial formations coalesced. First, it has analyzed the origins and institutionalization of the discipline, which were marked by national debates on the agrarian reform, the transition from feudalism to capitalism, and the role of culture and identity for revolutionary politics and evangelization. Foreign anthropologists contributed their knowledge and taught the discipline in Ecuador, but their external agendas were less central to the institutionalization of Ecuadorian anthropology than the need to understand a society in flux and to act upon it. This differs from the assumption that the anthropology of the South is a mere result of the diffusion of the discipline from the North Atlantic world in a neocolonial fashion (Krotz 2006; Lins Ribeiro 2006). In Ecuador, the anthropological agenda was not orchestrated by the nation-state, as happened in other national anthropologies of the Global South (Lins Ribeiro 2006), but by the Catholic Church and the political Left, which led indigenista racial projects of their own in the absence of a strong state.

Second, the chapter analyzes the fragility of Ecuadorian academia in the context of neoliberalization and during a period of economic crisis. However, the emergence of a powerful indigenous movement in this conjuncture benefited Ecuadorian anthropologists, as it revealed the importance of research on rural and indigenous topics, and increased the international funding to conduct this kind of work. Moreover, neoliberal multiculturalism provided opportunities and opened spaces for indigenous intellectuals, but also limited their options to bureaucratic and political jobs, thus leaving these intellectuals little time for scholarly writing and academic reflection. Their academic production shifted between an interest in showing that indigenous people are fully inserted into modern, global contexts and their use of strategic essentialism to reinforce the indigenous movement's claims.

How did living in an economically and politically unstable environment during the neoliberal period affect the intellectual work of anthropologists located in Ecuador? Instability does good and bad things to our ability to produce knowledge and to the kind of knowledge produced for those who not only study but also live in unstable places (Greenhouse 2002). It is important to note that during this period academic jobs were few, institutions tended to be fragile, and the state did not provide anthropologists a reliable framework within which to work. From the mid-1980s to the mid-2000s, Ecuadorian academics relied more on consulting work for international agencies like the World Bank, the Inter-American Development Bank, and the United Nations. Others were forced to work for private companies—including oil companies that financed some Amazonian anthropology. Still others had to work with the approval of the social actors they were studying. This had important ethical implications for those who wanted to maintain a perspective of critical distance. Even those who were lucky enough to work for stable academic institutions, such as universities, were required to bring in private funds that could sustain these institutions financially. While this process was certainly linked to the neoliberalization of academia that was also taking place in the North, the stakes were much higher in an "unstable," poorer country with virtually no safety net for intellectuals who did not succeed in the entrepreneurial world of consultancies (Escobar 2006). However, as Greenhouse (2002) and the authors of *Ethnography in Unstable Places* note, instability and fragility can also lead to insights and creative solutions. Ecuadorian anthropologists were able to overcome institutional obstacles and play major roles in public debates on important social and political transformations, and they tended to avoid trivial discussions in an environment where the contribution of academia to the understanding and improvement of a fragile reality was deemed fundamental.

Third, the chapter looks at the Correa decade and the commodity boom that offered both opportunities and constraints for white-mestizo and indigenous anthropologists. A stronger and better-funded state allowed academics to conduct the kind of basic, solid research that had not been possible in the previous period. On the other hand, the semiauthoritarian tendencies of the regime restricted freedom of expression. Within this context, anthropologists had choices: some supported indigenous social movements at some personal cost, others wrote intercultural propaganda for the government, others weakened and co-opted social actors, and still others decided to avoid a political discussion. A material understanding of intellectual production does not preclude awareness of individual and group agency.

During the Correa decade there were more jobs in academia, and these jobs were better paid. In addition, funding was available for attending international conferences. Institutional stability and international exposure helped improve the quality and visibility of Ecuadorian anthropological production. This situation only enhanced the cosmopolitanism of Ecuadorian anthropology, a characteristic that can be traced back to the origins of the discipline. Despite a decade of nationalist ideology, the tendency toward intellectual dependency persisted, as academics tried to keep pace with the latest foreign trends. However, anthropologists also adjusted the new paradigms to national context and needs. For instance, when they adopted the ontologies turn, they made it more political and applied. Moreover, Ecuadorian anthropologists might have been able to convince some practitioners from the Global North of the need to become politically involved in view of the current dangers faced by indigenous peoples and the environment, which might be more noticeable in the South than the North.

On the other hand, intellectuals operated within a semiauthoritarian context. Jobs, funding, and information were allocated selectively to those who supported—or did not oppose—the regime. Those who did not support the government were excluded from funding and information, or indirectly repressed. In this way, the government was able to silence and shape the opinion of experts. According to Andrés Ortiz Lemos (2015), who worked for the Ministry of Politics, this was not a coincidence, but a well thought-out strategy of the regime. In addition, intellectuals lost sources of independent funding from abroad and came to depend exclusively on the government. In this way, the regime increased its ability to control civil society.

The nationalist-extractivist decade also had mixed effects on indigenous scholars. Postneoliberal meritocracy allowed them to obtain full-time academic jobs, but the lack of a serious commitment to affirmative action and interculturalism constrained their job stability and protection in discriminatory environments. As did other academics, indigenous anthropologists made choices within the political conjuncture. Whereas one feared discussing politics openly, the other expressed opinions more candidly. However, given their special socioeconomic vulnerability, they faced an even greater risk of co-optation by the regime.

Despite public statements about interculturalism, plurinationalism, and affirmative action, the Correa regime did not enforce these concepts in academic spaces. On the contrary, if there was some affirmative action, it seems to be a legacy of the previous period. The government closed the only indigenous institution of higher education with the argument that integration was better than segregation. However, integration, as the regime defined it, was not so different from the previous paradigm of mestizaje and assimilation. As the regime's practices demonstrate, integration was expected to happen under the leadership of whites and mestizos. Under President Lenín Moreno, the Intercultural University of Indigenous Nationalities and Peoples has been reopened. However, it still confronts many challenges such as lack of funding and official support.

CHAPTER 6

THE SALESIAN MISSIONS

Navigating Neoliberalism and Nationalist-Extractivism with the Indigenous Movement

During his 2006 political campaign, Rafael Correa noted that his most important learning experience had taken place when he was a Catholic volunteer for a year at the Salesian Mission of Zumbahua. This was one reason that Correa organized his symbolic inauguration (discussed in chapter 2) at the heart of the mission. In his speech at the event, Correa emphasized the importance of being a Catholic volunteer, and thanked the missionaries who had facilitated the experience. In an extensively documented biography of Correa, Mónica Almeida and Ana Karina López (2017) argue that the mandatary was eager to publicize his religious volunteering to compensate for his lack of political militancy on the Left. During his time at the mission, Correa had managed a cooperative mill and taught some literacy classes (Almeida and López 2017).

This has not been the only time that the Salesian missions have been at the center of Ecuadorian politics. Since the 1960s, the missions have been key points for the organization of the modern indigenous movement and the creation and implementation of multicultural policies, including intercultural bilingual education and the recognition of indigenous territories. The missionaries were also instrumental in nurturing the antineoliberal political ideology of the social movements. The indigenous movement that missionaries helped organize led the struggles against neoliberalism and halted the implementation of some structural adjustment reforms (F. Guerrero and Ospina 2003). Furthermore, the activism of the Catholic Church and the social movements it was allied with created the fertile ground that made possible the turn to the Left and the election of Correa in the first decade of the twenty-first century. However, the order was shaken when the development priorities of the Correa regime, centered on the expansion of natural resource extraction, produced a confrontation with the very social movements that the missionaries had fostered. The order tried to take advantage of being close to a president who was a lay Salesian missionary, but it was also committed to continue working with indigenous and other social movements. This situation produced the tensions and contradictions that are examined in this chapter, which eventually confronted Catholic hierarchies with some priests working on the ground and weakened the indigenista project of this key actor of Ecuadorian civil society.

The creation of multicultural policies and an antineoliberal political culture was intimately linked to the development work conducted by the Salesian Order. Their understanding of development was multidimensional, focusing on the protection of indigenous peoples' territories, land acquisition, access to credit and technical knowledge for agricultural and animal husbandry, education, political organization, and, of course, evangelization. An important focal point of Salesian work with indigenous peoples was the promotion of pride in their heritage and identity, which the missionaries perceived as an important goal in itself and a necessary first step toward claiming territories and other rights. In the first half of the twentieth century, the Salesians emphasized the need for indigenous peoples to learn Spanish and Western ways and to become Christian as a way to "civilize" them. After Vatican Council II (1962–1965), the order changed its goals and struggled to preserve indigenous languages and customs—although purified by Christian ethics—as mechanisms to promote a better standard of living and what the missionaries understood as the integration of indigenous citizens into the nation-state.

Although they are a transnational Catholic order with European as well as Latin American and local staff, the Salesians have had a close relationship with the Ecuadorian state. After independence, the state lacked the infrastructure and perhaps the motivation to control and serve the totality of the national territory. Frontier areas populated by indigenous and Afro-Ecuadorian peoples were typically delegated to the Catholic Church (Martínez Novo 2007) or to evangelical organizations (Lu, Valdivia, and Silva 2017). This was just one aspect of a delegative state that also ceded the administration of native populations to the private domain of haciendas (A. Guerrero 1993). At the end of the nineteenth century, the Ecuadorian state granted the Salesian Order jurisdiction over the southern portion of the Amazon, a grant that has been renewed several times up to the present. After the Agrarian Reform of 1964 distributed public haciendas to peasants, an absent state also informally delegated the administration of *páramo* (high elevation) lands to religious orders. In these marginal regions, the missionaries were in charge of building roads, schools, and hospitals, enhancing the local economy, and even organizing people to claim their rights from the state.

Given his close relationship to the Salesian Order, Correa renewed state–church agreements in the first years of his presidency. However, a few years into his mandate, the regime reversed what the president and other government officials came to interpret as the neoliberal trend to delegate state responsibilities to third parties. In successive years, the state expanded its territorial and administrative grip, effectively displacing the missions (Juncosa 2017). In addition, the regime suspected that the missions and the progressive Catholic Church might be organizing other sectors of civil society to resist government policies. Thus, nationalist-extractivism worked to weaken the Catholic order as well as those other actors of the multicultural turn that had permitted Correa's rise to power.

First, I examine the complex ways in which the Salesian indigenist racial project was appropriated, internalized, and sometimes contested by its recipients, the indigenous peoples of the Amazon and the Andes. I show that indigenous identities and forms of political organization were not created in any simple way from below, but were also shaped by interaction with allies, such as the Catholic Church (Rappaport 2005). Various authors have acknowledged the important role played by the Catholic Church in the formation of indigenous social movements in Ecuador and elsewhere (Cornejo 1991; León 1992; Martínez Novo 2004; Rappaport 2005; Rubenstein 2005; Zamosc 1993). Others have emphasized the role of the Left, particularly the Communist Party through its Ecuadorian Federation of Indians branch (Becker 2008; A. Guerrero 1993). An emphasis on one ally or another can be explained by regional differences in the formation of the indigenous movement, the Left having had more influence in the northern highlands whereas the Catholic Church was more salient in the central highlands and some parts of the Amazon. However, many authors have argued that once the Confederation of Indigenous Nationalities of Ecuador (CONAIE) was created in 1986 and the first national indigenous uprising took place in 1990, indigenous movements were able to become independent from their allies (A. Guerrero 1993; León 1992; Lucero 2008). The desire to emphasize the recently acquired political voice of indigenous people and the fear of reproducing the colonial stereotypes of passive and manipulated Indians have precluded efforts to study in greater depth the relationships between the Catholic Church and the indigenous movement.

Some compelling studies have examined the interactions between missionaries and native peoples in Ecuador (Andrade 2004; Kohn 2002; Lyons 2001; Muratorio 1981; Rubenstein 2005). However, with a few exceptions, these have focused only marginally on the political ramifications of the relationship (see, for example, de la Torre 2002; Rubenstein 2005; Martínez Novo 2004). In addition, the literature has tended to emphasize the cultural transformations effected by missionaries rather than their efforts toward cultural preservation (Gutierrez 1991; Muratorio 1981).

Although it has been assumed that the Catholic Church aimed to assimilate indigenous people, this institution was deeply involved in the making of multiculturalism. It started to acknowledge the religious legitimacy of non-Western cultures and the need to respect and preserve them after Vatican Council II. More concretely, the Ad Gentes Decree on the missionary activity of the Church issued under Pope Paul VI in 1965 has been recognized as one of the foundational documents of the theology of inculturation. The main idea behind "inculturation" is that the Church no longer considers non-Western cultures profane. These cultures are also believed to contain the "seeds of the word of God." Pastoral agents should identify these seeds, which are those elements within a culture that are positive from the point of view of Christian ethics or that can be used for evangelization purposes such as solidarity, love for mother earth, and spirituality. Pastoral agents should learn the language, music, and other cultural elements of the people among whom they work and use these elements for evangelization purposes and in Catholic rituals. This theological trend has led to the development of branches of the Church or religious orders specializing in indigenous peoples, the African diaspora, and other identity-based groups. Examples of this are the Pastoral Indígena and Pastoral Afro in Ecuador.

Although the theology of inculturation emphasizes respect for diversity and cultural preservation, the Decree Ad Gentes also argues that cultures should be purified from those elements that are negative from the standpoint of Christian ethics. Ad Gentes is an interesting example of the tensions between the global identity of the Catholic Church, whose very name means "universal," and the desire to accommodate and incorporate cultural diversity. This chapter analyzes the meanings of indigenous culture and inculturation to missionaries and indigenous people in the Amazon and highlands, as well as the political consequences of these (mis)understandings.

Andrew Orta has defined the theology of "inculturation" as a trend within the Catholic Church to "codify and reinforce indigenous religiosity as part of the Church's broader effort to embrace 'local theologies' and 'inculturate' itself within specific cultural contexts" (Orta 2004, 105). After centuries of preaching that indigenous people should turn away from their traditional cultural practices to embrace Christianity, many Catholic missionaries now insist that indigenous ways were Christian all along: indigenous people must become more "Indian" and return to the ways of their ancestors that missionaries see as local cultural expressions of Christian values (Orta 2004, vii). Orta argues that "inculturation" theology follows on the heels of liberation theology, which proposed that Christians were called on to correct the sinful social injustices of poverty and oppression, and that tended to downplay ethnic distinctions and emphasized instead the homogenizing identity of "the poor." He adds that the theology of inculturation is a response to the relative failure of liberation theology to take hold in rural and indigenous contexts where the rationalizing and homogenizing discourses of the liberationists did not resonate strongly. For instance, liberation theology rejected popular religiosity based on the sacraments and syncretic Catholic rituals and emphasized instead evangelization based on reasoning and the written word. According to Orta, the move from liberation to inculturation also signals the Catholic Church's accommodation to the global shift from class based movements to identity politics. Orta (2004) locates the origins of inculturation theology in the mid-1980s and claims that this current only arrived in Bolivia in the early 1990s. However, the trend seems to have started earlier in Ecuador. In the project that the Salesians wrote for the Zumbahua mission in 1971, there was already concern for the preservation and reinforcement of indigenous identity as part of their human development and evangelization design. A 1975 document of the Apostolic Vicariate of Méndez in the southern Amazon already proposes a catechesis that takes into account Shuar culture (Gnerre 2012). Missionaries in Ecuador locate the starting point of inculturation theology directly in Vatican Council II, and the discontinuity between liberation and inculturation is not clear in the Ecuadorian documents or interviews.

I explore the indigenist project of inculturation theology as it has taken shape in Ecuador on the basis of field and archival research that I have conducted since 2002 in highland and Amazonian missions. I analyze how this racial project articulates with those of the state and indigenous organizations to shape the racial formations that characterize multicultural neoliberalism and nationalist-extractivism.

The Salesian Missions of Ecuador from Their Creation to the Neoliberal Period

Identity and Politics in the Salesian Missions of the Ecuadorian Oriente

In 1893 President Luis Cordero, a fervent Catholic and an indigenist who wrote a Quichua–Spanish diccionary and Quichua poetry, granted the Salesians the authority to "civilize and Christianize" the Shuar in the southeastern lowlands of Ecuador and, in the process, to ensure Ecuadorian presence along the highly contested border with Peru (Audiovisuales Don Bosco, *Misiones en el Oriente*, n.d.; Botasso 1986; Rubenstein 2005). Paradoxically, Italian missionaries were in charge of teaching native children Spanish and Ecuadorian national identity. As a result of these interactions, some Shuar elders speak Spanish with an Italian accent. The original goal of the Salesians was to transform Shuar culture into a Western Christian model. A first step was to compile information on Shuar language and myths in order to eradicate them, as the missionary Siro Pelizzaro did in the mid-twentieth century (Pelizzaro 1990). However, as Pelizzaro advanced with his research on Shuar mythology and worldview, he was seduced by the value and beauty of the culture and became one of the main advocates for inculturation theology in the southern Amazon and beyond (Gnerre 2012).

The Spanish conquerors called the Shuar "Jívaros," adapting the word "siwar" meaning "people" in Spanish phonetics (Taylor 1994). The conquerors perceived the "Jívaro" as an anarchic group that rejected any form of authority or social hierarchy beyond the family, inhabited a dispersed habitat, and were in a permanent state of internal war. The lack of hierarchical social organization in a large group endowed with a coherent culture puzzled the conquerors. After independence, Creoles came to perceive the Jívaros as the embodiment of rebelliousness, love of liberty, and virility because they were a polygamous society of warriors who struggled against an unforgiving rainforest. Ecuadorian Creoles saw these characteristics as virtues, while they still perceived the Shuar as savages whose allegiance to the fatherland was suspicious. On the other hand, European travelers were fascinated by the Shuar custom of reducing the heads of dead enemies to make *tsantsas*, the native word for shrunken heads. What called the attention of nineteenth-century travelers was what they interpreted as a combination of technical knowledge with moral depravity (Taylor 1994).

At the end of the nineteenth century, the rationalism, materialism, and perceived lack of spirituality and rituals of this group irritated the missionaries. Missionaries called the Shuar "a barbarous and atheist race . . . resulting from all the savage forces combined such as the cascades, ravines, the claws of beasts, and the venom of snakes" (Taylor 1994, 84, quoting Pierre and Alvarez). Because of their alleged cynicism, the missionaries argued that Shuar culture was of satanic inspiration. For the missionaries in this period, cultural change was a way to eradicate the work of Satan. The Salesians were also preoccupied by the lack of sexual mores of the Shuar, which they associated with the custom of polygyny (see chapter 4). The missionaries presented themselves as the advocates of native women whom, they thought, Shuar males treated as "slaves and prostitutes."

However, by the 1960s, the Salesians began to reflect on the importance of preserving an indigenous culture that was increasingly threatened by their own missionary work as well as by the colonization of the Amazon by peasants from the highlands.

The Salesians tried to transform the Shuar, a seminomadic group, into settled peasants in order to protect their territories from colonization. Although the agrarian reform and colonization laws of 1964 and 1973 benefited highland peasants with the distribution of public hacienda lands and the granting of plot titles to those who worked on private haciendas, the Shuar experienced the agrarian reform as harmful to their interests. According to the law, lands that were not in cultivation could be distributed

FIGURE 6.1. Father Marco Beltrame, SDB (Sociedad Don Bosco, Catholic Salesian missionary) and the anthropologist Kar Atamaint, member of the Shuar nation, February 26, 2008. Photo by the author.

to those in need. This meant that the Shuar, who moved periodically when their plots were exhausted and their hunting prey dwindled, were forced to become sedentary in order to be able to claim their territory. Trying to help the Shuar resist the colonists' land grabbing, the Salesians promoted subsistence agriculture, especially cattle raising, which was more appropriate given the thin Amazonian soils. Amazonian soils are not optimal for sedentary cultivation. Due to abundant rainfall, these soils are superficial and the traditional strategy of slash-and-burn agriculture makes more sense in this kind of natural environment when using rudimentary techniques. In addition, the Salesians encouraged the creation of agrarian and cattle cooperatives to help strengthen Shuar production.

The missionaries encouraged the formation of Shuar centers—groups of houses around a main square—that resonated with the colonial *reducciones*. In 1964, at the time of the first agrarian reform, Father Juan Shukta encouraged the centers to create a federation called the Interprovincial Federation of Shuar Centers (FICSH). This was one of the first modern indigenous organizations in Latin America. FICSH was a founding member of CONAIE, whose first president was Miguel Tankamash, a Shuar. FICSH, however, did not seek a return to an indigenous tradition. According to Steven Rubenstein (2005), the hierarchical character of FICSH, its well-defined territorial limits that mimicked the Ecuadorian state, and the concentration of the population in towns or centers, contrasted with traditional Shuar understandings of diffuse authority and vague territoriality.

Maurizio Gnerre (2012) has shown that the Salesians completely reorganized the physical and sociopolitical space of the southeastern lowlands. The order sought to create rural towns following a European model. This process preceded the agrarian reform and was accelerated by the legislation. Father Rouby conducted the first efforts at Shuar sedentarization in the 1920s, gathering a group of "Jivaros" in Sevilla del Oro. Then he changed the name of the town to Sevilla Don Bosco in honor of the founder of the Salesian Order. In the 1930s, Father Gomezcoello continued the process of sedentarizaton of the Shuar, founding Asunción, considered to be the first Shuar center. A native elder donated a large tract of land for this purpose. Since the Shuar had not previously lived in towns, they did not have a word for them. They borrowed the Kichwa word "llakta" to refer to a town, adapting it to Shuar Chicham phonology as "yakat" (Gnerre 2012). However, since the 1940s the missionaries preferred to use the word "centro" (center) in order to avoid the Andean reminiscences of the previous term. Moreover, the concept of a center was more appropriate to refer to a central square surrounded by the dispersed houses and plots that the Shuar preferred because they more resembled their traditional habitat.

In 1935 Father Vigna applied for official protection of the Shuar territory, which the Ecuadorian state was willing to grant in 1945. When enough centers had been established, Father Shukta and the Shuar authorities established FICSH. With the help of voluntary topographers, the federation mapped the territory of each center, which the missionaries envisioned as communal property with a global property title and family usufruct of specific lots. The centers were made up of single-family homes according to the Salesians' plan to curb polygamy (Gnerre 2012).

In 1972 the Salesians and the Shuar Federation founded the Shuar Intercultural Bilingual Radio Education System (SERBISH), one of the first ventures of this kind in Ecuador and Latin America. In order to educate a population dispersed in the rainforest and to intensively use scarce human resources, a "radio-teacher" transmitted the lesson through the radio, and a radio-teacher assistant reinforced the lesson directly in the community. With the help and financial support of the Salesians, the organization printed teaching materials in Shuar Chicham and Spanish. This system was the seed of intercultural bilingual education in the Amazonian province of Morona Santiago. Today, for a number of reasons, including the allocation of more human resources for intercultural education, modernization processes in the region, and the fact that the radio technology imported by the Salesians became obsolete, teachers conduct education in person in regular schools, even in remote centers.

The education system in Morona Santiago has been both public- and mission-led (*fisco-misional*) in accordance with church–state agreements, and was controlled first by the missionaries and later by the indigenous organizations. José Juncosa (2017) has argued that the shift from the original model of the mission boarding schools, where Shuar children were interns and were separated from their families, to the center schools that allowed children to live with their families and permitted community authorities and parents to manage the schools, was a key tool in allowing the Shuar to control their own education.

As happened with other pioneer experiences in indigenous education in Ecuador, after 1988, when the National Directorate of Intercultural Bilingual Education was created, there was some tension regarding who would own and manage the intercultural education system: the missionaries who implemented it in the first place or the indigenous organizations that the government put in charge. The indigenous organization wanted to control the system and make it public and secular, causing a conflict with the Salesian missionaries who also claimed ownership. Interestingly, according to interviews I conducted in several schools, Shuar parents preferred the supervision of the missionaries because they felt that mission education instilled more discipline and was of higher quality.

In addition to helping the Shuar claim their territory, founding a modern indigenous organization and an intercultural bilingual system of education, the missionaries also studied the Shuar culture and language. Siro Pelizzaro was the first to study Shuar mythology in order to eradicate what he saw as superstition. However, he soon became aware of the human and religious value of Shuar oral narrative. With Father Rampón, he created the Missionary Center for Scientific Research. The Salesians were able to appreciate the beauty of the Shuar language. On the other hand, when they standardized the language to be able to write it, these religious scholars also transformed Shuar Chicham. The language is conversational and sentences are uttered as part of a face-to-face dialogue with a specific interlocutor. When the missionaries wrote the language and used it to convey content unrelated to an interpersonal conversation, they changed it. Moreover, missionaries who only understood Shuar Chicham poorly also oversimplified it (Gnerre 2012).

These linguistic and anthropological debates led to novel religious perspectives. Shuar mythology was interpreted according to Christian values. The evangelization method proposed by Pelizzaro consisted in comparing a Shuar myth with a miracle of Christ. Ethical myths were compared to anecdotes from the life of Jesus. However, these interpretations produced resistance on the part of some missionaries as well as some Shuar. Father Juan Botasso encouraged caution and warned about the danger of stretching Shuar meanings to fit Christian values. Christianized Shuar accused Pelizzaro of reproducing superstition and ignorance. Traditionalist Shuar resented the missionary invasion of Shuar beliefs. Younger Shuar despised the worldviews of their elders. In addition, many disputes arose regarding how to interpret basic Shuar concepts (Gnerre 2012).

Despite the interest of the Salesians in the preservation of indigenous culture, the profound transformations effected in the Shuar culture and way of life during the first half of the twentieth century could hardly be reversed. In addition, the processes of "cultural preservation" such as the formation of a modern indigenous organization and the transformation of seminomadic people into settled subsistence peasants and cattle raisers radically transformed Shuar culture, even if conducted in the name of cultural resistance and identity politics. As noted above, Shuar Chicham also changed as it became a written language and was used to convey content rather than functioning relationally in face-to-face conversations. The perspective of some Shuar individuals helps illuminate the process.

Rosana Pichama and her father Carlos Pichama, an eighty-six-year-old Shuar who grew up in the Salesian Mission of Sevilla Don Bosco, interpret the transformations of Shuar culture and the role that the Salesians played in them as follows. Rosana notes:

> When we went to school they did not want us to speak the Shuar language. We spoke Shuar with our classmates because we did not know how to speak

correct Castilian, but the nuns thought we were insulting them. Today, they do not want us to speak Spanish. "Speak Shuar," they say. They used to call the parents and tell them that they [the Salesian nuns] commanded us to speak Castilian. And because we were young, we gradually lost our language. Today, our kids at the Shuar centers speak only Spanish. We still know a little, but our children don't. And now they [the Salesians] want us to return to our past. (Interview with author, February 19, 2006)

This quote illustrates some of the complexities of the process of cultural transformation as experienced by the Shuar. They were first forbidden to use their language and follow their customs, and when the process of cultural change was almost complete, they were asked to retrieve them. As seen in the quote above, both processes are perceived as being imposed from outside.

Rosana's father, Carlos, also makes reference to the misunderstandings enmeshed in the process of cultural recovery as undertaken by the missionaries. He complains of the new Catholic Mass implemented by the Salesians that makes use of Shuar language and music in the liturgy. Pichama notes:

Here, they celebrate the mass in Shuar. If God had been here and had made a miracle, if God-Arutam [a Shuar spirit] had said, "Come with me," I would believe. But I don't. That Father said that Arutam is God. He is writing a Bible [in Shuar Chicham]. I don't want the Shuar mass. My father and my grandfather used to sing that music [that they use in mass] when they killed. They are singing a song from the times of the hard *chonta* [kind of palm of the Ecuadorian Amazon]. My father would drink *chicha* and sing that song with our own rhythm. The priests should not use that [in the Catholic Mass]. That song is what they sang when they killed a person. I told the Father that the Bible that God wrote couldn't be amended. We cannot change what Christ has written. What Christ said, we must follow. But now they are writing another book, a book with Arutam, Iwia [a mythological Shuar giant], and what else. My father and grandfather used to say that Iwia ate people. . . . And there he was, Father José, I came in and he was there, standing and singing "Ahhhhh." Then, he raises the holy host and he invokes Arutam and Christ. If Christ were that powerful, why would he need Arutam to help him? Then, I said: "That's enough," I won't come back to mass. If they would sing in Shuar Chicham, speaking about God that would be nice. But they confuse everything. The

FIGURE 6.2. Carlos Pichama, an elder of the Shuar nation, Sevilla Don Bosco, February 19, 2006. Photo by the author.

song that they sang when they killed humans and made *tsantsas* [shrunken heads], the song that they sang to attract women, songs for demons and snakes . . . [they use in the mass]. I say no. I told them to be careful with Arutam. Arutam is a powerful demon. They [the Salesians] taught us that. They told us that Arutam was a demon almost equal to God. Arutam knows how to deceive. We did not know well before. All the Salesian priests and nuns who have prayed to Arutam have died or become ill. That Arutam gave strength to commit crimes. That is why I say that this is not a real mass. They already fed us [the idea] that there is only one God. Why do they have to bring in Arutam now? (Interview with the author, February 19, 2006)

Carlos Pichama again highlights the contradictions of the colonization process. First their culture is stigmatized and transformed. Later the Salesians want to retrieve it. However, they do so as if one culture is equivalent to another, as if one God is equal to another God. The priest was probably using the Shuar word "Arutam" to mean God in the native language. Pichama's sharp cultural analysis tells us, however, that cultures cannot be translated into one another literally without consequences. Furthermore, the missionaries have convinced the Shuar that their own culture included negative traits, particularly those related to violence. And it is problematic to return to these elements for both the Catholic Church and the indigenous organizations. Pichama's critique lies between the Christianized Shuar critique stating that the theology of inculturation is reproducing ignorant superstitions and the traditionalist critique requesting respect for the separateness and integrity of Shuar ontology. Thus, Pichama refuses to accept the new stereotyped and stylized version of his own culture that the Salesians try to promote in their search for "cultural preservation." He states, "I know everything, nobody can lie to me because my grandfather told me: 'This is like this, and that is like that. . . .' And, now they are creating a new law. That is why I don't like when they do Shuar things." Pichama rejects the "purification" of culture that the theology of inculturation proposes as unauthentic. Consequently, this Shuar elder perceives the process of "preservation and recovering" as yet another colonial imposition, or, in his own words, as a new "law."

Identity and Politics in the Salesian Mission of Zumbahua

In the 1970s, the Salesians decided to expand their missions to the highlands, opening several congregations in the northern, central, and southern Ecuadorian Andes, as well as in the city of Quito. The Salesian hospice where Tuaza lived when he was a graduate student in Quito (see chapter 5) was meant to serve temporary indigenous migrants, market porters, and others visiting the capital to participate in land lawsuits and demonstrations (Torres 2012).

I began my fieldwork at the Salesian Mission of Zumbahua in 2002. Peasants who speak the Kichwa language and Spanish live there. Differently from the Oriente missions, this one, which was founded in 1971, was informed from the start by liberation theology and the philosophy of inculturation. From the sixteenth century until the beginning of the twentieth, Zumbahua was a large hacienda property of the Augustinians, another Catholic order (Weismantel 1998). Due to the high altitude of most of its lands, the hacienda consisted largely of pastures used for sheep raising, an activity that provided wool for a textile factory that the order owned close to the provincial capital, Latacunga. In 1908, with a law that nationalized

Church assets, Zumbahua became the property of the Social Assistance, a public institution that rented agricultural lands to finance hospitals, orphanages, and other charities for the urban poor. Paradoxically, labor conditions were often harsher on these public haciendas. The Zumbahua hacienda subjected its workers to the systems of *concertaje* and later *huasipungo*, contracts based on custom through which the worker exchanged his and his family's labor for the usufruct of a small plot of land (*huasipungo*), a nominal salary that most of the time was not paid, and some benefits like clothing and seeds (A. Guerrero 1991; Weismantel 1998). In 1964, with the first agrarian reform law, Zumbahua, like other public haciendas, was distributed among the Kichwa peasants who worked there. Social differences that originated in the hacienda period were reproduced in the land distribution process, causing inequalities and tensions. The Salesians had to confront these tensions in their search for a more egalitarian peasant community.

The missionaries sought to combine peasant evangelization with human development in Zumbahua. They understood human development as helping and advising peasants in their struggle for access to the land and for a better use of this resource. In order to struggle to make the agrarian reform law effective, or to get government credit, or to have access to development funds and technical advice, peasants first needed to organize. Thus, the Salesians promoted social and political organization through implementing intercultural bilingual education or directly creating and strengthening peasant organizations.

From the point of view of rural development, the Salesians had goals that may seem contradictory to us: they sought both to promote a self-sufficient peasant community based on the Kichwa tradition and to modernize agriculture in the style of the green revolution. Among the first goals of the mission were the improvement of roads, the introduction of enhanced seeds, new agrarian techniques, and the selection of animal species. These goals and intentions, however, confronted limitations due to the low quality of eroded land, the difficulty of cultivating steep slopes, and the small size of land plots. Given these drawbacks, peasants in the Cotopaxi highlands have not been able to live solely on agriculture. They typically combine several economic activities that include trade, smuggling, temporary construction work in cities, crafts in the case of Tigua, and incipient tourism. Despite this reality, the Salesian priests wanted the inhabitants of this area to remain as subsistence peasants and criticized migration as a source of social disorganization, violence, and destruction of the traditional culture. This peasant-oriented focus resonated with the kind of education offered by the mission, which focused on rural and agricultural needs. The Salesians educated rural teachers as well as experts on agrarian and animal husbandry techniques. This *campesinista* (peasant-oriented) approach also resonated with the work of the nongovernmental organization Andean Center for Popular Action (CAAP; see chapter 5), which worked closely with the Salesian Order in the Zumbahua parish.

Young highlanders have questioned this rural-oriented curriculum: they prefer a professional, urban education based on the use of computers and knowledge of English and other modern languages. In their own words, they want to be ready for the modern world. However, they seek this kind of professional education without detriment to the study of the Kichwa language and culture, as well as political training that was useful for young people's insertion into the indigenous movement, an important source of social mobility during the last decades of the twentieth century.

A young woman from Zumbahua, I will call Gladys, exemplifies well the fluidity of economic alternatives available for young peasants as well as the complex relation of highlander youth to rural and urban spaces (Gladys, interview by the author, August 2002). Gladys was grateful for the opportunity the Salesians provided for her to attend high school in her own community at the pedagogical institute Jatari Unancha. This intercultural school protected her from the discrimination she had suffered as a child, when a teacher told her that "indigenous people can't make it." On the other hand, she thinks that the school's approach to educating rural teachers does not prepare them well for modern life. Thus, Gladys decided to continue her studies in the provincial capital, Latacunga, in a school that teaches both English and computer applications to students. Gladys noted: "Now the world is already modern and to do any job they want you to speak English and to be able to work on a computer, that is the reason why I changed schools."

To the Salesians' credit, it is important to note that mission education adapted to the desires of Kichwa youth, by offering some classes in computers and modern languages. The Salesians did not perceive a contradiction between the reinforcement of ethnic traditions and the education of youth in those aspects related to modernity. For instance, I attended a computer application workshop at the mission where indigenous students were eager

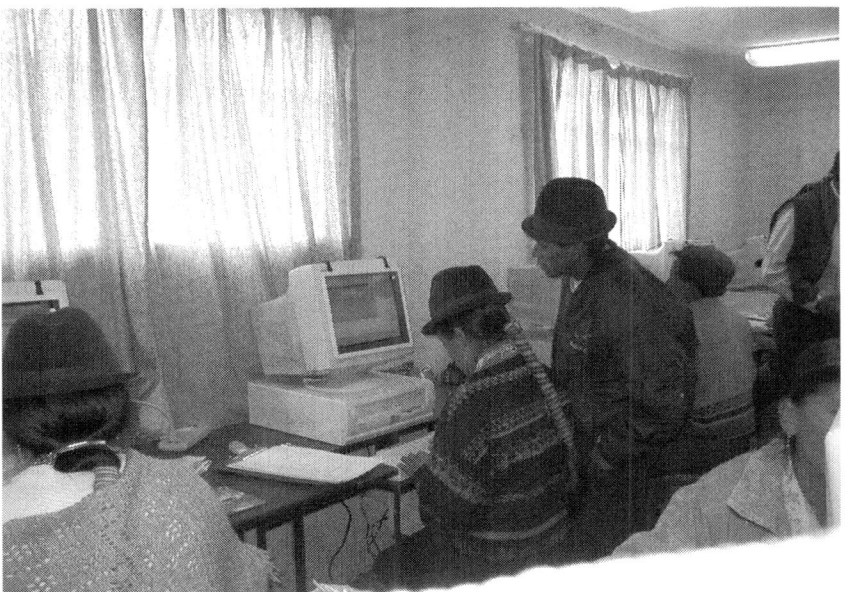

FIGURE 6.3. Programa Académico Cotopaxi, Computer Laboratory, August 2, 2002. Photo by the author.

to learn these skills. However, due to problems of infrastructure and frequent electricity cuts it was not easy to teach with technology in Zumbahua.

Gladys did not want to stay in the city after she graduated. Her dream was to return to her community as a journalist to communicate what happens there to the outside world. She wanted to conduct this work in Kichwa, her mother tongue. She says: "There are many problems here, there are criminals and thieves, but this information is not shared with the rest of the country." For Gladys there is no contradiction between being prepared for modernity and adhering to her indigenous Kichwa identity. She uses the traditional indigenous skirt called an *anaco*, an embroidered blouse, a special shawl, and a hat, speaks Kichwa well, and is a proud member of Pachakutik, the pro-indigenous political party. Gladys is Catholic, but she married a young evangelical man from a nearby community whose family earns a living from commerce. She traveled with her husband to Quito to buy clothing that they later sold across the border in Colombia. After the Ecuadorian currency was changed to the US dollar and Ecuadorian clothing became relatively expensive, Gladys traveled to Colombia to buy textiles that she then sold in the Ecuadorian Amazon. The couple did not own a vehicle, so they traveled by bus to conduct all their business. In Zumbahua a number of traders own trucks, which they use to sell highlands agricultural products on the coast and bring back coastal products such as fruits and vegetables to the highlands. This kind of trade across the Andes, connecting different ecological niches has been in use since preconquest times, as Frank Salomon has documented (Salomon 1986).

On Gladys's trips to Colombia, the guerrilla and paramilitary detained her several times and she became aware of the dangers of trading. She noted:

> In the city of la Valle is where the guerrillas lived. They stopped us and asked us what we thought of the guerrillas. And, because I new about the guerrillas, I gave my opinion. I said that here we live from barley and potatoes; there they live from cocaine. I gave that opinion. They had us tied [up] and interrogated us for about an hour. Then they talked among themselves and said: "Well, they are merchants." And a lady there also knew us, so they went to ask that lady. The lady said: "They are merchants, they are not what you think." And she requested that the guerrillas free the three *cachifucos* (Ecuadorians). We had a large suitcase and they thought that we might be carrying guns or cocaine inside. They took all the clothing out of the suitcase, and because they did not have anything to wear, they bought from us.

As we see, Gladys's skills go beyond those of an idealized subsistence peasant. She has contact with cities, has traveled internationally, and even knows how to survive in a situation as complex as the Colombian conflict. Gladys's skills resonate with the long tradition of contraband of *aguardiente* (sugarcane liquor) in Zumbahua that also connected the highlands with the coast, where sugarcane liquor was produced. A research report by the bishop of Latacunga in 1971 noted that smuggling sugarcane liquor was one of the main economic activities in Zumbahua.[1]

Gladys also notes that tourism is an important economic alternative for her parish. She says: "Because of the tourists that arrive here we have been helped. For instance, now we have an office of the phone company from which you can make international calls in Quilotoa [a nearby lake located in

---

1. Report of the Zumbahua team, January 20, 21, and 22, 1971. Archives of the Salesian Order in Quito, Casá Magón, Quito.

a volcano crater that is popular with tourists]. Because of tourism the area of Quilotoa has improved. Before, this area was completely abandoned." Thus, Gladys sees benefits in tourism even if indigenous people do not profit directly from it, as it results in better infrastructure and attracts attention to the area.

The Salesians, however, still think of Zumbahua as a peasant-oriented project. To confront the agrarian crisis in the area, they propose reforestation and the migration of highland peasants organized in cooperatives to subtropical lands. The Salesians do not perceive craft making, tourism, or migration to cities as valid long-term alternatives. The indigenous movement, strongly influenced by the Salesians, has reproduced this representation of indigenous people as subsistence peasants. This vision has important political implications as more complex economic realities and identities are not taken into account in the movement's political strategies. Even educated leaders, whose culture is urban and who live in the city and return to the countryside only occasionally, pretend to be peasants in order to be perceived as "authentic" Indians.

Since the 1970s, the Salesians have sponsored intercultural bilingual education in an area where 70 percent of men and 95 percent of women were still illiterate. Missionaries started with informal literacy programs in Kichwa in 1976, continued creating a network of elementary schools, and then founded Jatari Unancha, a pedagogical institute that trained rural teachers. In the early 1990s, the Salesians opened the Cotopaxi Academic Program, a branch of the Polytechnic Salesian University, to provide intercultural and bilingual higher education to prepare rural teachers and agrarian engineers.

As happened in the Shuar case, the Salesians who worked in Cotopaxi considered organizing on the basis of identity to be an appropriate way for indigenous peasants to claim land, improve their standard of life, and better integrate into the nation. The original project for Zumbahua written by the Salesians in 1971 noted: "It is important to create a new rural school that preserves and develops the culture that exists in the indigenous world and that in this way achieves integration into the national culture." The peasants of the area agreed with the Salesians on this point because they too perceived intercultural bilingual education and ethnic political organization as means for them to be recognized by the Ecuadorian state. Indigenous teachers wished not only to be officially recognized but also to become government officials. This is understandable because official recognition also carried economic benefits: the state began to pay bilingual educators the salaries and benefits that other mestizo teachers already enjoyed. In his thesis written on graduating from the pedagogical institute Jatari Unancha, Pedro Cunuhay (1993, 39) notes: "Because of the efforts of the System of Indigenous Schools of Cotopaxi, led by Father José Manangón and the teachers, we managed to get 27 positions from the Ministry of Education for the intercultural bilingual teachers."

Although the Salesians' motivations for integrating highland peasants into the nation while also reinforcing their indigenous identity and culture may have been largely idealistic in the beginning, peasants kept the projects and programs grounded. Salesian Father Javier Herrán states:

> We did well because, before the start of the [national] literacy campaign, we already had funding for teachers through the Provincial Directorate. There was a lot of interest on the part of the people to learn how to read and write. That is why they learned quickly. But we could not give them their official elementary school diplomas. Then, the Provincial Directorate in Cotopaxi gave us a hand because the Provincial Director was a good guy—I did not find opposition or difficulty, but support. He accepted that we give a special examination . . . and the supervisors were thrilled. They felt that the kids knew a lot, even more than those graduating from regular schools. And then, they gave them their elementary education diplomas. That gave a lot of strength to the people. Then the indigenous schools started to acquire prestige for the community. Because the teachers were not *cholos*, mestizos, or white, they were runa. And they said, "That runa does not know anything because he is a runa." But when they started to see official certificates . . . Then, their attitude changed. (Interview by the author, August 2002)

What is interesting here is that intercultural education and ethnic political organization are seen not as ways of segregating from the state (i.e., some form of ethnic separatism), but as a way to become recognized and included into the nation.

What, then, did the Salesians understand by promoting an indigenous identity and what impact did these ideas have on the political culture of the indigenous movement? The Salesians thought that one important reason to promote a cultural identity was to reinforce the self-esteem of peasants. For that reason they taught the Kichwa language and philosophy in rural schools. However, they did not learn it from the indigenous people. On the contrary, the missionaries believed that peasant Kichwa was corrupted by profuse influences from Spanish, and therefore, they sought to teach a purified, more classic version of the language, one used by university-based linguists and priests. Missionaries also thought that Kichwa culture should be preserved while also purifying it from aspects they found contrary to ethics such as the oppression of women.

Father Javier Herrán, a Salesian who worked at the Zumbahua mission in the early 1980s, and at the time of this writing is the president of the Salesian Polytechnic University in Quito, relates the following anecdote: "When intercultural bilingual education started in Zumbahua, many families did not want to send their daughters to school. Seeing that there were few girls in school, I insisted that the comuneros send them to school. The peasants answered that women did not need to study in order to take care of the home, children, and domestic animals. I then asked: Do you think that women are not human beings equal to men? If that is the case, from now on I will not baptize your women." According to Herrán, horrified by the threat, the peasants decided to send their girls to school.

Another Salesian priest who was influential in the Zumbahua mission, Father Luigi Ricchiardi (a theologian also known as Father Gigi), added that the well-known trait of Andean reciprocity should be transformed into the Christian value of altruism (he used *gratuidad*, the act of giving something without expecting anything else in return). He noted:

> From the point of view of the Church, or those of us who want to help indigenous people, this moment of change is a good moment to help introduce within their own culture new elements that help the culture develop in a certain way. The element that we want to emphasize is the element of solidarity. But from solidarity, they should evolve into altruism. Indigenous culture is a culture of solidarity. But their understanding of solidarity is based on the concept of *randi-randi*, meaning that you give something to me, and then I must give something to you. This is what we call Andean reciprocity. But Andean reciprocity mixed with the capitalist perspective can lead to selfishness. That is why we have to inject the value of altruism that immunizes Andean reciprocity against the neoliberal mentality of exploitation of others. I use the other for what he can give me, and I help him expecting something else in return. (Interview with the author, July 2002)

Father Gigi did not see indigenous culture as something that must change to adapt to modernity, but as a mixture of traditional and modern traits that must be purified from the standpoint of Christian ethics to give way to a more ethical society. This indigenous utopia is expected to immunize peasants against neoliberal logic. As the Ad Gentes Decree (1965, Chapter 1, Article 9) states: "But whatever truth and grace are to be found among the nations, as a sort of secret presence of God, He frees from all taint of evil and restores to Christ its maker, who overthrows the devil's domain and wards off the manifold malice of vice. And so, whatever good is found to be sown in the hearts and minds of men, or in the rites and cultures peculiar to various peoples, not only is not lost, but is healed, uplifted, and perfected for the glory of God." As in the Shuar case, this particular way of understanding culture by transforming and purifying it from its undesirable traits met with some resistance from Kichwa peasants. Communities did not always trust the indigenous teachers, and many peasants thought that learning Kichwa was a waste of time. Wasn't the whole point of going to school and learning Spanish to become stronger and less vulnerable in relation to the dominant culture? For instance, Rodrigo Martínez, a lay white-mestizo teacher who collaborated for decades with the Salesian education project stated:

> Why did we emphasize the philosophy of bilingual education? Because indigenous people were not convinced of the value of indigenous education. They always thought it was a second-class situation. They were not convinced that an education that is relevant to the cultural reality could also be an education with possibilities for achieving quality. Then we spent our time convincing them that the Indian is a person with value, that indigenous people are valuable as a people, that their culture includes important things. And so we spent our time until they were able to consolidate their collective identity. (Interview with the author, July 2002)

The struggles for land, rural development, and intercultural bilingual education were closely linked to the need for indigenous political organization: to get land and credit peasants required an organization that could become an interlocutor with the state and nongovernmental organizations. Intercultural education raised their political consciousness on the basis of ethnic pride and formed a new generation of leaders. The Salesians also promoted political organization directly. The original Zumbahua Project (Proyecto

Zumbahua-Guangaje 1971, 20) prioritized this aspect: "In order to solve the indigenous problem, indigenous peoples themselves have to become agents in liberating actions (. . .) through a consciousness raising process that leads them to transform every unfair socio-economic structure. Therefore, the main goal of all our action should be to lead the indigenous community to a true SELF-MANAGEMENT [in caps in the original document]. Our work as agents of change is just temporary, transient, and subsidiary." The Salesians did not aim to preserve traditional hacienda forms of indigenous social organization, but to promote the kind of politics that they understood as liberating. For instance, the missionaries had to struggle against forms of exploitation and inequality among peasants that were rooted in hacienda times. Those who were supervisors on haciendas (*mayordomos* or *kipus*) or those who had huasipungos (small plots) in usufruct were entitled to more and better land and remained in positions of leadership after the agrarian reform (Bretón 2015). Those who were just *arrimados* or *yanapas* (those who helped a family member cultivate a usufruct plot or worked on the hacienda in exchange for access to pasture, timber, water, or even right of way) were left with less land or none. Because of their fight against what they called the local caciques, the Salesians were close to being lynched and expelled from the Zumbahua area.

The style of work of the Catholic Church, which promoted social and political organization and then stepped aside to allow people to become self-sufficient, is one of the reasons that the Church's role has remained hidden to researchers. In addition, indigenous leaders have wanted to emphasize their own independent agency. Father Javier Herrán, however, highlights the outstanding role that the Salesians played in the creation of the Indigenous and Peasant Movement of Cotopaxi (MICC), a branch of CONAIE:

> We [Salesians] held the first meeting. It was in Chugchilán, if I remember correctly. We did everything. We called the people through the radio. We hired buses so the people could come. After three and a half years, our role continued to be central. We animated the meetings and were able to congregate the peasants. In that period, support for the struggle to acquire the land was central. In general, what we wanted was to create something that would help people make their own decisions. We did not find it appropriate to continue with the traditional organization systems of our area. (Javier Herrán, interview by the author, August 2002)

The theses of indigenous students who graduated from Jatari Unancha reinforce the Father Herrán's narrative. For instance, Cesar Pilaguano (1993, 5) notes: "MIC was founded by the organization of indigenous schools, by Father Javier Herrán. When Javier left, MIC failed." Fabiola Ante (1993, 58) adds: "After that [the founding of MIC], a leading committee was created. Juan Rivera from the community of Cachi Alto was elected president. With the enthusiastic collaboration of Father Javier Herrán from the Latacunga dioceses, the priests were included in the formation of this provincial organization [MIC]. Apart from raising the consciousness of the peasants regarding labor issues and the laws that affected the poor, they explained to us the importance of having such an organization." However, years later the Salesians have taken some distance from the indigenous movement. This happened in part because the leaders were able to become independent, but also because the missionaries understood that their goal was to keep their critical distance from political power. Father Gigi notes:

> I think that there are three categories of indigenous people: there is a leadership that is very political, has clear ideas, and a certain ambition for power. Then, I would say that there is a middle stratum of indigenous intellectuals: those who study, the teachers, the catechists. . . . And then, there is the mass of people who are not too conscious, but who know how to follow their leaders. Originally, the Church worked with the leaders of the indigenous people. Now we think that our work must be with the intermediate stratum and the intermediate space which is education, and with the poorest among them, so that we can remind the intellectuals and the political leaders that they should not forget [the people]. (Interview with author, December 2001)

Through thirty years of sustained work, the Salesians had a positive influence in the highlands of Cotopaxi. Although the process has not been without tensions and contradictions, the Salesians have successfully promoted indigenous organization and pride by tackling a series of quite concrete problems ranging from bilingual education, outdated agricultural techniques, and the development of infrastructure. From this point of view, the Salesians were key allies in the construction of the multicultural state.

Missionaries and Social Movements under Correa's Nationalist-Extractivism

When Rafael Correa was elected president in 2006, the Salesians enjoyed privileged access to his government. He often sought advice from the missionaries he knew better and renewed state–mission agreements (J. Manangón, interview July 30, 2015). On June 12, 2009, the president issued Executive Decree 1780, which delegated the administration of education, health, development, and infrastructure in the Amazon to the Catholic missions with the economic and political support of the state. The decree was received coldly by part of the Left, which argued that it was important to preserve the secular character that the Ecuadorian state had enjoyed since the Liberal Revolution of 1895. A similar debate had taken place two years earlier in the 2007–2008 Constituent Assembly, when the deputies discussed whether to include references to God in the preamble to the 2008 constitution. As a compromise, the name of God was invoked, but it was accompanied by the recognition of the diverse forms of religiosity existing in the country (Constitución 2008, Preámbulo, 23).

During the first two years of Correa's government, the indigenous movement that the Salesians had nurtured supported the regime. However, starting in January 2009, CONAIE protested the new mining and water laws. After that, Bosco Wisum, the Shuar teacher, died in confrontations between demonstrators and the police. The Shuar were protesting the laws as well as the ongoing changes to the intercultural bilingual system of education. Some Shuar were named "Bosco" in recognition of Don Bosco, the founder of the Salesian Order. Wisum was raised and educated in the Salesian Mission of Sevilla Don Bosco. As noted earlier in this book, the government blamed Shuar leaders for Bosco's death, and temporarily closed the federation's radio station, Radio la Voz de Arutam, with the argument that it had sparked the violence. The Salesian Order had created the radio station and put it at the service of the Shuar Federation.

As the government clashed with the indigenous organizations, the missionaries faced a sharp contradiction: on the one hand, they were close to the government, which they saw as progressive. Missionaries perceived the conjuncture as a unique opportunity to gain influence over the state and further their social and religious agenda. On the other hand, some priests working on the ground sided with the social movements against the state and the extractive industries it promoted. The missionaries also resisted the retrenchment of the previous multicultural gains that they had helped to achieve. Moreover, the priests disagreed with the abolition of the autonomy of intercultural bilingual education, with the consolidation of the community schools (see chapter 4), and with the closure of the iconic pedagogical institutes, which the progressive Catholic Church had also created in the 1980s. When the government punished the indigenous movement for its anti-extraction stance, it also affected the multicultural institutions that the missionaries had built and that the organizations had appropriated, such as the pedagogical institutes and the radio station. The religious order was divided: the hierarchies and some priests on the ground took different political positions. However, the vow of obedience and the effective use of ecclesiastical hierarchies were able to silence the voices of the most radical priests. There was also government vigilance and repression of religious activists. I saw a spreadsheet created by the Ministry of Politics of the Correa regime in which particular individuals within the Catholic Church were listed as possible threats to the country's security and as political agitators. We now turn to the ways that some individual missionaries understood the nationalist-extractivist conjuncture.

I attended a meeting of the Shuar Federation in January 2010, a year after the start of hostilities between CONAIE and the government. The discussions at the meeting revealed much confusion and internal division, as many still understood Correa as a progressive candidate sympathetic to the social movements, but others argued that the government's budget depended on natural resource extraction to the detriment of indigenous rights and livelihoods. The regime had just closed Radio Arutam.

The annual meeting of the federation was noteworthy. More than three hundred delegates from thirty-six associations of Shuar centers located throughout the southern Ecuadorian Amazon as well as strategic allies from environmentalist NGOs, the Catholic Church, and the military attended. Meanwhile, the regime had asked another Shuar leader working for the Ministry of Culture to organize a concurrent counterevent. It was a concert by the protest singer and songwriter Juan Fernando Velasco, the son of a late leftist intellectual known as Fernando (el Conejo) Velasco and Rosa María Torres, a Pachakutik-affiliated former minister of education. The choice was meant to confuse and divide the social movement.

The bishop of Méndez and Gualaquiza was also invited to the Shuar Federation's meeting, but excused himself and sent Ernesto Ankuash, a Shuar priest, to represent him. Marcelino Chumpí, the governor of the province and leader of Pachakutik, opened the meeting by criticizing Correa's orders to close Radio Arutam and arguing that the station had taught the Shuar how to read and write. Chumpí requested the Shuar Federation should be consulted regarding any mining or other resource extraction project. He then explained that he had been accused of financing the Shuar uprisings because the provincial government had funded projects to strengthen Shuar organizations. Nevertheless, he promised to continue supporting the associations. Chumpí ended by stating that the Shuar were not at war to cut off heads (a reference to the famous *tsantsas* or shrunken heads), but to defend their rights (field notes, January 2010).

After the governor, Gloria Chicaiza, a representative of the environmentalist NGO Acción Ecológica, gave a speech. She called Morona Santiago "the heart of the resistance that questions an exploitative economic model." She connected the closure of radio Arutam with the start of a Canadian–Chinese open-pit mining project in the province's Condor (also called Copper) Mountain Range. After Chicaiza's speech, it was the turn of Paco Moncayo, a social democrat army general who recruited the Shuar in the war against Peru in the 1980s. Moncayo stated that the revolution should not be the work of a messiah (in reference to Correa), but should be fought from below by the common people. Pepe Acacho, the president of the Shuar Federation, then stated that some Shuar wanted to sell themselves to the mining and oil companies and to the government, but that others, supported by the progressive Catholic Church, still resisted.

The following day, after the lengthy opening ceremonies, the business of the meeting started. The delegates elected assembly authorities, who are selected every three years, and discussed land conflicts among the Shuar, with colonists, and with the Salesian Mission, as well as local quarrels that were to be resolved through customary justice. The authorities of the Shuar Federation gave a report of activities and financial operations. Some delegates protested and requested clarification of particular expenses. After that, the elected authorities, governor Chumpí and the Pachakutik congresswoman Diana Atamaint, explained what they had achieved for the Shuar in the past year. The assembly then debated the current situation of intercultural bilingual education.

Following this discussion, the delegates discussed the possibility of creating a Shuar territory or *circunscripción territorial* according to the regulations established in the 2008 constitution. Finally, the assembly analyzed the project Socio Bosque (Partners for the Forest), a plan that paid the communities not to use the rainforest, but to preserve it. The initiative was funded by the European Union, but the Correa regime disbursed the money and presented the initiative as a government project.

The government had made an agreement with the association Pueblo Shuar Arutam to start Socio Bosque in Morona Santiago. Some Shuar stated that the plan was problematic because it could mean surrendering their territory to the state. There was some confusion among the delegates between Socio Bosque and the creation of an indigenous territory. The assembly concluded that it needed to learn more about the initiative before accepting it. They also agreed that individual associations like Pueblo Shuar Arutam were not authorized to compromise any territories under the jurisdiction of the Shuar Federation. Some proposed that the federation itself conduct the agreements with the Ministry of the Environment and manage the Socio Bosque plan for all the Shuar people. The delegates voted and agreed to work with the government, but strategically. However, after reaching this decision, someone proposed that the Shuar should work directly with the European Union, which funds Socio Bosque, instead of accepting the government as an intermediary. The delegate noted that the government was probably keeping most of the money.

The delegates ended the meeting with several sweeping resolutions, including: not to allow mining, oil, or timber extraction by national or international companies in Shuar territory; to make all agreements directly with FICSH and not with the smaller associations; to request signatures to appeal the closure of Radio Arutam; and to punish the Shuar associations that were signing independent agreements with the mining companies or with the government. It was a moment of confusion. The delegates feared that the government and the transnational companies might divide the Shuar organization.

As the federation wrapped up its business, Father Juan de la Cruz Rivadeneira, a Salesian missionary, asked everyone to stand and sing a hymn. The Shuar, respectfully, and now in complete silence, followed the priest's directions. Rivadeneira congratulated the Shuar for taking good care of Mother Nature. He then warned the delegates that they were confronting a great danger: the government was planning to open their whole territory to the oil and mining companies. He also cautioned that Socio Bosque was a potentially dangerous initiative because the government and the international community might appropriate Shuar territory and resources for just a handful of money. He asked the Shuar to continue their struggle to provide air and water to the whole world. Father Rivadeneira then argued that the Catholic Church had a strong commitment to the Shuar people. He asked the Shuar to make the bishops and the catechists well understand that they must join the fight to defend Mother Earth. Finally, Rivadeneira asked everyone to sing a special song in honor of Don Bosco, the founder of the Salesian Order. In the lyrics, the saint gave the Shuar people strength to battle the mining and oil companies.

In a private conversation with the me, Father Rivadeneira noted that he was trying to convince the bishops to draft a declaration supporting the Shuar and censoring the Correa government. He thought the alliance of the missionaries with Correa was a trap because it separated the religious order from the indigenous people. Years later, on March 5, 2015, Father Rivadeneira was invited to speak at the United Nations headquarters in New York City in an event celebrating the global work and influence of the Salesian Order. He explained the impact of the extractive industries on the lives, health, and culture of the Shuar and complained about the diversion of great quantities of water for industrial use.

The meeting of the Shuar Federation illustrates the confusion and divisions taking place in the indigenous organizations at the beginning of the Correa decade, the attempts of the government and the extractive industries to divide the organizations, and the ambivalent role played by the Catholic Church in this conflict. The bishop was unable to support the federation by attending the meeting personally. The priest working on the ground with the Shuar supported the indigenous organization against the government and the extractive industries and tried to convince the hierarchy of the Church to do as much. However, he did so indirectly, by asking the Shuar to address Catholic hierarchies.

In his doctoral dissertation, José Juncosa (2017), a lay Salesian, long-time editor of Abya Yala publishing, and vice president of the Polytechnic Salesian University in Quito, reflects on the challenges in the relationship between the religious order and the Shuar during the Correa decade. Juncosa focuses on Salesian efforts to "civilize," educate, and evangelize the

Shuar, on the interactions between Salesian and Shuar worldviews, and on how the Shuar were able to bend missionary efforts to their own purposes. According to Juncosa, Shuar wisdom holds that "in order to prevail, it is necessary to appropriate the opponent's tools" (Juncosa 2017, 19).

Juncosa argues that the relationship between the Shuar and the Salesian Mission is experiencing an impasse and has even ended in the past decade: the Shuar have become increasingly autonomous and have circumscribed the work of the mission only to evangelization. The links between the Salesians and the Shuar Federation have been weakened. Previously, the Salesians were advisers to the federation, particularly in educational matters. Today the Ecuadorian state has displaced the mission. The reinforcement of the state during the Correa decade rendered both the missions and the indigenous organizations irrelevant for the management of education, which was centralized in the executive, represented by the Ministry of Education (see chapter 4). Rejecting the government's offer to keep their pedagogical institute in Bomboiza (southern Amazon) operating as a branch of the National University of Education, the Salesians instead decided to close it.

After decades working with the Shuar, Juncosa (2017) claims to have learned two important lessons: First, the Shuar perceive nature as a spiritual realm of relationships where all beings coexist, and where even those creatures that could be harmful to the Shuar are conceived of as relatives. In contrast, Juncosa shows that the Salesians historically understood the Amazon as an inert and empty space full of natural resources ready to be exploited by men. For example, in 1926 Father Crespi noted: "We can affirm that in the current state of geological studies we have not yet found in our Oriente a true gold mine like the ones in Zaruma and Peru. However, that does not mean it cannot be found. I insist that oriental geology is still in its beginnings. When the hand of man penetrates the jungles, practices beneficial deforestation, and reaches the unexplored valleys, it is quite possible that something will be found that will enrich the nation. Another product that huge companies are avidly seeking is oil" (Crespi 1926, cited in Juncosa 2017, 232–233). Juncosa claims that the Salesians perceived the Shuar, as they lived traditionally, as an obstacle to the exploitation of these resources. The process of sedentarization and pacification undertaken by the order was a necessary step to render the Amazon exploitable to the national society.

Later, the Salesian Order, and the Catholic Church more generally, have transitioned from perceiving nature as a nonspiritual, inert realm to be exploited by man to following the environmental theology practiced by Father Juan de la Cruz Rivadeneira and discussed by Pope Francis in his encyclical letter "Laudato Si" (Pope Francis 2015). In my conversations with Father Rivadeneira in 2010, he compared the rainforest to the mantle of the Virgin Mary because it was able to protect fugitive Shuar who were escaping police persecution and mining company harassment. In this way, Rivadeneira transformed the rainforest into a domain of Christian spirituality.

A second teaching grasped by Juncosa from Shuar worldviews is that the group typically learns through the transmission of myths from the elders to the youth. The myths are passed on in specific conjunctures and are meant to be practical and practiced. These myths prepare individuals to be alert and ready for what is to come in the real world. Missionary education, on the contrary, relied on rote learning. Teachings were decontextualized and not immediately useful or applicable to the students' daily life. Juncosa suggests that the missionaries must study Shuar ways of teaching and learning because they are more effective and meaningful.

José Manangón (interviewed in chapter 4) was the salesian in charge of the mission in Zumbahua when Rafael Correa volunteered there. As a result, he became close to the man who would later become president. After many years as a Salesian missionary, Manangón left the order and became a regular priest in the indigenous pastoral of the Latacunga dioceses. Father Manangón is of Kichwa descent and originally from the northern highland province of Cayambe, where the Salesians also had a mission. Manangón has been highly influential in the development of intercultural bilingual education in the central highlands and is known for his commitment to raising indigenous consciousness as well as his anticapitalist and antineoliberal views (Martínez Novo 2004).

When I interviewed Manangón on July 30, 2015, the priest was an informal adviser to President Correa. He had direct access to the mandatory. At the time, the priest visited the Presidential Palace regularly, every three months or so. However, when the missionary started to disagree with the regime's direction and its development policies, Correa pretended to continue listening, but then delegated Manangón to low-level government officials who did not implement the priest's suggestions.

Manangón complained that Correa disregarded previous educational experience to start anew. For instance, SERBISH, the radio system of intercultural bilingual education founded by the Salesians in the southern Amazon, was closed. The System of Indigenous Schools of the Cotopaxi Province (SEIC) that Father Manangón led at the time, also lost its accreditation. Despite this, SEIC continued operating informally. Manangón objected that those making the decisions regarding education were not educators but economists who did not know the subject well. In addition, government officials ignored the history of intercultural education as well as the geography of the rural areas. The priest noted that Correa had subordinated the educational model to the ideas of production and productivity: the system was now aimed at training people in specific skills that are useful to business. The missionary regretted the closure of the pedagogical institutes created by the missionaries to educate intercultural teachers. The government was willing to reopen them, but only if they followed the regime's directions. For instance, the government closed Jatari Unancha, the pedagogical institute located in Zumbahua and founded by the mission. Jatari Unancha had educated leaders of the indigenous movement as well as Pachakutik-affiliated politicians. The government then allowed the educational facility to reopen, but downgraded it to a technical institute that trained workers for industry. Manangón also regretted the closure of the community schools and their consolidation in millennium schools (see chapter 4). According to the priest, the reason for consolidation was not educational quality as the government claimed, but economic savings. The priest also worried that the conservative branches of the Catholic Church, such as the Opus Dei, were becoming closer to Correa's government and thus important institutional actors. While the Opus Dei became increasingly influential through high government officials affiliated with the group, liberation theology priests humbly and silently continued working with the grassroots. As the regime closed the institutions founded by the missionaries in collaboration with the indigenous organizations, Manangón proposed resisting and working from the margins of the state as an alternative. This was not new to him, as he had already operated similarly in the 1970s.

Mission-Led and Indigenous Racial Projects

These examples of the work of the Salesians in different regions and with different native groups show that the racial project of the Catholic Church has not been homogeneous in time or space. From a historical perspective, the Salesians defended assimilation from the nineteenth century until the mid-twentieth century as well as their own understanding of cultural preservation after Vatican Council II. They also transitioned from seeing nature as an inert realm to be exploited by man, to being inspired by indigenous relational and spiritual understandings of the forest. In the early twentieth century, the missionaries, with the state or, better, for the state, were central actors of assimilationist policies in Ecuador and elsewhere. At a later historical moment, they became promoters of the multicultural agenda.

From a geographical point of view, the work of the order varied depending on the regions, the peoples, and the challenges that it encountered. It has been less problematic to work on cultural preservation with a Kichwa peasant group whose customs are purportedly based on solidarity, reciprocity, and love for mother earth, than with a group suffering from internecine warfare and violence such as the Shuar. However, in the Catholic Church's peculiar understanding of multiculturalism both cultures needed to be purified of their negative, non-Christian traits. This means that the cultural relativism of the Church has limits set by the tensions between the search for intercultural dialogue and a universal worldview. Moreover, because cultures need to be purified, the indigenous peoples from whom these cultural traits emerge no longer recognize them. For this reason, indigenous groups both in the Amazon and the highlands perceive cultural preservation as a project imposed from outside and alien to them. Native peoples may also reject an inculturation agenda for other reasons: they are victims of the kind of internalized prejudice that is a consequence of colonization.

Although the agendas of the Salesians and indigenous groups diverge in the ways outlined above, they coincide in their approach to modernization. For the religious order, cultural preservation is not opposed to the search for modernity and progress. In fact, the Salesians as an order specialize in offering technical training to popular groups, and are thus happy to learn and teach the newest technologies and methods. Both the Church and indigenous peoples are often perceived as the opposite of modernity, but the two groups have a surprising ability to bring themselves up to date.

The Salesians and indigenous people coincide in yet another aspect: they do not perceive the reinforcement of ethnic pride and identity politics as in opposition to integration into and love for the nation. Indigenous people are less worried about assimilation than about exclusion from citizenship. The idea that they reject the nation-state seems to originate in elite prejudices and their desire to justify the exclusion of ethnic minorities. For example, in all intercultural bilingual schools controlled by the indigenous organizations and the Church, native children are proud to honor the national flag and sing the national anthem both in their native language and Spanish. In contrast to what mestizo commentators and scholars often assume, indigenous people are far from being suspicious of or even indifferent to the nation-state.

Another aspect emerging from this discussion is the influence of the Catholic Church, and the Salesians in particular, on the political organization of the indigenous movement. The Shuar with the collaboration of the Salesians created the Shuar Federation in 1964 to protect this indigenous group from colonization and to prevent its disappearance. The order was also central to the creation of the Indigenous and Peasant Movement of Cotopaxi. By fighting for the implementation of the agrarian reform and promoting intercultural bilingual education, the missionaries educated the leadership that gave birth to the most active branches of CONAIE.

During the Correa decade, the order has played a more ambivalent role. Through its work in intercultural bilingual education and political organizing, the Salesians influenced the promotion of the kind of antineoliberal ideology and politics that brought Correa to power in 2006. This explains the importance of indigenismo in Correa's original project. The president found it necessary to ground his regime in this radical history and traditions. However, as Correa's government distanced itself from the social movements, missionaries doing grassroots activism were key to checking the power of the executive. To curb this resistance, the regime manipulated and weakened the Catholic Church in the same way that it manipulated and weakened other actors of civil society, by creating confusion and divisions in their midst. When Correa dismantled the gains of the multicultural period, he also dismantled the achievements of the long-term efforts of the Salesians. However, as Correa circumscribed indigenous rights and took apart the multicultural state, the Salesians became formidable critics of the undoing of multiculturalism.

To sum up, how should we characterize the racial project of inculturation theology during the neoliberal and national-extractivist conjunctures? The chapter has shown that this is a utopian project that goes beyond the superficial or symbolic politics of identity typical of neoliberalism. The Salesians did try to combine recognition with redistribution from the start (Fraser 1996). Furthermore, they thought that recognition was necessary to achieve redistribution. Inculturation and environmental theology also went hand in hand with trying to understand and reinforce native worldviews while also caring for the material aspects of people's lives. Similarly, during nationalist-extractivism missionaries working with indigenous organizations were not convinced that the fight to remediate poverty justified extractivism and the sacrifice of those living in the areas of extraction. The order did not accept that fighting poverty and keeping the so-called Citizens' Revolution required dismantling the indigenous organizations, intercultural education, and other gains of the previous multicultural period. Neither neoliberalism nor nationalist-extractivism were able to co-opt this multicultural and redistributive project.

CHAPTER 7

VENTRILOQUISM, RACISM, AND THE POLITICS OF DECOLONIAL SCHOLARSHIP

This chapter further examines the racial formation that emerged under Correa's rule. Although the living standards of the indigenous majority did not improve substantially during the multicultural neoliberal period, indigenous leaders, intellectuals, and organizations did achieve greater levels of participation and agency in their own affairs and those of the state. Under Correa, indigenous poverty persisted or increased (see chapter 3) and indigenous participation decreased, allowing the regime to develop a ventriloquist style: urban, middle-class, white, and mestizo government officials typically devised policies and spoke for indigenous people (see chapters 2 and 4). When these paternalist forms of representation failed because indigenous leaders and organizations challenged them, the regime resorted to crude racism and open repression. As the state's economic resources dwindled around 2014, and as the frontiers of natural resource extraction kept expanding over indigenous territories, open racism and violent repression became more common strategies. Despite a steep decline in indigenous rights and participation under Correa, some scholars continued praising the regime for its anticolonial achievements or, when praise became difficult, refrained from openly criticizing it. The praise or silence of prominent intellectuals were instrumental in consolidating a racial formation based on exclusion, stigmatization, and repression.

Ventriloquism is a strategy that allows some whites and mestizos to speak for indigenous people and permits other nonindigenous individuals to accept ventriloquist discourses at face value as if they had originated in the grassroots. Open racism takes place when authorities project negative stereotypes of indigenous leaders and organizations that they combine with racialized and gendered forms of repression. The example of ventriloquism that the chapter analyzes is the concept of Sumak Kawsay, Kichwa for Good Living. The examples of racism are taken from the repressive policies of the regime, particularly during the antigovernment demonstrations of 2015, as well as from presidential speeches.

Purportedly, Sumak Kawsay is an ancient Andean understanding of well-being (Quijano 2012). The concept, central to the 2008 Constitution of Ecuador and to several government development plans, condenses the regime's interpretations of—and relations to—indigeneity. Thus, Sumak Kawsay is an appropriate window to an understanding of the racial formation that took shape under Correa's regime. This chapter shows that Sumak Kawsay does not originate in the past or present of indigenous communities, but at the interface of development, indigenous intellectuals, environmentalism, and populist politics. The text examines the array of projects that fall under the umbrella of Sumak Kawsay and analyzes them as a form of ventriloquism, a discursive style that can be traced back to Latin America's colonial past. Similarly, the chapter notes that when Correa's government repressed indigenous leaders and organizations, the punishments resonated with humiliations typical of a past rooted in indigenous serfdom and the hacienda system.

The chapter also reflects on the role that decolonial theory—or the decolonial turn (Restrepo and Rojas 2010)—played in the racial formation of Correa's decade. "Decolonial turn" scholars are Latin Americans as well as some Latin Americanists interested in the relations between modernity and colonialism and in the meanings of those experiences to colonized groups (Restrepo and Rojas 2010). The group includes the authors Walter Mignolo, Arturo Escobar, Enrique Dussel, Aníbal Quijano, Edgardo Lander, Catherine Walsh, Agustín Lao Montes, among others. According to this intellectual current, the notion of coloniality originates in colonialism but also transcends it. Coloniality results from the naturalization of the geographical, racial, cultural, epistemic, and ontological hierarchies of colonialism. As a result, the identities, knowledge, experiences, and lifeways of those previously colonized are suppressed, silenced, or marginalized. The group proposes decoloniality as its privileged political project. According to the authors, decoloniality must move beyond decolonization: once political independence is achieved, the taken-for-granted racial and epistemological hierarchies originating in colonialism must also be subverted. Decolonial-turn authors understand indigenous and Afrodescendant peoples as the privileged agents of decolonial struggles, because these groups think and act based on the wounds of colonialism and the frontiers between what the decolonial group understands as Western and non-Western epistemologies.

Decolonial scholars were fascinated by the possibilities opened by the wave of progressive governments that were elected in Latin America in the decade of the 2000s (de la Cadena 2010; Escobar 2010; Mignolo 2006; Walsh 2009). They explained the turn to the Left as a result of the struggles of indigenous, Afrodescendant, and other social movements and claimed that the epistemologies of these groups had been able to break through mainstream politics. Enthusiasm led some of these scholars to become formal or informal advisers to these regimes, particularly in their initial constituent moments. The chapter shows that cultural studies scholars have called the Correa government decolonial even when the regime has increasingly used a colonial vocabulary and repertoire. Perhaps the colonial has been taken for the decolonial because ventriloquist concepts such as Sumak Kawsay have been interpreted as grassroots utterances. Moreover, some scholars may have taken ventriloquist stereotypes as Andean worldviews due to a lack of interest in discovering whether these ideas have ethnohistorical or ethnographic grounding. Finally, decolonial theorists, once they have taken some distance from the populist Left, have been insufficiently self-critical and reflective of their own complicity with the state's repressive project vis-à-vis indigenous communities.

Analyzing Subtle Discrimination

Although some scholars have called the policies of the Correa regime, and in particular the concept of Sumak Kawsay, decolonizing, I place Sumak Kawsay within the colonial and republican tradition that allows nonindigenous individuals to speak for and represent indigenous people, especially before state officials and courts. Andrés Guerrero (2010) has called this practice "ventriloquism." The practice originated in the colonial period when the population was legally divided between the republics of Spaniards and Indians. Indians were separated from Spaniards for the purpose of taxation, because only Indians paid taxes. To avoid abuses by those who collected tribute—and to protect what was left of the decimated indigenous population—the Spanish crown nominated special advocates for the indigenous population called *protectores de indios*, who represented these colonized groups. Protector representation was justified by the legal status of "miserable" assigned to the Indians. This status originated in sixteenth-century theological debates and was later codified in royal decrees and the Laws of the Indies.

After the independence of Gran Colombia in 1821, Simón Bolívar tried to abolish the Indian tribute, but he restored it again in 1828 to avoid bankruptcy and increase public revenues. The status of indigenous people was extremely ambiguous after independence. Indians were supposed to become citizens, but they were excluded from active citizenship. In order to vote and be elected, the newly formed republic required citizens to own a certain amount of property, to not be dependent on or work for others, to be literate in Spanish, and to have the status of *vecino*, conditions that indigenous people did not fulfill. The term "vecino" in particular was reserved for those classified as being of Spanish descent. In addition, the state continued assigning Indians the legal status "miserable." This status was explained as the result of "a history of oppression, social conditions of dependency, unintelligible language, biological degradation, the state of cultural development, and the psychological condition of being adult-children" (A. Guerrero 2010, 240). The miserable legal status meant that Indians were not allowed to exercise rights and were wards of the state. For these reasons, Indians continued to be protected by appointed advocates. The purpose of the *protectores* was to legally and politically represent the populations defined as miserable.

After the abolition of the Indian tribute in 1857, the legal figure of the protector was dropped, but the custom continued. Notaries public, local lawyers, and other local literati continued representing indigenous peoples before the legal system and the state. The "ventriloquism" of these advocates consisted in the translation of oral Kichwa into legal written Spanish that state officials could understand and recognize. In addition, "ventriloquists" helped indigenous petitioners strategize regarding which officials and institutions they would appeal to and how they would increase their chances of being heard.

In an influential chapter written after the 1990 indigenous uprising that paralyzed Ecuador and created awareness of the modern indigenous movement among urban mestizos, Andrés Guerrero (1993) declared that the phenomenon of ventriloquism was over. He saw indigenous leaders expressing their demands without the need of mestizo intermediaries. Other scholars after Guerrero have restated on numerous occasions that ventriloquism ended with the formation of the modern indigenous movement, which they perceive as nonmediated (e.g., Becker 2012b; Lucero 2008). I argue instead that the legacy of ventriloquism continues to be relevant to the contemporary experiences of Ecuador's indigenous peoples.

Based on his research on mestizo representation of indigenous traditional healers in the Mexican state of Chiapas, Pedro Pitarch (2007) argues that ventriloquism is also a discursive style. He notes that the ventriloquist effect is achieved through stylistic devices and themes that make the utterance seem to originate in indigenous communities in the eyes of urban mestizos and other outsiders. According to Pitarch, the ventriloquist effect is accomplished by mixing scattered words from indigenous language with Spanish. Another strategy is to combine these terms with new age and Marxist rhetoric. Pitarch sees ventriloquism as a Mexican phenomenon, arguing that the Mexican state has spoken for the indigenous population through its corporate organizations led by mestizos since the 1910 Revolution. However, the Mexican state seems to have replicated earlier and more widespread practices of colonial origin. In another article on the ventriloquism of Subcomandante Marcos and the Zapatista Army of National Liberation, Pitarch (2004) adds that one reason the ventriloquist message is so powerful is that it is very simple, repetitive, and full of commonplaces that different audiences can interpret as ancestral wisdom and appropriate at will. This also seems to explain the success of the Sumak Kawsay concept.

Analyzing ideologies of subtle discrimination such as ventriloquism is important to debunk paternalist forms of domination. Articles published in *Cultural Studies* (da Costa 2016; Mukherjee 2016) have worked toward this goal. Roopali Mukherjee (2016) discusses the history of color-blind ideologies in the United States. She argues that the idea of color-blindness first appeared in the 1970s to contain the antiracist movements of the 1960s.

Maintaining that the United States has already overcome racism, color-blind paradigms conceal white privilege and the connection between race and socioeconomic inequality. Alexandre E. da Costa (2016) examines the idea of racial democracy and its discriminatory effects in Brazil. The concept of racial democracy depicts Brazilian race relations as relatively harmonious and understands race as having minor importance in shaping identities or life outcomes. Black activists and scholars have criticized the concept because it denies racism and hinders activism.

Despite their differences, ventriloquism, color-blindness, and racial democracy strategies resonate with each other. Moreover, we could argue that color-blindness and racial democracy are ventriloquist concepts devised by the dominant groups to speak for—while denying the experiences of—communities of color. Subaltern groups feel pressured to accommodate to these apparently benign top-down constructs because they claim to question discrimination and pretend to include nonwhites. Although it is important to analyze these subtle forms of discrimination, it is also vital to discuss how paternalist discourses articulate with the reemergence of open racism. Whereas paternalism and racism have been two faces of the same coin, we are witnessing a shift from subtle to more crude expressions of discrimination.

State Ventriloquism under President Correa

Sumak Kawsay or Buen Vivir (Good Living) appear frequently in the 2008 Constitution of Ecuador as well as in national development plans. Within the constitution, Good Living figures more prominently in Title II, which spells out rights. Its second chapter is dedicated to the "Rights of Good Living," which include water, food, a healthy environment, culture, communication, education, housing, and a job. Title VII "On the Regime of Good Living" discusses equality, education, health, social security, housing, culture, science, ancestral knowledge, and human mobility (Constitución 2008). The 2007–2008 Constituent Assembly seems to have understood Sumak Kawsay as a subset of rights linked to the idea of substantive democracy, which goes beyond individual political and civil rights and emphasizes socioeconomic well-being. The articles that fall under the umbrella of Sumak Kawsay contain nothing particularly indigenous, except perhaps that these rights include the promotion of cultural diversity.

During Correa's presidency, the National Secretariat for Planning and Development (SENPLADES) was the institution that formulated national development plans and was one of the main advocates for the idea of Sumak Kawsay. SENPLADES demonstrated a problematic relation to indigeneity from its inception. When the agency presented its first National Development Plan 2007–2010 to the public (SENPLADES 2007), it did so at the Man's Chapel, a museum designed by the indigenista painter Oswaldo Guayasamín. As the actors of development, including elected indigenous officials, arrived at the chapel, a line of mestizo men and women disguised as the fourteen nationalities of Ecuador received them. Each "nationality" carried a banner spelling out a national development goal as defined by the urban middle-class government officials of SENPLADES. At the ceremony, the public servants delivered a lengthy PowerPoint presentation to the public. There was no time for dialogue between government representatives and the actors of development. There was time, however, to enjoy folkloric dances performed by mestizos in indigenous attire.

The dances impersonating the nationalities were performed by Ballet Jacchigua, a favorite of President Rafael Correa who granted this dance troupe the prestigious Espejo National Award in 2010. According to the ballet's website, the ensemble was founded in the 1990s and sponsored by Metropolitan Touring, a company owned by some of Quito's most aristocratic families. The official website of the ballet explains: "The name Jacchigua comes from 'jacchima,' a celebration that the *patrón* gave for his workers on the hacienda's patio. . . . There, *huasicamas* [those who served in the *patron's* house] and *huasipungueros* [hacienda workers who received a plot of land in usufruct in exchange for theirs and their family's labor] enjoyed a day of celebration with the *patrón* and his family" (Ballet Jacchigua website). Ballet Jacchigua is one among several neofolkloric performance troupes that emerged in the Andes in the second part of the twentieth century (Bigenho 2006; Roper 2019). These troupes were typically made up of mestizo performers who impersonated indigenous or Black individuals and their customs. Their stated goal was to recover and celebrate national traditions in the context of nationalist, revolutionary, or military regimes. Michelle Bigenho (2006) argues that these performances dignified indigeneity before urban nonindigenous audiences at a moment in which an indigenous person would not have been allowed in these spaces. Danielle Roper (2019) disagrees arguing that these performances can be read as fantasies of power that reenact the subjection of colonized people. Another way to look at these performances is as a form of ventriloquism in which whites and mestizos impersonate colonized populations. The intention of the urban, upper middle-class mestizo authorities of the Correa government to speak for, or perhaps through, the indigenous nationalities was quite apparent at this inaugural event.

Mestizos' impersonation of indigeneity became more widespread during Correa's presidency. For instance, when Pope Francis visited Ecuador in July 2015, he was not allowed to meet with representatives of the Confederation of Indigenous Nationalities of Ecuador (CONAIE), the largest indigenous organization. Rather, the government surrounded the Pontiff with mestizos in indigenous attire. Indigenous people from the communities that the costumes referred to denounced the impostors on social networks. In contrast, a supporter of Correa argued in social media that the president had done much for the country's indigenous peoples. As a proof, he posted a picture of the mestiza president of the National Assembly, Gabriela Rivadeneira, dressed as a stylized indigenous woman. Rivadeneira is from Ibarra, a predominantly mestizo city surrounded by indigenous and afrodescendent communities located in the northern highlands.

This understanding of diversity shows that the regime wished to associate with indigeneity as a concept or an aesthetic, but not as an identity embodied in real people, and even less as one embraced by autonomously organized and active citizens. This attitude is not new but grounded in the kind of indigenismo that existed before the indigenous uprising of 1990, when for the first time mestizos accepted indigenous individuals as political interlocutors.

Whites and mestizos posing as Indians have a long history in the Andes. Thomas Abercrombie (2001) has noted that colonizing cultures were also shaped by those they dominated. For non-Indians, the relationship with Indians was fundamental to their own identity, as both Indians and non-Indians were part of a single colonial situation. Urban whites and mestizos enjoyed playing Indian and appropriated an Indian ancestry for themselves and their nationalist projects. On the other hand, indigeneity worked in contrast to their white and mestizo "civilized" selves. For Abercrombie (2001) the Indian within often signals a nationalism in search of a legitimating identity.

Deborah Poole (1992) has noted that the Cuzco indigenistas of Peru cross-dressed as Indians, among other costumes, to demonstrate that their identities were fluid and that indigeneity was tied to the Andean landscape rather than to phenotype or ancestry. Early twentieth-century Cuzco indigenistas also cross-dressed as Indians to strengthen Cuzco's regional identity as the former capital of the Inca Empire, in contrast to Lima's Eurocentric cosmopolitanism. Paradoxically, Cuzco's landowners came to embody their own peons for Peruvian national audiences.

The authors cited above agree that Andean elites embodied indigeneity for the sake of legitimating their national and regional projects, as indigeneity was an important part of their own identity as colonizers. Correa's government also used mestizos in indigenous garb to legitimize his particular brand of "progressive" nationalism. However, masquerading as another does a great deal of symbolic violence to colonized populations. Besides domesticating what mestizos see as the dangerous features of indigeneity to show that Indians can be incorporated into the nation (Postero 2017), the culture and aesthetics of indigeneity are appropriated for the project of the dominant, indigenous individuals are excluded and silenced, and their messages are stylized to make them more palatable to white-mestizo audiences or, even worse, they are caricatured for elite entertainment. As Roper (2019) has argued, Latin American cross-racial impersonations by whites and mestizos resonate with "blackface" in the United States, a performance in which whites painted their faces black and donned exaggerated phenotypical features to perform demeaning renderings of African American lifestyle and culture. Dressing mestizos as indigenous people for the Pope might have been a strategy to control the message of this sector of the population and to render indigenous citizens docile and part of the background while also celebrating the national folklore. When the mestizo president of the National Assembly cross-dressed as an indigenous woman as the executive (of her political party) militarized communities and evicted *comuneros*, it could be interpreted as hypocritical. On the other hand, Gabriela Rivadeneira is from Imbabura, a province inhabited by the well-known Otavaleños who have been historically perceived as model Indians. Her practice of cross-dressing resonates with that of the Cuzco indigenistas and can be interpreted as a way of emphasizing her regional roots. Provincial whites and mestizos have been important constituencies in Correa's political movement (see chapter 5). Therefore, this regional aesthetics may have permeated the regime.

In Ecuador, where the indigenous nationalities and peoples had a strong and highly organized social movement and had been actors in politics since at least the 1990 uprising, the return of the masquerading mestizo signals a shift in racial formation, from one in which indigenous people were agents to one in which they are excluded from the public sphere and represented by others.

Returning to SENPLADES's policies, the second National Plan for Good Living 2009–2013 written under the leadership of René Ramírez, an economist and longtime second in command of Correa's government, provides an eclectic understanding of Sumak Kawsay (SENPLADES 2009). The plan vaguely alludes to the concept's indigenous origins, but the theories of Amartya Sen, winner of the Nobel Prize in Economic Sciences, environmentalists, and postdevelopment authors inform the plan (Walsh 2010; Zamosc 2013). Following Sen, the plan defines Good Living (Buen Vivir) as an increase in human capabilities and opportunities.

In another publication, René Ramírez (2010) reflects on the new social pact that the 2008 constitution entails. The pact is not only between the members of a community, but between them and the natural environment. The document foresees a new mode of accumulation in Ecuador. The strategy so far has been to export raw materials and agricultural products. Ramírez envisions a sustainable future based on biodiversity, Ecuador's comparative advantage. The country must take advantage of its biodiversity by developing ecotourism, organic agriculture, biotechnology, and bioresearch. In prioritizing biotechnology, Ramírez finds inspiration in the recent development strategies of Southeast Asian countries (Ong 2006). Despite Ramírez's goals, Ecuador has remained highly dependent on the export of hydrocarbons and agroindustrial products (Acosta 2016). Ramírez thought that a transitional reliance on hydrocarbons would provide the needed foundation to invest in a more diversified future. However, the country never reached during Correa's presidency the second phase of his project.

Ramírez was not the first to invoke Sumak Kawsay within Correa's political circles. The Amazonian Kichwa intellectual Carlos Viteri is regarded as the first to articulate the concept in Ecuador. He did so in his thesis for Universidad Politécnica Salesiana, from which he graduated with a degree in applied anthropology in 2003. Viteri worked for the Inter-American Development Bank in Washington, DC, from 2002 to 2009, and has been a member of Correa's political party, Alizanza País, since 2009. As a representative of Alianza País, Viteri was elected to the National Assembly as a congressman in 2013.. Sumak Kawsay as defined by Viteri (2002) emphasizes solidarity, reciprocity, the *minga* or collective work party, and the correct management of biodiversity.

The environmental economist and ex-president of the 2007–2008 Constituent Assembly Alberto Acosta picked up the concept of Sumak Kawsay from Viteri and included it in the text of the 2008 constitution. Acosta and the environmental activist Esperanza Martínez (Acosta and Martínez 2009) define Sumak Kawsay as an umbrella term for some of their own utopian ideas with varying connections to indigeneity. These projects included the rejection of aggressive resource extraction, a proposal for the promotion of universal citizenship to protect Ecuadorian migrants, and a plan for cooperative economic strategies based on solidarity and reciprocity. In a more recent article, Acosta (2015) acknowledges that Buen Vivir encompasses criticisms of development by Andean and Amazonian peoples, but not only by them. Sumak Kawsay also includes the contributions of environmentalists and postdevelopment theorists. He redefines the term as a search for alternatives grounded in popular struggles. Acosta, who left Correa's government after working on the draft of the 2008 constitution, argues that the governments of Ecuador and Bolivia have usurped and misused the concept of Sumak Kawsay.

Eduardo Gudynas and Catherine Walsh, scholars who informally advised Acosta in the 2008 Constituent Assembly, have also written extensively about Sumak Kawsay. Catherine Walsh (2009) cites the book *Filosofía Andina* (Andean Philosophy) by the Swiss theologian and philosopher Josef Estermann (1998) to flesh out the idea. However, the term as such does not appear in Estermann's influential book. Despite this, Estermann (2012) later appropriated the term "Sumak Kawsay" and has argued that the concept is both ancestral and Andean. Estermann's 1998 book is the one that Luis Cuji (2011) found to be very influential in the definition of interculturalism in indigenous higher education (see chapter 4).

For Walsh (2009) Sumak Kawsay is an important tool for the implementation of interculturalism. When colonizers arrived in the Americas, indigenous people were forbidden to worship nature, an activity that was then labeled idolatry. Therefore, changing our relation to nature is an act of decoloniality. Walsh praises Sumak Kawsay for not restricting its objectives to economic development but focusing on the spiritual and the epistemic. She finds it significant that the Constitution of Ecuador places ancestral knowledge on an equal footing with scientific and technological endeavors.

According to the author, ancestral knowledge is marked by the Kichwa idea of *ñaupa*, which she defines as the past that is able to shape the future. Walsh's use of "ancestral" and her emphasis on *ñaupa* seems to place indigenous cultures in the past in a way that resonates with classical indigenista representations.

Eduardo Gudynas (2011) shares a vague understanding of Buen Vivir as a platform for critical views of development. He agrees that Buen Vivir moves beyond the economic focus of traditional development to prioritize cultural, aesthetic, and spiritual values. With Buen Vivir, nature becomes a subject and human beings are not the only source of value. For Gudynas, the term is not only "postcapitalist" but also "postsocialist" because it rejects the eurocentrism in both models. To the social equality goals of socialism, Sumak Kawsay adds the importance of non-Western ontologies and the biocentric turn. Gudynas states that the concept is based on a mixture of older indigenous values, contemporary Andean peoples' reaction to development, the postdevelopment and decolonial ideas of the decolonial intellectuals Arturo Escobar and Walter Mignolo, and other approaches such as degrowth theories.

Another government institution promoting Buen Vivir was the secretariat of the same name led by Freddy Ehlers, a journalist and television producer. This secretariat was created by President Correa in June 2013, had the rank of a ministry, employed approximately thirty government officials, and had a reported budget of US$12 million for four years (Neira 2015). The secretariat understood Buen Vivir as "a sustainable model of harmonious life that would allow for the conditions that make possible the happiness of all" (Secretaría del Buen Vivir 2015, 3). It also argued that the concept was created by ancestral peoples such as the Kichwas, Aymaras, Guaraní, Tzeltales, Kunas, and Miskitos. In the midst of a civilizational and climate change crisis, the secretariat understood Buen Vivir as an ideology that directs us to live in harmony with nature and was spelled out in the form of the Rights of Nature in the 2008 Constitution of Ecuador. An official publication of this ministry connected Buen Vivir with the debate on the lack of correlation between development and happiness that was launched in the 1970s by a group of Economic Commission for Latin America (CEPAL) economists (Secretaría del Buen Vivir 2015). The sources of the secretariat were rather eclectic: besides citing CEPAL, it used concepts of positive psychology taken from Harvard University's and the University of

California–Berkeley's online classes. Another important source was Jigme Singye Wangchuck (1972–2006), the king of Bhutan who has advocated for the use of a Gross National Happiness Index rather than the gross domestic product to measure the well-being of the population in the context of his authoritarian regime.

In another section of the secretariat's official publications, details were provided regarding the more concrete activities of this government institution: it produced television programs about nature and happiness. It also organized international workshops to promote the concept of Buen Vivir. In addition, it was interested in promoting a conscious way of life based on Zen meditation and eating organic food. It is important to note that Minister Freddy Ehlers was an enthusiastic practitioner of Buddhism. The secretariat counted among its main achievements that more people learned about Buen Vivir through television shows. The institution also promoted the creation of quantitative indicators of Buen Vivir in a meeting about how to measure happiness that took place in the kingdom of Bhutan. Finally, Ehlers promoted meditation breaks in Ecuadorian schools, as well as leisure and sport breaks for government officials (Constante 2014).

Unsurprisingly, the Secretariat of Buen Vivir was the target of multiple jokes that called Correa's inner circle "the circle of Good Living," making reference to widespread accusations of corruption (Neira 2015). Others mocked the name of the secretariat changing it to "Buen Beber" (Good Drinking). In addition, journalists claimed that the citizenry was uncomfortable with the use of public funds for purposes of propaganda in a country with many unsatisfied needs (Neira 2015). One of the first things that the Lenín Moreno government did after coming to power in 2017, was to eliminate the Secretariat of Buen Vivir by an executive decree published on May 3, 2017, in an effort to cut the budget and fight corruption (Radio Huancavilca 2017).

To sum up, there seem to be two complementary understandings of Sumak Kawsay in Correa's regime: On the one hand, Sumak Kawsay is an umbrella term for an array of environmentalist, postdevelopment, and antineoliberal projects. On the other, it is a new age version of indigeneity with an emphasis on spirituality, communitarianism, and harmony with nature. Indigeneity helps legitimize and provides coherence and a catchy term for this array of eclectic projects. Occasionally, scholars stretch the concept of Sumak Kawsay to include other non-Western critiques of development and capitalist modernity by indigenous groups beyond the Quechua and Aymara, the African diaspora, and other non-Western cultures (Acosta 2015; Gudynas 2011; Walsh 2009). As Pitarch (2007) argued, particular stylistic devices make it credible to urban mestizo and international audiences that Sumak Kawsay originates in indigenous communities: the (mis)use of Kichwa and Aymara terms and the articulation of well-known stereotypes of indigeneity with environmentalist and leftist rhetoric.

Sumak Kawsay as a Form of Ventriloquism

Not surprisingly, Sumak Kawsay as a concept cannot be found in ethnohistorical or ethnographic records. According to Víctor Bretón (2014) Sumak Kawsay or Suma Qamaña do not appear, except as separate words, in the ancient dictionaries of the Quechua or Aymara languages, in colonial chronicles, or in academic texts on Andean culture or philosophy before roughly 2000. When I asked a number of prominent Andeanists, they asserted that they have only heard about the concept recently. Scholars writing about Sumak Kawsay and Suma Qamaña commonly cite two sources for Ecuador and Bolivia as the first to articulate the idea: Carlos Viteri (2002) and the Aymara Bolivian intellectual Simón Yampara (Yampara, Choque, and Torres 2001).

Leon Zamosc (2013) places the origins of the Sumak Kawsay concept in Ecuador in the early 1990s as an Amazonian instead of an Andean idea. The Organization of Indigenous Peoples of Pastaza (Organización de Pueblos Indígenas de Pastaza) organized a march to Quito in 1992 and achieved the recognition of indigenous jurisdiction over a large tract of Amazonian land. Zamosc argues that the Viteris, a prominent family of Kichwa leaders of which Carlos Viteri is a member, created the concept to negotiate funds with European nongovernmental organizations. The original 1990s concept resonated with traditional understandings of development. Zamosc states that the concept had little or no impact until Alberto Acosta rescued it. Acosta claims that he first heard about Sumak Kawsay in an op-ed piece by Carlos Viteri in *Diario Hoy*, a Quito newspaper. Zamosc (2013) adds that the concept was not in CONAIE's original proposals to the 2007–2008 Constituent Assembly, but the organization hurriedly adopted Sumak Kawsay after Alianza País first launched the idea.

Other indigenous activists seem to have appropriated Sumak Kawsay after it was included in the constitution. For example, Luis Macas, a historic leader and two times president of CONAIE, seems to struggle with the concept in a text first published in 2010. He writes: "What is the essence and origin of Sumak Kawsay? We depart from society's imaginary. It is believed that this indigenous phrase means development. For this reason it was incorporated into the Republic's Constitution, and thanks to the fact that it became a constitutional mandate, this indigenous phrase has acquired validity and strength" (2014, 183). He continues, stating that the term is based on millenary indigenous values such as community, connection to nature or *pachamama*, reciprocity, relationality, and complementarity, as well as more contemporary indigenous projects such as plurinationality. Other indigenous leaders and organizations have appropriated the term to argue that the government is not living up to the concept. In this way, some decolonial- and ontological-turn ideas have made it first into Ecuadorian policy and then into social movement discourse (see also chapter 5).

In his MA thesis for Universidad Andina, Guillermo Churuchumbi (2014) investigates the meaning of Sumak Kawsay to low-level indigenous leaders and *comuneros* in his native Cayambe. He is surprised that, although many claim that the term "Sumak Kawsay" originates in the indigenous world, there are few studies of what it means to indigenous communities. Churuchumbi argues that "Sumak Kawsay" is not used in Cayambe. "Alli Kawsay" seems a more correct expression in Kichwa. However, even "Alli Kawsay" is not an everyday term. Despite this, grassroots community leaders have decided to adopt the phrase because they realize its political potential. They have created workshops to train community leaders in how to use Sumak Kawsay.

Churuchumbi first analyzes the meaning of Sumak Kawsay for progressive mestizo intellectuals. He argues that for them, the concept entails critiques of development, capitalism, consumption, and materialism. It also conveys a renewed focus on human beings, nature, and spirituality. Churuchumbi then asks grassroots indigenous leaders how they compare Alli Kawsay to the Western concepts of development and progress. Interestingly, indigenous *comuneros* do not see Sumak Kawsay and development as opposites, but as synonymous. They argue that to bring both development and Sumak Kawsay, it is important to be politically organized, seek consent, avoid conflict, and keep Kichwa traditions alive so that communities can have access to enough land and water to produce and survive. Churuchumbi discovered that community members associate the word "progress" specifically with government provision of infrastructure such as roads and schools. Progress also resonates for them with Alli Kawsay. The interpretation of Sumak Kawsay as an indigenous criticism of development and economic growth is a ventriloquist idea that does not originate in the communities.

To sum up, Sumak Kawsay is a recent construct devised by indigenous intellectuals catering to the world of development. It is also a ventriloquist term that environmentalists, decolonial scholars, and other indigenistas have contributed to shape and popularize. Decolonial and ontology scholars contributed an emphasis on non-Western worldviews and the biocentric turn. Members of the environmentalist and social science circles who joined the government of Rafael Correa made a political tool of Sumak Kawsay. Indigenous intellectuals and grassroots leaders at the community level reappropriated the concept because of its political potential and positive reference, however vague, to indigeneity.

Sumak Kawsay helped provide coherence and legitimacy to a number of nonindigenous eclectic proposals. It is not only an indigenous idea but also a genuine urban, middle-class project. However, as a political tool, Sumak Kawsay has been used to legitimize a government that, as will be discussed below, has not been friendly to indigenous rights or the environment. The long-term habit of ventriloquism has facilitated acceptance of the concept without much inquiry into its origins. Furthermore, if the Correa regime uses Sumak Kawsay, and if Sumak Kawsay is an indigenous philosophy, audiences assume that indigenous people must support the regime, or alternatively, they conflate the regime with indigenous agendas and movements (e.g., de la Cadena 2010). Finally, the idea of Sumak Kawsay comes full circle when some decolonial scholars who in the first place influenced the mestizo activists who coined the concept, further promote it in international circles. With the concept, they also legitimize the governments that use this term as their brand.

The Reemergence of Public Racism

As the Correa administration appropriated indigeneity in the form of Sumak Kawsay and claimed to be working toward interculturalism, plurinationality, antidiscrimination, and the rights of nature, the conflict between the administration and the indigenous movement progressively worsened. As seen in previous chapters, the government of Rafael Correa reduced indigenous rights starting in 2009. The autonomy of the intercultural bilingual education system was abolished immediately after the indigenous movement protested a new mining law that launched large-scale, open-pit mining in the country. Approximately 13,000 community schools were closed beginning in 2013, and children were relocated to consolidated schools that were far from their communities and did not teach the indigenous language or culture. The budget of the Council for the Development of the Nationalities and Peoples of Ecuador (Consejo de Desarrollo de las Nacionalidades y Pueblos del Ecuador) was drastically cut, with the argument that that money had been used to finance anti-mining protests. The institution was subsequently closed (see Martínez Novo 2016). Indigenous legal autonomy, enacted in the 1998 and 2008 constitutions, was circumscribed to local and internal issues that strictly concerned indigenous culture through a 2014 ruling of the Supreme Court, an institution tightly controlled by the executive.[1] Correa's government attempted to end CONAIE's lease on the building it had used for decades as its headquarters in Quito on the grounds that the state needed it for the rehabilitation of drug addicts. After a national and international campaign, the administration allowed CONAIE to stay.

As indigenous people tried to speak up about these and other abuses through their own autonomous organizations, they were harshly repressed. The government used the penal code's vaguely defined figures of sabotage, terrorism, and resistance to curb and criminalize protest. Indigenous individuals suffered indiscriminate arrests and lack of due process. Those who challenged the regime risked becoming involved in lengthy, arbitrary trials staged by a judicial apparatus tightly controlled by the executive and used for political purposes. The government's strategy has been to punish a few dissenters in order to deter broader contestation. Indigenous people have been particularly vulnerable to this kind of judicial harassment. Judicial repression was complemented by Executive Decree 16, which states that only those civil organizations authorized by the government are licit (see chapter 5). The government can shut down organizations that deviate from their original stated purpose, participate in politics, or allegedly threaten national security (Conaghan 2015).[2]

---

1. Constitutional Court Sentence no. 113–14-SEP-CC, case no. 0731-10-EP, July 30, 2014.
2. The incoming president Lenín Moreno canceled Decree 16 on October 23, 2017.

The Correa regime charged over seven hundred people, most of them indigenous activists trying to protect their territories from mega-projects and asking for the implementation of prior, informed consultation. Consultation is an indigenous right under the 2008 Constitution of Ecuador as well as under the 2007 UN Declaration on the Rights of Indigenous Peoples, of which Ecuador is a signatory. Two deaths of indigenous environmental activists are still awaiting legal resolution (CONAIE et al. 2016).

The repression of an indigenous and labor union protest in August 2015 was among the most brutal in Ecuador's recent history. Protestors opposed a constitutional amendment that would allow for indefinite presidential reelection, questioned the government's defunding of workers' social security, the use of the army for internal security purposes, the closure of intercultural community schools, and the violation of the Rights of Nature (Colectivo Investigación/Acción Psicosocial 2015). Repression was harsher in Quito, the indigenous community of Saraguro, and the Amazon province of Morona Santiago.

In Quito, nationally known indigenous leaders were beaten, humiliated, and arrested. The arrests of Carlos (Yaku) Pérez Guartambel, the president of the Awakening of the Ecuadorian Runa (ECUARUNARI, an organization of Kichwa peoples from the highlands) and Salvador Quishpe, at the time the elected governor of the province of Zamora-Chinchipe for the indigenous party Pachakutik, were quite violent. Quishpe was dragged and beaten. The police surrounded him and attempted to throw him into a crowd of belligerent Correa followers who were staging a counterdemonstration. Quishpe, however, took a "selfie" with the police general who was holding him captive and sent it to his Facebook list. The general released Quishpe when he learned that the picture had been sent to social media.

Over a thousand police and military personnel invaded the indigenous community of Saraguro in Ecuador's southern highlands and arrested thirty-six *comuneros*. The community was militarized on August 17, 2015. The Saraguro people did nothing to provoke the aggression except for demonstrating peacefully and being an area of dense indigenous organization that has produced important national-level leaders. The Saraguro protesters demanded that their territories not be allocated to mining companies, that the government respect bilingual intercultural education, and that the state help strengthen peasant dairy production and commercialization, instead of promoting agribusiness (Ortiz Lemos 2016). The police used the government's

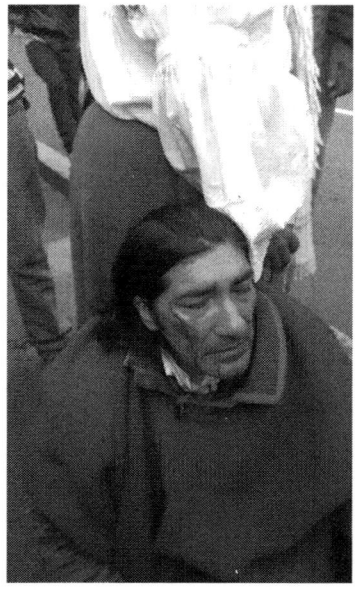

Figure 7.1. Beating of Carlos (Yaku) Pérez Guartambel in 2015 antigovernment demonstrations. Photo from Colectivo de Investigación/Acción Psicosocial, "Informe preliminar sobre las estrategias estatales de control social y represión en el marco del paro nacional en Ecuador, 13–23 Agosto 2015," Quito, August 2015, accessed June 2016, https://investigacion psicosocial.files.wordpress.com/2016/06/infor me-estrategias-estatales-de-control-y-represic 3b3n-social-durante-el-paro-nacional-y-las -marchas-indc3adgenas.pdf.

declaration of a state of exception to break into the homes of the Saraguro people. They threw tear-gas bombs into homes and beat up and arrested people who were uninvolved in the protests as well as pregnant women, minors, and elderly people. Indigenous women were kicked in their sexual parts, threatened with rape, humiliated with racial slurs, and pulled by the hair. A woman who was six months pregnant was beaten, and when other women tried to protect her, they were arrested.

The government's strategy was to simultaneously target the national indigenous leadership and the indigenous grassroots in those places where the organization was stronger (Colectivo Investigación/Acción Psicosocial 2015). Although the police beat up indigenous and mestizo protestors, they treated indigenous people worse. The police only invaded homes, beat uninvolved people, minors, and the elderly in indigenous areas. For instance, "M. J. C. a seventy-five-year-old woman states that twenty members of the military broke into her house, kicked her and pushed her toward the wall, pulling her by her two arms as if she were going to be crucified" (Colectivo Investigación/Acción Psicosocial 2015, 31).

Scholars who have praised Correa's government, and even those who later took some distance from the regime, seem to have paid insufficient attention to the regime's aim not only to repress but also to humiliate indigenous people. A close look at the punishments used by the security forces during the 2015 protests shows that these were based on humiliations previously inflicted in hacienda times, before the abolition of indigenous

FIGURE 7.2. Policeman pulling the shawl of a Saraguro woman. Photo from Colectivo de Investigación/Acción Psicosocial, "Informe preliminar sobre las estrategias estatales de control social y represión en el marco del paro nacional en Ecuador, 13–23 Agosto 2015," Quito, August 2015, accessed May 20, 2020, https://investigacion psicosocial.files.wordpress.com/2016/06/informe-estrategias-estatales-de-control-y-represic3b3n-social-durante-el-paro-nacional-y-las-marchas-indc3adgenas.pdf. Original source Plan V.

serfdom. For example, a photo published by Colectivo Investigación/Acción Psicosocial (2015) shows a policeman pulling the shawl of an indigenous woman. Salvador Quishpe was stripped of his hat, a symbol of his Saraguro identity. Several women were stripped of items of clothing that signal their indigenous identity such as the *anaco* (indigenous skirt).

Stripping indigenous people of an item of clothing also has a long history in the Andes. In the first half of the twentieth century, when hacienda or mestizo authorities wanted to humiliate, get free labor, or some payment from an indigenous individual, they would forcibly take an item of clothing, typically the hat, poncho, or shawl, and then ask the individual to perform a job or make a payment in order to recover the item. Some examples are found in Hugo Burgos's *Relaciones interétnicas en Riobamba* (Interethnic Relations in Riobamba) first published in 1970, soon after the abolition of indigenous serfdom. Burgos writes, "A mestizo child can kick off the hat of an adult Indian, despite the fact that the child has low status within his family, and even if the Indian were the governor or ruler of his parish group" (Burgos 1997 [1970], 250). He continues, "If an Indian uses a public restroom, the guard wants the Indian to pay for toilet paper even if he has not used it. If the Indian protests claiming that he does not have the money, the guard takes his hat until he pays the 10 cents" (263). "On paydays, cantina owners ask Indians to pay back what they owe. Some Indians only pay half of what they owe, others hide or claim not to have the money. This is when the *culebras* [lit. snakes, here referring to the cantina owners] prey on the less acculturated. They take an item from them. However, they do not want the hat because they think it may be old. They may take the *poncho* or some implement that the Indian has in his hands" (269).

Another form of humiliation that the police used profusely during the 2015 protests was to pull indigenous protestors by their hair. Some examples follow: S. L., a young woman arrested in Saraguro states: "They [the police] pulled me by the *jimba* [braided hair]. They dragged me, beat me up, and pulled off my clothes. The police insulted me and told me that they were going to rape me. They broke into our plots and houses. They stepped on our plants. They scared our little animals away. They kicked down our doors. Our children cried, they beat up our parents and then us" ("Violencia de estado" 2015). K. M., another Saraguro woman stated: "They [the police] pulled us by the braids. They insulted us with racist slurs. They said: 'Dirty Indian women, what are you doing here? Go to work with your husbands.' They said: 'Pull them by the braids, we are going to rape them'" ("Violencia de estado" 2015).

Pulling indigenous hair is a form of humiliation that law enforcement has traditionally used in Ecuador. *Relaciones interétnicas en Riobamba* includes a photograph of a policeman pulling an indigenous woman's hair as an elegant white couple passes by. The caption reads: "Transit campaign in Riobamba. Whites are kindly warned. Law enforcement beats Indians on the legs or pulls their hair 'benevolently' as shown in the picture" (Burgos 1997, 252).

Missionaries and other colonizers typically trimmed the hair of indigenous people to "civilize" them, because long hair was associated with savagery. Despite this, indigenous men and women have managed to keep their hair long in Ecuador. One of CONAIE's requests during the 1990 uprisings was that indigenous boys and men be allowed to keep their long, braided hair when they attended public school or fulfilled their military service (de la Torre 1996). The indigenous writer Raúl Cevallos associates the male braid with a sense of masculinity (Cevallos Calapi 2006).

VENTRILOQUISM, RACISM, & THE POLITICS OF DECOLONIAL SCHOLARSHIP   259

FIGURE 7.3. Meme circulated on social media, comparing Latacunga's "Mama Negra" with Governor Salvador Quishpe after his arrest and beating during the antigovernment demonstrations of August 2015.

Governor Salvador Quishpe also suffered from what seems to be a "traditional" form of humiliation when he was arrested during the 2015 protests. A poster distributed by protestors stated: "Salvador Quishpe, indigenous leader and governor of the Province of Zamora-Chinchipe, was humiliated yesterday by the police forces of the Correa regime in Quito. Salvador was stripped of his hat, the symbol of his identity, dragged, beaten up, and soiled with a dark substance. The Correa regime does not hesitate to harm the dignity of popular leaders." After Quishpe's assault, Correa's followers distributed a meme on social media that featured a picture of Governor Quishpe with a soiled face and body next to a picture of the Mama Negra (Black Mama).

Black Mama is the main character of a popular festival celebrated in the city of Latacunga since the eighteenth century. In the festival, a mestizo man disguised as a Black woman performs Mama Negra. The meme reads:

"Mama Negra" beneath the festival's character, and "mamarracho" (monstrosity, piece of crap) beneath the picture of Quishpe, an elected authority. The meme highlights Quishpe's nonwhiteness and also feminizes him. The Mama Negra festival celebrates the Virgen de las Mercedes (Our Lady of Mercy) who protected the city of Latacunga from an eruption of the Cotopaxi volcano. The Cotopaxi was erupting at the time of the 2015 protests and the government took advantage of this situation to declare a state of exception and suspend civil rights. The Mama Negra festival has two *priostes* (those who organize and pay for the celebration): The *prioste* of the whites, and the *prioste* of the soiled ones (*prioste de los tiznados*). Correa's followers continued to use the nickname *carita sucia* (little soiled face) for Quishpe. The script of Governor Quishpe's humiliation was not random, it had deep historical roots in the colonial period.

Danielle Roper (2019) notes that Black impersonation by non-Blacks such as Mama Negra is common throughout the Americas. In Latin America it has roots in Catholic rituals that represented slavery and the subjugation of Africans. For Roper blackface is a hemispheric phenomenon linked to slavery and its legacy travels internationally and borrows from different traditions. However diverse, the point of blackface rituals is to celebrate white power over subjugated African Americans. Interestingly, Salvador Quishpe was "blackfaced" to put him in his place. He was expected to refrain from being an uppity Indian and forced to accept his subordinate place in Ecuadorian society.

Public Racism in Presidential Discourses

President Correa's pejorative remarks against indigenous leaders and organizations during his weekly broadcast speeches were another manifestation of official prejudice. In them, he represented indigenous organizations as a minority of the population, as obstacles to development, and as violent groups. For example, Correa stated: "Let's have an uprising of thirteen million Ecuadorians against these troglodyte positions that want to keep our country in the past. Let's resist these aggressions because what the leaders of CONAIE are doing is not resistance, but aggression" (cited in Granda 2016, 24). On another occasion the president said: "I am not going to live in a country where a Carlos Pérez Somethingelse [mocking the leader's indigenous last name], a Marco Guatemal, any crazy individual who has not won half of an election, can throw stones at the car in which I am traveling with my family, beat up a police officer, burn an ambulance, throw rocks at my windows. Do you want to live in such a country? That would be punished in any civilized country!" (cited in Granda 2016, 23). In another instance the president stated: "We cannot allow those who are only a few to close a road with tree trunks and stones. What they did not achieve with the ballots they want to achieve now" (cited in Granda 2016, 24). The "we" that Correa uses refers to mestizo Ecuador, who for Correa represent the majority of the population, and who should be outraged by the lack of vision, the antiquated ways, and the violence of a minority of organized indigenous people. Correa's representation of indigenous leaders as violent justifies violent state repression against them. The representation of indigenous people as backward, attached to the past, and as obstacles to progress is typical of Latin American indigenismo. Moreover, the president uses his electoral gains to delegitimize civil society organizations: According to Correa, only those who have won elections can have a say in collective matters. His depiction of indigenous people as an insignificant minority was legitimized on the basis of census results (see chapter 3).

Correa's pejorative remarks have encouraged followers to perpetrate violence against indigenous leaders. For example, Correa repeatedly ridiculed the indigenous assemblywoman Lourdes Tibán calling her a "poor woman" and accusing her of using development money to finance protests against the government. After the 2015 nationwide protests, three women attacked Tibán when she was on her way to the National Assembly where she worked. The attackers threw rocks, pulled Tibán's hair, kicked her in the back, and threatened to kill her (El Universo 2015).

Correa does not believe that the indigenous grassroots express their own opinions and agency; instead, he argues that their leaders manipulate them. He stated: "I approached a peasant comrade and asked her: comrade, why do you think we are selling the water? She responded: 'Because you are selling the water to other countries.' . . . This is what they put in their head. They steal the mind and heart of our peasant comrades in this way" (cited in Granda 2016, 24). Correa then insisted that indigenous leaders do not represent their constituencies; instead Correa's government better represents the indigenous grassroots. He stated:

> Ask the indigenous people whether they support their leaders or the government . . . of course there are many discourses that indigenous leaders borrow

from coffeehouse intellectuals [*intelectuales de cafetín*], from infantile environmentalists. I was not wrong when I said that they were the main danger to our political project. They put discourses in the mouths of indigenous people . . . we, in contrast, believe in interculturalism, plurinationality, we have [enacted] that in the Constitution. But let's not lie to ourselves; the main problem that indigenous people face is poverty. And there is no government that has done more for interculturalism, plurinationality, water protection, and poverty reduction than the government of the Citizens' Revolution. That is why indigenous peoples, the communities, support us. (Cited in Granda 2016, 26–27)

This paragraph goes full circle, connecting the repression and humiliation of autonomously organized indigenous people back to ventriloquism. If indigenous people would only allow the government to speak for them and if they would stay in their place, repression would not be necessary. The paragraph also shows the importance given to the reduction of poverty in Correa's discourse to justify repression and the undoing of multiculturalism (see chapter 3).

The Decolonial Turn and Correa's Regime

Decolonial authors became interested in the turn to the Left in Latin America in the decade of the 2000s because they thought this political shift combined anticapitalist with indigenous and Afrodescendant approaches to politics. Arturo Escobar (2010) was one of the first to examine the possibilities of this political shift in Venezuela, Bolivia, and Ecuador. Escobar wondered whether these regimes were undertaking alternative forms of modernization (antineoliberal but still based on the Eurocentric values of modernity) or unleashing radical possibilities for the political activation of relational ontologies. According to Escobar, relational ontologies eschew the Eurocentric dichotomy between nature and culture and focus on communitarian values instead of the liberal principles of the individual, private property, and the state. Escobar was particularly fond of state declarations of plurinationality and interculturalism, direct and participatory democracy, and endogenous development on the basis of the Andean concept of Good Living (Sumak Kawsay in Kichwa, Suma Qamaña in Aymara). According to Escobar, Sumak Kawsay policies led Ecuador to take a biocentric turn: for the first time nature was endowed with its own rights. He argued, although not unambiguously, that the political changes taking place in Latin America were not only a turn to the Left, but also a decolonial turn.

Marisol de la Cadena (2010) agreed with Escobar that the understanding of nature as a subject of rights in the 2008 Constitution of Ecuador was the result of the emergence of indigenous ontologies into mainstream Latin American politics. On the basis of her research on spiritual leaders in communities near Cuzco, Peru, de la Cadena argued that indigenous people see natural features such as mountains—which they call earth beings—as capable of subjectivity and political action (de la Cadena 2015). For her, the Constitution of Ecuador meant the transformation of these insights into policy. She assumed, however, that grassroots indigenous worldviews inspired the legislation without researching how the idea started or how it got included in the text of the 2008 constitution.

Catherine Walsh's book *Interculturalidad, estado y sociedad* (Interculturalism, State, and Society) (2009) also praised the decolonial achievements of the regimes of Evo Morales (2005–2019) and Rafael Correa. According to Walsh, these regimes abandoned the neoliberal model and allowed ethnic and cultural differences to guide the debate. For Walsh, interculturalism was the most salient innovation. She understood interculturalism as a decolonial project, originating in indigenous and Afrodescendant thought, that sought the creation of a new society based on interactions, complementarity instead of competition, and a new relation to nature. Walsh interpreted the adoption of plurinationality in Ecuador and Bolivia as another decolonial endeavor that complemented interculturalism. The agenda of plurinationality was the full recognition of indigenous and Afrodescendant nationalities and peoples as historical and political entities with their own territories, cultures, and languages. As noted above, Walsh was an adviser in the 2007–2008 Constituent Assembly in Ecuador and helped develop articles on interculturalism and plurinationality for the 2008 constitution. More specifically, Walsh was an adviser to Assemblywoman Alexandra Ocles, a leader of the Afro-Ecuadorian movement and a member of Ruptura de los Veinticinco, a small group of younger politicians who started working for the Esquel Foundation, and later became part of Correa's political movement.

As Correa's and other radical populist governments in Latin America became more authoritarian, more focused on the extraction of nonrenewable natural resources, and more repressive of the social movements, decolonial scholars grew increasingly skeptical of these regimes, but some of their writings remained ambiguous and they have not developed a sound critique of their own role in launching and promoting these regimes. For instance, in a publication focusing on the crisis of the new Left in Latin America, Escobar (2016) insists that Latin American critical thought is not waning but still thriving in the proposals of social movements. He acknowledges in passing the exhaustion of the progressive, neo-extractivist, and developmental state model, but prefers to eschew that discussion and focus instead on the ideas sprouting from below. In an article on affirmative action in South America, Walsh (2015) praises the Ecuadorian government for its antidiscrimination and affirmative action policies, which she labels decolonial. She acknowledges that the laws have barely been implemented but justifies this fact on the grounds that the regime has prioritized its struggle against poverty. Like Escobar, she then shifts the focus to Afro-Ecuadorian activism and empowerment from below as a form of what she calls "affirmative action(ing)." When she stretches the concept of affirmative action to include grassroots cultural affirmation (rather than restricting the concept to public policies to remedy past injustices), she misunderstands and trivializes the term. Despite mounting evidence of Correa's assault on social movements and the environment, decolonial critiques of these developments have remained ambiguous and timid.

Subtle and Open Racism

The racial formation that developed under Correa was permeated by ventriloquism. When organized indigenous people rejected state representations and asked to speak in their own voices, repression ensued. During Correa's decade there seemed to be a progression from an emphasis on ventriloquism to a greater emphasis on open racism and repression. This progression seemed related to increasing popular discontent when redistribution decreased due to the reduction of oil prices and the state budget.

The colonial tradition of ventriloquism as discussed by Guerrero (2010) makes it easy, almost natural, and a form of habitus for whites and mestizos to speak for and represent indigenous people. This tradition also makes it natural for other nonindigenous citizens to accept the discourse as genuine, if the ventriloquist follows certain well-rehearsed patterns. For their part, indigenous people are used to accommodating to these representations, or are forced to do so, and sometimes try to employ them strategically.

If it were not for the legacy of ventriloquism, it would be difficult for the Correa regime and its advisers to appropriate Sumak Kawsay—a concept originated by indigenous intellectuals catering to development organizations—to fill it with the usual stereotypes or with an array of eclectic projects, and to project it to national and international audiences and then back to indigenous communities.

Government ventriloquism relies on simplistic understandings of indigeneity, understandings that are not based on long-term interaction, deep reflection, or a serious investigation of indigenous languages or cultures. As Pitarch (2004) notes, the power of the discourse arises precisely from its repetitive, simple, and even meaningless nature. It can then be associated with indigenous ancestral wisdom (which needs to be simple, right?) and then appropriated and resignified at will. The Correa regime impersonated this stereotyped indigeneity and used it to strengthen its own legitimacy in front of sympathetic audiences. The work of decolonial-turn and other scholars contributed to further legitimizing and circulating this discourse. Moreover, the legacy of ventriloquism allowed decolonial-turn scholars to freely define Sumak Kawsay without being concerned with gathering the necessary ethnohistorical or ethnographic materials that would ground the concept—or not—in the indigenous past or present.

Ventriloquism emerges from a history of colonization through indirect rule that generated measures of paternalist protection. Scholars who wrote about the end of ventriloquism (Becker 2012b; A. Guerrero 1993; Lucero 2008) thought that the empowerment of indigenous people after the 1990 uprisings and after the formation of the modern indigenous movement was enough to reinstate the power of self-representation to them. However, these scholars may have underestimated the persistence of discrimination and the continuing need of indigenous people to accept being represented by others. As was noted above, the role of *protectores de indios* was only justified because Indians were classified as "miserable." Thus, ventriloquism is the child of inequality and it contributes to perpetuate it. Furthermore, when indigenous people try to project their own voice and agency, they are harshly repressed. Violent repression forces them back into paternalist containment.

The reemergence of open forms of racism takes place under particular circumstances. Indigenous rights are curtailed in the context of expanding extractivism, which is threatened by indigenous autonomy and control of the territory. In addition, the grassroots are less inclined to accept ventriloquist representation when oil prices collapse and the redistribution of state rents diminishes. In the context of unacceptable retrenchment of rights and benefits, organizations question the state's ability to speak for them. However, the indigenous movement is sufficiently weak so that elites are able to choose open confrontation and backlash. Social movements had previously been weakened by co-optation through superficial multiculturalism and strategies of soft discrimination like ventriloquism. Furthermore, the Correa government fragmented popular organizations through a combination of patron–client practices and outright repression (see chapter 2). The state justified repression, representing autonomous indigenous people as violent and nonrepresentative of their constituencies. Similarly to ventriloquism, the language of repression also originates in an ancient—can we say ancestral?—colonial repertoire. As it impersonates indigeneity through ventriloquism and violently represses indigenous peoples, the government of Rafael Correa has drawn on what Ecuadorian elites, law enforcement, and the rest of Ecuadorian society know best—and what hurts and humiliates the most—colonial and hacienda legacies.

CONCLUSION

NEOLIBERALISM, NATIONALIST-EXTRACTIVISM, AND RACIAL FORMATIONS IN ECUADOR

This book has focused on two racial formations or "socio-historical processes by which racial categories are created, lived out, transformed and destroyed," the multicultural neoliberal and the nationalist-extractivist as they took shape in Ecuador (Omi and Winant 2015, 109). Under neoliberalization, a state that was historically weak retrenched even further. A smaller state allowed one of the most powerful social movements of the continent to emerge and thrive, something that did not take place in other countries with stronger state institutions and sizable indigenous populations such as Mexico or Peru (M. García 2005; Martínez Novo 2006). Moreover, the process of retrenchment of the state left enough leeway for nonstate actors such as missionaries, anthropologists, and ethnolinguists to freely interact with and support the indigenous movement in ways that reinforced indigenous consciousness and political organization. Under neoliberalization, the collective rights of indigenous peoples were recognized in the 1998 constitution. However, structural changes were insufficient, and indigenous poverty and exclusion continued. Neoliberalization produced a few jobs for indigenous leaders and intellectuals and opened some opportunities for them. However, the combination of the social mobility of the leaders with the lack of structural change for the communities eventually weakened the indigenous movement. It separated the grassroots from their leaders, and encouraged disaffected individuals to embrace the nonindigenous project of Rafael Correa, which prioritized the fight against poverty over the struggle for recognition. Thus, although Evo Morales, a self-identified indigenous president, was elected in 2005 in Bolivia, the indigenous candidate Luis Macas achieved only 2 percent of the national vote and 25 percent of the indigenous vote in 2006 in Ecuador (Báez and Bretón 2006).

On the other hand, neoliberalization and globalization brought to Ecuador an environment of relative tolerance in which racism retreated to the backstage and indigenous and Afro-Ecuadorian peoples began to have a space in the public sphere through their intellectuals and activists. Neoliberalization also encouraged ethnic participation and decentralization and constructed indigenous leaders and organizations as political actors and interlocutors. It allowed for their relative political and cultural empowerment as seen in the example of intercultural bilingual education.

Intercultural bilingual education was one of the main claims of an identity-based social movement because it promoted the preservation and reinforcement of such an identity as well as the political cohesion of the indigenous group. Indigenous activists achieved the creation of a separate and autonomous education system. Indigenous organizations, first the Confederation of Indigenous Nationalities of Ecuador and later the smaller indigenous movements, controlled the hiring of teachers and administrators and the curriculum. Thus, the system was participatory and decentralized. This situation was unique in Latin America, and perhaps only became possible due to the delegative nature of the Ecuadorian state, which typically transferred some of its functions to third parties. However, the finances of the system were still controlled by the Ministry of Education, which did not allocate sufficient funds for the system to work efficiently. During neoliberalization, the education system was characterized by tensions between recognition (the promotion of indigenous languages and cultures) and redistribution (the teaching of mainstream knowledge and the provision of official titles to allow for the social mobility of indigenous people). Another tension was between the utopian origins of the system and the legacies of an authoritarian pedagogy, poor public service, and sexual abuse.

Regarding the formation of official racial categories, in the previous period of import-substitution industrialization and military dictatorship, the Ecuadorian state avoided separating the population by ethnicity or race in its censuses, and instead promoted the project of mestizaje. This was a period of important structural reforms that included the agrarian reform and the expansion of the franchise to illiterates, which allowed indigenous people, Afro-Ecuadorians, and other rural poor to vote. During neoliberalization, the state began producing statistics disaggregated by ethnicity first based on language and later on self-identification and language. However, state strategies and practices reduced indigenous numbers in population censuses. Moreover, the state depoliticized ethnic identities, thus promoting the idea that ethnicity was a personal choice. It also imported concepts of race of North American origin such as hypodescent for Afro-Ecuadorians. On the other hand, in light of the environment of multicultural tolerance and participation, the interviewers for the census were indigenous.

The racial projects of nonstate actors during neoliberalization differed from those of the state. Anthropologists were important supporters of the indigenous movement as it emerged and grew in the 1980s and 1990s. Intellectual labor conditions were precarious due to the retrenchment of the state and the economic crisis, and anthropologists and other social scientists depended on siphoning off funds from international sources. On the other hand, a vibrant indigenous movement brought attention and funding to those who studied indigenous and rural issues. The intimacy of intellectuals with the indigenous movement sometimes precluded them from taking the necessary distance or time to produce critical academic analyses.

Missionaries were even more central to the creation and growth of a powerful indigenous movement. They often replaced the state in marginal areas it did not reach or from which it retrenched. The state historically delegated the jurisdiction of indigenous workers to haciendas. When some haciendas were dissolved in the process of the agrarian reform, the missionaries took over servicing and managing these populations. The racial project of the missionaries was to create a peasantry that was politically organized on the basis of their indigenous, Kichwa, or Shuar, identity. Indigenous peasants, aware of the precariousness of subsistence agriculture, had different goals. They were more mobile and cosmopolitan, and they prioritized their professionalization and preparation for a more globalized, rural/urban future.

During the period of nationalist-extractivism and President Correa's rule, there was a process of state formation fueled by oil extraction and the high prices of commodities. Extractivism and the consolidation of semiauthoritarian, centralized rule limited the expansion of multiculturalism, particularly in its territorial and self-government dimensions. Although the 2008 Constitution of Ecuador allows for the creation of indigenous territorial circumscriptions, the process established in the legislation makes their creation difficult, if not impossible. In fact, very few were approved after 2008 (F. García 2014b). This resonates with what has happened in other turn to the left and extraction-oriented countries like Bolivia and Venezuela. In the Constitution of Bolivia and the subsequent Law of Autonomies, the category of indigenous autonomy was watered down (Postero 2017). As in Ecuador, autonomy was only feasible in already existing municipalities and territorial demarcations. The law set down strict bureaucratic procedures for creating new indigenous territories. The requirements were so rigid that only eleven municipalities in the whole country were able to start the process (Postero 2017, 59). In Venezuela, the Chávez regime promoted the creation of communal councils rather than indigenous territories (Angosto Ferrández 2015). After seventeen years of the Bolivarian process no indigenous territories had been recognized. Indigenous rights, including previous and informed consultations, have not been applied because these rights are only applicable to officially recognized indigenous territories (Lander 2017). In addition, none of the three countries has conducted a sweeping agrarian reform because land redistribution would conflict with land grabbing by extractive industries (Gudynas 2009).

Despite the state's symbolic embrace of indigeneity as shown in the adoption of the Sumak Kawsay and Suma Qamaña (Good Living) philosophies, and in the indigenist performances of the various state officials, indigenous autonomy has not expanded or thrived in the first two decades of the new millenium. Meanwhile, a folkloric indigeneity has been deployed for the purpose of legitimating these regimes. Although both multicultural neoliberalism and nationalist-extractivism invoke folkloric indigeneity of the "indio permitido" kind, their styles are substantially different. While neoliberal multiculturalism allows for limited and orchestrated participation by indigenous leaders and intellectuals as well as organizations, nationalist-extractivism leans more toward impersonation, ethnic cross-dressing, and ventriloquism. This is because neoliberalism is relatively more "liberal" whereas nationalist-extractivism tends to be more authoritarian or paternalist. Some decolonial and other scholars have played an important role in promoting these nationalist-extractivist regimes, taking their official declarations at face value, and have contributed to legitimizing forms of impersonation and ventriloquism.

However, the tensions between the discourses and on-the-ground realities of extractivism eventually became too stark. Symbolic recognition and ventriloquism thus gave way to more open discrimination, which was able to reemerge in the public sphere. Another change has been a shift toward the repression and criminalization of indigenous protest. This happened in Ecuador as well as in other countries like Bolivia and Argentina (Briones 2015). In Venezuela, repression is so generalized that there are few accounts of specific repression against indigenous peoples (an exception is Lander 2017). Indigenous movements have been weaker in Venezuela than in Ecuador or Bolivia (Angosto Ferrández 2015).

The kind of cultural policy that allowed reinforcement of social movement cohesion and political organization was also curtailed. The Correa regime practically dismantled intercultural bilingual education during its decade of rule. It abolished the autonomy of the system, replaced the authorities with younger people who were easier to manipulate and sympathetic to the regime, and reverted to monocultural education in Spanish. In addition, community schools were closed and education became centralized, often although not always, in larger population centers. Indigenous teachers lost their jobs due to evaluations that were not relevant to their socioeconomic context, or they were encouraged to retire in exchange for severance. Centralized control of the jobs in intercultural bilingual education inflicted a significant blow on indigenous political organization. Some leaders lost their jobs, and the movement lost the ability to distribute employment and other benefits. The communities lost their intellectual guides; parents and elders lost control over the education of their own children and grandchildren. Once deprived of these essential services, the population started leaving the communities that were the backbone of the indigenous movement and the only indigenous institutions that had been able to survive colonization. Finally, *comuneros* began migrating to cities, thus opening additional territories to extractive industries.

Regarding the official construction of racial categories, during this period the state reinforced the idea that the indigenous population was a minority among others, and used population censuses to argue that indigenous peoples should not have a say in national issues or that they did not deserve special rights because they were few. Groups that were originally allied with the indigenous movement and were part of the imagined community of "the peoples and nationalities," such as Afro-Ecuadorians and Montubios, were encouraged to separate from, compete with, and oppose the indigenous movement. This strategy legitimized the retrenchment of indigenous rights, both territorial and cultural, as well as the retreat of social tolerance and the return of open racism.

Nonstate actors lost autonomy and relevance under nationalist-extractivism. Anthropologists were silenced, as was the rest of civil society. They lost international funding and became increasingly dependent on state moneys. The state used its funds and access to information to privilege those who were friendly and to punish opponents. There was open repression of some intellectuals who were harassed in presidential speeches, or by the administration of their own universities. Administrators were pressured by members of the executive to control and silence public intellectuals. However, some scholars resisted and continued supporting indigenous agendas against resource extraction. Others eschewed politics to avoid repression or to reap rewards. Still others collaborated with, and used their expertise to promote the regime and used their privileged access to social movements to weaken or co-opt them.

Missionaries found themselves in a double bind: they admired a progressive Catholic president who presented himself as a product of liberation theology. On the other hand, as Correa became more controlling, focused on resource extraction, and distrustful of social movements, priests on the ground chose to side with the social movements. This caused divisions in the progressive Catholic Church similar to the fissions that tore apart the social movements and the professional and intellectual groups. Meanwhile, and paradoxically, conservative branches of the Catholic Church such as the Opus Dei crept closer to power, and some of its members achieved positions in the executive. At the same time, some rebellious priests made it onto the Ministry of Politics list of those who needed to be closely watched. The Catholic Church had developed the theology of inculturation before and during the period of neoliberalization as its own style of multiculturalism. Under nationalist-extractivism, it shifted to an environmentally sensitive theology and practice. However, these theologians never separated inculturation or environmental theology from the struggle for redistribution and their commitment to the poor.

During the transition from neoliberalization to the government of Rafael

Correa my thinking and political position also evolved. During the period of neoliberalization, I was critical of shallow forms of multiculturalism because of their tensions and contradictions. I questioned superficial forms of recognition that justified the lack of substantial structural change. I was also wary of the collaboration of some indigenous leaders with neoliberal institutions for personal or political gain, while they left the grassroots of the movement behind. However, during the Correa decade, I saw myself in the position of defending multiculturalism, as imperfect as it had been before, as it was progressively dismantled and as the environment of tolerance and participation morphed into paternalism, ventriloquist impersonation, open racism, or outright repression. Interestingly, some of my previous arguments against neoliberal multiculturalism were used by the regime to justify dismantling the previous racial formation—of course, without referencing my work explicitly. This intellectual struggle resonates with what Wendy Brown (2003) has described regarding the North American Left, which was critical of liberalism and labeled it hypocritical, but then found itself in the position of defending liberal democracy when neoliberal values eroded liberal principles and brought about authoritarian tendencies and the resurgence of right-wing movements. I also found myself in the position of supporting the leadership of the indigenous movement that courageously struggled against extractivism and authoritarian rule, and I became more critical of the pragmatic middle leadership and commoners who, on occasion, chose to side with the regime in exchange for some meager benefits. It was an intentional strategy of the Correa regime to isolate the leaders and try to co-opt the middle leadership and the grassroots (Ortiz Lemos 2015).

The methodology of the book also deserves further reflection. The manuscript looks at race and ethnicity from multiple perspectives and timespace locations. It draws from multiple contexts, historical, social, economic, and political, building on the classical political economy paradigm. This methodology allowed me to see connections and trace trends (Wolf 2010 [1982]). It also allowed me to link what happens in the high spheres of power with what transpires in the communities. This kind of methodology requires a great deal of effort, from learning Kichwa and doing fieldwork in communities, to occupying other social spaces: institutional, power-ridden, or intellectual. I also draw information from several disciplines and sources to try to achieve a holistic perspective on racial formations under semiauthoritarian extractivism.

The methodology also poses some difficulties. Racial formations can be better apprehended if one works in multiple locations, historical periods, and social groups, but the work might not attain the depth that could be achieved in a monographic study of a particular community (Canessa 2012). On the other hand, much can be missed in a monograph when the connections and contexts are not fully apprehended. Another drawback of studying up is the personal cost for the researcher. In the discipline of anthropology it is relatively easy to write about subaltern groups and even about the state or the elites when referring to them in general terms or when reifying them. It is a different thing altogether when an anthropologist writes about the state and other institutions as made up of particular individuals who make choices and are accountable for their actions. This allows for a more interesting and realistic story, but the author may have to pay a price.

What can we learn from this particular case about racial formations in Latin America and globally? The retrenchment of multiculturalism has not only taken place in the countries that turned toward the Left. The high prices of commodities during the past two decades encouraged aggressive extractivism as well as threats to minority rights in neoliberal countries such as Mexico, Colombia, and Peru, as well as in other areas of extraction throughout the world (Bebbington and Humphreys Bebbington 2011). However, as Eduardo Gudynas (2009) noted, the contradictions were starker in turn to the left countries, because they had promised to undo both neoliberalism and the legacy of colonialism. In addition, turn to the left countries were more effective in justifying extractivism as a way to end poverty or achieve national development, and have been more skillful in dividing, repressing, and confusing the social movements. This has allowed for subsequent backlash by extractivist elites and disaffected mestizos.

As commodity prices plummeted around 2014, Latin American states had to confront their reduced ability to redistribute rents to the rest of society. In this situation, governments that want to stay in power have two options: greater repression or negotiation with the social sectors. Ecuador took the second path. Lenín Moreno, of Correa's same political party Alianza País, was elected in 2017. Moreno started as a less authoritarian ruler and was willing to open a dialogue with the different social sectors. He also prioritized the fight against corruption. However, the Ecuadorian state continues to depend on natural resource extraction. After a period of dialogue and indults for indicted social activists, repression and the criminalization of protest resumed, as did the expansion of the extractive frontier into the biodiverse Yasuní National Park. On the other hand, Moreno and the mining companies tried to convey the idea that more humane and responsible resource extraction was possible. Until new alternatives for development are imagined and implemented, indigenous groups will continue to be sacrificed (Postero 2017). When Lenín Moreno applied austerity measures and reduced subsidies to basic products in the fall of 2019 to respond to low commodity prices, an enlarged state, and mounting debt, indigenous mobilizations resumed. This was possible because Moreno had previously lifted some of the repression and social control. Correa's followers tried to take advantage of these indigenous mobilizations to avoid accountability for corruption and possibly to return to power. In this context, Moreno's government went back to harsh repression tactics.

Is the decline of multiculturalism and rights linked to the authoritarian leanings of a natural resource dependent state? Or is it linked to the commodity boom itself and the difficult position that indigenous peoples occupy between the state, the companies, and the resources? Does the rise of right-wing extremism and racism in the Global North have an additional impact in the shift toward more open forms of discrimination in Latin American contexts? Latin America and the world are facing a challenging moment for minoritized populations characterized by fewer rights and less tolerance. This has happened because neoliberalization previously weakened the social movements with superficial forms of recognition and co-opting of the activists. Resource dependent turn to the Left governments further watered down cultural and territorial rights and divided the indigenous movements. As the turn to the Left gives way to the election of several right-wing governments in Latin America, a right-wing scenario with aggressive extractivism and social movement repression is likely to reinvigorate again the social movements and their allies.

REFERENCES

Abercrombie, Thomas. 2001. "To Be Indian, to Be Bolivian: Ethnic and National Discourses of Identity." In *Nation States and Indians in Latin America*, edited by Greg Urban and Joel Sherzer, 95–130. Austin: University of Texas Press.

Abram, Matthias. 2004. "Estado del arte de la educación bilingüe intercultural en América Latina." Interamerican Development Bank Document, Washington, DC.

Abrams, Philip. 2006 [1988]. "Notes on the Difficulty of Studying the State." In *The Anthropology of the State*, edited by Aradhana Sharma and Akhil Gupta, 112–130. Malden, MA: Blackwell.

Acosta, Alberto. 2009. "Comunicación a los miembros de la Corte Constitucional sobre los efectos económicos, medioambientales, sociales y culturales de la Ley Minera." Corte Constitucional del Ecuador, June 9, 2009.

Acosta, Alberto. 2013. "A modo de prólogo. El correismo: un nuevo modelo de dominación burguesa." In *El correismo al desnudo*, edited by Alberto Acosta, 9–21. Quito: Montecristi Vive.

Acosta, Alberto. 2015. "El buen vivir como alternativa al desarrollo." *Política y Sociedad* 52, no. 2: 299–330.

Acosta, Alberto. 2016. "Maldiciones, herejías y otros Milagros de la economía extractivista." *Tábula Rasa* 24: 25–55.

Acosta, Alberto, and Esperanza Martínez. 2009. *El buen vivir: una vía para el desarrollo*. Quito: Abya Yala.

Ad Gentes Decree on the Missionary Activity of the Church. 1965. Accessed September 19, 2020, http://www.vatican.va/archive/hist_councils/ii_vatican_council/documents/vat-ii_decree_19651207_ad-gentes_en.html.

Agencia Efe. 2015. "La CIDH pide a Ecuador explicaciones por la muerte de tres líderes indígenas." *El Comercio*, March 17, 2015.

Aguirre Beltrán, Gonzalo. 1967. *Regiones de refugio*. Mexico City: Instituto Indigenista Interamericano.

Albro, Robert. 2010. "Confounding Cultural Citizenship and Constitutional Reform in Bolivia." *Latin American Perspectives*, 37, no. 3: 71–90.

Almeida, Ileana. 1996. *Temas y cultura quichua en el Ecuador*. Quito: Abya Yala.

Almeida, José et al., eds. 1993. *Sismo étnico en Ecuador*. Quito: CEDIME/Abya Yala.

Almeida, Mónica, and Ana Karina López. 2017. *El séptimo Rafael*. Quito: Aperimus.

Altares, Guillermo. 2014. "Es perfectamente legítimo tener una ley de comunicación." *El País* (Madrid), April 26, 2014.

Amnesty International. 2012. "'Para que nadie reclame nada' ¿Criminalización del derecho a la protesta en Ecuador?" London: Amnesty International.

Andrade, Susana. 2004. *Protestantismo indígena: Procesos de conversión religiosa en la provincia de Chimborazo, Ecuador*. Quito: FLACSO.

Angosto Ferrández, Luis Fernando. 2008. "Pueblos indígenas, guaicaipurismo y socialismo del siglo XXI en Venezuela." *Antropológica de la Fundación La Salle de Ciencias Naturales* 110: 9–33.

Angosto Ferrández, Luis Fernando. 2015. *Venezuela Reframed*. London: Zed Books.

Angosto Ferrández, Luis Fernando, and Sabine Kradolfer. 2012. "Race, Ethnicity and National Censuses in Latin American States: Comparative Perspectives." In *Everlasting Countdowns: Race, Ethnicity, and National Censuses in Latin American States*, edited by L. F. Angosto Ferrández and S. Kradolfer, 1–40. New Castle: Cambridge Scholars.

Ante, Fabiola. 1993. "Libro de experiencias vivenciales." Graduation thesis, Jatari Unancha-Instituto Pedagógico Intercultural Bilingüe Quilloac.

Antón Sánchez, Jhon. 2011. *El proceso organizativo afroecuatoriano: 1979–2009*. Quito: FLACSO.

Antón Sánchez, Jhon. 2014. "La experiencia afroecuatoriana en el censo de 2010." Manuscript. Quito: IAEN.

Antón Sánchez, Jhon, and Fabiana del Popolo. 2008. *Visibilidad estadística de la población afrodescendiente de América Latina: Aspectos conceptuales y metodológicos*. Santiago de Chile: CEPAL.

Archetti, Eduardo. 1997. *Guinea Pigs: Food, Symbol and Conflict of Knowledge in Ecuador*. London: Bloomsbury Academic.

Arcos Cabrera, Carlos. 2005. "Los avatares de la literatura ecuatoriana: El caso Chiriboga. *Letras* (Chile), September

Arnold, Denise, and Christine Hastorf. 2008. *Heads of State: Icons, Power, and Politics in the Ancient and Modern Andes*. Walnut Creek, CA: Left Coast Press.

Arnold, Denise, with Juan de Dios Yapita. 2006. *The Metamorphosis of Heads: Textual Struggles, Education, and Land in the Andes*. Pittsburgh: University of Pittsburgh Press.

Audiovisuales Don Bosco. n.d. *Abya Yala*. Quito.

Audiovisuales Don Bosco. n.d. *Misiones en el Oriente*. Quito.

Báez, Sara, and Víctor Bretón. 2006. "El enigma del voto étnico o las tribulaciones del movimiento indígena." *Ecuador Debate* 69: 19–36.

Ballet Jacchigua website. Accessed October 22, 2016, http:www.jacchiguaesecuador.com.

Bauer, Daniel. 2012. "Emergent Identity, Cultural Heritage, and El Mestizaje: Notes from the Ecuadorian Coast." *Journal of Latin American Cultural Studies* 21, no. 1: 103–121.

Bebbington, Anthony, and Denise Humphreys Bebbington. 2011. "An Andean Avatar: Post-neoliberal and Neo-liberal Strategies for Promoting Extractive Industries." *New Political Economy* 16, no. 1: 131–145.

Becker, Marc. 2006. "La historia del movimiento indígena escrita a través de las páginas de Ñukanchik Allpa." In *Estudios ecuatorianos, un aporte a la discusión*, edited by Ximena Sosa-Buchholz and William Waters. Quito: FLACSO and Abya Yala.

Becker, Marc. 2008. *Indians and Leftists in the Making of Ecuador's Indigenous Movements*. Durham, NC: Duke University Press.

Becker, Marc. 2011. *¡Pachakutik! Indigenous Movements and Electoral Politics in Ecuador*. Lanham, MD: Rowman and Littlefield.

Becker, Marc. 2012a. "In Search of Tinterillos." *Latin American Research Review* 47, no. 1: 95–114.

Becker, Marc. 2012b. "The Limits of Indigenismo in Ecuador." *Latin American Perspectives* 39, no. 5: 45–62.

Bigenho, Michelle. 2006. "Embodied Matters: Bolivia Fantasy and Indigenismo." *Journal of Latin American Anthropology* 11, no. 2: 267–293.

Botasso, Juan. 1986. "Las nacionalidades indígenas, el estado y las misiones en el Ecuador." *Ecuador Debate* 12: 151–159.
Bretón, Víctor. 2001. *Cooperación al desarrollo y demandas étnicas en los Andes ecuatorianos.* Quito: FLACSO.
Bretón, Victor. 2005. *Capital social y etnodesarrollo en los Andes.* Quito: CAAP.
Bretón, Víctor. 2014. "En busca del Sumak Kawsay." *Iconos* 48: 9–24.
Bretón, Víctor. 2015. "Tempest in the Andes? Peasant Organization and Development Agencies in Cotopaxi, Ecuador." *Journal of Agrarian Change* 15, no. 2: 179–200.
Briones, Claudia. 2015. "Políticas indigenistas en Argentina: entre la hegemonía neoliberal de los años noventa y la nacional popular de la última década." *Antipoda* 21: 21–48.
Brown, Wendy. 2003. "Neoliberalism and the End of Liberal Democracy." *Theory and Event* 7, no. 1. Accessed May 11, 2019, https://muse.jhu.edu/.
Buitrón, Aníbal, and John Collier Jr. 1971 [1949]. *El valle del Amanecer.* Otavalo: Instituto Otavaleño de Antropología.
Burgos, Hugo. 1997 [1970]. *Relaciones interétnicas en Riobamba.* Quito: Corporación Editora Nacional.
Bustamante, Teodoro. 1988. *La larga lucha del kakaram contra el sucre.* Quito: Abya Yala.
Cabodevilla, Miguel Angel. 2004. *El exterminio de los pueblos ocultos.* Quito: CICAME.
Calderón, Guido. 2010. "Mestizos trasnochados." *El Telégrafo,* June 13, 2010.
Canessa, Andrew. 2004. "Reproducing Racism: Schooling and Race in Highland Bolivia." *Race, Ethnicity and Education* 7, no. 2: 185–204.
Canessa, Andrew. 2006. "Todos somos indígenas: Towards a New Language of National Political Identity." *Bulletin of Latin American Research* 25, no. 2: 241–263.
Canessa, Andrew. 2012. *Intimate Indigeneities: Race, Sex and History in the Small Spaces of Andean Life.* Durham, NC: Duke University Press.
Castells, Manuel. 2012. *Networks of Outrage and Hope: Social Movements in the Internet Age.* Cambridge: Polity Press.
Centro Andino de Acción Popular (CAAP). 1981. *Comunidad andina: alternativas políticas de desarrollo.* Quito: CAAP.
Centro Andino de Acción Popular (CAAP). 1984. *Estrategias de supervivencia en la comunidad andina.* Quito: CAAP.Cevallos, Raúl. 2007. "Informe de la investigación Racismo y Ciudadanía en el sistema de educación básica ecuatoriano." Manuscript prepared for the project "Racism and Citizenship in the Ecuadorian Educational System," directed by Carmen Martínez Novo and Carlos de la Torre. Quito, FLACSO Ecuador.
Cevallos Calapi, Raúl. 2006. *Desde San Juan, San Pedro y Santa Lucía: Hacia la construcción social y política del Inti Raymi en Cotacachi, Imbabura.* MA thesis, Quito, FLACSO Ecuador.
Chiriboga, Manuel. 1980. *Jornaleros y gran propietarios en 135 años de explotación cacaotera.* Quito: CIESE.
Chiriboga, Manuel.1988. *El problema agrario en el Ecuador.* Quito: ILDIS.
Chiriboga, Manuel. 2014. *Las ONGs ecuatorianas en los procesos de cambio.* Quito: Abya Yala and Comité Ecuménico de Proyectos.
Chisaguano Maliquinga, Silverio. 2012. "El enfoque étnico cultural en la estadística: una propuesta de los pueblos indígenas." Paper presented at the Fifth Congress of the Latin American Association of Population, Montevideo, Uruguay, October 23–26.
Churuchumbi, Guillermo. 2014. *Usos cotidianos del término Sumak Kawsay en el Territorio Kayambi.* MA thesis, Universidad Andina Simón Bolívar, Quito.

Clark, A. Kim. 1998. "Race, Culture, and Mestizaje: The Statistical Construction of the Ecuadorian Nation, 1930–1950." *Journal of Historical Sociology* 11, no. 2 (June): 185–211.

Cohen, Abner. 1981. *The Politics of Elite Cultures: Explorations in the Dramaturgy of Power in a Modern African Society*. Berkeley: University of California Press.

Colectivo Investigación/Acción Psicosocial. 2015. "Informe preliminar sobre las estrategias estatales de control social y represión en el marco del paro nacional en Ecuador." Quito.

Colloredo-Mansfeld, Rudi. 2009. *Fighting Like a Community: Andean Civil Society in an Era of Indian Uprisings*. Chicago: University of Chicago Press.

Colloredo-Mansfeld, Rudi, Paola Mantilla, and Jason Antrosio. 2012. "Rafael Correa's Multicolored Dream Shirt: Commerce, Creativity and National Identity in Post-neoliberal Ecuador." *Latin American and Caribbean Ethnic Studies* 7, no. 3: 275–294.

Conaghan, Catherine. 2015. "Surveil and Sanction: The Return of the State and Societal Regulation in Ecuador." *European Review of Latin American and Caribbean Studies* 98: 7–27.

Conaghan, Catherine. 2016. "Ecuador under Correa." *Journal of Democracy* 27, no. 3: 109–118.

Conaghan Catherine. 2017. "Contraasociational Strategy in a Hybrid Regime: Ecuador 2007–2015." *Bulletin of Latin American Research* 36, no.4: 509–525.

CONAIE, frente popular, plataforma por los derechos de las mujeres, red interamericana de derechos humanos. 2016. *Criminalization of Social Protest: Ethnic Discrimination and Criminalization of Indigenous Peoples in Ecuador, 2016, Alternative Report*. Human Rights Committee of the United Nations, Session 117, June 20–July 15.

Consejo regional indígena del Cauca (CRIC). 2009. *¿Qué pasaría si la escuela? 30 años de construcción de una educación propia*. Popayán, Colombia: PEBI.

Constante, Soraya. 2014. "La felicidad es un asunto de estado." *El País Internacional*, October 21.

Constitución de la República del Ecuador. 2008. Quito: Asamblea Nacional, Registro Oficial, October 20.

Cornejo, Diego, ed. 1991. *Indios: una reflexión sobre el levantamiento indígena de 1990*. Quito: ILDIS, Duende, Abya Yala.

Coronil, Fernando. 1997. *The Magical State: Nature, Money, and Modernity in Venezuela*. Chicago: University of Chicago Press.

Correa, Rafael. February 18, 2009. "Executive Decree 1585: Sobre educación intercultural bilingue." Accessed March 14, 2009, www.presidencia.gob.ec.

Correa, Rafael. September 28, 2009. "Executive Decree 60: Sobre la eliminación de todas las formas de racismo y discriminación." Accessed January 2010, www.presidencia.gob.ec.

Cortina, Regina. 2014. "Introduction." In *The Education of Indigenous Citizens*, edited by Regina Cortina, 1–18. Bristol: Multilingual Matters.Cucurella, Leonella. 2005. *Abya Yala: tierra en plena madurez*. Quito: Abya Yala.

Cuji Llugna, Luis Fernando. 2011. "Educación superior e interculturalidad." MA thesis, FLACSO Ecuador.

Cunuhay, Pedro. 1993. "Libro de experiencias vivenciales." Graduation thesis, Jatari Unancha-Instituto pedagógico intercultural bilingüe Quilloac.

Da Costa, Alexandre E. 2016. "The (Un)happy Objects of Affective Community." *Cultural Studies* 30, no. 1: 24–46.

Das, Veena, and Deborah Poole. 2004. *Anthropology in the Margins of the State*. Santa Fe: School of American Research Press.

De la Cadena, Marisol. 2010. "Indigenous Cosmopolitics in the Andes: Conceptual Reflections beyond Politics." *Cultural Anthropology* 25, no. 2: 334–370.

De la Cadena, Marisol. 2012. "Women Are More Indian: Ethnicity and Gender in a Community Near Cuzco." In *Ethnicity, Markets and Migration in the Andes*, edited by Brooke Larson and Olivia Harris, 329–348. Durham, NC: Duke University Press.

De la Cadena, Marisol. 2015. *Earth Beings: Ecologies of Practice Across Andean Worlds*. Durham, NC: Duke University Press.

De la Cuadra, José, and Humberto Robles. 1996. *El montuvio ecuatoriano: ensayo de presentación*. Quito: UASB.

De la Torre, Carlos. 1996. *El racismo en el Ecuador. Experiencias de los indios de clase media*. Quito: CAAP.

De la Torre, Carlos. 2002. *Afroquiteños: ciudadanía y racismo*. Quito: CAAP.

De la Torre, Carlos, and Andrés Ortiz Lemos. 2016. "Populist Polarization and the Slow Death of Democracy in Ecuador." *Democratization* 23, no. 2: 221–241.

De la Torre, Carlos, and Jhon Antón Sánchez. 2012. "The Afro-Ecuadorian Social Movement: Between Empowerment and Co-optation." In Rahier, *Black Social Movements*, 135–150.

Descola, Philippe. 1986. *In the Society of Nature: A Native Ecology in Amazonia*. Cambridge: Cambridge University Press.

Descola, Philippe. 1996. *The Spears of Twilight: Life and Death in the Amazon Jungle*. New York: New Press.

DeYoung, Alan, and Craig Howley. 1990. "The Political Economy of Rural School Consolidation." *Peabody Journal of Education* 67, no. 4: 63–89.

DINEIB. 2008. "El Quichua es una novelería según Correa." Email communication, July 23.

Ecuador Inmediato. 2009. "Lourdes Tibán pone a disposición su cargo por recorte de presupuesto de CODENPE." January 21. Accessed October 10, 2019, http://www.ecuadorinmediato.com/index.php?module=Noticias&func=news_user_view&id=96093.

Ecuadorenvivo. June 16, 2011. "Asambleistas denuncian mal manejo de recursos del Ecorae." June 16. Accessed December 10, 2012, www.ecuadorenvivo.com.

El Comercio, 21 Febrero 2006, p. 19.

El Comercio, redacción. 2012. "El prefecto César Umajinga apelará su destitución." *El Comercio*, June 13, 2012.

El Universo. 2015. "Asambleista Lourdes Tibán denuncia agresiones físicas y verbales cerca de su oficina." *El Universo*, September 23.

Elbein, Saul. 2017. "The Youth Group That Launched a Movement at Standing Rock." *New York Times Magazine*, January 31.

Elwood, Sarah, Patrick Bond, Carmen Martínez Novo, and Sarah Radcliffe. 2017. "Learning from Post-neoliberalisms." *Progress in Human Geography* 41, no. 5: 676–695.

Erazo, Juliet. 2013. *Governing Indigenous Territories: Enacting Sovereignty in the Ecuadorian Amazon*. Durham, NC: Duke University Press.

Escobar, Arturo. 2006. "Revisioning Latin American and Caribbean Studies: A Geopolitics of Knowledge Approach." *Latin American Studies Association Forum* 37, no. 2: 11–14.

Escobar, Arturo. 2010. "Latin America at a Crossroads: Alternative Modernizations, Post-Liberalism, or Post-development." *Cultural Studies* 24, no. 1: 1–65.

Escobar, Arturo. 2016. "Desde abajo, por la izquierda y con la tierra." In *Rescatar la esperanza: más allá del neoliberalismo y el progresismo*, edited by Eduardo Gudynas, 336–369. Barcelona: Entrepobles.

España, Sara. 2017. "Un caso de abusos sexuales a 100 niños en un colegio alarma a Ecuador." *El País Internacional*, October 15, 2017.

Espinosa Andrade, Alejandra. 2017. "Space and Architecture of Extractivism in the Ecuadorian Amazon Region." *Cultural Studies* 31, no. 2–3: 307–330.

Estermann, Josef. 1998. *Filosofía andina: Sabiduría indígena para un mundo nuevo*. La Paz: ISEAT.

Estermann, Josef. 2012. "Crisis civilizatoria y vivir bien: Una crítica filosófica del modelo capitalista desde el allin kawsay/suma qamaña andino." *Polis* 11, no. 33: 149–174.

Estrada, Jenny. 1996. *El montubio: un forjador de identidad*. Guayaquil: Banco del Progreso.

Farga, Cristina, and Almeida, José. 1981. *Campesinos y haciendas de la sierra norte*. Otavalo-Ecuador: Instituto Otavaleño de Antropología.

Farthing, Linda, and Nicole Fabricant. 2018. "Open Veins Revisited: Charting the Social, Economic and Political Contours of the New Extractivism in Latin America." *Latin American Perspectives* 45, no. 5: 4–17.

Field, Les, and Joanne Rappaport. 2011. "Special Issue Introduction." In *Collaborative Anthropologies in Latin America*, guest-edited by Les Field and Joanne Rappaport. *Collaborative Anthropologies* 4: 3–17.

Figueroa, José Antonio. 2015. "Educación superior intercultural y post-neoliberalismo en el Ecuador: el caso de la universidad Amawtay Wasi." In *Pensamiento político y genealogía de la dignidad en América Latina*, edited by Analuisa Guerrero, Jorge Olvera, and Julio César Olvera, 59–81. Mexico City: Universidad Autónoma del Estado de México.

Fine-Dare, Kathleen. 2007. "Más allá del folklore: la yumbada de Cotocollao como vitrina para los discursos de la identidad, de la intervención estatal y del poder local en los Andes urbanos ecuatorianos." In *Estudios ecuatorianos: un aporte a la discusión tomo II*, edited by William Waters and Michael Hamerly, 55–72. Quito: FLACSO and Abya Yala.

Foucault, Michel. 2006 [1991]. "Governmentality." In *The Anthropology of the State*, edited by A. Sharma and A. Gupta, 131–143. Malden, MA: Blackwell.

Fraser, Nancy. 1996. *Justice Interruptus: Critical Reflections on the Post-socialist Condition*. New York: Routledge.

Freire, Paulo. 2000 [1968]. *Pedagogy of the Oppressed*, 30th anniversary ed. New York: Continuum Press.

García, Fernando.1980. "Introducción." *Revista de la Universidad Católica* 8, no. 26: 7–14.

García, Fernando. 2002. *Formas indígenas de administrar justicia*. Quito: FLACSO.

García Fernando. 2006. "De movimiento social a movimiento político: caso del movimiento de Unidad Plurinacional Pachakutik Ecuador," In *Movimiento indígena en América Latina: resistencia y proyecto alternativo*, vol. 2, edited by Raquel Rodríguez and Fabiola Escárzaga. Mexico City: Juan Pablos.

García, Fernando. 2011. "La construcción del pensamiento antropológico ecuatoriano: derroteros y perspectivas." *Alteridades* 21, no. 41: 61–68.

García, Fernando. 2014a. "La relación entre la antropología Mexicana y Ecuatoriana: ¿Un camino de ida y vuelta?" *Revista Antropologías del Sur* 1: 105–118.

García, Fernando. 2014b. "Territorialidad y autonomía, proyectos minero-energéticos y consulta previa." *Antropológica* 32: 71–85.

García, María Elena. 2005. *Making Indigenous Citizens: Identities, Education, and Multicultural Development in Peru*. Stanford, CA: Stanford University Press.

Giménez, Jaime. 2017. "Las despojadas de la Cordillera del Cobre." *El País*, February 18, 2017.

Gnerre, Maurizio. 2012. "Los salesianos y los shuar construyendo la identidad cultural." In

La presencia salesiana en el Ecuador: perspectivas históricas y sociales, edited by Lola Vázquez, Juan Fernando Regalado, Blas Garzón, Víctor Hugo Torres, and José E. Juncosa, 573–636. Quito: Abya Yala.

González Casanova, Pablo. 2006. "Colonialismo interno (una redefinición)." In *La teoría marxista hoy: problemas y perspectivas*, edited by Atilio Borón, Javier Amadeo, and Sabrina González, 409–434. Buenos Aires: CLACSO.

Goodale, Mark, and Nancy Postero. 2013. "Revolution and Retrenchment: Illuminating the Present in Latin America." In *Neoliberalism Interrupted*, edited by Mark Goodale and Nancy Postero, 1–22. Stanford, CA: Stanford University Press.

Granda, María P. 2016. *El macho sabio: racismo y sexismo en el discurso sabatino del presidente Rafael Correa*. BA thesis, Universidad Central del Ecuador, Quito.

Greenhouse, Carol. 2002. "Introduction." In *Ethnography in Unstable Places: Everyday Lives in Contexts of Dramatic Political Change*, edited by C. Greenhouse, E. Mertz, and K. Warren, 1–34. Durham, NC: Duke University Press.

Grossberg, Lawrence. 2006. "Does Cultural Studies Have a Future?" *Cultural Studies* 20, no. 1: 1–32.

Gudynas, Eduardo. 2009. "Diez tesis urgentes sobre el nuevo extractivismo." In *Extractivismo, política y sociedad*, edited by Jurgen Schuldt, 187–225. Quito: CAAP.

Gudynas, Eduardo. 2011. "Buen vivir: Today's tomorrow." *Development* 54, no. 4: 441–447.

Guerrero, Andrés. 1980. *Los oligarcas del cacao*. Quito: El Conejo.

Guerrero, Andrés. 1983. *Haciendas, capital y lucha de clases andina*. Quito: El Conejo.

Guerrero, Andrés. 1991. *La semántica de la dominación: el concertaje de indios*. Quito: Libri-Mundi.

Guerrero, Andrés. 1993. "La desintegración de la administración étnica en el Ecuador." In *Sismo étnico en el Ecuador*, edited by José Almeida, 91–112. Quito: CEDIME and Abya Yala.

Guerrero, Andrés. 1994. "Una imagen ventríloqua: el discurso liberal de la desgraciada raza indígena a fines del siglo XIX." In *Imágenes e imagineros*, edited by Blanca Muratorio, 197–252. Quito: FLACSO.

Guerrero, Andrés. 2000. "El proceso de identificación: sentido común ciudadano, ventriloquía y transescritura." In *Etnicidades*, edited by Andrés Guerrero, 9–61. Quito: FLACSO Ecuador.

Guerrero, Andrés. 2010. *Administración de poblaciones, ventriloquía y transescritura*. Quito: FLACSO.

Guerrero, Fernando. 2005. "Población indígena y afroecuatoriana en Ecuador: diagnóstico sociodemográfico a partir del censo de 2001." Santiago de Chile, Documentos de proyectos CEPAL.

Guerrero, Fernando, and Pablo Ospina. 2003. *El poder de la comunidad: ajuste estructural y movimiento indígena en los Andes Ecuatorianos*. Quito: CLACSO.

Gutierrez, Ramón. 1991. *When Jesus Came, The Corn Mothers Went Away: Marriage, Sexuality and Power in New Mexico 1500–1846*. Stanford, CA: Stanford University Press.

Gutiérrez Aguilar, Raquel. 2014. *Rhythms of the Pachakuti: Indigenous Uprising and State Power in Bolivia*. Durham, NC: Duke University Press.

Haboud, Marleen. 2004. "Quichua Language Vitality: An Ecuadorian Perspective." *International Journal of Sociology of Language* 167: 69–81.

Hale, Charles. 2002. "Does Multiculturalism Menace? Governance, Cultural Rights and the Politics of Identity in Guatemala." *Journal of Latin American Studies* 34: 485–524.

Hale, Charles. 2005. "Neoliberal Multiculturalism: The Remaking of Cultural Rights and

Racial Dominance in Central America." *Political and Legal Anthropology Review* 28, no. 1: 10–28.

Hale, Charles. 2006. *Más que un Indio: Racial Ambivalence and the Paradox of Neoliberal Multiculturalism in Guatemala*. Santa Fe: School of American Research Press.

Hale, Charles, Pamela Calla, and Leith Mullings. 2017. "Race Matters in Dangerous Times." *NACLA Report on the Americas* 49, no. 1: 81–89.

Hale, Charles, and Rosamel Millaman. 2018. "Privatization of the Historic Debt? Mapuche Territorial Claims and the Forest Industry in Southern Chile." *Latin American and Caribbean Ethnic Studies* 13, no. 3: 305–325.

Harris, Olivia. 2008. "Alterities: Kinship and Gender." In Poole, *Companion to Latin American Anthropology*, 276–302.

Harvey, David. 1990. *The Condition of Post-Modernity*. Malden, MA: Blackwell.

Harvey, David. 2005. *A Brief History of Neoliberalism*. Oxford: Oxford University Press.

Hoffman French, Jan. 2009. "Ethnoracial Identity, Multiculturalism, and Neoliberalism in the Brazilian Northeast." In *Beyond Neoliberalism in Latin America? Societies and Politics at the Crossroads*, edited by John Burdick, Philip Oxhorn, and Kenneth Roberts, 101–116. New York: Palgrave Macmillan.

Hoy, Consejo de redacción. 2011. "Umajinga denuncia retaliación por el no." *Hoy*, May 19.

Ilaquiche, Raúl. 2004. *Pluralismo jurídico y administración de justicia indígena en Ecuador*. Quito: Hans Seidel.

Illicachi, Juan. 2007. "Discriminación discursiva y dominación étnica en la educación." Manuscript prepared for the project "Racism and Citizenship in the Ecuadorian Educational System," directed by Carmen Martínez Novo and Carlos de la Torre. Quito, FLACSO Ecuador.

Illicachi, Juan. 2014. *Diálogos del catolicismo y protestantismo indígena en Chimborazo*. Quito: UPS.

Iturralde, Diego. 1980. *Guamote: Campesinos y comunas*. Otavalo-Ecuador: Instituto Otavaleño de Antropología.

Jackson, Jean, and Kay Warren. 2005. "Indigenous Movements in Latin America, 1992–2004: Controversies, Ironies, New Directions." *Annual Review of Anthropology* 34: 549–573.

Jaramillo, Pío. 1922. *El indio ecuatoriano*. Quito.

Jimeno, Myriam. 2008. "Colombia: Citizens and Anthropologists." In Poole, *Companion to Latin American Anthropology*, 72–89.

Jintiach, José Vicente. 1976. *La integración del estudiante Shuar en su grupo social*. Quito: Mundo Shuar.

Juncosa, José. 2017. "Saber para prevalecer: civilización, educación y evangelización en el territorio shuar." PhD diss., Universidad Andina Simón Bolívar, Quito.

Junka-Aikio, Laura, and Catalina Cortés-Severino. 2017. "Cultural Studies of Extraction." *Cultural Studies* 31, no. 2–3: 175–184.

Karsten, Rafael. 1935. *The Head-hunters of Western Amazonas: The Life and Culture of the Jíbaro Indians of Eastern Ecuador and Peru*. Helsinki: SSF.

Kingman Garcés, Eduardo, and Blanca Muratorio. 2014. *Los trajines callejeros: memoria y vida cotidiana, Quito, siglos XIX–XX*. Quito: FLACSO.

Klinkicht, Susana. 2010. "El censo 2010." *Hoy* (Quito) November 22.

Knapp, Gregory. 1987. *Geografía Quichua de la Sierra del Ecuador*. Quito: Abya Yala.

Kohn, Eduardo. 2002. "Infidels, Virgins and the Black Robed Priest: A Backwoods History of Ecuador's Montaña History." *Ethnohistory* 49, no. 3: 545–582.

Kohn, Eduardo. 2013. *How Forests Think*. Oakland: University of California Press.
Kohn, Eduardo. 2015. "Anthropology of Ontologies." *Annual Review of Anthropology* 44: 311–327.
Krotz, Esteban. 2006. "Las antropologías latinoamericanas como segundas: situaciones y retos." In *Memorias del II Congreso Ecuatoriano de Antropología y Arqueología*, edited by Fernando García. Quito: Abya Yala-Banco Mundial.
Krupa, Christopher, and David Nugent, eds. 2015. *State Theory and Andean Politics: New Approaches to the Study of Rule*. Philadelphia: University of Pennsylvania Press.
Kuper, Adam. 1973. *Antropología y antropólogos: la escuela británica*. Mexico City: Fondo de Cultura Económica.
La Republica. 2016. "Correa anuncia retorno a flexibilidad laboral." *La República*, February 12. Accessed April 14, 2016, http://www.larepublica.ec/blog/politica/2016/02/06/correa-anuncia-retorno-flexibilidad-laboral/.
Lander, Edgardo. 2017. "Venezuela: la experiencia bolivariana en la lucha por trancender el capitalismo." Paper presented at the workshop "Beyond Development." Quito, May 10–18.
León, Jorge. 1991. "Las organizaciones indígenas: igualdad y diferencia." In *Indios*, edited by Diego Cornejo, 373–417. Quito: ILDIS, Duende, Abya Yala.
León Guzmán, Mauricio. 2003. "Etnicidad y exclusión en el Ecuador: una mirada a partir del censo de población de 2001." *Íconos* 17 (September): 116–132.
Ley orgánica de educación intercultural (LOEI). 2011. Registro Oficial: órgano del gobierno del Ecuador, administración del economista Rafael Correa Delgado, year II, n. 417, Thursday March 31.
Lins Ribeiro, Gustavo. 2006. "Cosmopolitics for a New Global Scenario in Anthropology." *Critique of Anthropology* 26, no. 4: 363–386.
López, Luis Enrique. 2014. "Indigenous Intercultural Bilingual Education in Latin America: Widening Gaps Between Policy and Practice." In *The Education of Indigenous Citizens*, edited by Regina Cortina, 19–49. Bristol: Multilingual Matters.
Lu, Flora, Gabriela Valdivia, and Néstor Silva. 2017. *Oil, Revolution and Indigenous Citizenship in Ecuadorian Amazonia*. London: Palgrave Macmillan.
Lucero, Jose Antonio. 2008. *Struggles of Voice: The Politics of Indigenous Representation in the Andes*. Pittsburgh: University of Pittsburgh Press.
Luykx, Aurolyn. 2000. "Gender Equity and Interculturalidad: The Dilemma in Bolivian Education." *Journal of Latin American Anthropology* 5, no. 2: 150–178.
Lyons, Barry. 2001. "Religión, Authority and Identity: Intergenerational Politics, Ethnic Resurgence and Respect in Chimborazo, Ecuador." *Latin American Research Review* 36, no. 1: 7–48.
Lyons, Barry J. 2006. *Remembering the Hacienda*. Austin: University of Texas Press.
Lyson, Thomas. 2002. "What Does a School Mean to a Community? Assessing the Social and Economic Benefits of Schools to Rural Villages in New York." Arlington, VA: National Science Foundation.
Macas, Luis. 2014. "El Sumak Kawsay." In *Antología del pensamiento indigenista ecuatoriano sobre el Sumak Kawsay*, edited by A. Hidalgo-Capitán, A. Guillen, and N. Deleg, 179–192. Huelva: CIM.
Maldonado, Gina. 2004. *Comerciantes y viajeros: de la imagen etnoarqueológica de "lo indígena" al imaginario del kichwa otavalo "universal"*. Quito: FLACSO/Abya Yala.
Mallon, Florencia. 2011. "Introduction: Decolonizing Knowledge, Language and Narrative." In

Decolonizing Native Histories, edited by Florencia Mallon. Durham, NC: Duke University Press.

Marcus, George. 1983. *Elites: Ethnographic Issues*. Albuquerque: School of American Research.

Martínez, Alexandra. 1998. "La producción de esteras en Yahuarcocha y la construcción del significado de ser mujer y ser hombre." In *Memorias del primer congreso ecuatoriano de antropología*, edited by C. Landázuri, vol. 1. Quito: PUCE-Marka.

Martínez, Alexandra. 2007. "Naturaleza y cultura: un debate pendiente en la antropología ecuatoriana." *Ecuador Debate* 72: 135–150.

Martínez, Luciano. 1984. *De campesinos a proletarios*. Quito: El Conejo.

Martínez Novo, Carmen. 2004. "Los misioneros salesianos y el movimiento indígena de Cotopaxi, 1970–2004." *Ecuador Debate* 63: 235–268.

Martínez Novo, Carmen. 2006. *Who Defines Indigenous? Identities, Development, Intellectuals and the State in Northern Mexico*. New Brunswick, NJ: Rutgers University Press.

Martínez Novo, Carmen. 2007. "¿Es el multiculturalismo estatal un factor de profundización de la democracia en América Latina? una reflexión desde la etnografía de los casos de México y Ecuador." In *Ciudadanía y exclusión: Ecuador y España frente al espejo*, edited by V. Bretón , F. García, A. Jové, and M. J. Villalta,182–203. Madrid: Catarata.

Martínez Novo, Carmen. 2009. *Repensando los movimientos indígenas*. Quito: FLACSO.

Martínez Novo, Carmen. 2013. "The Backlash against Indigenous Rights in Ecuador's Citizen's Revolution." In *Latin America's Multicultural Movements: The Struggle Between Communitarianism, Autonomy, and Human Rights*, edited by Todd Eisenstadt, Michael Danielson, Moisés Bailón, and Carlos Sorroza, 111–134. Oxford: Oxford University Press.

Martínez Novo, Carmen. 2014. "The Tension between Western and Indigenous Knowledge in Intercultural Bilingual Education in Ecuador." In *The Education of Indigenous Citizens in Latin America*, edited by Regina Cortina, 98–123. Bristol: Multilingual Matters.

Martínez Novo, Carmen, Shannon Bell, Subhadra Channa, Annapurna Pandey, and Luis Alberto Tuaza. 2018. "Indigenous Social Movements in Mountain Regions." In *Global Mountain Regions*, edited by Ann Kingsolver and Sasikumar Balasundaram, 83–120. Bloomington: Indiana University Press.

Martínez Novo, Carmen, and de la Torre, Carlos. 2010. "Racial Discrimination and Citizenship in Ecuador's Educational System." *Latin American and Caribbean Ethnic Studies* 5, no. 1: 1–26.

Mato, Daniel. 2014. "Universidades Indígenas en América Latina." *ISEES* 14: 17–45.

Mena, Maria Soledad, and Rosemarie Terán. 2014. "Implicaciones educativas y socio-culturales del modelo de territorialización y circuitos escolares en las redes históricas del Sistema de Educación Indígena de Cotopaxi." Informe de Investigación, Universidad Andina Simón Bolívar.

Mercurio, Consejo de Redacción. 2012. "En Cotopaxi se agrava disputa por prefectura." *El Mercurio*, June 13.

Mignolo, Walter. 2003. "Globalization and the Geopolitics of Knowledge: The Role of the Humanities in the Corporate University." *Nepantla: Views from the South* 4.

Mignolo, Walter. 2006. "Evo Morales en Bolivia: ¿giro a la izquierda o giro decolonial?" In *Ensayos en sociedad civil y política en América Latina*, edited by J. da Cruz, 93–106. Montevideo: Coroscoba.

Mijeski, Kenneth, and Scott Beck. 2011. *Pachakutik and the Rise and Decline of the Ecuadorian Indigenous Movement*. Athens: Ohio University Press.

Ministerio de Educación y Cultura. 1993. *Modelo de educación intercultural bilingüe*. Quito: Ministerio de Educación.

Ministerio de Educación del Ecuador. 2011. Ley Orgánica de Educación Intercultural (LOEI). Accessed May 19, 2012, www.educacion.gob.ec.

Ministerio de Educación del Ecuador. 2009. El gobierno de la Revolución Ciudadana fortalece la educación intercultural bilingüe, March. Accessed March 16, 2009, https://educacion.gob.ec/.

Mintz, Sidney. 1985. *Sweetness and Power: The Place of Sugar in Modern History*. New York: Penguin.

Moreno Yánez, Segundo. 1985. *Sublevaciones indígenas en la Audiencia de Quito desde comienzos del S. XVIII hasta finales de la colonia*. Quito: PUCE.

Moreno Yánez, Segundo. 1992. *Antropología ecuatoriana: pasado y presente*. Quito: Ediguias.

Moreno Yánez, Segundo, and José Figueroa. 1992. *El levantamiento indígena del Inti Raymi*. Quito: Abya Yala.

Moya, Ruth. 1981. *Simbolismo y ritual en el Ecuador Andino*. Otavalo-Ecuador: Instituto Otavaleño de Antropología.

Mukherjee, Roopali. 2016. "Antiracism Limited: A Pre-history of Post-race." *Cultural Studies* 30, no. 1: 47–77.

Muratorio, Blanca. 1981. *Etnicidad, evangelización y protesta en el Ecuador: una perspectiva antropológica*. Quito: CIESE.

Muratorio, Blanca. 1991. *The Life and Times of Grandfather Alonso: Culture and History in the Upper Amazon*. New Brunswick, NJ: Rutgers University Press.

Muratorio, Blanca. 1992. "Ensayo introductorio: en la mirada del otro." In Blanca Muratorio. *Retrato de la Amazonía*, 9–27. Quito: Libri Mundi.

Muratorio, Blanca. 2000. "Identidades de mujeres indígenas y políticas de reproducción cultural en la Amazonía ecuatoriana." In *Etnicidades*, edited by Andrés Guerrero, 235–266. Quito: FLACSO.

Muratorio, Blanca. 2001. "History and Cultural Memory of Violence against Indigenous Women in the Ecuadorian Upper Amazon." Manuscript.

Murra, John V. 2017 [1969]. Reciprocity and Redistribution in Andean Civilization: The 1969 Henry Lewis Morgan Lectures. Chicago: HAU, University of Chicago Press.

Nader, Laura. 1969. "Up the Anthropologist-Perspectives Gained from Studying Up." In *Reinventing Anthropology*, edited by Dell Hymes, 284–311. New York: Pantheon.

Neira, Mariana. 2015. "Esto se podría pagar con la plata del Buen Vivir del Freddy Ehlers." *Plan V*, August 17. Accessed September 25, 2017, http://www.planv.com.ec/historias/politica/esto-se-podria-pagar-con-la-plata-del-buen-vivir-freddy-ehlers.

Nobles, Melissa. 2000. *Shades of Citizenship: Race and the Census in Modern Politics*. Stanford, CA: Stanford University Press.

Observatorio sobre discriminación racial y exclusión étnica. 2012. "Las acciones afirmativas y el decreto 60." *Boletín Informativo* (April–June), FLACSO, Ecuador.

Omi, Michael, and Howard Winant. 2015. *Racial Formation in the United States*. New York: Routledge.

Ong, Aiwa. 2006. *Neoliberalism as Exception: Mutations in Citizenship and Sovereignty*. Durham, NC: Duke University Press.

Orta, Andrew. 2004. *Catechizing Culture: Missionaries, Aymara and the New Evangelization*. New York: Columbia University Press.

Orta, Andrew. 2013. "Forged Communities and Vulgar Citizens: Autonomy and Its Limites in Semineoliberal Bolivia." *Journal of Latin American and Caribbean Anthropology* 18, no. 1: 108–133.

Ortiz Lemos, Andrés. 2015. "Taking Control of the Public Sphere by Manipulating Civil Society: The Citizen's Revolution of Ecuador." *European Review of Latin American and Caribbean Studies* 98: 29–48.

Ortiz Lemos, Andrés. 2016. "El miedo a la voz indígena: un diálogo con Carlos Perez Guartambel." *Plan V* 19 (July).

Ospina, Pablo. 2009. "Nos vino un huracán politico: la crisis de la CONAIE." In *Los Andes en movimiento: identidad y poder en el nuevo paisaje político*, edited by Pablo Ospina, Olaf Kaltmeier, and Christian Buschges, 123–146. Quito: Corporación Editora Nacional.

Pallares, Amalia. 2002. *From Peasant Struggles to Indian Resistance: The Ecuadorian Andes in the Late Twentieth Century*. Norman: University of Oklahoma Press.

Pallares, Amalia. 2007. "Montub(v)ios and Political Activism in the Ecuadorian Coast." Paper presented at the twenty-seventh International Congress of the Latin American Studies Association, Montreal, September 5–8.

Peck, Jamie, Nik Theodore, and Neil Brenner. 2010. "Postneoliberalism and Its Malcontents." *Antipode* 41: 94–116.

Pelizzaro, Siro. 1990. *Arutam: mitología Shuar*. Quito: Abya Yala.

Pérez Anrango, Rafael. 2007. *Tierra comunitaria de Tunibamba por fin eres nuestra*. Quito: Fundación Pueblo Indio del Ecuador.

Petrich, B. 2016. "Agotados modelos de gobiernos progresistas." *Latin American Perspectives*, Political Report 1105.

Picq, Manuela L. 2012. "Between the Dock and a Hard Place: Hazards and Opportunities of Legal Pluralism for Indigenous Women in Ecuador." *Latin American Politics and Society* 54, no. 2: 1–33.

Pijal, Luis Fernando. 2014. "¿Cómo estamos las nacionalidades y pueblos indígenas según el censo de población y vivienda de 2010?" Manuscript. Quito, CODENPE.

Pilaguano, César. 1993. "Libro de experiencias vivenciales." Graduation thesis, Jatari Unancha-Instituto intercultural bilingüe Quilloac.

Pitarch, Pedro. 2004. "The Zapatistas and the Art of Ventriloquism." *Journal of Human Rights* 3, no. 3: 291–312.

Pitarch, Pedro. 2007. "The Political Uses of Maya Medicine: Civil Organizations in Chiapas and the Ventriloquist effect." *Social Analysis* 51, no. 2: 185–206.

Poeschel, Ursula. 1986. *La mujer salasaca*. Quito: Abya Yala.

Ponce Icaza, Isabela. 2019. "The Ghost of Nankints." https://dialogochino.net/26310-the-ghost-of-nankints.

Poole, Deborah. 1992. "Figueroa Aznar and the Cusco Indigenistas: Photography and Modernism in Early Twentieth Century Peru." *Representations* 38: 39–75.

Poole, Deborah, ed. 2008. *A Companion to Latin American Anthropology*. Malden, MA: Blackwell.

Pope Francis. 2015. *Laudato Si: On Care for Our Common Home*. Encyclical Letter. Vatican City: Librería Editrice Vaticana.

Postero, Nancy. 2007. *Now We Are Citizens: Indigenous Politics in Postmulticultural Bolivia*. Stanford, CA: Stanford University Press.

Postero, Nancy. 2017. *The Indigenous State: Race, Politics and Performance in Plurinational Bolivia.* Berkeley: University of California Press.

Postero, Nancy, Helene Risor, and Manuel Prieto Montt. 2018. "Introduction: The Politics of Identity in Neoliberal Chile." *Latin American and Caribbean Ethnic Studies* 13, no. 3: 203–213.

Postero, Nancy, and León Zamosc. 2004. *The Struggle for Indigenous Rights in Latin America.* Brighton: Sussex Academic Press.

Pozo, José. 2005. "Estudio social y de salud para las organizaciones Shuar-Achuar." Manuscript.

Prieto, Mercedes. 1980. "Haciendas estatales: un caso de ofensiva campesina." In *Ecuador: cambios en el agro serrano*, edited by O. Barsky. Quito: FLACSO/CEPLAES.

Prieto, Mercedes. 1998. "El liderazgo en las mujeres indígenas: tendiendo puentes entre género y étnia." In *Mujeres contracorriente*, edited by E. Cervone. Quito: CEPLAES.

Prieto, Mercedes. 2004. *Liberalismo y temor: imaginando los sujetos indígenas en el Ecuador Post-colonial 1895–1950.* Quito: FLACSO.

Prieto, Mercedes, ed. 2017. *El Programa Indigenista Andino, 1951–1973: las mujeres en los ensambles del desarrollo.* Quito: FLACSO.

Prieto, Mercedes, Clorinda Cuminao, Alejandra Flores, Gina Maldonado, and Andrea Pequeño. 2005. "Las mujeres indígenas y la búsqueda del respeto." In *Mujeres ecuatorianas: entre la crisis y las oportunidades*, edited by Mercedes Prieto, 147–188. Quito: FLACSO.

Proyecto Zumbagua-Guangaje. 1971. Archivo Histórico de la Sociedad Salesiana del Ecuador, Inspectoría Salesiana, Magón house, Quito. Signed by Alfredo Costales Samaniego, P. Pedro Creamer, P. Javier Cattá, and P. Juan Botasso.

Quijano, Aníbal. 2012. "'Bien Vivir': entre el 'desarrollo' y la (des)colonialidad del poder." *Viento Sur* 122: 46–56.

Quintero Lopez, Rafael, and Erika Sylva Charvet. 2010. "Ecuador: la alianza de la derecha y el corporativismo en el putch del 30 de septiembre de 2010." Web page of Partido Socialista Frente Amplio del Ecuador. Accessed May 15, 2011, www.psecuador17.org.

Radcliffe, Sarah. 2012. "Development for a Postneoliberal Era? *Sumak Kawsay*, Living Well and the Limits to Decolonization in Ecuador." *Geoforum* 43: 240–249.

Radcliffe, Sarah. 2015. *Dilemmas of Difference: Indigenous Women and the Limits of Postcolonial Development Policy.* Durham, NC: Duke University Press.

Radio Huancavilca. 2017. "Secretaría del Buen Vivir y Plan Familia suprimidas tenían planes para este año." May 28. Accessed September 25, 2017, http://radiohuancavilca.com.ec/noticias/2017/05/28/secretaria-del-buen-vivir-plan-familia-suprimidas-tenian-planes-este-ano/.

Rahier, Jean M. 1998. "Blackness, the Racial Spatial Order, Migrations and Miss Ecuador 1995." *American Anthropologist* 100, no. 2: 421–430.

Rahier, Jean M. 2012. *Black Social Movements in Latin America: From Monocultural Mestizaje to Multiculturalism.* New York: Palgrave.

Rahier, Jean M. 2013. *Kings for Three Days: The Play of Race and Gender in an Afro-Ecuadorian Festival.* Urbana: University of Illinois Press.

Ramírez, Franklin. 2010. "Postneoliberalismo indócil: agenda pública y relaciones socio-estatales en el Ecuador de la Revolución Ciudadana." *Temas y Debates* 14: 175–194.

Ramírez, René. 2010. "Socialismo del Sumak Kawsay o biosocialismo republicano." In *Los nuevos retos de América Latina: Socialismo y Sumak Kawsay*, edited by SENPLADES, 55–76. Quito: SENPLADES.

Ramón, Galo. 1987. *La resistencia andina: Cayambe 1500–1800.* Quito: CAAP.
Ramón, Galo. 1991. "Ese secreto poder de la escritura." In Cornejo, *Indios*, 351–372.
Ramón, Galo. 1994. "Los territorios indígenas en el Ecuador." Manuscript. Quito, CAAP.
Ramos, Alcida Rita. 1990. "Ethnology Brazilian Style." *Cultural Anthropology* 5, no. 4: 452–472.
Ramos, Alcida Rita. 1998. *Indigenism: Ethnic Politics in Brazil.* Madison: University of Wisconsin Press.
Ramos, Alcida Rita. 2007. "¿Hay algún lugar para el trabajo de campo etnográfico?" *Revista Colombiana de Antropología* 43: 231–261.
Rappaport, Joanne. 2005. *Intercultural Utopias: Public Intellectuals, Cultural Experimentation, and Ethnic Pluralism in Colombia.* Durham, NC: Duke University Press.
Redacción política. 2013. "Asamblea aprobó la ley de consejos de la igualdad." *El Comercio.com.* Accesssed July 24.
Regalado, Juan Fernando. 2010. *Ecuador y México: vínculo histórico e intercultural (1820–1970).* Quito: Museo de la Ciudad.
Restrepo, Eduardo, and Axel Rojas. 2010. *Inflexión decolonial: Fuentes, conceptos y cuestionamientos.* Popayán: Universidad del Cauca.
Rival, Laura. 2002. *Trekking through History: The Huaorani of Amazonian Ecuador.* New York: Columbia University Press.
Rodriguez Cruz, Marta. 2018. *Educación intercultural bilingüe, interculturalidad y plurinacionalidad en el Ecuador.* Quito: Abya Yala.
Roitman, Karem. 2009. *Race, Ethnicity and Power in Ecuador: The Manipulation of Mestizaje.* Boulder, CO: First Forum Press.
Roper, Danielle. 2019. "Blackface at the Andean Fiesta: Performing Blackness in the Danza de Caporales." *Latin American Research Review* 54, no. 2: 381–397.
Roseberry, William. 1989. *Anthropologies and Histories.* New Brunswick, NJ: Rutgers University Press.
Roseberry, William. 1994. *Anthropologies and Histories: Essays in Culture, History and Political Economy.* New Brunswick, NJ: Rutgers University Press.
Rubenstein, Steven. 2005. "La conversión de los Shuar." *Iconos* 22: 27–48.
Rubenstein, Steven. 2002. *Alejandro Tsakimp: A Shuar Healer in the Margins of History.* Lincoln: University of Nebraska Press.
Rubio Orbe, Gonzalo. 1973. "Prólogo." In G. Villavicencio, *Relaciones interétnicas en Otavalo.* Mexico City: Instituto Indigenista Interamericano.
Rueda, Marco Vinicio. 1982. *La fiesta religiosa campesina.* Quito: Ediciones de la Universidad Católica.
Sacher, William. 2017. *Ofensiva megaminera en los Andes: acumulación por desposesión en el Ecuador de la Revolución Ciudadana.* Quito: Abya Yala.
Sacher, William, Michelle Baez, Manuel Bayón, Fred Larreátegui, and Melisa Moreano. 2015. "Entretelones de la megaminería en el Ecuador: Informe de investigación." Quito: Acción Ecológica y PUCE.
Salomon, Frank. 1986. *Native Lords of Quito in the Age of the Incas: The Political Economy of North Andean Chiefdoms.* Cambridge: Cambridge University Press.
Sánchez Parga, José. 1990. *¿Por qué golpearla? etica, estética y ritual en los Andes.* Quito: CAAP.
Sánchez Parga, José. 1996. *Población y pobreza indígenas.* Quito: CAAP.
Sánchez Parga, José. 2002. *Crisis en torno al Quilotoa: mujer, cultura y comunidad.* Quito: CAAP.

Santana, Roberto. 2004. "Cuando las élites dirigentes giran en redondo: el caso de los liderazgos indígenas en Ecuador." *Ecuador Debate* 61: 235–258.

Schavelzon, Salvador. 2014. "Mutaciones de la identificación indígena en el censo de 2012 en Bolivia: mestizaje abandonado, indigenidad estatal y proliferación minoritaria." *Journal of Iberian and Latin American Research* 20, no. 3: 328–354.

Scheper-Hugues, Nancy. 1992. *Death without Weeping: The Violence of Everyday Life in Brazil*. Berkeley: University of California Press.

Scott, James C. 1998. *Seeing Like a State: How Certain Schemes to Improve the Human Condition Have Failed*. New Haven, CT: Yale University Press.

Secretaría del Buen Vivir. 2015. *Buen Vivir: Sumak Kawsay. ¿Porqué? ¿Para qué? ¿Cómo?* Quito.

Seligman, Linda. 2008. "Agrarian Reform and Peasant Studies: The Peruvian Case." In Poole, *Companion to Latin American Anthropology*, 325–351.

Sell, Randall, and Larry Leistritz. 1997. "Socioeconomic Impacts of School Consolidation on Host and Vacated Communities." *Community Development* 28, no. 2: 186–205.

SENPLADES. 2007. *Plan Nacional de Desarrollo 2007–2009*. Quito.

SENPLADES. 2009. *Plan Nacional para el Buen Vivir 2009–2013*. Quito.

SERBISH. 2000. Reglamento. Sucua: SERBISH.

Shakia, Prabinda, and Gretchen Gordon. 2016. "The World Bank Bizarre Retreat in Indigenous Rights." Accessed October 16, 2018, https://truthout.org/articles/theworldbankbizarre retreatatindigenousrights.

Sharma, Aradhana, and Akhil Gupta. 2006. *The Anthropology of the State*. Malden, MA: Blackwell.

Shore, Cris. 2002. "Introduction: Towards an Anthropology of Elites." In Shore and Nugent, *Elite Cultures*, 1–21.

Shore, Cris, and Stephen Nugent. 2002. *Elite Cultures: Anthropological Perspectives*. London: Routledge.

Sieder, Rachel. 2002. *Multiculturalism in Latin America: Indigenous Rights, Diversity, and Democracy*. Hampshire: Palgrave Macmillan.

Stolen, Kristi Anne. 1987. *A media voz: relaciones de género en la sierra ecuatoriana*. Quito: CEPLAES.

Striffler, Steve. 2001. *In the Shadows of State and Capital: The United Fruit Company, Popular Struggle and Agrarian Restruturing in Ecuador*. Durham, NC: Duke University Press.

Stutzman, Ronald. 1974. *Black Highlanders: Racism and Ethnic Stratification in the Ecuadorian Sierra*. PhD diss., University of Washington, Ann Arbor, University Microfilms.

Stutzman, Ronald. 1981. "El Mestizaje: An All-inclusive Ideology of Exclusion." In Whitten, *Cultural Transformations*, 45–94.

Szeman, Imre. 2017. "On the Politics of Extraction." *Cultural Studies* 31, no. 2–3: 440–447.

Tapias, María. 2015. *Embodied Protests: Emotions and Women's Health in Bolivia*. Urbana: University of Illinois Press, 2015.

Tarrow, Sidney. 2004. *El poder en movimiento: los movimientos sociales, la acción colectiva y la política*. Madrid: Alianza Editorial.

Taylor, Anne-Christine. 1994. "Una categoría irreductible en el conjunto de las naciones indígenas: los jíbaro en las representaciones occidentales." In *Imágenes e imagineros: representaciones de los indígenas ecuatorianos. S XIX y XX*, edited by Blanca Muratorio, 75–108. Quito: FLACSO.

Torres, Rosa María. 2013. "Adiós a la educación comunitaria y alternativa." *La línea de fuego: Pensamiento crítico*, November 14.

Torres, Víctor Hugo. 2012. "Misiones, pueblos indígenas e interculturalidad: introducción." In *La presencia salesiana en el Ecuador*, edited by Lola Vázquez, Juan Fernando Regalado, Blas Garzón, Víctor Hugo Torres, and José Juncosa, 563–572. Quito: Abya Yala.

Tuaza, Luis Alberto. 2010. "Interviews with Petrona Pilamunga, Cicalpito, Chimborazo." Unpublished raw material.

Tuaza, Luis Alberto. 2011. *Runakunaka ashka shaikushka shinami rikurinkuna, ña mana tandakunata munankunachu: la crisis del movimiento indígena ecuatoriano*. Quito: FLACSO.

Tuaza, Luis Alberto. 2017. *La construcción de la comunidad desde los imaginarios indígenas*. Riobamba: UNACH.

Unidad de investigación. 2017. "Ecuador: 102 casos de abuso sexual en centros educativos al año." *El Telégrafo*, December 11.

Universo, Consejo de redacción. 2012. "PAIS denuncia a prefecto César Umajinga." *El Universo*, May 29.

Uzendoski, Michael. 2009. "La textualidad oral napo kichwa y las paradojas de la educación bilingüe intercultural en la Amazonía." In Martínez Novo *Repensando los movimientos indígenas*, 147–172.

Uzendoski, Michael. 2018. "Amazonia and the Cultural Politics of Extractivism." *Cultural Studies* 32, no. 3: 364–388.

Vallejo, Ivette. 2014. "Petróleo, desarrollo y naturaleza." *Anthropologica* 32: 115–137.

Van Cott, Donna Lee. 2005. *The Friendly Liquidation of the Past: The Politics of Diversity in Latin America*. Pittsburgh: University of Pittsburgh Press.

Van Cott, Donna L. 2009. "Indigenous Movements Lose Momentum." *Current History* 108, no. 715: 83–89.

Villavicencio, Gladys. 1973. *Relaciones interétnicas en Otavalo: ¿Una nacionalidad india en formación?* Mexico City: Instituto Indigenista Interamericano."Violencia de estado contra mujeres indígenas que defienden sus derechos en Ecuador." 2015. Accessed December 15, 2016, http://resistiresmiderecho.org/violencia-estado-mujeres-indigenas-defienden-derechos.

Viteri, Carlos. 2002. "Visión indígena del desarrollo en la Amazonía." *Polis* 1, no. 3: 1–6.

Viveiros de Castro, Eduardo. 2000. "Cosmological Deixis and Amerindian Perspectivism." *Journal of the Royal Anthropological Institute* 4: 469–488.

Wade, Peter. 1997. *Race and Ethnicity in Latin America*. London: Pluto Press.

Walsh, Catherine. 2007. "Shifting the Geopolitics of Critical Knowledge: Decolonial Thought and Cultural Studies 'Others' in the Andes." *Cultural Studies* 21, no. 2–3: 224–239.

Walsh, Catherine. 2009. *Interculturalidad, estado y sociedad: luchas decoloniales de nuestra época*. Quito: Abya Yala.

Walsh, Catherine. 2010. "Development as Buen Vivir: Institutional Arrangements and (De)colonial Entanglements." *Development* 53, no. 1: 15–21.

Walsh, Catherine. 2012. "Afro In/Exclusion, Resistance, and the Progressive State: Decolonial Struggles, Questions and Reflections." In Rahier, *Black Social Movements*, 15–34.

Walsh, Catherine. 2015. "Affirmative Action(ing)s and Postneoliberal Movement in Latin America and Ecuador." *Cultural Dynamics* 27, no. 1: 19–41.

Warren, Kay, and Jean Jackson. 2003. *Indigenous Movements, Self Representation, and the State in Latin America*. Austin: University of Texas Press.

Webber, Jeffery. 2010. "Indigenous Liberation and Class Struggle in Ecuador: A Conversation with Luis Macas." Interview, July 17. Accessed March 18, 2011, http://upsidedownworld.org.
Weismantel, Mary. 1998. *Food, Gender and Poverty in the Ecuadorian Andes*. Long Grove, IL: Waveland Press.
Weismantel, Mary. 2001. *Cholas and Pishtacos: Stories of Race and Sex in the Andes*. Chicago: University of Chicago Press.
Weyland, Kurt. 2009. "The Rise of Latin America's Two Lefts: Insights from Rentier State Theory." *Comparative Politics* 41, no. 2: 145–164.
Whitten, Norman. 1981. Introduction. In Whitten, *Cultural Transformations*, 1–41.
Whitten, Norman, ed. 1981. *Cultural Transformations and Ethnicity in Modern Ecuador*. Urbana: University of Illinois Press.
Whitten, Norman. 1986 [1974]. *Black Frontiersmen: Afro-Hispanic Culture of Ecuador and Colombia*. Long Grove, IL: Waveland Press.
Whitten, Norman, and Diego Quiroga. 1998. "To Rescue National Dignity: Blackness as a Quality of Nationalist Creativity in Ecuador." In *Blackness in Latin America and the Caribbean: Social Dynamics and Cultural Transformations*, edited by Norman Whitten and Arlene Torres, 75–99. Bloomington: Indiana University Press.
Williams, Raymond. 1978. *Marxism and Literature*. Oxford: Oxford University Press.
Wolf, Eric R. 2010 [1982]. *Europe and the People without History*. Berkeley: University of California Press.
Yampara, Simón, R. Choque, and M. Torres. 2001. "Búsqueda de la camaña del ayllu andino." *Revista Pacha* 6: 150.
Yánez, José.1988. *Yo declaro con franqueza: Cashnami causashcanchic*. Quito: Abya Yala.
Yánez Cossío, Consuelo. 1996. *La educación indígena en Ecuador*. Quito: Abya Yala.Yashar, Deborah J. 2005. *Contesting Citizenship in Latin America: The Rise of Indigenous Movements and the Postliberal Challenge*. Cambridge: Cambridge University Press.
Zamosc, Leon. 1993. "Protesta agraria y movimiento indígena en la sierra ecuatoriana." In Almedia et al., *Sismo étnico en el Ecuador*.
Zamosc, Leon. 1994. "Agrarian Protest and the Indian Movement in the Ecuadorian Highlands." *Latin American Research Review* 29, no. 3: 37–68.
Zamosc, Leon. 1995. *Estadística de las áreas de predominio étnico de la sierra ecuatoriana*. Quito: Abya Yala.
Zamosc, Leon. 2007. "The Indian Movement and Political Democracy in Ecuador." *Latin American Politics and Society* 49, no. 3: 1–34.
Zamosc, Leon. 2013. "La ideología del Buen Vivir en Ecuador: ¿Una nueva ventriloquía?" Paper presented at the Third ERIP Conference, Oaxaca, Mexico, October 23–25.

INDEX

Abya Yala, 163
affirmative action, 55, 186
Afrodescendant (Afro-Ecuadorian), 71–72, 76, 78, 82–84
agrarian reform, 8, 22, 25, 29, 37–38, 39, 270; and anthropology, 153, 161, 166; and colonization, 209; and missions, 205; oral narratives of, 124; and poverty, 95, 100; in Zumbahua, 217
Amerindian perspectivism, 124
antidiscrimination, 55–56, 186
anthropology of the state, 50, 69

CAAP (Centro Andino de Acción Popular), 158, 165, 168, 218
Carlos (Yaku) Pérez Guartambel, 43, 255, 256, 260
CEPAL (Comisión Económica Para América Latina; ECLA), 249
Chávez, Hugo, 47
Chumpí, Marcelino, 43, 178, 229
citizenship: and census, 68, 70, 81, 101; and education, 105, 107, 112, 147; and exclusion, 241; and neoliberalism, 17; postneoliberalism, 48
Citizens' Revolution, 4, 47, 53, 262
CODENPE (Consejo de Desarrollo del Pueblo Montubio de la Costa), 40
CONAIE (Confederación de Nacionalidades Indígenas del Ecuador): and Catholic Church, 39; and Correa, 8, 47; crisis of, 51, 54, 58; and education, 126, 136; history of, 40–43
communities (community): and anthropology, 165, 168; and CONAIE, 39; Correa's attack on, 143; crisis of, 50, 51; and education, 106, 109–10; extractivism, 42–45; and identities 76, 84, 89; and indigenous knowledge 123–24; and schools, 32–33, 138–41
conjuncture, 14, 70, 155, 171, 175
Correa, Rafael, 51, 62, 150, 154, 269; introduction to, 4–5, 7, 15; and creation of postneoliberal state, 21–22; first investiture, 46–47; and missions, 272–73

decolonial turn, 239–40, 252, 262, 270
DINEIB (Dirección Nacional de Educación Intercultural Bilingüe), 55, 113, 137
discrimination, 160, 169, 271

ECSA (Ecuacorriente S.A.), 142
Ecuador Estratégico, 26
environmental theology, 233, 237
ethnolinguists, 113, 168
extractivism, 11, 24–25

Father Javier Herrán, 222, 223, 225
Father José Manangón, 139, 141, 151, 168, 233
Father Juan Shukta, 201
Father Luigi Ricchiardi, 223, 226
FICSH (Federación Interprovincial de Centros Shuar), 39, 178, 210, 228, 230
FLACSO (Facultad Latinoamericana de Ciencias Sociales), 6, 30, 163–64, 174, 187–88, 193–94
Freire, Paulo, 114, 120

gender complementarity, 170
gender discrimination, 107, 131, 171
Guayaquil Group, 72–73
Gutiérrez, Lucio, 40

hacienda system: and anthropology, 166, 169; and Catholic Church, 225; and education, 109–11, 123; history of, 36–39; public haciendas, 217
hyperdescent, 78–79, 100
hypodescent, 78–79, 83, 100

inculturation theology, 206–7
indigenismo, 12, 65–66
indigenous intellectuals, 89, 173–75, 186–99

295

INDEX

indigenous knowledge, 59, 106, 117–18, 123, 126, 128
indigenous migration, 217–218
indigenous territories, 56–57, 211, 212, 230, 270
interculturalism, 54, 125, 116–27, 136–37, 263
Intercultural University of Indigenous Nationalities and Peoples, 126–27, 184–85

Liberation Theology, and education, 110, 114; and anthropology, 162, 163; and indigenous intellectuals, 187, 191, 198; and the missions, 207, 216, 234; 272
LOEI (Ley Orgánica de Educación Intercultural), 58, 60, 136

Macas, Luis, 51, 64, 126, 268
merit, 9, 89, 136, 156, 195
meritocracy, 146, 186, 198, 201
methods, 29–31, 273
millennium schools, 138, 144
montubios, 72–73, 80
Morales, Evo, 47, 51, 66, 102
multiculturalism, 4–5, 18, 270

nationalist-extractivism: definition of, 4, 15; and indigenous intellectuals, 201; and indigenous rights, 23–29; and missions, 205, 228; and race, 101–2; and racial formations, 267, 269, 270
neoliberal multiculturalism, 18–19, 100, 123, 151, 199, 267, 270
neoliberalism, 15–17, 21, 65, 204
neoliberalization, 16, 17, 154, 172, 199, 267, 272

ontologies paradigm, 181–182, 252
open-pit mining, 8, 10, 27, 43–44, 48, 61, 142, 229
Otavalos, 160, 174, 246

PAC (Programa Académico Cotopaxi), 126
Pachakutik, 41, 42, 51–52, 54
paternalism, 5, 13, 125, 242
plurinationalism, 54, 263
postneoliberalism, 20–23
PRODEPINE (Programa de Desarrollo de los Pueblos Indígenas y Negros), 40, 173
PUCE (Pontificia Universidad Católica del Ecuador), 158, 161–62, 168, 174

racial formation, 12, 238, 264–65, 267, 273–74
racism, 13
radical contextualism, 14
rape, 132–33, 134

salesians (Salesian Order), 46, 121, 126, 129–30
Santi, Marlon, 42, 53
SEIC (Sistema de Escuelas Indígenas de Cotopaxi), 120, 121, 123, 150, 234
self-identification, 71, 77, 86, 92, 101, 103
SENPLADES (Secretaría Nacional de Planificación y Desarrollo), 244
SERBISH (Sistema de Educación Radiofónico Bicultural Shuar), 130, 131, 211, 233
sexual harassment, 132, 134–35
Shuar, 8, 33, 39, 87, 108; and environmental conflict, 43–45; and social conflict, 51, 53, 55; and censuses 90, 95; and education 117–19, 129–30; and missions, 208–16, 227
study up methodology, 29–30
Sumak Kawsay, 9, 239–40, 243, 247–48, 251–53, 270

Tibán, Lourdes, 136, 178, 261
turn to the Left, 23–25, 48, 179, 240, 275
twenty-first-century Left, 3, 66
2008 Constitution: and Afro-Ecuadorians, 82; and indigenous rights, 54–57; and montubios, 73; and indigenous peoples, 85; and ontologies 263; and prior consultation 255; and religion 227; and Sumak Kawsay, 239, 243, 248; and territories, 230, 270
2007–2008 Constituent Assembly, 7, 54, 83, 170, 227, 243, 248

UNDRIP (United Nations Declaration of the Rights of Indigenous People), 255

ventriloquism, 239–42, 264
Viteri, Carlos, 247
Voz de Arutam, 227, 228, 229, 230

whiteness, 81

Zumbahua, 46, 216–27